Afterlives of Revolution

Afterlives of Revolution
Everyday Counterhistories in Southern Oman

Alice Wilson

With a Foreword by
Abdel Razzaq Takriti

Stanford University Press
Stanford, California

STANFORD UNIVERSITY PRESS
Stanford, California

© 2023 by Alice Wilson. All rights reserved.

Foreword © 2023 by the Board of Trustees of the Leland Stanford Junior University. All rights reserved.

No part of this book may be reproduced or transmitted in any form or by any means, electronic or mechanical, including photocopying and recording, or in any information storage or retrieval system without the prior written permission of Stanford University Press.

Printed in the United States of America on acid-free, archival-quality paper

Library of Congress Cataloging-in-Publication Data

Names: Wilson, Alice, 1980- author.
Title: Afterlives of revolution : everyday counterhistories in southern Oman / Alice Wilson.
Description: Stanford, California : Stanford University Press, 2023. | Includes bibliographical references and index.
Identifiers: LCCN 2022039388 (print) | LCCN 2022039389 (ebook) | ISBN 9781503634572 (cloth) | ISBN 9781503635784 (paperback) | ISBN 9781503635791 (ebook)
Subjects: LCSH: Revolutionaries—Oman—Dhofar. | Collective memory—Oman—Dhofar. | Oman—History—Dhofar War, 1964-1976—Influence. | Dhofar (Oman)—Politics and government. | Dhofar (Oman)—Social conditions.
Classification: LCC DS247.O68 W56 2023 (print) | LCC DS247.O68 (ebook) | DDC 953.5305/3—dc23/eng/20220822
LC record available at https://lccn.loc.gov/2022039388
LC ebook record available at https://lccn.loc.gov/2022039389

Cover design: Alex Robbins
Cover photo: Trevillion Images
Typeset by Newgen in Adobe Garamond Pro 11/13.5

For Raphaël

Contents

Foreword, by Abdel Razzaq Takriti ix
Acknowledgments xv
Note on Transliteration and Translations xix
List of Acronyms xxi
Map of Dhufar xxiii

INTRODUCTION Former Revolutionaries, Lasting Legacies 1

1 Anti-colonialism and Counterinsurgency 37

2 The Messiness of Social Change 62

3 Patronage, Coercion, and Transformed Spaces 98

4 Kinship, Values, and Networks 137

5 Everyday and Extraordinary Interactions 169

6 Resources of Unofficial Commemoration 200

CONCLUSION Postrevolutionary Platforms for Progressive Politics 235

Notes 245
Bibliography 277
Index 299

Foreword

The second half of the twentieth century witnessed the launch of numerous revolutions across the three continents of Asia, Africa, and Latin America. All of them were anti-colonial, most were republican in their political outlook, and many were socialist or Marxist in their economic orientation. Militant in their strategies and tactics, their leaderships often adopted armed struggle and guerrilla warfare and raised the banners of women's liberation, workers' rights, and peasant empowerment. The Dhufar revolution in Oman belonged to that family of tricontinental revolutions, its journey shadowing their global trajectory.

The revolution—typically downplayed by its opponents as a mere insurgency or a rebellion—was born out of the coincidence of growing local grievances and a rising Arab regional revolutionary tide. Its most prominent leaders and organizers came of age in Oman's southernmost province, socialized in its isolated environs that sustained a rural economy dependent on herding, ghee butter production, fishing, frankincense gathering, and trade in staple goods. Many of them had also experienced exile. Dispersed across the Arabian Peninsula, a good number were employed in the oil industry, seeing how the black gold they were extracting with their hard labor paid for a massive expansion in healthcare, education, and infrastructure. Others joined newly established Gulf armed and security forces, acquiring modern military training. A select few received education in Kuwait, Baghdad, and Cairo, accessing a privilege that their peers were denied in Salalah.

Their local experiences gave them a sense of opposition to Sultanic rule propelled by political marginalization, economic destitution, and everyday oppression. Their regional exposure equipped them with new frameworks and languages grounded in visions of anti-colonialism and social justice. It spurred in them a lifelong attachment to emancipatory causes such as the liberation of Palestine. It further allowed them to acquire new political practices and models of organization and to join pan-Arab clandestine formations, foremost among which was the Movement of Arab Nationalists. Akin to other cadres of that movement, they were pulled by the gravitational force of Nasserism after the Tripartite Aggression of 1956, firmly moving to the Marxist-Leninist orbit after the 1967 Naksa.

As they became more integrated into the Arab anti-colonial sphere, Dhufari exiles tapped into new sources of military and economic resource mobilization from the Egyptian and Iraqi republics as well as Kuwaiti civil society. For a very brief while, some were even receiving Saudi assistance. This enabled them to announce their armed struggle on June 9, 1965. Over the course of the following decade, they held territory in Dhufar's highlands, sheltered by its forests, caves, and rugged terrain. After their sharp turn to the left in 1968, they secured modest support from a variety of forces, including China, the Palestinian revolution, Cuba, the USSR, Vietnam, and, above all, South Yemen. Revolutionaries from across the region—Bahrainis, Palestinians, Iranians, Saudis, Kuwaitis, and Lebanese—lent them varying levels of solidarity. Their struggle underwent ideological twists and turns, accompanied by changes in liberatory objectives, social outlooks, and international alliances. Thus, what started as the Dhufar Liberation Front morphed in 1968 to the Popular Front for the Liberation of the Occupied Arab Gulf. That name was changed in 1971 to the Popular Front for the Liberation of Oman and the Arab Gulf, after unity was achieved with revolutionaries from northern Oman, Trucial Oman, and Bahrain. It was yet again altered to the Popular Front for the Liberation of Oman in 1974, reflecting a narrowing of the geographic scope of the struggle and a readjustment to the growing strength of the state. Many developments accompanied these shifts in nomenclature, but what stayed constant was the opposition to Sultanic rule and Britain's imperial role in Oman. That opposition persisted even after the withdrawal of revolutionary forces to South Yemen in the spring of 1976, its power waning gradually over the following decade and a half, and its leadership finally collapsing after the fall of the socialist government in Aden.

The revolution was militarily defeated by a coalition of international forces committed to Anglo-Sultanic rule in the context of the Cold War.

Britain remained the key player throughout, but it had galvanized around it help from various Middle Eastern conservative powers. Iran and Jordan sent troops, and Saudi Arabia and the United Arab Emirates offered financial aid. Their interventions were crucial to the reestablishment and extension of regime authority. But the battle over Oman was not merely geopolitical; it had profound ideological and social implications, especially in Dhufar, the heartland of the revolution. As Alice Wilson shows in this book, the reestablishment and extension of regime control was accompanied by a reorientation of social values. Against the egalitarianism embraced by the revolution—enhancing the status of women, marginalized tribes, and the formerly enslaved—the past few decades, she illustrates, witnessed a reintroduction of gendered, tribal, and racialized hierarchies. The secularism promoted by the revolutionary leadership was replaced by growing religiosity and social conservatism, fueled by a framing of events that presented the victory of the sultan as an Islamic defeat of communism. Crucially, this was accompanied by the attempted burial of revolutionary memory and the suppression of political dissent.

Given the triumph of Sultanic rule and the pervasive presence of the state in Dhufari life, is there anything left of the revolution? This is the core question posed in this work. Wilson's nuance in answering it is unsurprising. Having already studied the Sahrawi experience in the western extremities of the Arab Maghreb, she came to the easternmost part of the Arab Mashriq with a keen understanding of the lasting social impact of revolutions, even after moments of military and political defeat. Conceptually, Wilson builds upon a growing literature on revolutionary afterlives, examining the ongoing relevance of ideas, values, networks, and social relations that were glaringly evident during older eras of struggle, only to become hidden after the imposition of official silence. This is a subject that has been overshadowed by the emphasis on "rehabilitation" of former insurgents in counterinsurgency studies, by critical analyses of success and failure in historical sociology, and by auto-critiques on the part of former revolutionary scholars. Wilson has identified a major gap in these literatures, convincingly arguing that contemporary realities in societies that have experienced suppressed revolutions cannot be understood without accounting for the long-term impacts of radical mass mobilization.

In filling this scholarly lacuna, *Afterlives of Revolution* draws on ethnographic research that was carried out against considerable odds. Researchers investigating revolutionary legacies in Oman should prepare for potential surveillance by the state and auto-censorship on the part of revolutionary veterans. They must also account for the possibility that their research could pose a risk to themselves and—even more gravely—their interlocutors. After all, suppressing the search for knowledge, as well as the sharing of experience, is an essential aspect of the official silencing of revolution that is so thoroughly discussed in this book. Despite these serious hurdles, Wilson was able to gather a rich source base through participant observation in a wide range of settings: evening gatherings of revolutionary veterans, visits to private homes, interactions at malls, encounters in the public library, and conversations in taxicabs. She was also able to consider a wide range of debates, exchanges, and discussions unfolding in cyberspace and over social media.

The result is a rich study that demonstrates deep familiarity with the literature on the revolutionary past, all the while making an essential and original contribution by documenting, and reflecting upon, the presence of the revolution in the present. This study deserves close reading by scholars of Oman, the Arabian Peninsula, and the Gulf, as well as students of suppressed revolutions across the world. From it, readers can learn much about state interventions in the private and public spheres, and the efforts of absolutist regimes to enforce dominance through patronage, spatial transformation, and social engineering. Perhaps more importantly, there is much on offer here for those wishing to learn about the persistence of alternative narratives, kinship networks, social interactions, and unofficial commemoration despite the grinding power of the state.

Combining attention to everyday life and fragmentary moments without losing sight of broader political themes, socioeconomic realities, and historical context, this book is a chronicle of survival and resilience, but it is also a testimony to the ongoing role of revolutionary legacies in regenerating contemporary popular challenges to authority. The protests that erupted across Oman at the onset of the Arab uprisings, as well as more recent mobilizations witnessed as late as 2021, undoubtedly entailed an ongoing search for a new counterhegemonic politics. The young organizers that participated in them are confronted by realities different than those surrounding their forebearers in the 1960s and 1970s. They are not living in the era of great Afro-Asian movements for independence, tricontinental anti-colonial quests, or raging Cold War ideological battles. They have not established popular fronts, nor have they organized clandestine formations akin to those that led past liberation struggles. Nevertheless, they are confronted by state repression, deep social inequities, and oppressive hierarchical structures. They have witnessed the ongoing horrors resulting from neocolonial paramountcy and the spread of US power in their region: from ongoing settler colonialism in Palestine to the dismantlement of Iraq and the sectarianization of Syria and Yemen. They are all too aware of the precariousness of their country's dependence on oil and are feeling the brunt of the retreat of the welfare state and the dominance of neoliberal economics. In grappling with their present, they are reflecting, as Wilson shows, upon the radical events of the past, events that unfolded in their cities and countryside, ones that left an enduring mark on their society. Challenging the idea of a strictly delineated end to revolution, this thoughtful, engaging, and important book suggests the latent possibility of new beginnings.

Abdel Razzaq Takriti
Mahmoud Darwish Visiting Professor
in Palestinian Studies, Brown University
Arab-American Educational Foundation
Chair in Modern Arab History, University of Houston

Acknowledgments

In a project that has presented challenges that have been as much ethical and emotional as intellectual, these lines are among the hardest to write. For while many people in and from Oman, and especially Dhufar, made this research and fieldwork possible, it is prudent that in these pages I try to thank most of them without naming them. Of those living in Oman, I thank by name here only Salim Tabook (d. 2019), seeking to honor his memory and pioneering anthropological study of Dhufar. The many others to whom I am grateful include former revolutionaries, family members, hosts, researchers, writers, professors, teachers, politicians, entrepreneurs, administrators, students, cab drivers, and those to whom I am indebted for a lifetime supply of frankincense. Thanks to their many and moving acts of welcome, kindness, patience, generosity, courage, and good humor I have had the privilege of beginning to learn about revolutionary experiences and afterlives in Oman.

Those who helped me during fieldwork were kind enough to correct and forgive my errors. I have endeavored to learn from their expertise, and from comments on draft material. Wherever this book demands it, I ask again here for their forgiveness for mistakes for which I alone am responsible. I have also learned from Omanis who publish, beyond official censorship, about sensitive topics that such writing can help expand the opportunities for Omanis to share progressive visions. Whether or not research participants agree with my argument that former revolutionaries' everyday and occasional extraordinary acts create afterlives of revolution, I hope that they can share my aspirations for this book to play a part in those progressive discussions. Amid Omanis' growing memory work about the revolution, I also hope that this book can bring to new audiences experiences that Dhufaris wanted to share.

None of this would have been possible without generous material support for this project. Initial preparations began thanks to a Junior Research Fellowship at Homerton College, University of Cambridge. Fieldwork in 2013 and 2015 was possible thanks to Homerton College, a Cambridge Humanities Research Grant with the support of the Department of Middle Eastern Studies at the University of Cambridge, and the Addison Wheeler Fellowship at Durham University. The Addison Wheeler Fellowship also generously supported writing time and assistance with Arabic sources. I am equally indebted to those who supported the ongoing writing process. After further progress at the University of Sussex, a Leverhulme Research Fellowship 2019–2020 provided the transformative opportunity to turn drafts into a manuscript, as well as funding for disseminating work in progress, translations from Farsi, and archival research at the University of Exeter. A semester of research leave at the University of Sussex, for which I am particularly grateful given the challenges of the pandemic, brought me to the first submission. I have been especially fortunate to submit the revised manuscript while enjoying a Visiting Fellowship at the Prince Alwaleed Bin Talal Centre of Islamic Studies at the University of Cambridge, and, in the final stages, a Derek Brewer Visiting Fellowship at Emmanuel College, University of Cambridge. Emmanuel provided the intellectual inspiration, resources, and nourishment, in all senses, to meet the deadline.

I am grateful to colleagues who shared feedback on work in progress. I learned from valuable comments during workshops and conferences on "(In)Security in Everyday Life" at the Arab Council for Social Sciences, "Permanence" at Bristol University, "The Event(s) of Citizenship" at the University of Cambridge's Centre for Research in the Arts, Social Sciences, and Humanities, "Claiming Justice after Conflict" at the Fondation Maison des sciences de l'homme, "Tribe and State in the Middle East" at the London School of Economics and Political Science, "After the Event" at University College London, and the MacMillan Political Violence and its Legacies workshop at Yale University, as well as meetings of the Association of Social Anthropologists in 2018 and the Royal Anthropological Institute/Royal Geographical Society in 2020. Among colleagues who share the book's regional focus, the research benefited from feedback during presentations at the Prince Alwaleed Bin Talal Centre of Islamic Studies at the University of Cambridge, the Middle East Institute at Columbia University, King's College in the University of Cambridge, the Institute of Middle Eastern Studies at King's College London, the Middle East Institute at the National University of Singapore, the Middle East and North African Studies Program at Northwestern

University, the Middle East Centre at the University of Oxford, Pembroke College in the University of Cambridge, the School of Area Studies, History, Politics, and Literature at the University of Portsmouth, and the Sharmin and Bijan Mossavar-Rahmani Center for Iran and Persian Gulf Studies at Princeton University. I am likewise grateful for the comments of colleagues in anthropology and related disciplines at the Geneva Graduate Institute, the University of Kent, the University of Lisbon, the London School of Economics and Political Science, the University of Manchester, Maynooth University, Utrecht University, and University College London. Thank you in particular to the colleagues who made these invitations possible.

Many people generously shared feedback on drafts, pitches, and ruminations. They include the colleagues at each of the institutions that generously supported the research. In particular, at Cambridge I am especially grateful to Paul Anderson, 'Abdullah Baabood, Devon Curtis, Alex Jeffrey, Yael Navaro, Mezna Qato, Marilyn Strathern, and Molly Warrington. Sertac Sehlikoglu made it possible to invite Bjørn Thomassen to comment on my work, and I thank both of them for their inspiring engagement. At Durham and thereafter, Catherine Alexander provided crucial mentorship, Jeroen Gunning helped the project grow, and Emma Chapman extended a helping hand. At Sussex, Meike Fechter and Anke Schwittay were invaluable, patient, and generous writing companions. Demet Dinler heroically read and commented on the first iteration of a complete manuscript. Along the way, colleagues and visitors in Sussex shared ideas and encouragement. I am especially indebted to my mentor, Becky Prentice, as well as Jane Cowan, Diana Ibanez-Tirado, Raminder Kaur, Magnus Marsden, Jon Mitchell, Geert de Neve, Dinah Rajak, Ben Rogaly, Margaret Sleebaum-Faulkner, and Ibtisam al-Wahaibi, alongside Katharyn Lanaro and colleagues in the research office.

At crucial stages, Lori Allen, Laleh Khalili, and Marlene Schäfers shared rigorous feedback. The manuscript benefited from conversations with Charlotte Al-Khalili, Charis Boutieri, Dawn Chatty, Susanne Dahlgren, Alice Elliot, Behrooz Ghamari-Tabrizi, Leslie Gross-Wyrtzen, Martin Holbraad, Helen Lackner, Darryl Li, Toby Matthiesen, Anne Meneley, Michelle Obeid, Nathalie Peutz, Ross Porter, Madeline Reeves, Nerouz Satik, Yezid Sayigh, Vivian Solana, Marc Valéri, Natalya Vince, Jessica Winegar, Jonathan Wyrtzen, and Naor Ben Yehoyada. I am happily indebted to Danny Postel for sharing many suggestions that shaped the project.

From when I first began to plan this research, and thereafter, Abdel Razzaq Takriti offered invaluable input. As the project continued, Mandana Limbert helped me find pathways at critical junctures. Their inputs were crucial for the project to progress. At the post-review stage, Abdel Razzaq Takriti and Miranda Morris generously provided insightful suggestions and pointed out many ways to improve the manuscript. I am honored and humbled that Abdel Razzaq Takriti has written the foreword, that Miranda Morris has taught me so much, and that scholars who have inspired me have supported this project.

Special thanks to James Downs, the wonderful archivist of the Middle East Collections at the University of Exeter, and his colleagues in the Old Library. As well as introducing me to many key sources, James went extra miles on many fronts with grace and patience, especially to facilitate access to images. John Wilkinson kindly gave permission to cite from his papers at the University of Exeter. Jean-Michel Humeau kindly gave permission to reproduce his images. Alex Halliday and Helen Lackner gave permission to reproduce images from the Gulf Committee Archive at the University of Exeter. Samaher Fahy (née AlAhmed), Kate Giles, Anahita Hosseini-Lewis, and Lia James provided tremendous assistance with Arabic texts, proofreading, Farsi translation, and editing.

It has been an immense privilege and pleasure to learn from the brilliance of Kate Wahl at Stanford University Press. Thanks also to Cat Ng Pavel for expert guidance, to Tiffany Mok and Erin Ivy for their patience and expertise during production, and to copy editor RF, to cartographer Erin Greb, and to indexer Jo Betts for their excellent work. Two anonymous reviewers for the press shared marvelously constructive, insightful, and detailed comments. I thank them for their care and vision.

No project of this nature can thrive without the support of family and friends. I am blessed to complete this book with my parents, my earliest supporters, at my side. My sisters, their growing families, and my in-laws have brought welcome smiles and hugs. Friends have willed this project to continue at many junctures, including Emma Abotsi, Sarah Albrecht, Demet Dinler, Mark Green, Jessica Johnson, Louise Joy, Nayanika Mathur, Fiona McConnell, Kameswarie Nunna, Sally Painter, Natalie Ramm, Sertac Sehlikoglu, Gyda Sindre, Kathryn Telling, and Fiona Wright. I am grateful for the forbearance of housemates who have also lived with this manuscript.

At every moment, especially the most difficult ones, my husband Raphaël has been at my side. He took to new levels what it means to be a loving and supportive partner. I have done my best for this book to reflect all that his wisdom, unfailing moral compass, strength, and compassion teach me every day. I dedicate the book to him.

Note on Transliteration and Translations

Seeking to make the text accessible for Anglophone audiences, I have used a simplified transliteration from Arabic without diacritics except for *'ayn* (') and *hamza* (').

Where a conventional transliteration for a published source, author, place, or term follows an alternative approach to transliteration, for these terms I have used the conventional form that will already be familiar to some readers.

Translations from Arabic are mine with assistance from Samaher Fahy (née AlAhmed). Translations and transliteration from Farsi are by Anahita Hosseini-Lewis. Translations from French are mine.

Acronyms

BATT	British Army Training Team
CAT	civil action team
CAD	Civil Aid Department
CSAF	Commander of the Sultan's Armed Forces
DCA	Dhufar Charitable Association
DF	Dhufar Force
DLF	Dhufar Liberation Front
DSO	Dhufar Soldiers' Organization
FCO	Foreign and Commonwealth Office
FO	Foreign Office
GCC	Gulf Cooperation Council
MSAL	Modern South Arabian languages
MAN	Movement of Arab Nationalists
NDFLOAG	National Democratic Front for the Liberation of Oman and the Arabian Gulf
OWO	Omani Women's Organization
PDRY	People's Democratic Republic of Yemen
PLA	Popular Liberation Army
PRSY	People's Republic of South Yemen

PDO	Petroleum Development Oman
PFLO	Popular Front for the Liberation of Oman
PFLOAG	Popular Front for the Liberation of Oman and the Arabian Gulf (1971–4)
PFLOAG	Popular Front for the Liberation of the Occupied Arabian Gulf (1968–71)
RAF	Royal Air Force
SAS	Special Air Service
SOAF	Sultan of Oman's Air Force
SAF	Sultan's Armed Forces
SWANA	Southwest Asia and North Africa

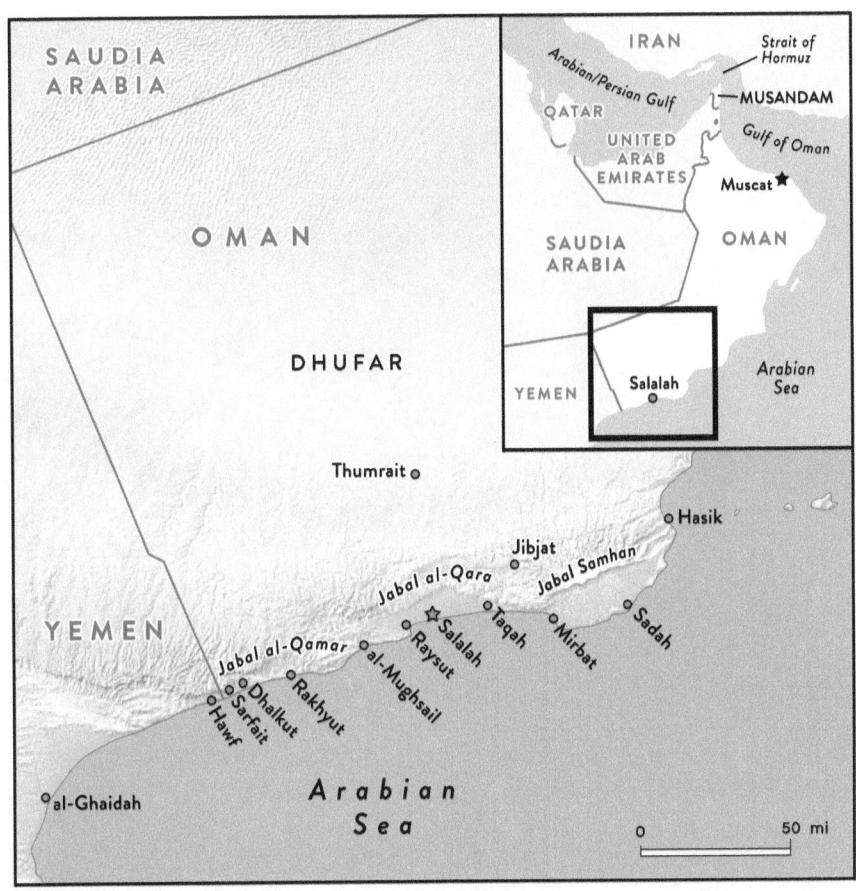

MAP. Map of Dhufar, with inset of Oman

Introduction

Former Revolutionaries, Lasting Legacies

THE JOURNEY BEGAN in an ordinary way. It was a pre-monsoon hot and sticky post-siesta afternoon in 2015. I was searching for a cab to take me several kilometers from one side of Salalah to another, where I was headed to visit a Dhufari family in their home. I felt an acute self-consciousness. It was rare for an unaccompanied woman to take a cab in Salalah. Most Dhufari women, whether of urban or rural background, conformed to prevalent social expectations that when circulating in Salalah they should avoid unnecessary contact with unrelated Omani men, including cab drivers. Women from global north backgrounds typically had their own cars. Many women of global south backgrounds were low-paid domestic workers with limited opportunities, reasons, or resources to take cabs. A roadside lone female cut an awkward figure. Uncomfortably familiar with this predicament, I initially struggled to hail a cab and settle a fare.

Eventually a driver who looked in his sixties agreed to take me. I followed the family's instructions to call them and hand the phone to the driver, so that the family could explain the directions. I got through to Musallam (a pseudonym), a male member of the household of a similar generation to the driver. Musallam began to explain the route. After a few exchanges, the driver joyfully exclaimed: "Musallam!" The two began to greet each other anew, exchanging news as if they were acquaintances who were glad to be in touch again after some time.

When the driver eventually hung up, he handed the phone back to me saying: "Musallam wants to talk to you."

I called back, and Musallam told me: "He is one of our group. Maybe he will talk to you." At this moment, the journey ceased to be ordinary.

I began to sweat beyond the effects of the oppressive heat. Musallam had used a term meaning "group" or "gathering" in classical Arabic (*jama'ah*). I most often heard Dhufaris use it to refer to their extended family or tribe. But I immediately understood that Musallam had employed the term in another sense.

Musallam and others in his close family had formerly been members of Dhufar's liberation movement (henceforth, "the Front"). Launching its revolution in 1965, the Front fought an anti-colonial insurgency for ten years against the British-backed, Muscat-based al-Busaid dynasty of sultans. From 1968 on, and in an increasingly internationalized conflict, the movement pursued Marxist-inspired, anti-tribalist, and egalitarian-leaning programs of social change. These continued until 1992 through the Front's mobilization and eventual exile in southern Yemen. Members gradually left the movement between the 1970s and the 1990s, taking up lives in Oman as citizens loyal to Sultan Qaboos bin Said (ruled 1970–2020). But for some of these former revolutionaries, the Front's values of egalitarianism, social inclusivity, and anti-tribalism remained influential.

The "group" to which Musallam referred, then, was not an extended family or tribe, but former members of the Front. The government of authoritarian absolutist Qaboos had nevertheless imposed an official silence regarding the Front and its armed and, later, political opposition. Only in private, informal circles could Dhufaris make reference to the Front without fear of consequences such as increased government surveillance or punishment. Musallam's suggestion that "maybe" the driver would talk to me was therefore significant. Many Dhufaris were understandably reluctant to speak to a British and British-based researcher about the Front. But Musallam was telling me that the driver might be willing to help me learn more about the movement and its afterlives.

Hence, I sweated in the cab. How could I—or should I—broach the sensitive topic of the Front with the driver, even if Musallam's overture suggested that he judged that it was safe to do so? After speaking with Musallam, I resumed small talk with the driver. I eventually ventured that I was a researcher studying social change in Dhufar in the 1970s and after. These were terms broad enough to include euphemistic reference to the revolution and its programs that a Dhufari could easily recognize. In adopting purposefully open-ended language I sought to give interlocutors the choice about whether or not to direct conversation toward the Front. The driver proceeded to tell me, equally euphemistically, that Musallam had a "background" (*khalfiyyah*), as did members of Musallam's family, male and female, whom the driver named to me. But the driver went no further, and following his cue I did not pursue the topic.

When we arrived at the house, I telephoned to say that I was outside. The driver heard me greeting Khiyar, a female senior member of the family also of a similar generation to Musallam and the driver. He asked for the phone. He and Khiyar then exchanged warm greetings, again as if between longstanding acquaintances who were glad to speak after some time. Just as gendered norms frowned upon most Dhufari women taking cabs in Salalah, similarly they generally discouraged unrelated Dhufari males and females from seeking social contact. Although such expectations applied less stringently to postmenopausal women of Khiyar's generation, the effusive greetings between her and the driver still struck me as unusual. Had they been relatives, they would likely have had opportunities to hear each other's news through kinship networks. This seemed not to be the case. Rather, they greeted one another as if reconnecting in the light of a shared past: the "background" in the Front at which Musallam and the driver had hinted.

In the end, the driver's reluctance to speak to me explicitly about the revolution had not foreclosed revelation. On the contrary, his recognition of Musallam's voice, and his subsequent conversation with Khiyar, proved suggestive. Did the enthusiastic greetings between this man and woman echo the well-known gendered egalitarianism of Dhufar's revolution? The interactions between Musallam, Khiyar, and the driver evoked possibilities that some former revolutionaries acknowledged social networks that linked them to one another and reproduced values of social—including gendered—egalitarianism and inclusivity. The cab journey had reached an extraordinary climax. It showed me firsthand how former militants reproduced lasting legacies of revolution.

Everyday Counterhistories

What happens to revolutionary ideas, networks, and values *after* military defeat, and *after* an authoritarian government has imposed official silence? How do afterlives of revolution persist despite censorship? Which kinds of revolutionary legacies survive authoritarian repression? What means are available for former revolutionaries, and others, to reproduce afterlives of revolution? What combinations of ordinary and extraordinary interactions produce revolutionary legacies? And what light do those afterlives shed on the processes and meanings of revolution?

These questions have hung for years over Dhufar's former revolutionaries, who have raised children and buried peers in Qaboos's Oman. The longevity of their presence in the Sultanate, and the inevitable dwindling of their numbers with each passing year, make Dhufar a compelling case for asking what legacies endure beyond official silence. These questions have become urgent to address.

Empirically, the revolutions that began in 2010–2011 in many countries in Southwest Asia and North Africa (SWANA)—the dubbing of which as the Arab Spring reflects Eurocentric categories—have produced new generations and growing numbers of disappointed revolutionaries.[1] They live under authoritarian governments that repress revolutionary mobilizations. In Tunisia, Egypt, Bahrain, Yemen, Syria, and beyond, how do those living under authoritarianism experience and create revolutionary aftermaths? How does their revolutionary past remain an inspiration for ongoing emancipatory projects? Their peers in Oman have preceded them in facing the dilemmas and possibilities of claiming a revolutionary past as a crucible of personal and national identity and aspiration.

Conceptually, attending to officially silenced revolution offers a novel perspective on revolution. Commentators and activists alike have most often approached revolution as ongoing protest, insurgency, experimentation, or governance. Beyond and alongside this familiar lens is the less examined alternative of afterlives of revolution. These afterlives are the lasting values, networks, ideas, and legacies that persist, despite political repression. The study of officially silenced revolution challenges and expands upon the conventional focus on what *makes* a revolution. It brings into view revolution understood through the optic of those values, ideas, and legacies that *survive*, despite discouraging odds. Such a focus calls for attention to the means for maintaining and reproducing those legacies.

In privileging moments of uprising, insurgency, and governance, many studies have probed revolutionary mobilization and transformation (as I have in previous work).[2] The experiences of revolutionaries in Oman have enriched such analysis of revolution-in-progress. Activist scholars produced eyewitness analyses of the Front.[3] Accounts of revolutionary schooling foreground the movement as a beacon of education aiming at social change.[4] The landmark revisionist retelling of the Front's mobilization until 1976 highlights revolutionaries' agency, institutions, and cultural production.[5]

FIGURE 1. Rally of PFLOAG combatants, 1971, Dhufar. © Jean-Michel Humeau. Reprinted with permission.

When revolutionary movements have fallen short of achieving the transformation of state power and social relations to which they aspired, analysis has tended to address two angles. On the one hand are attempts to understand the reasons for failure.[6] On the other are assessments of how former revolutionaries navigate disappointments, dreams, and ongoing activism in conditions of exile or multipartyism.[7] When it comes to officially silenced revolutionaries living under authoritarianism, repression raises difficulties of access and of how to shield research participants from harm. Until recently, a handful of studies navigated such constraints.[8] Inquiry into postrevolutionary lives under authoritarianism is nevertheless growing in the wake of the 2010–2011 uprisings in SWANA.[9] More usually, though, inquiry into revolution has focused on either revolution-in-progress or revolutionary legacies in contexts that afford greater political freedoms than does authoritarian official silence.

In contrast, there is a plethora of counterinsurgency narratives that address officially silenced revolutionaries. These perspectives, however, uphold questionable premises. They typically cast revolutionaries as threats to national security and morality, while lauding victorious interventions against them. A case in point is Egypt's post-2013 counterrevolutionary government.[10] Its discourses have presented the consequences of the 2011 deposition of President Mubarak as a threat to national security. Conversely, they portray President Sisi as the savior of security and stability. Such endorsement serves the interests of ruling classes whom revolutionaries defied, as well as neocolonial agendas. Similarly, in the Dhufari case, Oman's British counterinsurgency backers created evocative propaganda.[11] It cast Dhufar's revolutionaries as terrorists and godless communists who threatened a glorified stability, security, and morality that the sultan's rule and colonial intervention promised to safeguard.[12] The accounts of some British veterans, and of some scholars, have echoed such depictions of the Marxist-inspired Front as a political, economic, and moral threat.[13]

In parallel to the demonization of Dhufar's revolutionaries, the accounts of some veterans and scholars depict a successful, even exemplary, counterinsurgency. This approach emphasizes the distribution of resources and services to Dhufaris as a means to "win hearts and minds."[14] Such a narrative is not merely empirically flawed.[15] It also rests on colonialist premises. It assigns to counterinsurgency forces the competence and right to decide which of Dhufaris' claims to grant or dismiss. It also implies white men "saving" brown men and women from other (here, communist) brown men and women.[16] In both demonizing and colonialist varieties, narrations of successful counterinsurgency distort the lives of officially silenced former revolutionaries. These narratives can offer their strongest insights into revolutionary experiences when read "against the grain." This book pursues such an impulse to question, destabilize, and decolonize dominant narratives.[17]

It is not satisfactory that the most frequent representations of officially silenced revolutionaries are narratives of counterinsurgency achievement. These accounts have produced a glut of problematic images of victorious counterinsurgency that obscure nonconforming alternatives. In privileging the perspectives of the victorious, these narratives neglect counterhistories: histories that recover the experiences of the marginalized.[18] Conventional narratives cannot advance an understanding of the officially silenced revolutionaries whose experiences it has become empirically and conceptually urgent to address. But the retrieval of counterhistories can destabilize dominant and official narratives and histories. This book takes up precisely these tasks.

This book begins to trace counterhistories of the postwar lives of male and female ex-revolutionaries in Dhufar who live alongside postrevolutionary generations, under varying degrees of surveillance. In doing so, this study takes inspiration from counterhistories of Dhufar's revolution-in-progress.[19] Placing a new focus on the postwar lives of Dhufari former revolutionaries, the book shows that there are lasting legacies—afterlives—of revolution that breach official silencing. These afterlives were manifest in Dhufar in ongoing legacies of revolutionary values, networks, and relationships. Afterlives were especially, but not exclusively, present in everyday interactions. Some veteran revolutionaries used kinship to reproduce a counterhegemonic, more egalitarian social order. In their daily socializing, they reproduced revolutionary values of egalitarianism. They also unofficially commemorated the revolution through ordinary acts, such as funeral attendance. More occasionally, those with personal or family connections to former militancy created revolutionary afterlives by undertaking extraordinary actions, such as unusual electoral candidacy or hosting a gathering to mark an ex-revolutionary's return to Oman. In all these interactions, Dhufaris were ever mindful of the Omani government's official silence about the war. In that context, the everyday interactions that created afterlives of revolution did not evince resistance that attracted the concern of the Omani state. Yet in these constrained conditions, former revolutionaries, and some close to them, nevertheless maintained *social* afterlives of revolution. An understanding of these afterlives foregrounds everyday counterhistories—as well as occasional extraordinary counterhistories—that illuminate new perspectives on revolution, patronage, and postwar everyday life.

From "What Makes a Revolution" to "What Survives of Revolution"

The dominant meaning of "revolution" shifted in the late eighteenth century. Until then, the term had referred to the restoration of circumstances to their original position. The newer meaning, prevalent today, refers to the upheaval of a given state of affairs and their replacement with alternative, new arrangements.[20] The notion emerged of an all-encompassing revolution in the way a society organizes political legitimacy and rule as well as social and economic relations. This is the kind of revolution to which militants in Dhufar aspired.

Revolution in this sense is a profound transformation of social order that undermines, often with speed and violence, former political and social organization, ruling authorities, and supporting myths, and propagates new replacements of each.[21] The scope of change entails not just institutions, but the very premises of political legitimacy.[22] Revolution on this scale is a "social revolution" involving not just change in the way a society organizes the means of production (an "economic revolution" such as the Industrial Revolution), or a change in political rulers (a "political revolution" such as a coup). It involves change in the organization of both political authority and of the social differentiation that political authorities legitimize.[23] Revolutionary subjects experience transformations on personal and collective scales.[24] Such attempted transformation of both political and socioeconomic life characterized revolution in Dhufar.

Dominant approaches in history, political science, and related disciplines have focused on the conditions and causes of revolution, its defining features, and the wide-ranging outcomes when revolutionary mobilizations operate, at least for a time, as state(like) powers governing civilian populations.[25] These outcomes include the possibility that seizing state power does not necessarily lead to a revolutionary transformation of society.[26] In contrast, anthropological and some historical approaches are concerned less with whether particular events "qualify" as a revolution. Rather, for the ethnographer, a revolution is an "event" in the sense of a rupture of the routine that makes alternative horizons visible and possible.[27] Anthropologists thus interrogate revolution as a social experience. Such inquiry dates back as far as the pioneering study during anthropology's formation of the Soviet revolution as a "gigantic social phenomenon."[28] Since then, through a combination of studies of longer-term revolutionary scenarios, accidents that saw anthropologists happen to be in situ when a revolution erupted, and growing awareness of how anthropological lenses predisposed some researchers to overlook emerging mobilizations, a growing field of anthropological studies of revolution has emerged.[29] Dhufar's revolution resonates with these discussions of revolutionary experience, social change, and legacies.

Typically, anthropologists heed the local—what ethnographers call the "emic" or "insider"—interpretation of what people experience as a revolution according to local terminology. Focused on understanding the relationship between local, national, and global experiences and narratives, anthropologists trace revolutionary transformations in everyday lives as "micro-processes" that constitute "a countlessly repeated uprooting of social relations, in thousands of local communities, in millions of lives."[30] Processual approaches illuminate how revolutionary phenomena that people may experience in terms of *rupture* nevertheless *connect* with existing wider ritual, economic, and political phenomena. Hence, revolutionary experience is always intersectionally inflected with gender, class, ethnicity, race, and sexual orientation.[31] Dhufar foregrounds how intersectionality is as relevant for revolution as for its afterlives.

Inevitably, "new" revolutionary experiences recycle and rework existing political, economic, and social relations.[32] The social dynamics of exceptional revolutionary spaces and times (e.g., those found in communities and spaces of resistance or in protests) echo rites of passage (such as transformations from childhood to adulthood). Both contexts see people experience liminality, a temporary suspension of social hierarchy, and communitas, egalitarian-leaning social bonds that the suspension of ordinary hierarchies facilitates.[33] In another social reverberation, the perceived need to find a solution to the crisis of revolutionary liminality creates opportunities for a leader who claims to be a savior. In practice, however, this leader can resemble devious "trickster" figures, such as those that feature in some folk tales.[34] In a further reprise, revolutionary discourse follows religious injunctions in demanding that devotees be ready for self-sacrifice.[35] Revolution is clearly a social process.

These social dimensions have implications for revolutions that end in disappointment, whether military defeat or disillusion. Whatever the outcome, persons still lived through and engaged with revolutionary process and feel lasting, potentially irreversible, impacts.[36] A disappointing denouement does not make the lived experiences of militants, including Oman's, any less revolutionary.

The localization of revolutionary processes within broader social relations illuminates connections with wider temporal contexts. This is especially relevant to inquiry into the aftermaths of revolution. On the one hand, past experiences of revolution can become an inspiration and resource for those articulating agendas for new revolutionary transformation—or other emancipatory projects.[37] In Dhufar, demonstrators in Salalah in February–May 2011 referred to events of the 1970s in their protest chants.[38] On the other hand, when confronted with futures radically different from those to which they aspired, militants who failed in their goals to take power or transform society can find that previous revolutionary experiences continue to define and influence their lives. For some, disappointment becomes a defining postrevolutionary experience, assuming postcolonial and postsocialist forms.[39] Disillusionment manifested in Dhufar too.

Yet those disappointed with revolutionary-era ambition may still continue to mobilize for their own rights and for the rights of marginalized groups. They may do so under other banners, such as social movements and human rights, as have former Sandinistas in Nicaragua, ex-Maoists in France, and Bahraini former Front member ʿAbd al-Nabi ʿIkri in a career that spanned exile before his return to Bahrain.[40] Indeed, "it may be precisely *after* the revolution that the long struggle for democratization and economic justice will be waged."[41] In Oman, no Dhufaris suggested to me that former revolutionaries engaged in ongoing political resistance of concern to Oman's governing authorities. But some of the country's political activists engaged in memory work about the revolution in Dhufar.[42] This suggests that later generations of activists construe the revolution as an episode of national significance. More discreetly, in their day-to-day lives some of Dhufar's former revolutionaries engaged in egalitarian-leaning interactions. Their kinship practices, everyday socializing, acts of unofficial commemoration, and occasional extraordinary acts reproduced revolutionary values and networks.

The experiences of Dhufaris and other erstwhile militants show how revolutions that failed to take power, lost power, or failed in wider social, political, and economic goals nevertheless have afterlives. An afterlife is a continuing influence, a later stage of life, or a life after death.[43] More expansively, an afterlife implies the anticipated collective continuation of projects after persons previously involved can no longer continue them.[44] All of these meanings cohere in *afterlives* of revolution—life after "death" in a form such as military, political, or ideological defeat and official silencing, ongoing influence of revolutionary ideas, later stages of life for revolutionary agendas, and the possibility of future generations' continuation of projects. Afterlives, then, see political projects seep into and "haunt" their successors as "the past extends into, interrupts, or impinges on the present."[45]

The plurality of after*lives* reflects these diverse meanings. Moreover, the very experience of revolution is plural, diverse, and entails "fragments."[46] Accordingly, by no means do the ongoing influences of revolution constitute a unitary experience. After*lives* of revolution are necessarily plural, multiple, and diverse. The experience of revolutionary legacies is as intersectional as is that of revolution. Former militants in Oman were differently positioned according to gender, race, ethnicity, tribe, and social status in their opportunities and motivations to create afterlives of revolution.

The afterlives of revolution, then, concern not only veteran revolutionaries who, however disenchanted, navigate disappointments, dreams, or ongoing activism. They also encompass officially silenced revolutionaries. The repression of state authorities precludes their survival as a political movement in their home country or, in some cases, in exile. We must continue to probe the reasons for these movements' failure and heed the voices of formerly imprisoned militants.[47] But we must also ask what happens to ideas, people, and their networks beyond the official silencing of a revolution. These afterlives invite exploration. Iranian Marxists who failed in their political goals nevertheless "succeeded in bringing many new ideas to the social arena and even into the Islamic movement."[48] Former Maoists in Bengal maintained some social aspects of their revolutionary projects. As old men they continued to avoid the two dominant forms of masculinity that they had rejected as revolutionaries, namely the male provider for a household, and a religious renouncer.[49] Among Sri Lanka–based Tamil ex-militants of leftist groups active in the 1980s and subsequently repressed, female friendships outlived militancy.[50] These insights have inspired this inquiry into the lives of former revolutionaries in Dhufar.

"Officially silenced revolution" is an awkward turn of phrase. It can nevertheless avoid pitfalls of alternatives. "Defeated revolution" risks reiterating the narrative of the overwhelming victory of Oman's government and its colonial backers. It also ignores the dissenting views of Dhufaris who hold that they in fact won the war by virtue of forcing the government to change its policies. "Repressed revolution" is likewise problematic in that it highlights government repression while neglecting Dhufaris' circumvention thereof. "Silenced revolution" is similarly flawed, for although the government seeks to impose a silence about the war—such as by omitting it from textbooks, museums, and monuments, and censoring print and digital publications—Dhufaris and other Omanis privately discussed, remembered, and unofficially commemorated the revolution in Oman, and published about it outside the confines of Oman's Ministry of Information censorship. "Officially silenced revolution" acknowledges both the fields of government coercion that constrained Omanis and the possibilities nonetheless for circumventing that silence, reproducing revolutionary networks and values, and creating revolutionary afterlives.

Making the afterlives of officially silenced revolution the focus of attention foregrounds new perspectives on revolution. First, by bringing into view, on the one hand, the intersectional diversity of afterlives of revolution, and on the other hand, their heterogeneous reach—across electoral politics in Latin America, former guerilla in Mozambique, ex-Maoist human rights activists, and officially silenced revolutionaries in Oman—the book opens a novel window onto revolution. We can apprehend revolution not only through its causes, characteristics, typologies, and defining features, in other words, "what makes a revolution." We can also appraise revolution through its legacies despite inauspicious political odds, through "what survives of revolution." An officially silenced revolution, such as Dhufar's, illuminates what persists even when so much imperils survival.

Second, by recognizing afterlives of revolution across both official silence and more permissive environments, we can question conventional distinctions between "failed" and "successful" revolutions. The empirical and conceptual investigation of revolution-in-progress has already questioned teleological narratives through which revolutionaries anticipate advancement and progress. Similarly, the analysis of afterlives of revolution highlights that the boundaries between "failed" and "successful" revolutions are not necessarily as clear as intuition might initially suggest. Of course it matters—perhaps most of all to militants themselves—whether revolutions succeed or fail in the goals to which activists have aspired, such as transforming social, political, and economic life in the promotion of greater justice, inclusivity, and participation. But revolutions with a range of outcomes, whether capturing state power, competing for it, or succumbing to defeat, produce persistent legacies as well as lasting frustrations. A focus on the afterlives of revolution disrupts conventional distinctions between successful and failed revolutions. It favors instead greater exploration and acknowledgment of diverse long-term revolutionary outcomes and influences. Failure to achieve some goals may still create conditions for alternative successes, including the pursuit of other afterlives. This has been the case in Oman.

Third, and relatedly, emphasis on the afterlives of revolution extends the temporality and spatiality of revolutionary experience and impact. It looks beyond conventional chronologies and mappings in the hegemonic narratives of revolutionary as well as counterinsurgency and colonial actors. The Omani government declared victory over the Front on December 11, 1975. It agreed to a ceasefire with the Front's provider of an exilic base, the People's Democratic Republic of Yemen (PDRY) on March 10, 1976. Nonetheless, Dhufaris' experiences question those official endpoints. It is not merely that some Dhufaris believe that they, and not the government, won the war. In addition, small numbers of Front fighters continued armed resistance in Dhufar until at least March 1980.[51] The Front held its last official conference in Yemen in 1992. Protestors in Salalah in 2011 warned the government not to forget the 1970s. During my first visit to Dhufar in 2013 some Dhufaris discussed their belief that the government was actively seeking to persuade the Front's former secretary general, ʿAbd al-ʿAziz al-Qadi, to return to Oman. In 2016, a year after my main fieldwork, the government imprisoned Omani journalist and activist ʿAbdullah Habib after he wrote on Facebook that the authorities should allow, forty years on, mothers to mourn at the graves of executed revolutionaries.[52] The list of follow-ups to Dhufar's revolution only extends.

Instead of apprehending revolution through putatively clearly delineated times and spaces, a focus on afterlives of revolution posits dynamic, unfolding revolutionary times, spaces, impacts, and legacies. A metaphor that captures such unfolding potential would be to conceptualize the afterlives of revolution—especially those of an officially silenced revolution—not as a dead stump of a felled tree that obstinately remains and, with the passing of time or with greater effort, might disappear. Rather, the afterlives of revolution resemble a living tree. Its branches and roots continue to grow. The branches produce new afterlives, and the roots extend as later generations look back on revolutionary predecessors and understand their experiences in new ways.

Limits of Patronage

The afterlives of revolution in Dhufar invite reevaluation of the social and political scope of patronage in authoritarian resource-rich security states. Patronage is the distribution of material benefits from the politically privileged and powerful to their dependent constituencies in order to shore up loyalty and support. The Dhufar counterinsurgency entailed patronage (that escalated over time) in forms such as food, access to water, wages, cash incentives, housing, medical and veterinary services, and subsidies for buying livestock. Many commentators refer to this patronage as part of a campaign to "win hearts and minds" alongside strategies such as propaganda promoting the government and defaming the Front. But these measures coexisted with military interventions such as food and water blockades, bombings, land mines, forced relocations, and the destruction of grazing and agricultural resources necessary for the prewar subsistence economy. The Dhufar counterinsurgency thus epitomizes two interlinking strategies at the core of governance in Gulf monarchies: coercion (the suppression of political opposition with actual or threatened coercion) and patronage.

Governance through coercion and patronage requires both economic and political resources. As rentier states that gain income (rent) from selling in-country resources (in the Gulf, oil and gas) to out-of-country purchasers, the rulers of these states access significant revenue. With this they can finance both coercion and patronage. They can fund a repressive security state that crushes political opposition. In parallel, they can provide subsidies to nationals in the form of a welfare state, public sector salaries, and zero or low personal taxation, with these subsidies encouraging citizens' loyalty. This combination of coercion and patronage has not only sustained Gulf monarchies but is also the model to which Gulf rulers turn in times of crisis. Through coercion and patronage, Gulf monarchies faced down protests that began in Bahrain and Oman in 2011 and fears that this unrest would spread.[53] During the Dhufar war, British counterinsurgency experts counseled and executed the application of coercion and patronage. Britain's role therein signals how the backing of imperial and (neo)colonial powers provides political and material resources that enable governance through coercion and patronage.

The repressive governance of Gulf monarchies has attracted both media and scholarly attention. In parallel, their patronage has proven key to analyses of the political economy of Gulf monarchies and comparisons with alternative, tax-raising liberal democracies.[54] Whether in a rentier state, a formal democracy, or another political environment, reliance on patronage implies a relationship of political hierarchy between a patron figure and dependents or clients.[55] By contrast, a liberal democracy connotes a hypothetical political equality between polity members, any of whom could, in theory, seek elected office. When patronage relations manifest in a formal democracy, this may correspond to each party's practical expectations of one another. But at least formally, patronage and its associated hierarchies are an apparent pathology or anomaly in liberal democracy.[56]

In Gulf monarchies, by contrast, hierarchical patronage relations allegedly represent a "healthy" state of affairs. The smooth running of governance *requires* the ruler to be a patron, and his subjects his protégés. The reliance on patronage has underpinned theories of a distinctive social contract between governing authorities and governed constituencies in rentier states.[57] If citizens of a liberal democratic social contract expect political representation, and on those grounds accept taxation, then citizens of rentier states—these theories suggest—differ. They accept that they have limited or no opportunities for meaningful political participation or holding rulers to account. In return, though, they expect to benefit from the state's material support for welfare, employment, and education. From such a perspective, patronage in postwar Dhufar would be essential to maintaining Dhufaris' compliance and submission.

To understand Gulf monarchies primarily through the lens of a distinctive "benefits-without-representation" social contract is flawed, however. Such accounts are incomplete, since they "[hide] the reality of political contestations, resistance to economic and political inequality, repression and corruption and citizens' desire for accountability and self-determination."[58] Protests that began in Gulf monarchies in 2011 were recent episodes of longer histories of dissenting voices there that include the revolution in Dhufar.[59] This recurring dissent reiterates the crucial role of coercion, in addition to patronage, in maintaining authoritarian rule in Gulf monarchies, including in postwar Dhufar. Coercion is also a feature of liberal democratic rule. But the degree of the reliance on coercion for maintaining Gulf monarchies makes these polities particular—in the form (but not the fact) of their divergence from fictions of a social contract based on mutual consent from governing and governed constituencies.[60]

An interrogation of counterinsurgency redistribution in the light of revolutionary afterlives can advance critical evaluation of rentier state political economies and the role of patronage therein. Lasting legacies of revolution bring to light the limitations of patronage for quelling political dissatisfaction. The problem is not a question of whether patronage has been a major strategy in Dhufar's counterinsurgency—and in the oil-era governance of Gulf monarchies more broadly. Gulf monarchies clearly distribute material benefits to citizens and intensify such activities in times of crisis.

Similarly, wartime and postwar counterinsurgency measures in Dhufar that "win hearts and minds" have relied on patronage. After counterinsurgency strategists advocated in 1970 offering resources to Dhufaris as a means of encouraging them to support the government, by 1971–1972 pro-government paramilitaries were receiving wages and resources for their families and had benefited from livestock subsidies, while Dhufaris in areas of government control were accessing medical services and schools.[61] During the final years of the war and early postwar years, Oman spent 40 percent of its national budget on development and military projects in Dhufar, even though Dhufaris constituted an estimated 10 percent of the country's population.[62] Patronage eventually funded the provision of roads, schools, health care centers, wells, subsidies, and payouts to former revolutionaries. In the late 1970s it even entailed the distribution of a school stipend to children. This stipend was higher in value for the children of parents whose loyalty the government especially sought given that they hailed from the Front's original stronghold, the *jabal* ("mountain, mountain range, highlands").⁶³ Decades on from the Front's defeat, Dhufari ex-revolutionaries were still receiving government handouts, some of their peers assured me. Meanwhile, Dhufari pro-government paramilitaries, the *firaq* (sing. *firqah*, "team, company, troop") continued to receive reservist salaries. Patronage has been a long-term postwar governance strategy in Dhufar.

The problem instead lies in the depiction of patronage as so *successful* in securing political loyalty and quelling dissenting voices in Gulf monarchies, and in allegedly winning hearts and minds in Dhufar. Recurring dissenting voices qualify the successes of patronage in dispelling political dissatisfaction, just as evidence from Dhufar questions the supposed winning of hearts and minds there. Dhufaris were subject to intensive counterinsurgency coercion: food and water blockades, the bombing of livestock, crops, and grazing resources, and threats of cutting off food and water for communities who resisted. Given that sources of water on the *jabal* were scarce and that cattle, a major part of Dhufar's subsistence economy, need watering every two days, water blockades threatened swift lethal consequences for people and livestock. Those whom the "hearts and minds" campaign targeted were either starving or at risk of starvation and death if they resisted. They cooperated with government rule under intense coercion.

Moreover, despite this coercion some Dhufaris continued to dissent, even after the Front's formal defeat. In the late 1970s, the government continued to discuss how to curb ongoing resistance, while some Dhufaris destroyed government housing facilities before heading for the hills. Such evidence of the limits of patronage's desired impacts suggests that any successes in securing Dhufaris' acquiescence were more properly the result of *both* coercion *and* patronage. The two were not separate, but operated in tandem. It is misleading to laud the apparent impacts of patronage without also acknowledging the effects of coercion.

A further limitation to patronage evident in Dhufar is that the subjects of patronage may create and maintain social relations that contradict patronage-related hierarchies. These include social relations that reproduce contrasting egalitarianism along tribal, ethnic, racialized, and gendered lines. Through their kinship, everyday socializing, unofficial commemoration, and occasional extraordinary acts, Dhufari ex-revolutionaries reproduced revolutionary networks and values of egalitarianism. Ex-militants' valorization of egalitarianism jarred with Dhufar's prevalent social distinctions as well as with the hierarchical patronage networks that underpinned the counterinsurgency, postwar life, and authoritarian rule.

This book thus shows how recipients of patronage who remain embedded in hierarchical patron-protégé relations can still reproduce alternative, more egalitarian social relations. Across the Gulf, citizens contest gendered and generational boundaries of social convention.[64] The afterlives of Dhufari ex-revolutionaries foreground the further possibilities for Gulf citizens, including coopted persons, to reproduce counterhegemonic values that contrast, and yet coexist, with patronage relations. The fact that protestors in Dhufar in 2011 chanted slogans referencing the 1970s suggests moreover how appetites for alternative, progressive politics and social relations resurface over time. Although governing authorities use patronage and repression to avoid such eventualities, their efforts do not foreclose these possibilities. The ongoing revolutionary values and platforms for progressive politics of postwar Dhufar signal the shortcomings of counterinsurgency patronage for "winning hearts and minds."

Everyday Life in Postwar Times

A focus on the afterlives of revolution sheds fresh light on everyday relations in postwar settings.[65] How much do quotidian relations such as kinship, daily socializing, and other ordinary interactions allow survivors to reproduce the "normal" life that recent or ongoing conflict threatened? Can the resumption of everyday interactions offer comfort?

When seeking reprieve from political violence, survivors and former perpetrators alike may eschew the pursuit of a transcendental experience. Survivors of Partition and ethnic riots in India preferred a "descent into the ordinary" as a way of coping with their trauma.[66] Former insurgents who had carried out political violence in 1980s Sri Lanka similarly steeped themselves in the everyday to rebuild new lives.[67] During the second Palestinian Intifada, some West Bank Palestinians turned to ordinary kinship obligations as a means of preserving a sense of everyday life.[68] Getting married and planning a family was a means of "going on as usual" for Palestinians in both Intifadas.[69] Both during and after organized political violence, then, kinship and the everyday can sustain or recreate a social world that violence threatened.

These findings draw on two wider insights into kinship and everyday interactions: their importance in social reproduction and in subtle resistance.

On the one hand, since Marxist criticism of the role of the family in reproducing capitalist exploitation and prevalent power structures, generations of anthropologists have stressed kinship's role in the social reproduction of dominant values, relationships, hierarchies, and foundational intellectual narratives. Similarly, quotidian gestures, choices of words, ways of greeting, interacting, or avoiding others normalize and reinforce dominant power relations and hierarchies. On the other hand, though, the quotidian nature of kinship and social relations accommodates subtle resistance against a status quo. The fact that kinship and the everyday can help survivors of conflict to resist its ravages by reestablishing "normal" life draws on these wider implications of kinship and the everyday for social reproduction and resistance.[70]

The afterlives of revolution, and especially those in contexts of official silence, nevertheless interrogate the role of postwar kinship and the everyday. That role is not necessarily to reproduce the "normal" life that conflict threatened, nor accommodate resistance of concern to opposition-crushing state authorities. Rather, the afterlives of revolution disrupt the association of the everyday with postwar survival and, more generally, social reproduction, while also qualifying links to resistance. Revolutionary afterlives expose a postwar challenge that differs from the desire to recreate normal life. What if, without forging an agenda of resistance that would risk repression, people sought not so much a "descent into the ordinary," but to preserve values, networks, and social relations forged in times of conflict such as revolution, and that the official postwar status quo has marginalized?

Dhufari ex-revolutionaries living under authoritarian surveillance used everyday interactions of kinship and socializing to maintain networks, values, and relations once associated with the subsequently silenced revolution. Postwar kinship relations and everyday socializing, then, can reproduce relations and values that are not so much "ordinary" and "normal," but counterhegemonic. In Dhufar, former revolutionaries' relations and values were counterhegemonic to the extent that they reproduced egalitarianism along tribal, ethnic, racialized, and gendered lines. These connections contrasted with the iterations in Dhufar of social hierarchies of tribe, ethnicity, and social status that exist across Oman.[71] These egalitarian-leaning tendencies also struck a counterpoint to the hierarchical patronage relations in which Omanis (including former revolutionaries) participated.

The relationship of former revolutionaries' everyday interactions and counterhegemonic values to resistance is not straightforward, though. In an authoritarian context where interlocutors practiced discretion with me and also with each other, it is hard to interpret the meanings and intentions behind their actions. Ambiguity may be a necessary feature of afterlives of revolution under authoritarianism. Oman's governing authorities seemingly did not manifest concern at everyday practices of kinship, socializing, or routine forms of unofficial commemoration. These circumstances suggest the absence in these everyday interactions of resistance of concern to Oman's governing authorities.

Indeed, many possibilities for creating afterlives of revolution in Oman are likely dependent on the perceived absence therein of resistance of concern to the Sultanate's security apparatus. Omani authorities' different reactions to two of Dhufaris' more extraordinary acts suggest as much. In the first case, a Dhufari woman of elite background, Fahima, ran for election as a means of promoting a message of gender equality. Her action attracted conservative backlash from other Dhufaris. Those who disapproved of an elite woman's assuming a public profile criticized Fahima, her husband, and her brothers. Eventually, the sultan intervened to show his support for her. Had the authorities judged her action an act of resistance of concern to them, this outcome would have been unlikely. But in the second case, some of my interlocutors surmised that intelligence officers curbed plans for an exceptional gathering of elite former revolutionaries. They had intended to host the Front's former secretary general, 'Abd al-'Aziz al-Qadi, after his return to Oman in 2014. In contrast to these incidents of extraordinary actions, when it came to everyday acts such as kinship practices, informal socializing, and low-profile unofficial commemoration, signs of disciplinary intervention were seemingly lacking. This implies the perceived absence therein of resistance of concern to the authorities.

Apparent *perceived* absence begs a question: to what extent might everyday interactions of Dhufar's former revolutionaries be coded, subtle, but intentional "hidden transcripts" of resistance that authorities, whether deliberately or otherwise, neglected to discipline?[72] This book cannot address this question. Given ongoing conditions of surveillance and repression in Oman, a condition of writing about afterlives of revolution there must be to prioritize the safety of research participants in Oman. This book therefore defers from evaluating any intentional resistance to Oman's ruling authorities in the interactions of Dhufaris tracing revolutionary histories. Instead, the focus here is on the indications that neither Dhufaris nor their governing authorities perceived resistance of concern to the state in the everyday interactions of former revolutionaries or those close to them.

This book does, however, rethink the associations of kinship and the everyday with social reproduction and resistance, both in postwar contexts and more broadly. Postwar kinship and everyday relations can reproduce counterhegemonic values that reflect legacies of social life during past upheaval, including revolution. The role therein of resistance is not straightforward, however. The perceived absence of resistance of concern to the state was crucial for navigating the ethical and methodological challenges of research under authoritarianism.

Research Dilemmas in a Postwar Authoritarian Security State

All research raises questions of ethics and permissions. What risks might arise for research participants, including the researcher? How can the researcher mitigate against these risks? What is the scope, and limitations, of the informed consent that interlocutors can give to participate in research? What institutional permission is necessary for conducting research? What implications arise for future access for researchers? Addressing these questions is especially challenging when planning, conducting, and disseminating research about a postwar authoritarian security state that restricts freedoms of expression and association. These are the conditions in Oman.[73]

How far, I had to ask, can an interlocutor's consent to interact with a researcher during fieldwork, given with awareness of the risks as understood at the time, serve as ongoing consent should circumstances, and potential risks, change? Can the anonymization of interlocutors through changing names and biographical details offer sufficient protection? Is such protection adequate when the researcher must consider whether the government has surveilled the researcher's movements? Even when interlocutors give consent, to the best of each party's understanding of potential risks, what if institutional permission is unfeasible for a topic that an authoritarian government views unfavorably? There are no straightforward answers to these questions. I have endeavored to take the best precautions I could for research participants' safety.

Before my fieldwork, I was aware that it was sensitive to discuss the Front publicly in Oman. Yet I also knew that other researchers, Omani and foreign, had conducted research in Dhufar entailing meetings with ex-revolutionaries.[74] They included Dhufaris—Muhammad al-'Amri, Salim 'Aqil, and Mona Jabob—whose books addressing the revolution did not, at least initially, receive a Ministry of Information permit for sale in Oman, but nevertheless circulated privately there. Dhufari scholars continued to live and work in both the public and private sector in Oman, and to enjoy a public profile.[75] This suggested some reassurance about the possibility of conducting research on a sensitive subject.

Nevertheless, as the 2016 imprisonment of journalist ʿAbdullah Habib demonstrates, in Oman crossing a red line in the public mention of the Front risks repression and imprisonment. Omani political scientist Khalid Al-Azri notes that in Oman, "going beyond mainstream culture is quite dangerous not only politically but also socially."[76] Yet the boundaries of red lines were sometimes uncertain. Ambiguous red lines that necessitate intensive decision-making for self-censorship may be more efficient for governing authorities than heavy-handed repression.[77] In Oman, repression was a real possibility for the wrong kinds of public discussion of a sensitive topic. But as long as conversations were unofficial in the eyes of the government, red lines were ambiguous. Omanis had to engage in their own decision-making of how far to self-censor.

Weighing up conditions, I spoke with persons who had relevant experience, whom it is prudent not to name here and who are not responsible for my decisions. They anticipated that it would be possible for me to talk with and later write about ex-revolutionaries and other Omanis without posing a risk to them. They nevertheless also envisaged that it would be unlikely that I would receive institutional permission or affiliation in Oman to conduct research on topics of interest to me. Taking into account these views, as well as indications that it would be possible to conduct this research without posing a risk to interlocutors, the university where I was then a postdoctoral researcher gave ethical approval for fieldwork.

The lack of an institutional affiliation in Oman has been an ongoing worry for me, however—even as I am mindful that if research addressed only those topics for which authoritarian governments will grant permission, resulting gaps in scholarship would risk reproducing official silences and biases. Given the sensitivity of the topic, during five months of fieldwork in 2015 I typically introduced my research in the euphemistic terms that I evoked with the cab driver, which allowed interlocutors to steer discussion. I also thereby hoped to minimize the risk of causing distress to those for whom memories of the revolution and counterinsurgency were painful. This approach nevertheless meant that at times the revolution went unmentioned, as was the case in my conversation with electoral candidate Fahima. When an interlocutor brought up the revolution of their own accord, as happened when I learned about the family connections to the revolution of college student ʿAli, this was a lucky break. My open-ended entry points to conversations also meant that it was in situ that kinship, everyday socializing, and unofficial commemoration emerged as themes in the afterlives of revolution.

My lack of a research permit was also a worry for interlocutors. Commonly, on first meeting me an Omani would soon ask me, or the person introducing me: "What's your/her affiliation?" ("*Tabiʿah li aish?*", literally, "Following what?"). I always replied that I did not have an affiliation in Oman, which usually led to an awkward pause. Because I lacked an affiliation in the Sultanate, some potential interlocutors declined to meet or speak with me.[78] Some interlocutors informed me that some well-known figures from the revolution, who knew themselves to be under close surveillance, only talked to researchers who had a permit. I ended up meeting some of them informally through spending time with other ex-revolutionaries. But I did not attempt to interview them.

Some former militants who agreed to interact with me still preferred not to address the revolution directly. Instead, they warned me that "there is no benefit in [studying] this." The Front was not the only sensitive topic, though. I also received negative responses to requests for meetings in relation to my parallel interests in platforms for progressive politics in postwar Dhufar, such as efforts to diversify those elected to Oman's Consultative Council.[79] The sensitivity of revolutionary legacies was only one of several factors, amid concerns about surveillance, that made some wary of speaking to me.

There were gendered and generational contours to interlocutors' willingness, or otherwise, to discuss the Front. Of the twenty-six ex-revolutionaries whom I met, no one among the handful of women I encountered wanted to discuss the revolution directly. This resonates with wider gendered postwar experiences that often see female former militants face higher barriers than male peers in the quest to regain social acceptance.[80] Female ex-revolutionaries' experiences remain an ethnographic gap in the research that I was able to conduct. My engagement with Dhufaris' and others' testimonies and memories about their lives only partially mitigates that absence.

Despite the challenges of political sensitivity and surveillance, some interlocutors did choose to share stories of a revolutionary past with me. Does their desire to do so validate disseminating some of their experiences through publication? I hope that it can. Perhaps in some cases interlocutors told their stories *as a response* to surveillance. Sharing experiences with a researcher offered a means of challenging official erasure and disseminating to wider audiences stories that government narratives silenced.

I encountered greater willingness to discuss the revolution among interlocutors aged under forty who had close relatives (siblings, parents, and grandparents) who had lived through the revolution, counterinsurgency, and/or exile. Ex-revolutionaries and other older generations tended to refer to "the Front" (*al-jabhah*). This abbreviation conveniently sidestepped the challenge of the movement's multiple name changes. But interlocutors under forty more commonly spoke of "the revolution" (*al-thawrah*). One man, born toward the end of the war and aged around 40 when I met him in 2015, reflected openly on the sensitivity of referring to the revolution. He was telling me (in a public place, the mall, and speaking in front of a group of other Dhufari young men) about the experiences of members of his family in the Front. He began by using the circumlocution "the phenomenon of the rebellion" *(dhahirat al-tamarrud)* but then broke off to explain: "The government calls it the rebellion *(al-tamarrud)* but we call it the revolution *(al-thawrah)*." Thereafter, he continued to refer to the revolution, disregarding official avoidance of this term. Bearing in mind the sensitivity in Oman of reference to the revolution, I write here of *former* revolutionaries.

A further tension arose from Dhufaris' conviction that *who* shared information, and that person's expected loyalties along lines of ethnicity, tribe, status group, or political faction, determined its reliability. I encountered frequent warnings that I "had to speak to a lot of people" (even though this was precisely one of the hard things for me to do) to get multiple sides of a story.[81] Some interlocutors qualified their expertise in the light of their own positionality. Someone from a town background might refrain from commenting on the *jabal*, saying: "I don't know the *jabal*, so I don't know." Meanwhile, reports of local reactions to Dhufaris' publications on the Front highlighted controversies surrounding the reliability of sources. Several interlocutors described that some sources later claimed that authors had introduced mistakes. One author had apparently issued the challenge: "Let's sit down with [the source], and [the source] can show me the mistakes that I made." The source, however, had refused to meet the author again. Such postwar intellectual cross fire also existed among former revolutionaries.[82] It added to my anxieties.

Amid these constraints, much of my fieldwork consisted of joining in and observing everyday activities, what anthropologists call "participant observation." In addition to meeting ex-revolutionaries, I visited eighteen homes of Dhufaris and met more than twenty relatives of ex-revolutionaries for informal conversations and, more occasionally, more formal interviews. We met in places such as the mall, Dhufar University, all-male informal evening social gatherings, a hillside café that overlooked the coastal plain, and Salalah's first public library. The event of a foreign woman using this library was enough of a talking point for me to get into conversation with other (mostly male) readers. As I talked with Dhufaris, some preferred to speak in English but more usually we spoke in Arabic. I adapted the North African dialect of Arabic that I had learned in my previous research on revolutionary state power and social change among Western Sahara's refugees, which had led to my interest in legacies of revolutionary social change in Dhufar. I gained insights into everyday social dynamics, as well as distinctions between ex-revolutionary and nonrevolutionary families.

I was rarely alone with any interlocutor, male or female. Some revealing conversations took place during occasional one-on-one "offstage" conversations. These usually arose when an interlocutor drove me across the city from one destination to another. With no other Omani present to hear our conversation, interlocutors sometimes spoke more frankly about sensitive subjects not limited to the revolution.

It was during such car journey conversations that some male and female interlocutors of sub-Saharan African and enslaved heritage, whom Dhufaris call *sumur* (literally, "dark"), described to me racialized experiences of discrimination and exclusion. Dhufar's *sumur* descend from dark-skinned enslaved persons whom slavers brought from Zanzibar and East Africa. The emancipation of enslaved persons in Dhufar, and Oman more broadly, took place within living memory for older generations of my interlocutors. The Front abolished enslavement in 1968, and Sultan Qaboos in 1970. Official discourse since the accession of Qaboos asserts the equality of all Omanis. The government penalizes reference to formerly enslaved Omanis and their descendants as *'abid* ("enslaved persons").[83] The putative absence of discrimination was the state of affairs of which non-*sumur* interlocutors usually assured me. In practice, however, discrimination against Oman's formerly enslaved and their descendants persists in everyday life, as well as in some state-sanctioned practices.[84]

Sumur interlocutors usually broached experiences of discrimination with me once they had learned that as a white European I was going to marry (and married during the fieldwork) a dark-skinned man whose ancestry encompassed enslaved persons of sub-Saharan African heritage. The reactions of some non-*sumur* Dhufaris were also, albeit less self-consciously, revelatory of post-enslavement legacies, including discrimination and prejudice.

A middle-aged mother who hailed from a prestigious town tribe background, and who learned of my marriage, asked me: "Don't you mind that your children will be black?" Though recognizable to her, my husband's blackness reflected a process of racialization different from that of *sumur*. Blackness is a social construct that takes historically specific and varying forms across different contexts of racialized enslavement, colonialism, and their aftermaths.[85] In southern Arabia, this woman's question did not require specific knowledge about the appearance of potential children. In Muslim-majority settings, the question of belonging to a community of enslaved persons and their descendants, as well as racialized identities of blackness and whiteness, is not reducible to skin color or other phenotypical features.[86]

In southern Arabia (and elsewhere in SWANA), membership in a racialized community of enslaved persons and their descendants inheres from ancestry, specifically the exclusion from honorable ancestry (*asl*). (Criteria of descent likewise determine membership in other social groups.) Among patrilineal tribes (the most common pattern of tracing ancestry in Dhufar), the children of a father of free status married to a mother from the *sumur*, whether enslaved or the descendant of the formerly enslaved, belong to the father's tribe and not to the *sumur*, regardless of appearance. There is not a straightforward "taboo of racial miscegenation," such as that which manifests in some European settler colonial and imperial contexts of enslavement and post-enslavement.[87] In a context such as Dhufar, interracial mixing produces persons whose appearances do not, and cannot, define their social status. The possession of physical features associated with sub-Saharan African heritage is insufficient for ascertaining the "social blackness" of Dhufar's *sumur*.[88] Ancestry is decisive, with southern Arabians understanding that blackness also has social, linguistic, and ethical dimensions.[89] Nevertheless, some in Dhufar stigmatized racialized features such as dark skin. Such prejudice reflects wider antiblack racism in SWANA.[90]

Accordingly, the woman who "read" my marriage through local values needed only to make a judgment about my husband in order to project a social status onto future children. As her concern signaled, in Dhufar this social status mattered. A middle-aged male interlocutor from a similarly prestigious background suggested to me that, should my husband visit Salalah, he would "sit with his own people" as "this is where he will be comfortable." Such everyday segregation was just one form of discrimination that *sumur* faced, and that contrasted with official assertions of post-enslavement equality. In highlighting post-enslavement discrimination, the reactions to my marriage made the egalitarian leanings and socially inclusive gatherings of former revolutionaries stand out all the more.

My own positionality in interlocutors' eyes inevitably opened and foreclosed avenues of insight. Dhufaris weighed me up as a light-skinned childless British woman then in her mid-thirties (an age when some Dhufari women, including from my own generation, were grandmothers), who held a PhD and yet did not at that time have a long-term job, and who was embarking on an interracial marriage. Interlocutors regarded me as occupying an ambiguous position that spanned perceptions of me as privileged, vulnerable, naïve, a sympathetic outsider, a threat, and an opportunity. Many were impressed by the fact that I held a PhD. But female interlocutors in particular were concerned to learn that neither my natal family nor my government would provide me with land or housing. Male and female interlocutors were aghast at the cost of living in the UK, and especially income and sales taxes that did not then exist in Oman. My interracial marriage, and its reproductive prospects, concerned some interlocutors while inviting overture from others.

Perceptions of me as an assumed neutral or even sympathetic outsider encouraged some interlocutors to confide in me about things that worried them in Dhufar. But some older Dhufaris who had experienced British counterinsurgency attempts to securitize Dhufar as an occupation found my Britishness threatening. One grandmother, who had survived British soldiers repeatedly raiding her home as they sought her relative, became anxious when she saw me writing notes about the stories that family members were telling me, and left the room. For other interlocutors, though, suggesting interviews for me and accompanying me to them was an opportunity to set up meetings of interest to them: to meet a historian, an archaeologist, a senior administrator in a major business, a writer, or a figure of historical importance in Dhufar; to communicate to a key audience something dear to the arranger of the interview; to ask an expert on Dhufar's archaeology the million-dollar question of *who* were the first people in Dhufar (a claim that several groups disputed). Whatever the risks of interacting with me, some interlocutors also leveraged my research as an opportunity for their own networking and interests.

Ethical dilemmas took on new forms once my task shifted to publication. I was troubled making each decision about if and how to write about interactions with and between interlocutors, and how to shield them. The red lines of what might endanger interlocutors remained blurred. When I read about 'Abdullah Habib's arrest a year after my fieldwork, I wondered whether the red lines had hardened. Would interlocutors who had talked with me about certain topics still want me to know the information in question? Was it safe to ask them over the phone? The effectiveness of a system of censorship that operates via ambiguity—living not with a fire-breathing dragon or a man-eating tiger but under an overhead "anaconda in the chandelier"—is that the message of the anaconda is always the same: "You yourself decide."[91] These decisions continue to haunt me.

Whenever it seemed prudent for interlocutors' safety, I self-censored. After I shared early draft material with Dhufaris, I saw from their feedback that using pseudonyms and altering biographical details of interlocutors was not always reassuring enough. In response, I self-censored more. I took material out. I decided to include only material that reflected the kinds of interactions of which Oman's intelligence officers would already be aware. They know that in postwar Dhufar persons with revolutionary histories meet one another by habit and by chance in family celebrations, homes, cabs, cafés, the mall, educational spaces, and hospital wards. They are well aware that in private conversations and online, Omanis skirt official censorship to discuss the revolutionary past and its significance for the futures to which they look forward. They know about 'Abdullah Habib's Facebook posts, Fahima's electoral candidacy, and the thwarted celebrations for al-Qadi's return. The book makes no empirical revelations that go beyond the kinds of knowledge that Oman's intelligence personnel already hold about Dhufaris. It makes no argument for resistance of concern to the state that the authorities have neglected to identify. I alone am responsible for my argument that some former militants and their relatives created afterlives of revolution that reproduced counterhegemonic networks and values of egalitarianism and social inclusivity.

For material where I felt that an interlocutor might prefer to have the option of claiming that they had not made a particular remark, I introduced further "noise." I split conversations with one interlocutor over several pseudonyms. I amalgamated conversations from multiple interlocutors into one pseudonym flagged as a fictive composite. I camouflaged potentially sensitive comments within social contexts from which I could remove or disguise identifying information. Self-censorship has seemed the best way to live with my own decisions surrounding the ambiguous red lines of discussion about Dhufar's revolution.

Some of the topics that interlocutors preferred not to address with me were partially accessible through other sources. A rich historiography, including the work of Dhufari researchers, analyzes the revolution and the counterinsurgency.[92] Original and translated memoirs, diaries, and audiovisual material documented eyewitness experiences of those who took part in and supported the Front's efforts.[93] Counterinsurgency personnel authored memoirs too.[94] The vast archival resources on the conflict surpass the scope of a fieldwork-driven project. These archives necessarily house their own gaps. It is not only that the revolutionary archives did not survive the war in Yemen in the 1990s, or that archives by their very nature necessarily both include and exclude. The sensitivity of the topic has also created gaps. Some British documents addressing the 1970 coup and UK arms sales to Oman during the war remained classified or redacted at the time of writing.[95] Still, the depth of the available archival and other historical sources enables a conversation between surviving records and interlocutors' postwar lives as well as their memories of revolution and counterinsurgency.

There are two fields to which I had limited or no access. Dhufaris sometimes asked whether I was familiar with online resources that addressed the revolution. But they demurred from sharing digital lives with me, typically telling me that they no longer had access to sources. This response perhaps reflects caution in the context of the state's penalization of online activities that it perceived as seditious, of which ʿAbdullah Habib fell foul.[96] Although Omanis engage in online controversies that address sensitive topics, relevant posts can become inaccessible following removal.[97] Amid such constraints of access, this book attempts only an initial exploration of cyberspaces beyond the reach of official censorship that Omanis use to debate the revolution.[98]

Contemporary heated exchanges in cyberspace echo debates that historically many Dhufaris carried out through the medium of poetry in Modern South Arabian languages (MSAL). Often using oblique turns of phrase, this poetry has commemorated political landmarks, controversies, and griefs of MSAL speakers.[99] The unpublished corpus on Dhufar's revolution and counterinsurgency was linguistically and socially inaccessible to me. Poetry and cyberspace promise rich grounds for further research about legacies of Dhufar's revolution, for which this book lays groundwork.

Omanis' avid discussion of research about Dhufar's revolution indicates the readiness of many to contravene official silences. This keen reception is worth recalling when it comes to evaluating the impacts on interlocutors—and on researchers' future access—of politically sensitive research to which interlocutors consent but that lacks the approval of state authorities. Khalid Al-Azri argues that it is "worthwhile" to publish research about the sensitive topics that the Omani government seeks to silence. He contends that "overcoming such fears [of repression]" has "huge potential for changing the current status quo."[100] His optimism suggests grounds for cautious hope. It is possible that the more that research about sensitive topics circulates in Oman, the more people discuss these topics in person and on social media, and the less effective censorship becomes in practice. It might be that more research helps bring aperture, facilitating, rather than jeopardizing, future research access.

In Oman, writing and research about taboo topics such as Dhufar's revolution has already achieved change by breaking official silence. A further step toward change in which this book plays a part is to challenge persistent myths about revolution and counterinsurgency.

Controversies of Revolution and Counterinsurgency

Hegemonic narrations about revolution and counterinsurgency reflect political interests. Dhufar is no exception. Common discourses about Dhufar express underlying biases that are favorable to Sultan Qaboos and his British backers while denigrating the Front. Recurring themes include praise for the "model" counterinsurgency, condemnation of the Front for conducting a "red terror" campaign of violence, skepticism about Dhufaris' support for Marxist-inspired agendas, and celebration of Sultan Qaboos's enlightened modernization of Oman. Yet an ethnographically inspired analysis of revolution, counterinsurgency, and their afterlives foregrounds problems with each of these contentions.

A distinctive history and geography contributed to some Dhufaris developing anti-colonial aspirations that *preceded* the Front (Chapter 1). During the movement's programs for social transformation, militants engaged with revolutionary agendas in ways that laid grounds for lasting legacies (Chapter 2). Dhufaris drew on revolutionary experiences to shape wartime and postwar space, despite counterinsurgency agendas (Chapter 3). Former revolutionaries and some close to them created afterlives of revolution in postwar kinship (Chapter 4), social interactions spanning everyday gatherings and extraordinary electoral candidacy (Chapter 5), and unofficial commemoration (Chapter 6). These afterlives nourish platforms for progressive politics in Oman (Conclusion). Familiar myths unravel as they encounter ethnographic interrogation.

Some scholars, many British veterans of the war in Dhufar, and some military training manuals have represented the post-1970 campaign as a "model" counterinsurgency. In such idealized accounts, the operation "won hearts and minds" through a successful political campaign without relying heavily on conventional military and counterinsurgency violence.[101] Revisionist studies of the counterinsurgency have, however, shown the extent to which the government victory relied on conventional military interventions, such as increases in troop numbers and equipment, as well as counterinsurgency measures that impacted both combatants and civilians, such as food and water blockades, air strikes, and free-fire zones (Chapter 3).

Training an ethnographic lens onto the revolution and its afterlives further undermines the "hearts and minds" thesis by bringing closer into view Dhufari perspectives and experiences. The starvation conditions among Dhufaris changing sides to join the government highlight that generalizing narratives about "winning hearts and minds" mask lived realities. Dhufaris suffered greatly from counterinsurgency coercion, taking up lives in government-controlled areas under conditions of duress (Chapter 3).

Nor is it tenable to claim that (post-1970) counterinsurgency violence in Dhufar was "selective," causing only limited human damage because of the region's sparse rural population.[102] In addition to the indiscriminatory effects of blockades and free-fire zones, claims of "low" civilian casualties as a result of counterinsurgency violence exist despite the apparent absence of comprehensive documentation of Dhufari deaths and injuries, whether civilian or military (Chapter 1). A focus on civilian deaths and injuries from bombings and land mines would, in any case, be too narrow.[103] It would overlook the suffering and damage that ensue from the targeting of a subsistence economy. Counterinsurgency violence destroyed homes, livestock, grazing and water resources, and rain-fed agricultural plots and blockaded food and water resources. Coercion that affects a whole subsistence economy belies claims of "selective" violence. A "model" campaign narrative cannot account for the effects of counterinsurgency violence in Dhufar. But it does resound wholeheartedly with troubling colonialist tendencies to justify and downplay colonial violence.[104]

Any winning of hearts and minds is necessarily an unfinished project. Ongoing policies of both coercion and patronage throughout the war and postwar years, as well as ongoing acts of resistance, point to the incomplete nature of "winning hearts and minds" (Chapter 3). Protestors' warnings in 2011 "not to forget" the 1970s similarly expose the contingency of a "hearts and minds" victory (Conclusion).

An ethnographic interest in local perceptions raises the further complication that many in Dhufar disagree that a government campaign "won" their hearts and minds. Dhufaris of different political backgrounds believe, for potentially divergent reasons, that they won the war against the government. As early as 1977–78, *jabal* residents asserted that they were the war's true winners.[105] Some former members and sympathizers of the Front also claim revolutionary success.[106] Such convictions credit the revolution with deposing Said and establishing a modernization agenda that Sultan Qaboos's government then appropriated. As a Dhufari former revolutionary told me: "The government gave us everything we wanted: development, education, roads, hospitals . . ." Similarly, former revolutionary cadre Muhammad al-Ghassani reportedly explained on his return from Yemen to the Sultanate in 1987 that his "decision was based on his conviction that the Sultanate's achievements had matched his desired goal."[107] Some Dhufaris may have found further evidence of their victory in counterinsurgency policies that accommodated Dhufari demands for welfare services and the demands of pro-government paramilitary recruits for the government to relocate and purchase livestock at an inflated price favorable to herders (Chapter 3). Diverse government policies convinced many Dhufaris of their own victory.

The view that Dhufaris were among war's winners exists beyond Dhufar and former revolutionaries and sympathizers. In 2011, a northern Omani political activist suggested that "[i]n Dhofar . . . they won the war and pushed out Qaboos' father."[108] A British veteran officer agreed that Dhufaris were "hugely successful" in "[forcing] their opponents to adjust their own attitudes and approaches."[109] Besides these alternative interpretations of victory and success, decades after the formal end of the war, ex-revolutionaries participated in ongoing networks, reproduced counterhegemonic values of egalitarianism, and unofficially commemorated the officially silenced past (Chapters 4-6). These afterlives question the extent and nature of the alleged winning of hearts and minds.

Apologists have justified the counterinsurgency not only on the grounds of a "domino theory" of communist threat—a perceived danger that allegedly warranted saving Dhufar from communism in order to safeguard shipping access for oil tankers through the Strait of Hormuz in northern

Oman. In addition, apologists have also defended the war on the grounds that the Front exerted a reign of "red terror" in Dhufar's mountains. They accuse the Front of kidnapping children to take them for indoctrination in the Front's schools, killing practicing Muslims, and terrorizing the population with violence (Chapter 2).

Portrayals of the Front as a hotbed of "red terror" overlook contradictory evidence that an ethnographic eye for minutiae foregrounds. Each strand of the "red terror" narrative merits scrutiny. The Front sought consent for pupils to attend its schools. Dhufaris later recalled wanting to send their children to the school as a way of protecting them from counterinsurgency bombing. This casts doubt on kidnapping accusations. Sultan Qaboos, however, did plan to use armed intervention to capture and relocate Dhufari schoolchildren (Chapter 2).

Concerning Islam, a 1974 Front decree stipulated punishment for those who mocked religion. This implied that there were issues with the application of other Front resolutions that supported religious freedoms. But with some revolutionaries openly admitting that they prayed, the grounds on which to claim that the Front was "against Islam" need qualification. There are firmer grounds for two conclusions. It was undoubtedly part of the counterinsurgency propaganda campaign to portray the Front as anti-Islamic. At the same time, the Front called upon people in new ways to make choices about whether and how to practice Islam (Chapter 2).

Accusations that the Front terrorized Dhufaris merit scrutiny in order to unpack underlying political biases and contexts. Other than for reasons of political predilection, it is unclear why executions on the part of only one party to the war, rather than both, stand accused of provoking terror. The Front operated a policy of trying those accused of treason in military courts and executing those found guilty (Chapter 2). But the Omani government also brought captured Front activists to trial, submitted them, with the help of British instructors, to "interrogation techniques," issued death sentences, and executed revolutionaries.[110] Narratives of "red terror," however, highlight Front violence while neglecting counterinsurgency violence.

Moreover, accounts of communist-inspired killings in the Front's mountain strongholds may misread entangled categories of political violence. These narratives may misattribute to one form of political violence, the Front's internal violence, killings that may have resulted from individual Dhufaris' pursuit of another category of political violence, revenge killings. After the Front banned revenge killings, the movement's anti-treason policies presented an opportunity for Dhufaris so inclined to pursue revenge through a remaining category of officially legitimate violence, namely the punishment of convicted traitors. Such intra-Dhufari revenge killing took place among members of the pro-government paramilitaries during and after the war. Counterinsurgency authorities sometimes protected the killers.[111] If Dhufaris in counterinsurgency ranks took advantage of available opportunities to pursue revenge, it is plausible that some peers in revolutionary ranks also used accusations of treason to settle scores. Yet some commentators have likely drawn upon these killings to bolster the "red terror" narrative.

Another category of violence of which the Front stands accused is sexual violence. Without indicating sources, one commentator suggests that "[g]uerrillas . . . raped Dhofari women."[112] At issue for the present purposes is not a discussion of the truthfulness or otherwise of that accusation. This question falls beyond the scope of this research project.[113] In the context of problematizing the bias within "red terror" narratives, what is striking is the imbalance between the stating of such an accusation without reference to supporting sources and the scant acknowledgment, in many accounts, of counterinsurgency abuses against Dhufari civilians. Yet British memoirs documented such abuses. Having served as an officer with the Sultan's Armed Forces (SAF) between 1968 and 1970, Ranulph Fiennes recalled a raid in which an SAF fighter "climbed into the upper 'room' [in a family's cave dwelling] to fondle a little girl." During the same raid, the SAF soldiers took "an elderly man and boy" away in lorries, despite the remaining female relatives' protests that "they will all die if there is no one to collect wood for [*sic*] Salalah and buy food."[114] Dhufaris themselves later recalled fears of air strikes and starvation.[115] A problem with the "red terror" narrative, then, is the neglect of counterinsurgency raids, food and water blockades, and the bombing of fields, livestock, and homes as experiences that caused terror among Dhufaris.

By no means did coercion "peter out" in the move after 1970 toward a revised counterinsurgency with increasing patronage distribution (Chapter 3). Even as food and water blockades and bombings intensified after 1970, this coercion nevertheless fell short of the new sultan's ambitions. Qaboos made requests to bomb the al-'Amri tribe for being too slow to join the pro-government paramilitaries.[116] He also requested attacks on the Front's schools to capture the pupils (Chapter 2) and the use of napalm bombs (Chapter 3). British officials refused both suits. The British role in restraining Qaboos's appetite for violence is present in the archives—but it is usually absent from those memoirs and studies where, by contrast, "red terror" narratives abound. These narratives were and remain a potent ideological tool. They reiterate colonial stereotypes of colonized subjects' alleged irrational violence.[117] In doing so, these narratives aided the propaganda campaign to demonize the Front. They also diverted attention from the suffering of Dhufaris as a result of counterinsurgency violence.

It follows for some commentators that if the Front was so violent, Dhufaris' support for its Marxist-inspired programs is doubtful.[118] The notion that in its Marxist-leaning incarnation the Front lacked local support not only plays into the "hearts and minds" victory thesis but also feeds into debates about the war's outcome. There is speculation that the Front was unable to continue effective resistance once its "leaders no longer had any faith in the willingness of increasingly anti-Marxist Dhofaris to supply and conceal insurgents."[119]

The idea that Dhufaris did not "really" support Marxist-inspired initiatives deserves interrogation. The notion that the Front could not conceal fighters among a local population hostile to Marxism makes a number of questionable assumptions. It presumes the feasibility of such support in the actual conditions on the ground. Yet settlements in the *jabal* were sparse, limiting human coverage for Front fighters.[120] Moreover, from 1971 the counterinsurgency began its strategy of "clear and hold." Government-supporting forces cleared an area of Front fighters and then concentrated the population into surveilled settlements.[121] Counterinsurgency forces threatened to cut off water supplies if anyone supported the Front.[122] This policy has attracted comparison to "New Village" forced resettlement in the Malaya Emergency.[123] The viability of civilians concealing Front fighters in such conditions is open to question.

The putative lack of local support for Marxist-inspired programs also contradicts data from both the time of the revolution (Chapter 2) and its aftermath (Chapters 3–6). Archival material and Dhufaris' memories of the revolution show how Dhufaris actively engaged with revolutionary programs. They exceeded the timescales and scopes of official initiatives, negotiated forms of change acceptable in their own eyes, and made choices about social change (Chapter 2). This active engagement helps explain the possibility of long-term legacies arising from those programs. In the postwar period, the government had to keep reiterating coercive policies against those who supported remaining guerrilla fighters (Chapter 3). This indicates that at least some Dhufaris continued to be sympathetic to Front members.

Furthermore, ongoing postwar kinship practices, everyday socializing, unofficial commemoration, and occasional extraordinary acts showed how some former revolutionaries reproduced revolutionary networks and social values (Chapters 4–6). Feminist consciousness forged during the revolution survived in everyday and extraordinary acts (Chapter 5). Marxist-inspired programs elicited both early and long-lasting forms of engagement.

Many conventional narratives laud Qaboos as a "progressive" ruler, crediting him with the avoidance of the perceived potential catastrophe of a communist Dhufar.[124] These narratives stress how Qaboos brought a program of modernization to Dhufar and to the rest of what became the Sultanate of Oman. Dhufaris' subsequent access to roads, schools, health care, housing, and other welfare provisions, these narratives hold, was thanks to what Omanis would come to call Qaboos's "renaissance" (*al-nahdah*).

These accounts of a Qaboos-led renaissance transformation have met extensive criticisms. Other factors facilitated the Sultanate's modernization. These include oil revenues and the prior existence of plans that Qaboos's father, Sultan Said bin Taimur (ruled 1932–1970), had made. More broadly, the character of Gulf monarchies' plans for spatial transformations has been authoritarian and coercive, rather than "enlightened" (Chapter 3).

Ethnographic attention to revolution and its afterlives foregrounds two further interventions. Revolutionary agency had provoked the British to organize the coup against Said.[125] Similarly, popular agency has shaped Gulf urban spaces against the grain of ruling authoritarian projects.[126] These insights inspire this book's emphasis on ongoing revolutionary agency and legacies in transforming both wartime and postwar Dhufar. Dhufar's revolutionaries established agendas for social transformation. The counterinsurgency-focused government later took these up, albeit in altered forms. The government's programs also had very different social effects of increased tribalization and social inequalities. In addition, former revolutionaries who had studied in the revolutionary schools in an environment critical of tribalization were key to delivering postwar development programs. These former revolutionaries were willing to work on projects that would benefit any tribe and not just their own. Revolutionary agency helped transform wartime and postwar Dhufar (Chapter 3).

In parallel to highlighting revolutionary agency, the Dhufari case foregrounds that the transformation of space in the Gulf was not merely a project of authoritarianism. It was also a counterinsurgency prerogative. This counterinsurgency agenda bore infrastructural fruit in Dhufar in particular.

But the wartime and postwar spatial transformation of Dhufar attracted support and participation from Oman's colonial backer, Britain, and its allies, Saudi Arabia and Kuwait (Chapter 3).

Training an ethnographic lens on Dhufar's revolution and its afterlives, then, unseats myths at the very heart of conventional narratives about revolution, counterinsurgency, and their aftermaths. Such a project of ethnographic and conceptual interrogation can advance ongoing efforts to decolonize dominant and official narratives and histories. That work is especially fraught in contexts of anti-colonial aspiration and internationalized colonial counterinsurgency, whose arcs in Dhufar the next chapter charts. The Front did not achieve the form of political decolonization to which its militants and sympathizers aspired. But the unfinished business of multiple decolonizations continues. As an effort toward decolonizing narratives of revolution and counterinsurgency, this book aspires to be one among many afterlives of revolution.

1

Anti-colonialism and Counterinsurgency

"DHUFAR IS GREAT BRITAIN'S VIETNAM." This was the slogan with which student sympathizers of the revolution in Dhufar began solidarity meetings in France in the early 1970s.[1] The slogan cast the conflict as an anti-colonial revolution facing an internationalized, imperially backed anti-communist counterinsurgency. Unlike their peers in Vietnam, however, revolutionaries in Dhufar would not achieve the anti-colonial liberation for which they fought. In contrast to the United States in Vietnam, Britain would emerge as a victor in Dhufar. It would avoid contemporaneous international scrutiny of its counterinsurgency interventions there. With Sultan Qaboos subsequently imposing official silence about the war in Oman, Dhufar's revolution would lose much of its international attention. The conflict would fall into relative international obscurity, except among circles interested in the mythologization of a "model counterinsurgency."

In the context of such postwar relative obscurity-cum-mythologization, this book does not attempt a history of the conflict or a review of existing historiography such as others have provided.[2] Rather, this chapter locates the revolution and counterinsurgency in Dhufar within local, national, regional, and global contexts of political, social, and economic histories. Dhufar's distinctive history in southern Arabia positioned its residents to resist their exploitation as a colonial possession of the British-backed al-Busaid dynasty. By the 1960s, Dhufaris' histories of resistance to exploitative external rulers intersected with their engagements with Arab nationalism and leftist ideas. This led to the formation and evolution of the Front. The geopolitical context of insurgents' location close to strategic oil reserves ensured an increasingly internationalized counterinsurgency.

Crucibles of Anti-colonialism

How did Dhufaris in the late twentieth century come to harbor anti-colonial aspirations that aligned with global decolonization movements? To understand these developments requires going back further in time. Dhufar has a long history of political, economic, social, and religious distinctiveness compared with Muscat and the north of present-day Oman. Moreover, hinterland Dhufaris have long resisted coast-based rulers. This resistance continued after Dhufar became a personal dependency of the sultans of Muscat and Oman in the late nineteenth century. Sultan Said bin Taimur (ruled 1932–1970) intensified the dependency's exploitation. The Front would emerge as an insurgency against his British-backed rule.

Today, Dhufar is the southernmost governorate of the Sultanate of Oman. The country adopted that name and territorial form in 1970. In its contemporary form, Dhufar borders to the north with Saudi Arabia's "Empty Quarter" desert, to the west with Yemen's Hadhramawt region, to the south with the Indian Ocean, and to the east with the Jiddat al-Harasis desert that stretches for 800 km between Dhufar and the rest of the present-day Sultanate. The 2010 census, the most recent at the time of my fieldwork, identified a population in Dhufar of 249,729 Omanis and foreigners (mostly from South Asia, but others hail from the Arabophone world and the global north), out of a total population in Oman of 2,773,479.[3] The contemporary governorate of Dhufar covers some 99,300 km^2—about one-third of the Sultanate's land mass. This places the governorate as similar in size to South Korea, somewhere between the US states of Indiana and Kentucky, and larger than Scotland.

In previous centuries, however, the term "Dhufar" has referred to territory of varying scope. There has been "no continuous historical thread of a single unit 'Dhofar' to be traced with any certainty through the sources."[4] Likewise, the territorial scope to which "Oman" refers has changed. The post-1970 Sultanate of Oman includes Dhufar. But it excludes the former Trucial Oman—now the coastal areas of the present-day United Arab Emirates. This area had been under the influence of the rulers of Muscat before becoming part of Britain's formal empire in the nineteenth century. A notion of Oman that included Trucial Oman and Dhufar would become the focus of the Front's aspirations for anti-colonial liberation.

Once famous for the production of frankincense, Dhufar prospered in Hellenistic times. The fragrant gum resin was in high demand for burning in temples and at funerals.⁵ Dhufar has the rare climate and terrain suited to frankincense.⁶ From June to September, monsoon rains reach Dhufar's central mountain plateau, bringing rain, fog, and mild temperatures. The resin grows on trees on the southern slopes of the central Jabal al-Qara mountains, in the hinterland of al-Mughsail, and on the dry plateau north of the Jabal al-Qara.⁷ Demand for frankincense dramatically declined by the end of the third century CE, however. Dhufar's economy weakened over the following centuries. The bustling port city that Ibn Battuta visited in 1327 fell into decline between 1500 and 1700.⁸ The remains of this port city are today's al-Baleed archaeological park in Salalah.⁹ One interlocutor described the unsettling experience of seeing the ruins as he traveled by foot or by donkey between the then villages of Salalah and al-Dahariz in the 1960s: "We saw the big stones. We knew that there had been a lot of people living here, that our fathers had been great. But where had all the people gone?"

With the decline of the frankincense trade, Dhufaris increasingly relied on a subsistence economy of exchanges among the diverse populations of the region's three geographical zones: coastal plain, hinterland mountains, and desert beyond. Dhufaris interacted across these zones and across ethnic, tribal, and racialized social distinctions for trade, seasonal migration, and marriage. Accounts of Dhufar in the nineteenth and twentieth centuries describe not only a situation fluctuating between "uneasy truce" and periodic tensions between settled populations of the plain (*ahl al-hadr*, "settled people") and seasonally mobile populations in the interior.¹⁰ They also attest to stratified economic interdependence across the coast, mountains, and desert amid widespread poverty.¹¹ In economic terms, inter-reliance and exchange and their associated demographics predominated until, from the 1960s and 1970s, conflict, displacement, dispossession, immigration, and oil revenues greatly altered Dhufar's demographics and livelihoods.

The social hierarchies prevalent in the context of the pre-oil economy have continued in modified forms and relationships among contemporary Dhufaris (those tracing pre-1970 family histories in Dhufar). Dhufaris command detailed knowledge of the relative prestige of different tribes, ethnic groups, and those historically excluded from the privileges of tribal membership. These hierarchies structured daily life in Dhufar for many of my interlocutors, as they had for earlier generations.¹²

In the pre-oil economy, Dhufar's coastal plain, called *jarbib*, stretching from Raysut to Taqah, nearly fifty kilometers wide and up to ten kilometers deep, supported irrigated agriculture thanks to its tropical climate, as well as fishing and seasonal transhumant herding.[13] The main population center after circa 1700 was a cluster of villages that would later form the core of present-day Salalah. By the nineteenth century, al-Husn contained the sultan's palace and the suq.[14] To the east was al-Hafah, and beyond al-Hafah were the al-Baleed ruins. East of al-Baleed was al-Dahariz. North of al-Husn and al-Hafah, beyond irrigated coconut plantations, was the village that locals then knew as "Salalah."[15]

The plain had a diverse population. Arabophone elites there included Kathiri tribes, *sadah* families tracing descent from the prophet Muhammad, and tribes with Somali origins.[16] Their protégés included Arabophone low-ranking families associated with professions such as trade, and historically known as *duʿaf* (literally, "weak.") Interlocutors nevertheless warned me that this term had become derogatory, and that for some years prior to my fieldwork those concerned had avoided using it about themselves.

Further down the social hierarchy of Arabophone coastal non-elites were client fishing families (*bahharah*) and Dhufar's community of dark-skinned persons of African and enslaved heritage (*sumur*). Until the 1970s, many were enslaved persons (*ʿabid*). Both elite and non-elite Arabophone families owned enslaved persons. In the nineteenth and twentieth centuries, many of the enslaved worked irrigated farms to produce cereals, millet, sweet potato, sugar cane, tomatoes, cucumber, onions, bananas, papaya, and coconut, among other foodstuffs.[17]

Besides these Arabophone populations, the coast was also home to speakers of the MSAL Shahri. They lived in coastal villages such as Mirbat and Rakhyut, respectively to the east and west of the villages that make up present-day Salalah.

The mountains, *jabal*, rise as a steep escarpment to the north of the plain, with Jabal al-Qamar to the west, Jabal al-Qara in the center, and Jabal Samhan to the east. The mountain range reaches heights of up to 1,200 m, dropping beyond to hilly pastures and deep wadis. Thanks to the monsoon (*kharif*, literally, "autumn" in standard Arabic), these varied *jabal* landscapes supported the raising of cattle, camels, and goats, as well as post-monsoon rain-fed agriculture: "As soon as the rains, the heavy clouds and the thick mists were over, the sunshine would reveal a spectacular landscape, green and flower-bedecked on the hills and in the valleys, with blue pools and leafy oases, and with animals delivering calves and yielding plenty of milk."[18] Such scenes of bounty were transient, though. For most of the year those living in Dhufar's interior faced severe shortages of water.

Some families owned different species of livestock, while others specialized in raising one kind of livestock. In the Jabal al-Qara mountains, settlement patterns ran "south-north in a fan-like structure whose handle is the Salala plain." In this metaphorical fan, "each 'rib' stretches from the upland plateau, across the grasslands, down the escarpment and to the foothills and the plain." A particular tribe "more or less occupied the area between two such 'ribs.'"[19] As a result, one tribe could have families specializing in each kind of herding. Some families also traded frankincense.

Mobile pastoralist inhabitants of the mountains, known collectively as *jabbali* people, were ethnically diverse. They comprised speakers of MSAL: Shahri, Mahri, and Hobyot. Elites included Qara tribes (also present in eastern and western coastal villages), *mashayikh* religious elites, mountain-based Kathir al-jabal, and Mahra tribes.[20] The latter speakers of Mahri spanned the northeast *jabal* and desert beyond, with other Mahra living in the western coastal region bordering with Yemen. The Qara's subordinates and clients were the *shahrah*. In the late twentieth century and early twenty-first century, Qara and their former *shahri* clients were two of the groups who hotly disputed claims to be the longest-standing inhabitants of Dhufar's *jabal*. *Jabbali* families moved seasonally according to the availability of grazing resources and their rights of access to them. Their homes and shelter for livestock ranged, according to season and terrain, from caves to one-room dwellings made of wood and stone, and shelters constructed around trees.[21]

The gravel plains to the north of the *jabal*, leading beyond to the Najd sand desert, were home to mobile pastoralist Arabophone Bedouin Bait Kathir tribes and Mahra tribes. These populations engaged in transhumant camel and goat raising, with the frankincense trade remaining significant until the 1960s.[22]

The interconnectedness between populations of coast, mountains, and desert intersected with high levels of social stratification. This would provide scope for the Front's radical policies promoting social egalitarianism. Seasonal climatic variation saw people move back and forth between regions. These movements underscored communities' mutual, if stratified, interdependence. Herders relied on dried sardines purchased on the coast to get their livestock through the lean pre-monsoon dry season. Pastoralists also moved flocks between mountain and desert, and between mountain and coastal plain, according to the season and suitable environments for the animals in question.²³ Some coast-based MSAL speakers relocated during the monsoon to the *jabal* to engage in rain-fed agriculture.²⁴ Some coast-based families, including Arabophone families, spent the cool post-monsoon *sarb* season in the mountains. They enjoyed access to plentiful fresh milk, as older generations of Dhufaris recalled to me. These families collected clarified butter through which *jabbali* families repaid debts incurred during the purchase of dried sardines.²⁵ Ties of marriage facilitated seasonal migrations. Common practice in Dhufar (as elsewhere in SWANA) saw women marry within or above, but not normally below, their social status. Within these constraints, families made marital and other connections across desert, mountain, and coast.

There is scant documentation about historical population numbers for each of these groups. British estimates placed Dhufar's early twentieth-century population at a total of 11,000 (Table 1). In the 1960s estimates for the total population rose to between 30,000 and 50,000.²⁶ Dhufar's first census took place in 1977 after the demographic disruption of war, exile, internal displacements, and immigration. It identified a population of 67,200 (Table 2).

Politically, over the centuries, "[v]arious semi-independent dynasties came and went" in Dhufar.²⁷ Rulers from Yemen to the west and Muscat to the north competed for control that in practice did not extend far from the coastal plain. The "most persistent and longest-lasting" of these rulers were Kathiris who also ruled Yemen's Hadhramawt region in the fourteenth century.²⁸ Close links with the Hadhramawt reflected Dhufar's geography that resembled a metaphorical island. Encircling Dhufar were the hinterland mountains and desert, the Jiddat al-Harasis, the rough monsoon winds that

TABLE 1. Population Estimates for Dhufar in the Early Twentieth Century

Villages near Salalah	3,000
Settled population elsewhere on coast	1,500
Qara	4,250
Kathir Bedouin	2,000
Other Bedouin	250
Total	11,000

Source: Lorimer, *Gazetteer*, 2:444.

TABLE 2. Census of Dhufar's Population in 1977

Salalah	35,000
Mirbat	3,000
al-Dahariz	650
ʿAwqad	1,500
Other coastal settlements	3,092
Jabal	16,470
Najd	4,578
The West	2,217 (This low figure perhaps represents low population in the western area that had seen the war's final battles.)
Other (location not specified)	693
Total	67,200

Source: Sichel, "Sultanate," 36.

closed Dhufar's ports for several months a year, and the single road (still unpaved by the 1960s) that linked Salalah to Thumrait north of the *jabal* and to Muscat some nine hundred kilometers beyond.

This geography of separation only compounded Dhufar's distinctiveness as opposed to Muscat and present-day Oman's northern mountain hinterland, al-Jabal al-Akhdar. The inhabitants of al-Jabal al-Akhdar, as well as the Muscat-based al-Busaid dynasty and most of the population in Muscat and the surrounding plain, practice Ibadhism.[29] This branch of Islam originates in a movement that broke away from both Sunni and Shiʿa branches of Islam in the seventh century CE. Adherents supported the choice of a caliph on the grounds of faith rather than hereditary leadership.[30] At various times until the 1960s, Ibadhis in the mountain interior chose a religious ruler, an imam. The rule of an imam was especially appealing when inhabitants of the northern interior were frustrated with the rule of the Muscat-based al-Busaid dynasty that came to power in 1749. By contrast, Dhufaris, like their Hadhrami peers, are Sunni Muslims who follow the Shafiʿi school of jurisprudence. In Dhufar, as in the Hadhramawt, religious elites are *sadah* families tracing descent from the prophet Muhammad. *Sadah* families first moved from the Hadhramawt to Dhufar in the twelfth century.[31]

Dhufar, then, has a very different ethnic, political, economic, and cultural history from Muscat and the north of present-day Oman. Intermittently, northern-based projects of political rule attempted, and struggled, to exert and maintain influence over Dhufar. Portuguese tenure in Muscat and the Gulf in the sixteenth and seventeenth centuries left oral histories among Dhufaris of battles with the Portuguese.[32] The northern Omani Ya'aribah dynasty (ruled 1624–1742), which displaced the Portuguese, briefly sent troops to Dhufar's coast.[33] In 1829 Sultan Said bin Sultan, who greatly expanded the maritime empire under al-Busaid rule, claimed Dhufar, but dropped these claims once he established his capital in Zanzibar.[34] The current period of al-Busaid formal political authority over Dhufar dates to 1879.

In a foreshadowing of late twentieth-century events, the late nineteenth century saw Britain pursue its colonial interests by facilitating al-Busaid claims to Dhufar. In the mid-1870s, Dhufari tribal leaders had invited a renowned Sufi who was descended from a Hadhramawti *sadah* family, Sayyid Fadhl bin 'Alawi, to settle tribes' disputes and govern Dhufar. Sayyid Fadhl governed Dhufar from 1875 to 1879, until British fears that he would extend Ottoman influence in the area led the British to push him out.[35] Thereafter, some Dhufari tribal leaders invited Turki bin Said, sultan of Muscat and Oman, to govern. Dhufar became, officially, a dependency of the sultan. In practice, like their predecessors, the sultans had little authority over Dhufar beyond a palace complex and its immediate surroundings. They also faced recurrent uprisings from Dhufar's hinterland tribes in 1880, 1888, 1895–97, and 1907.[36]

The sultans were, in turn, from the latter half of the nineteenth century, increasingly reliant on British finance and military support. As Britain became the dominant maritime power in the Indian Ocean, the sultan's dominions became part of Britain's "informal empire."[37] The advent of steamships had allowed trade routes to bypass ports in the al-Busaid Indian Ocean empire, leading to its decline. Keen to control sea routes to India, Britain sought dominance over, and stability in, routes via Arabia. Accordingly, in 1861 Britain formalized recognition for two separate polities: on the one hand, the ruler of Muscat and Oman, and, on the other hand, the ruler of Zanzibar. An annual subsidy (the Canning Award) from Zanzibar to the sultan of Muscat and Oman underpinned this arrangement, with Britain guaranteeing payment. This gave Britain political and financial influence over the rulers of Muscat.[38] These payments continued until 1956, with other subsidies following shortly after.[39]

Subsequent sultans became increasingly indebted. Economic decline and British political influence added to the frustrations with the rule of the al-Busaid on the part of inhabitants of the northern interior, the Ibadhi heartland. In 1913, they elected a new imam and declared jihad against

British-backed Sultan Taimur bin Faisal.[40] To resolve the ensuing conflict, in 1920 the British brokered the Treaty of Seeb. It established a distinction between "Oman" as an interior territory over which the imam ruled, and Muscat and its surrounding area, over which the al-Busaid sultan governed. The sultan retained Dhufar as a personal dependency. Dhufar was not formally part of either the polities of Muscat or Oman as defined in the treaty. When Taimur abdicated in 1932, Said bin Taimur inherited a situation of indebtedness, reliance on British financial support, dependence on British military intervention for dynastic survival, and fragmented territorial sovereignty.

Over his nearly forty-year reign, Said acquired a reputation—for his (many) critics, a notorious reputation—that would last well beyond his lifetime for being averse to political and social change. This reputation is not without foundation. Said feared that contact with the outside world and Western-style education would introduce his subjects to ideas that would encourage revolt. He told an advisor: "This is why you [the British] lost India, because you educated the people."[41] Consequently, Said sought to restrict the possibility of such contact for his subjects. Both boys and girls could attend privately run Qur'anic schools where local communities provided these.[42] But Said restricted access to Western-style education. He founded the first Western-style primary schools for his subjects in Salalah in 1936, in Muscat in 1940, and in Bait al-Mandhari (later relocated to Muscat's Corniche) in 1959.[43] Said restricted entrance, however.[44] By 1970, these schools reportedly catered to 909 male pupils among a population estimated by the 1960s to number some 500,000 across the territories then known as Muscat, Oman, and Dhufar.[45]

Said restricted other activities that he feared reflected contact with foreign influences, such as owning a radio or riding a bicycle.[46] He allowed his subjects few opportunities to pursue education or work abroad and personally controlled access to passports. As a result, many young men, including from Dhufar, fled clandestinely in order to pursue education and work in the Gulf, Iraq, and Egypt. Ironically, clandestine students' lack of an approved passport pushed some of them into closer contact with leftist governments that Said feared. Some students went on to pursue higher education in communist countries that were willing to accept them without an official passport.[47]

It was not only access to education that Said's subjects lacked. Health care services were limited, and in Dhufar they were virtually nonexistent.

Communication and travel were challenging: according to one of the more generous estimates, by 1970 there were thirty to fifty kilometers of paved roads in the whole Sultanate.[48] After the coup in 1970 that deposed Said, British press coverage further tarnished the reputation of the man whom until then Britain had been protecting as an ally. Reports circulated of Said's stockpile of weapons in the palace in Salalah and of his alleged mistreatment of enslaved persons.[49] Furthering Said's reputation for harshness are British diplomatic papers that record him making derogatory comments, such as that Dhufari young men were "like rats."[50]

Undoubtedly, then, Said's rule was harsh for the majority of his subjects. The situation of Dhufaris as subjects of a dependency that Said treated as his private estate was particularly dire. Said expropriated valuable agricultural land in the plain, introduced taxes higher than those that he imposed elsewhere, and directed revenues from Dhufar into his private bank account.[51] Many Dhufaris experienced his rule as colonial exploitation at the hands of a ruler whom they perceived as an outsider from the north. Moreover, this ruler relied principally on military personnel whom Dhufaris also perceived as foreign: Britons, northern Omanis, and Baluchis (an ethnic group from Makran in present-day Pakistan, where the al-Busaid sultans possessed the enclave port of Gwadar from 1783 until 1958). This colonial experience contributed to Dhufari resistance to the British-backed Said and, eventually, their support for the Front.

Recognition of Dhufaris' colonial experience under Said, however, should not preclude interrogation of one-sided portrayals of Said as a tight-fisted despot averse to change.[52] Vilifying portrayals of Said reproduce colonial stereotypes of an "oriental despot." Such representations all too neatly support clichéd narratives. They tidily cast Said as the villain who stands in contrast to Qaboos as the apparent savior of the Sultanate of Oman.[53] Equally, the demonization of Said plays to celebratory depictions of Dhufar's revolutionaries as oppressed victims of Said's harshness.[54] Said's notorious reputation neglects the fact that, once he expected oil revenues, he began plans for investment in services and infrastructure, such as a hospital for Salalah. (Qaboos would later complete Said's plans, adding fuel to the "Qaboos transformation" myth.) These plans situate Said as an advocate of conservative colonialism, open to minimal change while maintaining the status quo.[55] Indeed, though opposed to change that he believed would threaten his rule, Said sought other forms of transformation. He was determined to alter to his advantage the challenging political and economic situation that he had inherited. Those changes that he achieved, and the continuity of his reliance on British imperial backing for political survival, ultimately reinforced the scope for Dhufaris to experience his rule as colonial, imperially backed exploitation.

Through frugal rule, Said initially balanced his country's finances.[56] He also leveraged British military intervention to end the Treaty of Seeb's fragmented sovereignty between Muscat and Oman. Between 1954 and 1959, a series of conflicts erupted in al-Jabal al-Akhdar.[57] Anglophone convention and Omani government discourses refer to them as a war or rebellion, but some decolonial approaches refer to a "revolution."[58] British military intervention eventually secured the area under the imam's rule for Said and, by extension, Petroleum Development Oman (PDO).[59] Counterinsurgency established a form of territorial sovereignty suitable for the needs of capitalist oil exploration.[60] The imam and his supporters fled into exile in Saudi Arabia. The prospect of oil revenues allowed Said to envisage financial independence from the British. With the first revenues projected for March 1967 (and arriving in August that year), Said announced plans for new infrastructure.

Said was not alone in anticipating greater financial independence thanks to oil revenues. In March 1967 Britain ended the subsidies for development projects in Muscat and Oman that it had stipulated in 1958 as a condition for further military intervention in al-Jabal al-Akhdar.[61] Britain had insisted on these projects, and on paying for the Development Department of Muscat and Oman, as an investment against future insurgency. Without such investment, Britain feared that Omanis would be frustrated with the lack of development and likely rebel again. Dhufar, though, as a dependency that was not part of Muscat and Oman, did not fall within the remit of the Development Department.[62] This exclusion fitted wider British complicity in Dhufar's separate treatment. British officials excluded Dhufar as a "special case" from efforts to pressure Said to lighten restrictions on his subjects.[63]

Despite the power imbalance between Britain and Said in the 1958 agreements about military and development agendas, Said had nevertheless been able to achieve some advantage for himself. The concessions that he secured further cemented colonial rule over Dhufar. The agreement granted access for Britain's Royal Air Force (RAF) to the air base at Masirah Island located between Salalah and Muscat. In return, Said required Britain to maintain the RAF base in Salalah. Britain had developed an air base at Salalah during WWII as part of an alternative air route between Aden and India. Once this route no longer connected two British colonies, this air base was of limited interest to Britain. The Salalah air base nevertheless offered Said an escape route out of Salalah should his worst fears of rebellion materialize. Consequently, even when Britain later pressured to close the base, Said would insist on its maintenance. Four years into the war in Dhufar, British officials had begun to look upon RAF Salalah not merely as an unnecessary expense but also as a political liability. There was a risk of bad publicity in the event of the death of RAF personnel "in a war which is not our business and in which our involvement, given the Sultan's character, would be particularly unpopular."[64] Said, however, insisted on keeping the base open. He would eventually leave Dhufar from that base—but only when the British had turned against his rule.

Once he had assured the future of the RAF base at Salalah, Said extended his previous habit of spending several months a year in Dhufar's favorable climate. From 1958 he took up permanent residence in Salalah. There he was comfortably distant from the visits of northern tribal leaders that incurred inconvenient expenses. His wife, Mazoon bint ʿAli Ahmad, who hailed from Dhufar's al-Maʿshani Qara tribe, and their only son, Qaboos, born in 1940, were already living in Dhufar. Once permanently resident in Salalah, Said ruled Muscat at a distance. He spoke several times a day by telephone to his administrative deputy Major Chauncy, a former British consul general in Muscat—whom one British official described as the sultan's "unofficial Prime Minister."[65]

In Dhufar's distinctive history, the resistance of mountain hinterland tribes to rulers on the plain is long-standing, the claims of the al-Busaid dynasty to Dhufar are recent, and imperial backing facilitated Said's colonial exploitation of the dependency. All these factors contributed to many Dhufaris' resistance against the rule of the al-Busaid dynasty. These Dhufari trajectories intersected in the 1960s with regional and global political crucibles of anti-colonialism, Arab nationalism, and Marxism. Many Dhufaris came to understand their situation in explicitly anti-colonial terms. They included those who founded the Front.

The Emergence of a Liberation Movement

Dhufari migrants in the Gulf escaping Said's restrictive policies found not only opportunities for work and education; they also encountered anti-colonial, anti-imperialist, and nationalist movements and ideologies, in particular the Movement of Arab Nationalism (MAN), Nasserism, and

Marxism. This political context of intersecting global, regional, and local mobilizations produced a movement that would eventually pursue both national liberation and Marxist-inspired social transformation.[66]

Dhufari migrants grew in number in Kuwait, Bahrain, Qatar, Iraq, and Egypt in the 1950s and 1960s. At the same time, political mobilization around nationalism, anti-imperialism, and leftist political ideologies was growing in the region and globally. Egypt's Nasser had seized the Suez Canal from Britain in 1956, Iraq's British-backed monarchy fell in 1958, and Kuwait gained independence from Britain in 1961. Activists were mobilizing against ongoing British imperialism in Aden, the Trucial States, Bahrain, and Qatar, where Britain was the formal colonial power. In the Sultanate of Muscat and Oman, Britain officially denied being the colonial power.[67] In practice, all bar one of Said's advisors were British, including those holding top military and security positions.[68] Britain represented the sultan in the country's limited diplomatic relations (the country being a member of neither the Arab League nor the United Nations).[69]

These conditions were among the reasons leading to several UN General Assembly resolutions that condemned Britain's colonial relationship with Sultan Said.[70] Anti-colonial UN member states made their criticisms publicly. But they were not alone in considering Britain to be a de facto colonial power in Muscat and Oman. Privately, a 1965 internal PDO report recommended that, in order to address growing political threats in the Sultanate, the "fiction of the Sultan's independence should be put aside."[71] The colonial situation of the sultan and his subjects struck multiple audiences—including Dhufaris who sought to tackle this predicament.

Dhufari migrants who frequented student and workers' gatherings in the Gulf, Iraq, and Egypt founded both public and clandestine Dhufari political associations.[72] These associations nurtured emerging Dhufari identity and opposition to foreign rule and exploitation. In 1962, Dhufari migrants in Kuwait founded the Dhufar Charitable Association (DCA). This organization was pioneering in bringing together Dhufaris from different tribal backgrounds around a shared Dhufari identity that surpassed tribes.[73] Ostensibly the DCA raised money for building mosques and education, but in practice members mobilized funds for buying weapons to oppose Said. Their slogan was "Dhufar for Dhufaris." In addition, in the late 1950s Dhufari migrants formed Dhufari branches of MAN.[74] A third organization, the Dhufar Soldiers' Organization (DSO), was composed of covert cell members across the security and police forces of the Gulf. A fourth organization, The Black Hand (*al-kaff al-aswad*), mobilized Dhufar's enslaved persons to achieve emancipation.[75] ʿAmer al-Bahraini, a Dhufari of enslaved heritage who had migrated to the Gulf, founded this organization in the early 1950s.[76] Meanwhile, opposition to Said also emerged within Dhufar. Musallam bin Nufl was a Bait Kathir shaikh who hailed from the area where the PDO was carrying out oil prospecting. He organized attacks on PDO targets, from vehicles to the sultan's military personnel, in April 1963 and from August to November 1964.[77]

With Dhufaris mobilizing to oppose Said's rule both in Dhufar and abroad, in December 1964 leaders of the DCA, the Dhufari branch of MAN, and the DSO agreed to work together. In early June 1965, at their first Congress in a cave near Wadi Nahiz in central Dhufar, they formally founded the Dhufar Liberation Front (DLF).[78] Bringing together multiple organizations and mobilizations, the DLF housed divergent political tendencies: Arab nationalist members of MAN, who included left-wing sympathizers; Dhufari nationalist members of the DCA who privileged Dhufari (rather than Arab) nationalism; and those who saw the uprising as part of long-standing patterns of tribes mobilizing against the claims to Dhufar of the British-backed sultan of Muscat and Oman. Their shared aim was to liberate Dhufar. Early Front broadcasts from the Cairo-based Voice of the Arabs radio station couched that goal in terms of armed struggle for independence and social justice. In December 1967, broadcaster Yusuf bin ʿAlawi called for "armed revolution" that aimed at "achieving for the people freedom, national independence and a dignified free life." He asserted that "every Dhufari citizen is today ready to sacrifice his life for the public interest, the interest of the people, the interest of the poor and the sick, the unemployed and the victims of injustice."[79] Revolutionary appeals to social justice preceded the movement's formal embrace of Marxism-Leninism.

Inaugurating the revolution on June 9, 1965, the DLF undertook its first action of armed insurrection: attacking and killing the driver of an oil company vehicle northwest of the road from Salalah to Thumrait.[80] In members' own accounts, the fighters at this stage numbered thirty-seven men and nine rifles.[81] By March 1966 British intelligence estimated that Front fighters numbered between eighty and two hundred.[82] Despite these relatively low numbers, Front fighters had several advantages over the Sultan's Armed Forces (SAF). Front combatants knew the mountain terrain well. Many had previous military training experience, having served in Gulf security forces.[83] They also had the support of Dhufaris from different tribes and social statuses, as a March 1968 British intelligence report acknowledged.[84] Popular support for the Front in fact extended further than a report focused on male Dhufaris could acknowledge. Women living in the *jabal* supported Front fighters. Both Front and counterinsurgency sources acknowledged women's early support.[85]

Nevertheless, the Front struggled to make military advances. The counterinsurgency forces operated a blockade on supplies to Dhufar. This left Front fighters short of weapons and both fighters and civilians in the mountains in starvation conditions. One Front fighter recalled that prior to supplies from the People's Republic of South Yemen (PRSY from November 1967 to November 1970)—later the People's Democratic Republic of Yemen (PDRY from November 1970)—weakening the blockade's effects, Front soldiers would go for three or four days eating only leaves from trees.[86] As the Front's leadership sought ways to overcome these difficulties, over 1967 and 1968 internal and external factors pushed the leadership toward an ideological shift to the left.

From within the movement, Front leaders were reflecting on how to overcome the difficulties that they faced. Regional and global developments suggested that a shift to the left could offer ways forward. Left-wing ideologies were in the ascendant in liberation movements. In the wake of the crisis of Arab nationalism after Israel's defeat of Egypt and allies in June 1967, activists in Gulf nationalist movements shifted to the left. With the USSR advocating "peaceful coexistence" with colonial and imperial powers, Maoist China emerged as the global leader supporting liberation movements. When in early 1967 a DLF mission sought aid from multiple embassies in Cairo, China was the only country to offer DLF delegates support. A follow-up delegation from the Front to China in June 1967 saw the delegates return bearing weapons and copies of Mao's Red Book.[87] Where China showed interest in Dhufar, Maoism's espousal of rural insurgency was also appealing in the Dhufari context of pastoral and agricultural economies lacking an urban proletariat.

In addition to these shifts toward leftist politics in Arab nationalism and in liberation movements globally, Dhufar gained a socialist neighbor in November 1967 when Aden gained independence from the UK. Military and food supplies from socialist Yemen weakened the effects of the counterinsurgency blockade on food and weapons supplies to the Front. Global and regional developments, then, both increased the influence of leftism on Dhufar's Front and made some nationalists in Dhufar, and beyond, more receptive to leftist ideas.[88]

The pace and scope of the spread of Marxist-Leninist sympathies in the Front is not straightforward to trace from surviving accounts. This topic also proved too sensitive for me to broach with interlocutors. A year after the Front's first delegation to China, British intelligence officials were still uncertain as to the extent of Maoist leanings in the Front. In June 1968 counterinsurgency forces recovered the corpse of a Front cadre "found with a Chinese or Russian automatic, a Mao Tse Tung badge, and a further metal badge showing crossed automatics of communist design and the Arabic words 'Dhofar Liberation Front.'" Derrick Carden, British consul general in Muscat, reported to Robert Crawford, political resident in the Persian Gulf, that "one can still only guess at the significance of these facts."[89]

In September 1968 some of the Front's leaders made their intentions clear. The Front held its second Congress at Hamrin in the liberated territories of Dhufar from September 1 to 20, 1968. The majority of the circa sixty-five delegates voted to espouse Marxism-Leninism and scientific socialism.[90] Delegates thereby endorsed the notion of a small vanguard guiding the masses toward socialist emancipation. Signaling the Front's departure in new directions, delegates elected a new General Command. Only three of them had previously served in the eighteen-strong leadership.[91] The Front's change of name to the Popular Front for the Liberation of the Occupied Arabian Gulf (PFLOAG) reflected the expansion of the movement's ambitions to liberate not only Dhufar but all of the occupied Gulf, including Said's dominions of Muscat and Oman, Bahrain, and the Trucial States.

The Hamrin Congress adopted a new National Charter that evinced Maoist influence.[92] Maoism is a dynamic movement that urges adaptation to local context. It has thus manifested differently from context to context.[93] In Dhufar, Maoism influenced the place and use of violence. The Front adopted Maoist strategies such as "organized violence." This involves the attempt to hold territory from which to launch attacks and the development of disciplined troops enjoined to behave respectfully toward the local population on whose support the movement relied.[94] The Front also followed the Maoist principle to "correct mistakes" and expunge internal threats.[95] The movement legislated for the execution of those whom its courts judged to have betrayed the revolution, such as those who mutinied against the

Front in September 1970, of whom the Front executed more than thirty.[96] Maoist influence likewise manifested in the Front's wide-ranging policies for social change, from the active mobilization of women to mass literacy and education campaigns. The new plans for social emancipation included the abolition of enslavement. This encouraged some members of The Black Hand to join the movement.[97]

A few months after Hamrin, the nature of Maoist influence over the Front no longer seemed mysterious to British observers. When British intelligence reported in January 1969 that "Chinese clothing and Mao badges [had] been found on the jebal," there was no accompanying speculation as to the meaning of these multiple finds.[98] Front leaders were claiming the movement's place among national liberation movements, Maoist and otherwise.

The Front embraced multiple horizons of national liberation. It governed "liberated" populations of civilian and combatant Dhufaris in mountain strongholds and in exile. Aspirations for national liberation would evolve, eventually coming to focus on a notion of Oman that incorporated Dhufar and included the former Trucial Oman. The map in the PFLO logo depicted this geography of anti-colonial aspiration (Figure 2). Two further name changes reflected this evolution. In 1971, the movement merged with its northern sister organization the National Democratic Front for the Liberation of Oman and the Arabian Gulf (NDFLOAG). The combined movements became the Popular Front for the Liberation of Oman and the Arabian Gulf (also PFLOAG). Then in 1974 the movement became the Popular Front for the Liberation of Oman (PFLO). As it evolved, the Front comprised members from Dhufar as well as today's northern Oman.[99] There were also some twenty activists from Bahrain and Kuwait.[100]

These activists ran offices in Cairo, Aden, Baghdad, Tripoli, and Algiers. They exchanged delegations with China, Vietnam, the USSR, and Cuba. The Front sent students to friendly socialist states such as Iraq, Syria, the USSR, and Cuba. The movement received military, financial, diplomatic, educational, and medical support at various points from socialist and anti-imperial allies, including the PDRY, China (until 1972), the USSR, Iraq, Libya, and Cuba.[101] It also hosted individual volunteer revolutionaries, such as from Palestine and Iran.[102] The adoption of Marxism-Leninism pushed Front leaders to combine their pursuit of anti-colonial liberation with radical ambitions for social emancipation. The turn toward Marxism-Leninism also triggered a scaling up of the counterinsurgency.

FIGURE 2. English-language logo of *Saut al-Thawra* newspaper of the People's Front for the Liberation of Oman. Courtesy of Special Collections, University of Exeter.

Counterinsurgency Agendas

At its outset, the counterinsurgency was already of cosmopolitan composition by virtue of the Baluchi, Omani, and British SAF personnel. After 1970, the internationalized counterinsurgency took on an expanded character. By 1974, the number of counterinsurgency personnel had risen to eleven thousand from four nations.[103] The Front guerrillas and militia whom they faced were an estimated eighteen hundred.[104] The latter's numbers were by then diminishing in the context of high casualties and of Dhufaris changing sides to join pro-government paramilitaries. The counterinsurgency mobilized military, logistical, and financial resources from Britain, Jordan, and Iran, as well as financial resources from Saudi Arabia and Kuwait. The sultan needed this support. Even when oil revenues had significantly increased after the 1973 hike in oil prices, and even when the government was spending 40 percent of its national budget on Dhufar in the final war years, the expensive war still pushed Oman into deficit.[105]

These counterinsurgency resources easily overshadowed the support that the Front was able to mobilize from its allies. Said's deposition had ended his more frugal approach to equipping the SAF. The conflict soon pitted the resources of a counterinsurgency "Goliath" against the far more meager resources available to the Front.[106] The territory at stake had only a subsistence economy barely sufficient to sustain its prewar population. The oil exploration that had begun in Dhufar in 1948 had led to finds in 1956, declared commercially unviable shortly after.[107] For whom and for what reasons, then, did counterinsurgency success in Dhufar matter so much?

To address these questions requires looking beyond Dhufar. However much al-Busaid rulers enjoyed having a palace in Salalah's tropical climate, for the British officials who made crucial decisions to sustain the counterinsurgency, Dhufar did not hold strategic interest for its own sake. This was a long-standing pattern in Britain's attitude to Dhufar. Salalah had been important to keep within the sphere of British influence in the nineteenth-century steamship age, and then in the twentieth-century age of air routes, not for its own sake but because of the connectivity it offered between Aden and India. With the independence of India and Aden, Britain's interests lay further north of Salalah: in the Strait of Hormuz, shared between the sultan of Muscat and Oman and the shah of Iran. This passage was crucial for Britain and other countries in western Europe to access the 60 percent of their petroleum needs for which the vast oil reserves of Saudi Arabia, Abu Dhabi, and Kuwait provided.[108] Dhufar was, in the view of Consul General Carden in January 1968, expendable to British interests. In the event of Sultan Said's death, he suggested, Britain should do "nothing to disuade [sic] a new government from cutting their losses in Dhofar if the Dhofaris are determined to secede."[109] But when, in September of that year, Dhufar's Front adopted a Marxist-Leninist leadership on the doorstep of socialist PRSY, this elicited alarm that Marxism would spread across Arabia to threaten control over shipping waters and oil reserves. In the light of these fears, counterinsurgency victory in Dhufar seemed worth fighting for.

Britain's eventual commitment to seeing the war through to victory nevertheless raised political difficulties. Although British veterans and military training manuals would later mythologize the war and British involvement, at the time Britain initially strove to keep the extent of its interventions out of the public domain.¹¹⁰ The colonial dimensions of Britain's involvement in Dhufar risked public controversy. This was an especially sensitive topic given that Britain officially denied being in a colonial relationship with the sultan of Muscat and Oman. Thus, during their mission to Dhufar, Special Air Service (SAS) and other British personnel received instruction not to talk about their deployment.¹¹¹ Deployed Britons wore no ID discs so that in the event of capture the Front could not document British military intervention.¹¹² For most of the war, and as late as 1974, the counterinsurgency denied journalists access to Dhufar.¹¹³

Similarly, Britain shrouded in secrecy the extent of its involvement in planning and executing the coup on July 23, 1970, that saw Sultan Qaboos assume the throne and the deposed Said go into exile in Britain. The brief and apparently mistaken declassification of British archival documents (subsequently swiftly reclassified) made clearer the context and extent of British involvement.¹¹⁴ Only a few months before the coup, British advisors had discounted the possibility of removing Said from office. Britain then discovered an ultimately unsuccessful NDFLOAG attempt to assassinate Said on June 12, 1970. British officials made the decision that it was necessary to remove Said before revolutionaries could claim the prestige of having done so.¹¹⁵ Said's reign ended in a "colonial coup" in which imperial powers removed a dependent ruler once they perceived that his rule no longer offered the best means of pursuing their interests.¹¹⁶ British intelligence officers nevertheless disseminated myths that hid revolutionary and British agency for the coup and instead attributed agency to Qaboos.¹¹⁷

After the coup, counterinsurgency success would still be out of reach for some time. Defence Secretary of Oman Colonel Hugh Oldman expressed uncertainty in August 1971 as to "whether [the war] can be won or not."¹¹⁸ Multiple crucial factors facilitated the counterinsurgency's eventual victory.¹¹⁹ Containment strategies of food and water blockades starved civilians in the Front-controlled *jabal*. These blockades and other containment strategies, such as barriers and land mines, cut off food, water, weapons, and other resources from Front combatants. The counterinsurgency had significant advantages in airpower for attacks and for logistics. British, Jordanian, and Iranian personnel manned airpower, with Britons on loan or on contract. The increase in counterinsurgency boots on the ground, and especially of Iranian troops, was key for the government retaking of the Salalah–Thumrait road in December 1973 and the final clearing of Front fighters from western Dhufar in 1975. The counterinsurgency made strategic use of intelligence and propaganda. It forged cooperation with local elites such as *firaq* leaders. Counterinsurgency welfare provisions met some of Dhufaris' economic grievances—but not political demands for autonomy and political participation.

Indeed, the counterinsurgency's scaling up of welfare provisions *after* it had secured the military upper hand in 1974 has prompted discussion that welfare policies in Dhufar *followed* rather than helped *achieve* counterinsurgency victory.[120] This approach rightly questions assumptions—in both "good governance" approaches to counterinsurgency and the Dhufar "model campaign" thesis—that "hearts and minds" measures are necessary for or lead to counterinsurgency victory.[121] A different question is how Dhufaris perceived aid, including in "scattered" and "irregular" pre-1974 initiatives.[122] From the perspectives of starving Dhufaris who were participating in or initially supportive of an armed movement calling for and attempting to deliver improved social and economic development, early counterinsurgency aid appears to have held significance. Front documents from 1971 (which the British later captured) revealed that as part of a plan to boost its local popularity, and in response to counterinsurgency welfare provision, the movement intended to increase medical training in its units.[123] Dhufari perspectives that take counterinsurgency welfare provision seriously do not, however, warrant a revived "model campaign" thesis. For many Dhufaris, their opportunities to engage with "hearts and minds" measures were evidence not of counterinsurgency success but of their *own* victory in reversing earlier government neglect of their welfare. Moreover, no analysis of the conflict's outcomes should overlook the significance of conventional military and counterinsurgency violence for countering Dhufari resistance.

State-backed record keeping indicates some of the material costs, and profits for some parties, of pursuing the counterinsurgency in Dhufar. Prior to the hike in oil prices that boosted Oman's budget, in 1972 Britain subsidized the counterinsurgency by giving Oman a grant worth $8.6 million covering ammunition, equipment, and SAS costs.[124] By 1973, the costs of British support to Oman made Britain fear that Oman might look to competing suppliers. To prevent this, Britain subsidized half the cost of seconded military personnel.[125] The war in Dhufar still offered lucrative prospects for Britain, though. In the twelve months to May 1974, Oman spent £10.3 million of its defense budget buying equipment from the UK. Where for 1974–75 Britain foresaw a cost of £300,000 for running RAF Salalah, and some £500,000 more on "overseas expenditure," it anticipated that the

Sultanate would spend a little over £2.2 million on "UK assistance."[126] In addition to profits from supplying military services and equipment, Britain also did well from construction contracts in Dhufar.[127]

The costs of the war in human terms are more elusive. Britain and the Front documented casualties on both sides. But these sources struggle to capture the scale of different categories of loss.

Some sources reflect politically motivated inaccuracies, omissions, or controversy. The Front's reports of SAF, British, and Iranian casualties are the subject of criticism for alleged exaggeration.[128] Conversely, the Front under-reported its own losses, such as during its failed attempt in 1972 to capture Mirbat.[129] On the counterinsurgency side, there seem to be only estimates of Iranian casualties through to the end of 1975. The high estimated numbers of Iranian casualties may explain the apparent ongoing lack of transparency about these figures on the part of Iran's successive governments.[130]

Estimates of casualties also suffer from the incompleteness of missing records. The Front's most complete published list of Front military and civilian casualties covers 1965 through 1979. The Front nevertheless gave this list the subtitle "part one" to acknowledge its incompleteness due to "the loss of some records and documents . . . which are still being searched for."[131] But missing records do not only reflect losses that defeat and exile inflict on archives; they may also result from the absence of attempted documentation in the first place. It is not clear that Britain tried to keep records about Dhufari civilian casualties of counterinsurgency violence. If Britain did attempt such documentation, these records are not forthcoming. In fact, Britain actively undermined possibilities for such documentation through its policy of preventing journalists from accessing Dhufar for most of the conflict.

Available data suggest a pattern of higher casualties for the Front than for the counterinsurgency. Counterinsurgency sources covering 1967 to February 1974 suggest a combined figure of 482 confirmed Front deaths, and 150 for counterinsurgency forces (Tables 3 and 4). This asymmetry is unsurprising given the imbalances in resources by the latter years of the war.

Those figures nevertheless omit both the early years of the war and the final years of intense bombing and fighting. The Front's incomplete list of military and civilian casualties between 1965 and 1979 covers 357 individuals' biographies.[132] This falls well below the 482 Front military deaths that counterinsurgency sources confirmed for the period of 1967 to February

TABLE 3. Dhufar Military Casualties 1967–70. Peterson, *Oman's*, 222.

	Front		
Killed			
Confirmed	98	*Reported*	59
Wounded	103		
Captured	35		
	SAF		
Killed	24		
Wounded	75		

Source: Peterson, *Oman's*, 222.

TABLE 4. Dhufar Military Casualties, January 1, 1971, to February 28, 1974

	Front		
Killed			
Confirmed	384	*Reported*	545
Wounded			
Confirmed	156	*Reported*	463
Surrendered enemy personnel	767		
Captured enemy personnel	28		
	Counterinsurgency		
British killed	9	British wounded	16
SAF killed	97	SAF wounded	313
Firaq killed	12	*Firaq* wounded	30
Iranian killed	8	Iranian wounded	12
Total killed	126	Total wounded	371

Source: FCO 8/2233, "Oman Intelligence Report 61," stamped March 19, 1974, App 2, https://www.agda.ae/en/catalogue/tna/fco/8/2233/n/36.[141]

1974 alone. The Front's decision to create a collection of biographies, rather than names only, may help explain that discrepancy.

For the counterinsurgency, estimates of total casualties by January 1976 are a few under four hundred, with a quarter estimated to be Iranians.[133] Some estimates for Iranian casualties nevertheless go as high as one thousand.[134] Even the lower estimate suggests that the conflict was most deadly for the counterinsurgency in its final two years. Higher mortality in the final years is likely to have been the case too for the outnumbered, less well-equipped, and increasingly starving Front fighters, as well as Dhufari civilians vulnerable to counterinsurgency violence.

The party to the war that generated the most complete records of its own casualties seems to be the British. The UK's Ministry of Defence places deaths among UK forces in Dhufar between October 1, 1969, and September 3, 1976, at twenty-five.[135] The former commander of the SAF Dhofar Brigade, John Akehurst, names thirty-five British casualties for the entire conflict.[136]

To date, no precise figures compile the human costs of the war for Dhufari civilians and fighters subject to death, injury, displacement, dispossession, air strikes, land mines, and starvation of food and water. In its weekly newspaper, *Saut al-Thawra*, the Front reported the names of killed and injured civilians and combatants. These names would have been familiar to Dhufari audiences, who would have been able to recognize and, later, verify reports. Possibly, then, the movement's reports of civilian casualties may be more reliable than its underreported military casualties. The newspaper also reported the destruction of livelihoods and livestock, the loss of which jeopardized survival. Taking stock over the year to June 1975, the Front claimed that in the previous twelve months the counterinsurgency had wounded forty-seven Front fighters and nine Dhufari civilians, killed twenty Front fighters and eleven civilians, burned eighty-four houses, and killed an "unestimated" number of livestock.[137] Figures estimating equivalent losses over the ten years of conflict are as yet lacking. But even in their absence, there can be no doubt that the counterinsurgency violence at stake had deadly consequences not just for Front fighters but also for Dhufari civilians.

There has been too little recognition of these Dhufari losses in conventional accounts of the war. The myth of Dhufar as a "model counterinsurgency" has propagated claims that the Dhufar counterinsurgency was "successful" in deploying "discriminate violence" that minimized casualties.[138] These claims are conceptually and empirically problematic. These assertions overlook the indiscriminate impacts of food and water blockades, of the destruction of essential resources of a subsistence economy such as livestock-raising, and of air strikes and land mines. Moreover, the empirical basis for these claims is unsatisfactory. It is not the case that counterinsurgency forces documented low civilian casualties. Instead, claims of minimal or low civilian casualties apparently rest on the *absence* of investigation into, and documentation of, Dhufar's civilian casualties. The Front began compiling its own records of these losses, but the vicissitudes of exile prevented completion.

In postwar Oman, the national government's official silence about the war neglects Dhufari losses. Dhufaris and other Omanis have partially circumvented this censorship. In the mid-1970s, a corpus of poetry in MSAL was already circulating that made discreet references to the war.[139] Since the demonstrations in 2011, Omanis have created internet forums to discuss the revolution and remember the conflict's victims.[140] Beyond such initiatives, though, official silence in Oman about the war overwhelmingly obscures Dhufari casualties. Those who break this silence, as did 'Abdullah Habib when he called for mothers to be able to mourn at the graves of revolutionaries whom the government executed, risk imprisonment. There are too few opportunities in the official public domain in Oman to acknowledge and commemorate Dhufaris who died, sustained wounds, or experienced dispossession as a result of being supporters or sympathizers of the Front.

Recognizing Revolution

Oman's official silence regarding Dhufaris' experiences of wartime loss and upheaval may have been among the underlying reasons why some Dhufaris chose to engage with me as a researcher. At the same time, though, these interlocutors lived under the authoritarian rule of the government that, with British backing, had waged the counterinsurgency. They identified me as a British researcher. Understandably, many Dhufaris avoided speaking explicitly with me about counterinsurgency violence. In replying to a question from me about female casualties during the war, one person was visibly ill at ease. This person's tone and expression conveyed discomfort when acknowledging Dhufari civilian death and injury during air strikes in which British seconded personnel piloted fighter jets for Oman's air force. This interlocutor quickly changed the subject.

That person was more willing, though, to share family histories of revolutionary projects for social change. Despite the context of violence, dispossession, and destruction, Dhufaris engaged with revolutionary social transformation. It is to the social contexts in which revolutionaries forged emancipatory agendas, and to Dhufaris' experiences of such social change, that the next chapter turns.

2

The Messiness of Social Change

FROM 1968, DHUFAR'S LIBERATION movement proclaimed its ambitions for both anti-colonial and social emancipation. At a time of worldwide attention to anti-colonial struggles, and widespread criticism of imperial intervention therein, some international audiences were sympathetic to these goals. In her documentary film on the revolution in Dhufar, *The Hour of Liberation Has Arrived* (*Saʿat al-thawrah daqqat*), Lebanese filmmaker Heiny Srour depicted striking scenes of the armed struggle and of the Front's social programs, such as mixed-gender schooling and military training. Critics selected the film to compete at the Cannes Film Festival in 1974.[1]

For audiences less steeped in that political moment, however, the testimonies of Srour and other sympathizers regarding the Front's programs foreground some unsettling entanglements of emancipatory aspiration with control and exploitation. Srour and fellow sympathizer Fred Halliday documented adolescent recruits in Revolution Camp, the Front's military training center. Halliday conducted interviews with female trainees aged twelve and fifteen, while Srour noted that trainees' "ages ranged from 12–25 though the majority of them are adolescents."[2] Some of these adolescents went on to die in combat, as did Fatma Musallam Muhad, who was born in 1958, joined the Front's Popular Liberation Army (PLA) in 1970, and died in battle in 1972.[3] At that time, adolescence was the age at which, outside the context of the revolution, Dhufaris became eligible to undertake adult roles such as becoming a spouse and, for males, an actor in indigenous categories of political violence. This local context, as well as the imperative of anti-colonial resistance and the urgency of exposing counterinsurgency violence, may be among the reasons that Srour and Halliday did not at the time publicly reflect on the military recruitment of adolescents as problematic. Yet for those whose efforts to understand revolution diverge from the overwhelming fervor that sympathizers apparently experienced at the time, it is troubling to encounter adolescents training for and dying in a very different category of political violence: a counterinsurgency war pitting parties with access to vastly asymmetrical weaponries. The entanglements within the Front of emancipation, control, and exploitation raise questions about revolutionary social change.

Overlaps of emancipation with control and exploitation speak to a predicament that overshadows revolutionary movements like Dhufar's Front. What are the implications of the fact that mobilizations pursuing transformed social relations, egalitarianism, and emancipation are fraught with contradiction? Both sympathizers and critics of revolutionary projects have found in these shortcomings reasons to diagnose failure—either failed revolutionary idealism or the violence of "red terror." Shortcomings, though, do not speak only of failure, but also of "complexity" in revolutionary experiences.[4] Such complexity invites reconsideration of revolution through a lens that eschews the rigidity of "failure" versus "success." An alternative analytical lens can instead explore revolutionary social change as "messiness."

The messiness at stake in revolutionary social change is not a synonym of randomness or chaos. Rather, it is an antonym of neatness. Experiences of revolutionary social change are messy in that they do not fit tidy official revolutionary narratives, with their precise beginnings, endings, and attributions of agency. Adopting messiness as an analytical framework means avoiding a "cookie-cutter" conceptualization of (revolutionary) social change where precise plans achieve intended outcomes. Instead, an attention to the messiness of revolutionary social change acknowledges the likely absence of neatness in beginnings, processes, and results.

Such messiness may arise when people have been involved in navigating their own forms of social change *before* the advent of revolutionary (or other) programs, when they negotiate and reinterpret their participation *during* initiatives for social change, and when they experience ambiguous *results* of programs. Messiness, then, does not imply randomness or a lack of patterns. Patterns exist within messiness, but crucially they are not necessarily those that correspond to official revolutionary narratives. An exploration of messiness avoids equating revolutionary shortcomings with failure in a way that narrows the possibilities for understanding the complexities of revolutionary experiences. Instead, attention to messiness allows for inquiry into the breadth of revolutionary experiences—and into the counterhistories and afterlives of revolution.

Analysis of the messiness of revolutionary social change retrieves counterhistories that reflect those experiences that conventional historical narratives neglect. In Dhufar, once the Front adopted programs that challenged long-standing social hierarchies of tribe, social status, unfree labor, and gender relations, the forms of emancipation that Dhufaris may have experienced were nevertheless riven with shortcomings. These shortcomings included contradictions within revolutionary programs, their problematic outcomes, and gaps between different subjects' experiences of initiatives. Yet these shortcomings also reveal messiness within Dhufaris' experiences of revolutionary social change. The scales of Dhufaris' engagement with revolutionary social change at times preceded and surpassed formal programs. Dhufaris furthermore negotiated for forms of social change acceptable in their own eyes. They also made choices about how to engage with change. These messy, heterogeneous experiences of revolutionary social change do not fit neatly with either the (initially) laudatory narratives of sympathizers or the condemnatory narratives of critics who have doubted that Dhufaris were ever really interested in socialist programs.[5] Instead, counterhistories foreground the "un-neatness" and messiness within Dhufaris' experiences of revolutionary social change.

Dhufaris' navigation of the scales, negotiations, and choices at stake in revolutionary social change imply an underlying engagement with social change. That is to say, if Dhufaris were choosing terms of involvement, they were engaged with revolutionary change. The fact of that engagement alerts us to the possibilities of afterlives of revolution. Messiness, and the engagement it implies, provide a framework for inquiry into the afterlives of revolution. How might a revolution that fails to survive as an explicit political movement nevertheless go on to produce lasting social legacies? The very possibility of afterlives of revolution might be partially contingent upon revolutionary subjects having been *engaged* in revolutionary social change, such as by navigating scales, negotiations, and choices, as Dhufaris did. The prospect emerges that afterlives of revolution arise not *despite* the messiness of revolutionary social change but *because* of such messiness and the engagement it implies.

In addition to shedding light on counterhistories and the afterlives of revolution, an analysis of messiness advances insights into revolutionary social change. First, an examination of messiness advances understandings of revolutionary vernacularization among those not in positions of formal leadership. In the context of unequal opportunities for different actors to record and narrate their experiences of revolutionary social change, more documentation typically survives about top-down initiatives and vernacularization of revolutionary ideals. Piecing together messiness from archival glimpses and from snapshots of Dhufaris' memories brings into view, however fleetingly, the everyday revolutionary vernacularization of those not in positions of authority.

Second, an examination of messiness can eschew some of the problems of polarized representations of revolutionary social change, whether laudatory from sympathizers or condemnatory from opponents. Such accounts risk overemphasis on (dis)proving Dhufaris' putative underlying support for, or rejection of, revolutionary social change. Instead of casting doubt over whether Dhufaris ever supported leftist programs, it may be more compelling to ask why—for reasons that surely varied—some Dhufaris supported the Front at all, especially given that it was "more profitable and far less risky" to support the counterinsurgency.[6] Arguably more compelling still is to look beyond flawed assumptions of necessarily clear distinctions between support for and rejection of a revolutionary movement. Instead, an examination of the range of people's experiences better illuminates how they engage with projects for social change in contexts of revolutionary wartime and exilic struggles for survival.

Unpacking Revolutionary Social Change

Revolutionary social change takes wide-ranging forms that, furthermore, vary in relation to the explicit and implicit intentions of those involved. On the one hand, revolutionary social change manifests in liminal settings such as protests or clandestine gatherings. From the demonstrations that spread across SWANA from 2010, including those in Salalah, to private illicit parties of Iranian youth in the early twenty-first-century Islamic Republic, people cooperate, demonstrate, and mobilize together along new lines of connection.[7] Activists in these liminal spaces may not necessarily harbor a project to take over state power.[8] Even so, militants may still experience new gendered, national, and political subjectivities, with potentially lasting effects despite the eventual absence of long-term institutional political change.[9]

On the other hand, revolutionary movements that act as state authorities have directed institutionalized projects for social transformation. Social scientists and historians have charted such revolutionary agendas across continents.[10] Potentially sharing aspects of both liminal and institutionalized state-backed revolutionary social change are the social transformation agendas of insurgencies and liberation movements, including Dhufar's.

Liberation movements and insurgencies seek to take over state power, with some eventually achieving long-term success in doing so. But as the governing authorities of "liberated territories" and/or exile civilian populations, these movements at least initially operate, and pursue projects for social change, in materially and politically precarious conditions.[11] These movements' social change programs are an "investment" in civilian governance, with movements that espouse socialist, and especially Maoist, ideologies being more likely to invest not merely in security and policing but also in education and health care.[12] In Dhufar, revolutionaries adopted the Maoist-inspired slogan "thought leads the rifle."[13] This reflected the conviction that a movement should educate and politicize the wider population about the goals of the conflict. The aim was for engagement with ideas to drive the conflict, rather than vice versa.

Unavoidably, contexts of wartime and/or exile impact on insurgents' plans for social change. These projects face resource shortages and political pressure to prioritize survival at the potential cost of ideals. At the same time, war and/or exile can increase the stakes of policies affecting civilians, including social change programs. A movement's treatment of the civilian population may influence whether an insurgency can survive or not. In the absence of local support to provide food, resources, and shelter (support that counterinsurgency measures seek to make unviable), an insurgency may lack the means to continue fighting. In Dhufar, revolutionaries' programs for social change faced significant material and political constraints, especially in the context of the counterinsurgency's blockades, bombings, and resettlement. But counterinsurgency strategists evidently believed that the Front's policies for social change were significant in attracting local support. Counterinsurgency authorities surmised that their own chances of attracting and retaining such support would benefit from their introducing alternative, rival services, such as in education, health care, and access to water.

Revolutionary projects for social change do not necessarily play out in the ways that those involved may have anticipated, though. Many of the issues that arise span three overlapping areas. First, tensions arise *within* revolutionary agendas when movements pursue programs that encompass inherent contradiction. For instance, the simultaneous promotion of socialist internationalism and nationalist identities, or of gender equality and a gendered division of labor, can pose contradictions. Such tensions have emerged across continents and also arose in Dhufar.[14]

Second, beyond questions of inherent contradictions within revolutionary programs are the problematic outcomes that can arise in applying these programs. These include unintended outcomes that undermine revolutionary goals. Movements committed to reducing inequalities can nevertheless introduce new hierarchies, such as between vanguard and grassroots, or between those included in and those excluded from opportunities for education or political participation.[15] Revolutionary policies may have uneven or incomplete outcomes, with policies reaching only certain groups, or going only so far in challenging exploitation and marginalization. For instance, only urban educated women could take up new opportunities to work in previously male-dominated areas in revolutionary Algeria.[16] The revolutionary emancipation of enslaved persons from Western Sahara could not protect those of historically enslaved backgrounds from an increasingly ethnicized market for commodified labor.[17] Other outcomes end up compromised when a movement, facing constraints, chooses to prioritize the achievement of some goals over others, as Nicaragua's Sandinista leadership prioritized national liberation over women's emancipation.[18] Dhufar's revolution had its share of problematic outcomes in unintended, incomplete, and compromised varieties.

Third, there are gaps between the visions, experiences, and practices of social change on the part of different constituencies within the vanguards and those beyond it. Regarding recruitment, adherents may not have found motivation for joining a movement in the conditions of exploitation that vanguards envision as the origin of their struggle.[19] Some of those joining may have already engaged in their own emancipatory projects prior to the revolution. This might entail making personal choices that challenge existing authority figures, participating in organized mobilization outside a revolutionary movement, or pursuing emancipation through routes such as education, migration, romance, and religious salvation.[20] It may not be revolutionary theories of liberation that attract popular support, but everyday gestures of intimacy and respect infused with egalitarianism.[21] Nor is it the case that everyone wants, or is able, to participate in revolutionary agendas in the same way. Class, gender, and ethnicity, among other characteristics, affect ability or willingness to mobilize.[22] Revolutionary movements nevertheless narrate more homogenous versions of mobilization, expunging where necessary those whose reasons for rebellion do not conform to official revolutionary narratives.[23]

Whatever their experiences of recruitment, revolutionary subjects may experience policies for social change in diverse ways. They do not encounter social change agendas as "automatons" but negotiate, vernacularize, and create their experiences of new subjectivities and temporalities by drawing on their own historical context.[24] People may experience "new" social arrangements as familiar rather than novel.[25] Some may not experience the kind of change that revolutionary activists intended, for instance when they experience new gender roles not as emancipation but as increased burdens.[26] Militants also chart their own trajectories of change, where popular interpretations of revolutionary agendas may fall short of, or go beyond, the vanguard's intentions.[27] Revolutionary subjects furthermore pursue initiatives of their own choosing, sometimes understanding these initiatives as resistance even when the acts in question are parasitic on the resources that the revolution provides.[28] Gaps in people's experiences of both recruitment and ensuing revolutionary transformation characterize Dhufar's revolution too.

Contradictions, problematic outcomes, and experiential gaps constitute shortcomings in projects for revolutionary social change (as well as other revolutionary goals). These shortcomings catalog revolutionary failures: failures to end exploitation, to protect from abuses and discrimination, and to achieve meaningful forms of emancipation. Growing acknowledgment over time of these shortcomings and failures has contributed to shifts in the narration of revolution, from the hopeful genre of romance to the conflicted genre of tragedy.[29] Those looking back on the militancy of their own youth or of earlier generations through the lens of growing awareness of revolutionary failures feel nostalgia for bygone activist optimism.[30] For many who dedicated themselves to revolutionary movements, and who made sacrifices for the sake of projects for emancipation, revolutionary failures provoke feelings of betrayal, disappointment, disillusionment, and fatigue.[31] Such feelings would come to haunt some of Dhufar's revolutionaries.

The acknowledgment of revolutionary shortcomings has nevertheless also provided the impetus for narrations that draw on the hope but not the naïveté of romance, and the realism but not the pessimism of tragedy. Such an approach reframes revolutionary shortcomings as signs not of incoherence or "pathological" forms of state power but rather of "complexity" and "compromises."[32] Engagement with this complexity sheds light on the meanings of revolutionary social transformations for those living through them. It also illuminates how divergent constituencies vernacularize and reinterpret agendas for social change. Ultimately, reflection on revolutionary shortcomings is a necessary step toward imagining different political futures that resist current forms of exploitation and marginalization.[33]

Such reinterpretation of revolutionary projects and their shortcomings in terms of complexity, rather than of failure or inauthenticity, opens up arresting insights and questions for the analysis of revolutionary social change and its legacies. First, this reinterpretation requires acknowledgment of the "messiness" of experiences of revolutionary social change. It is precisely in the light of messy details—such as that people may have already been pursuing forms of emancipation before the formalization of those agendas in the revolution, and that people negotiate forms of social change acceptable for them—that shortcomings become signs of complexity.

Second, acknowledgment of the messiness of revolutionary social change raises the question of how this messiness signals possibilities for revolutionary projects to produce lasting legacies. Messiness produces and results from engagement: it is through people negotiating, interpreting, and engaging that messiness arises. How, then, might messiness, with all that it implies for engagement, ultimately contribute to the survival of revolutionary legacies beyond a movement's formal existence as an (un)armed mobilization that makes claims on the state? In sum, how might messiness contribute to legacies of lasting social relations and subjectivities?

In the absence of ongoing formal mobilization, revolutionary survival in social relations and subjectivities is possible. In permissive political circumstances of postrevolutionary multipartyism, those who do not necessarily identify as revolutionaries may experience multiple revolutionary legacies and survivals. These can take forms such as public mobilization around the lasting appeal of ideas of emancipation and political freedom, and the institutionalization and embedding of revolutionary change in political, economic, and social life. Those living in the wake of revolution may experience revolutionary legacies and survivals in a sense of voice, self, and the right and capacity to make decisions about the self and to interrogate one's circumstances.[34] Even after a movement's formal demise, erstwhile militants experience changes in subjectivity, such as a new sense of the self that cannot merely be "cast away."[35] In hostile political conditions, such as the absolutist authoritarianism of Sultan Qaboos's Oman, survivals in social relations and subjectivities are among the possibilities for ongoing revolutionary legacies.

One of the factors enabling such survival would surely be that people had earlier engaged with revolutionary social change. Exploring the messiness of revolutionary social change in Dhufar, then, is a crucial step toward understanding the creation of afterlives of revolution there.

Dynamic Social Inequalities in Dhufar

When the Front introduced radical policies promoting social egalitarianism, the movement faced long-standing and pronounced patterns of social stratification in Dhufar. The economic interdependence that linked Dhufaris of different social backgrounds accommodated spectrums of social difference spanning inequality, privilege, and exploitation. Dhufaris distinguished between settled and transhumant, noble and dependent, free (e.g., tribute claimant) and unfree (e.g., tribute payer or enslaved person).[36] In Dhufar, these social hierarchies also intersected with ethnic distinctions between speakers of different varieties of Arabic and speakers of MSAL. Dhufaris determined social status principally by tracing patrilineal descent. The historical exceptions concerned two groups. Some Mahra tribes are matrilineal, although this practice is becoming less common.[37] The other exception concerns *sumur*, Dhufaris of African and enslaved heritage. Until the abolition of the formal status of enslavement, the children of an enslaved woman were free if born of her marriage to her owner, but enslaved (and the property of her slaveholder) if born in other circumstances.[38]

In the context of a fragile subsistence pre-oil economy where most Dhufaris went hungry for most of the year, for many (and likely most) Dhufaris inequalities did not necessarily manifest themselves in extreme material differences of consumption. When Bertram Thomas, the Briton who served Sultan Taimur as minister of the Council of State of Oman, visited Salalah in a personal capacity in 1930, he observed that "[t]he general standard of life is so low—just above the line of bare sufficiency—that the slave-owner, in his own interests, has to feed and clothe the slave nearly as well as himself."[39] Among my interlocutors, those who had grown up owning enslaved persons similarly recalled that "we [free and enslaved] ate the same thing," and stressed the poverty of that diet. Some older interlocutors also recalled that in the prewar village of Salalah, neighboring families of mixed backgrounds—*sadah*, non-elites, and *sumur* of free status—had shared celebrations of religious and life cycle festivities: "There was no difference in economic standards between the different families, *sadah* and the others. Other families could be richer than *sadah*. The only difference was that *sadah* did not let others marry their daughters. But we did everything together—celebrations, festivals. . . . In Ramadan every family took its turn to provide iftar [the evening meal that breaks the fast] for all the neighbors." Such memories were tinged with nostalgia for a perceived lost community of reciprocity of the kind that helped pre-oil Gulf communities survive recurring times of scarcity.[40]

Instances of neighborly reciprocity notwithstanding, inequalities manifested in Dhufar in intersections of the material and the social. Relations of exploitation between patron and client households, and within households along lines of gender, generation, and unfree labor, evinced these hierarchies. For instance, residence patterns were informally segregated in some prewar coastal neighborhoods. An older woman from Salalah, Nada, explained to me that in al-Hafah, elite Yafaʻi and Shanfari tribes originally lived along the seafront, with *sumur* and *bahharah* living north of them. She contrasted this with al-Dahariz, where *bahharah* and *sumur* originally lived along the coastline and elite families lived to the north of them. Evidence of intra-household hierarchy surfaced as some of those who recalled that they "ate the same thing" as enslaved members of the household also casually pointed out segregated sleeping arrangements. While they and other free members of the household had slept on the upper story of the family home, the enslaved had slept at ground level "next to the cows."

A further means of reproducing social differentiation between privileged and subordinate Dhufaris was marriage. Marriage gifts on which the groom's and bride's parties needed to agree—and that Islam required—facilitated tribal and familial control over the contracting, and dissolution, of marriages. This familial control enabled the avoidance of women marrying "below" their social status.[41] Marriage practices further entrenched social inequalities.

Particularly vulnerable to marginalization and exploitation were the *bahharah* and *sumur*. They were excluded altogether from the privileges of tribal membership because of their respective low social status and enslavement. Dhufar's enslaved population dates back "centuries."[42] In the 1930s, the population that Bertram Thomas referred to as "[t]he negro community" (despite the differences in concepts of race between southern Arabia and European settler colonial contexts) was "the biggest single element in the population of the Dhufar capital."[43] In the 1970s, Dhufaris of African and enslaved heritage formed 30–50 percent of the coastal and urban population.[44] By the 1960s, Sultan Said owned a significant portion of the enslaved population. In 1968, the British chief of intelligence in Salalah reported that Said owned most of Dhufar's enslaved, who included 200 palace guards and, in addition, the rank and file of the Dhufar Force (DF), who numbered around 145 in 1969.[45] Given that these numbers excluded women and children, and that in 1972 Qaboos suggested plans for the education of some 200 children of enslaved persons, accounts from Said's critics that he owned some 500 enslaved persons seem plausible and perhaps even conservative.[46]

Said certainly needed an agricultural labor force, which enslaved persons could provide. He had claimed all the agricultural land in the plain for which another party could not claim ownership.[47] But one of my interlocutors recalled that Said also sought enslaved persons for their perceived loyalty. This interlocutor explained: "Said didn't trust Dhufaris so he bought lots of slaves from [a prestigious Salalah family]." By some accounts, Said bought more than a thousand enslaved persons in the early 1930s.[48] Four of Said's enslaved persons were his trusted final companions, traveling with him to London after the coup to live with him in exile at London's Dorchester Hotel.[49] But the lot of other enslaved persons was by no means luxurious. After Said's deposition, the new governing authorities showed visiting foreign journalists members of Said's retinue who had allegedly "been forced, under pain of beating, not to speak" and "had become mutes," while others "stood with their heads bowed and eyes fixed on the ground, their necks now paralysed."[50]

Inequalities of tribe and exclusion from the privileges of tribal membership intersected with inequalities along lines of gender. Gender relations nevertheless varied among and within Dhufar's different communities. Front militants would go on to note—without specifying how these dynamics intersected with distinctions among Qara, *shahrah,* and other mountain residents—that in the *jabal* women enjoyed greater opportunities for economic participation, movement, and remarriage after divorce without social stigma compared with their peers in Arabophone coastal communities: "[Women from Dhufar's rural areas] talk to whoever they want to—male or female—and go for visits without having to obtain the permission of their husbands or fathers. To run their family's affairs, they travel as they please and stay away from home for long hours sometimes all day, looking after livestock."[51] In these *jabal* contexts of transhumant pastoralism, women's mobility was essential for survival.

When *jabbali* women experienced formal exclusion, they sometimes improvised means of informal inclusion. At tribal meetings in the *jabal*, each man had a right to speak. Women, however, sat "within earshot" and shouted out "comments from time to time."[52] But even when some Dhufari women enjoyed greater relative freedoms, none could take up the full range of economic, political, and social opportunities available to male peers. Women and girls had no access to Salalah's sole Western-style primary school that catered only to "sons of Salalah merchants or sons of Sultan's slaves," with its pupils numbering just 150 in 1970.[53] Social customs, ranging from female genital cutting to taboos preventing women from bearing arms or milking cattle, constrained women. Women, like junior males, were under the authority of male elders.

Social inequalities tracing lines of tribe, status, ethnicity, race, and gender ran through Dhufaris' social relations, then. But these lines were not necessarily rigid. British intelligence officers liked to envisage fixed ethnic and tribal distinctions. They documented each of Dhufar's social groups, contemplating possibilities for exerting political control through the exploitation of social divisions in Dhufar.[54] While the British-led counterinsurgency in Dhufar would ultimately draw on tribal distinctions to counter Dhufari resistance, in 1969 J. S. Longrigg, first secretary at Britain's Persian Gulf Residency in Bahrain, would complain that Dhufari tribes "are broken into very numerous sub-sections," with the result that "the Sultan's system, which works very well in the rest of the country, of governing through large tribal sheikhs" was, for Dhufar, "inappropriate between rulers and ruled."[55] In practice, Dhufar's town, mountain, and desert residents were interconnected through economic exchanges, seasonal migrations, and intratribal mixed livestock holding. Lines of social distinctions and inequalities, as well as connections, could be fluid.

In parallel to this potential fluidity on the ground, during the twentieth century Dhufaris developed novel collective identities. When Dhufar became a dependency of the sultan of Muscat and Oman, colonialism contributed to an emerging, anti-colonial collective identity that went beyond local divisions. With Dhufar's resources barely enough to feed Dhufaris year-round, increased centralized political exploitation brought the threat of starvation.[56] Sultan Said's land grabs and taxes intensified Dhufaris' economic exploitation. Furthermore, many Dhufaris were frustrated that oil exploration had brought them few benefits. Dhufari emigrants told the UN General Assembly's ad hoc committee investigating conditions in Muscat, Oman, and Dhufar in 1964 that "in 1957 when the oil company came, people from outside the country were given the jobs, although local people had wished to work. However, the young people of Dhofar had held secret meetings about these matters and although they had had no education, some of them had travelled and they all knew their rights."[57] The shared experience of Said's exploitation, and the possibility of a foreign-owned company exploiting Dhufar's oil, helped foster an emerging Dhufari identity.

Migration also contributed to this budding Dhufari identity. Those who succeeded in leaving Dhufar forged connections with other Dhufaris beyond differences of tribe and status that held in Dhufar. One former migrant, Mustahail, who later became a political supporter of the Front while he was living in one of the Gulf states, explained to me: "Dhufaris outside [Dhufar] are all brothers."

Any emerging collective Dhufari identity as a result of colonialism and migration necessarily intersected with Dhufaris' positions of tribal, ethnic, racial, and gendered privilege and exploitation. For instance, according to the Front, all of Dhufar's migrants to the Gulf were male. In the view of the Front, this contributed to the discrimination that Dhufari women experienced under Sultan Said in that they lacked opportunities to seek education and work abroad.[58] While not everyone could participate to the same degree in an emerging Dhufari identity, from various positions Dhufaris nevertheless challenged traditional social hierarchies through personal and collective actions. I heard of one mountain family who were eager for their son to access education at the al-Saidiyyah school in Salalah, despite the school not accepting boys from the *jabal*. The family arranged to smuggle the boy into the school—from which he was expelled once discovered. Another Dhufari man who had migrated to the Gulf, going on to marry and start a family there, explained to me that he sent both his sons and daughters to school there. He thereby made available to his daughters a formal education that was impossible in Dhufar in the early 1960s. Dhufaris also challenged traditional social hierarchies through collective organization, including through the founding of political organizations. The longest-lasting of these was the Front.

The Hour of Liberation Strikes

After the Hamrin Congress, the Front's new leadership set about promoting Marxist-inspired social emancipation. Front militants promoted wide-ranging programs that aimed to challenge Dhufar's long-standing social hierarchies and encourage greater social egalitarianism and emancipation.

These interventions surpass the scope of what it is possible to discuss here. A nonexhaustive account of interventions targeting tribalism (including the stigma of exclusion from tribal origins) and gender relations, as well as Front educational and military institutions, must suffice. This can illuminate the Front's ambitions to promote greater social egalitarianism and emancipation in political, economic, social, kinship, and religious life.

Front leaders were skeptical about tribalism for reasons similar to those of their peers in contemporary anti-colonial national liberation movements from the Gulf to North Africa and sub-Saharan Africa.[59] They were critical that tribal relations reproduced the social differences and hierarchies that the revolution sought to undermine. Tribes also represented a potential vehicle of complicity with colonial rule to the extent that tribal leaders cooperated with colonial rulers, collecting taxes on the sultan's behalf.[60] Mindful of such concerns, the Front cultivated a supra-tribal Dhufari identity that nurtured the identities emerging from Dhufaris' experiences of migration and colonialism. Mustahail recalled his experience of a supra-tribal identity in the context of revolutionary mobilization: "People came to fight the government and the British. We had to be comrades. They fought to liberate the country, not their tribe. There was a rule between fighters: there is no difference between black and white, that tribe and that tribe." Mustahail's recollection of a "rule between fighters" hints at potential contextual limitations of that supra-tribal identity. After Hamrin, the Front attempted to bring this anti-tribalist agenda to the heart of its activities.

In its Marxist-inspired incarnation, the Front tackled tribal hierarchies in access to land and water resources. In 1969, the movement set up three agricultural committees. They determined that tribes would no longer control land and water resources on the *jabal*, and that cooperatives would run agricultural production.[61] At the third Congress in 1971, the Front declared that all land in the Front-controlled "liberated" areas was collective property.[62] During visits to the liberated territories in 1970 and 1973, British sociologist and activist Fred Halliday learned of the kinds of changes, potential tensions, and their (idealized) resolution that arose from these reforms: "[A] former tribal leader hit a woman near Dhalkut because she 'dared' to water her cattle before his. The man was arrested by the local PLA. He was then taken to the scene of his crime, where the woman related what had happened. The Committee then pointed out the incident's political lesson: all citizens have equal rights over land and water. In the end the local people attending the trial decided to pardon the sheikh, since it was his first offence."[63] This incident points to the Front's further undermining of tribalism through the introduction of new institutional means of resolving conflicts.

Before the revolution, in conflicts over land, animals, marital disputes, injuries, or killings, tribal authorities negotiated solutions, often under the mediation of religious elites.[64] At the Hamrin Congress, the Front ordered the settling of outstanding revenge killings via compensation. It also introduced a death penalty for the perpetrators of future murders as well as for those found guilty of treason. The movement thereby claimed for itself the monopoly over legitimate violence that, previously, powerful tribes had enjoyed. After Hamrin, the Front established the Committee for the Solution of Popular Problems, setting up one such committee for each of the eastern, central, and western areas of Dhufar. Dealing with feuds, divorces, and "personal conflicts," the committees moved within the regions to solve disputes—a kind of mobile justice resolution forum.[65] In August 1972, the Front replaced this Committee with a People's Council for each of the by then four administrative regions.[66] The People's Council was composed of between eight and eleven members, according to the size of the population. Members represented the citizens, the militia, and the PLA, with the citizens' representatives forming the majority. Those aged over sixteen had the right to vote in annual elections. The Council was responsible for "political, social and productive organisation and the development of community life."[67] The Council met monthly, needing a two-thirds majority to enforce its decisions. It was not only national resources that the Front redistributed but also political power and decision-making.

To further undermine the privileges of tribal elites, the Front also reshaped agricultural labor. Formerly, tribal leaders appropriated a crop surplus from which they paid taxes to the sultan.[68] In revolutionary agriculture, members of tribes continued to work together as the unit of production and to consume their own produce.[69] But crucially, laborers and their families no longer had to set aside a portion for the shaikh. If there was a surplus, the Front bought this for cash.[70] These political changes accompanied technological transformations. The Front introduced seeds, pumps, new wells, a model farm, and irrigation from rain-fed dams.[71] These technologies sought to lessen the effects of the counterinsurgency's food and water blockades, while the new labor arrangements aimed to undermine social inequalities.

Front interventions also undermined tribal hierarchies in the labor of herding. Previous herding arrangements reflected tribal relations. Family members herded their relatives' livestock, with client groups tending the livestock of patron families. A February 1973 government radio broadcast that aimed to encourage Dhufaris to leave the Front addressed the movement's altered arrangements. Salim ʿAqil Salim, the Front's former political director who had recently joined the pro-government paramilitaries, described the new provisions: "The unarmed section [of Front supporters] supervises the herding of the cattle that belongs to those fighting in the Army of Liberation [PLA]."[72] These unarmed supporters lived in their home areas in family and tribal groups. In contrast, the PLA members—the owners of the cattle in question—were of diverse tribal backgrounds and moved between different territories. These herding patterns, whereby locals tended the cattle of the socially heterogeneous PLA, were politically charged in that they broke with tribally shaped precedents. ʿAqil Salim, noting that the militia was also "charged with indoctrinating the people with Communist ideology,"[73] highlighted the ideological role of these supporters.

A major intervention in both the organization of labor and the undermining of tribal privilege was the emancipation of enslaved persons excluded from the privilege of claiming tribal membership. The National Charter committed the Front to the "complete erasure" of enslavement.[74] As there were in practice few enslaved persons in the *jabal*, the emancipation of enslaved persons may have had a limited economic impact in the liberated areas.[75] But this emancipation had major political and social implications. In the Dhufari context where most enslaved persons belonged to the sultan, the emancipation of enslaved persons undermined the sultan's power. Their emancipation also further undermined tribal privileges. In the revolutionary context, those of free and those formerly of unfree status fought and worked side by side. In addition, those formerly of unfree status assumed positions of authority—as did Rajab Jamʿan, a formerly enslaved person who had belonged to the sultan and became a member of the PFLOAG General Command.[76] Enslaved persons' emancipation also intersected with the Front's transformation of kinship and marital relations and the related transformation of gender relations.

The Front sought to reshape multiple social distinctions and hierarchies in which gender intersected with tribe, racialized identities, and ethnicity. Gendered transformations run through revolutions.[77] The Front, in line with Marxist analyses, understood women's subjugation as the result of their exploitation as both workers and women.[78] In a statement that recurs in publications about the Front, multiple militant women recounted: "We [women] suffered from four sultans. We had the political sultan—the Sultan of Muscat; the tribal sultan—the Sheikh; the religious sultan—the Imam; and the family sultan—the father, brother and husband."[79] The Hamrin Congress established the Front's ambitions to emancipate women from exploitation.

The drive to emancipate women saw the Front reform Dhufar's marriage practices that reproduced long-standing social inequalities. After Hamrin, the Front ended polygamy and unequal access to divorce for men and women.[80] In 1970, the movement set a standard, token rate for the bride-price.[81] The stated aim was to "allow men and women to choose freely their partners without compulsion or intervention from any third party."[82] By 1975, either spouse could request divorce for reasons of "suspicion of the partner's political position; lack of material support or total disagreement between the partners."[83] New conceptions of bride-price, spousal prerogatives, and divorce reconfigured marriage as a potential means of reproducing not inequality but greater equality.

Marriages became possible that before the revolution would have been impossible because of the spouses' different backgrounds. Men previously of enslaved background could marry women of free background, and women of *sadah* background (who historically considered women marrying "out" to be unacceptably marrying "down") could marry men of other backgrounds. Revolutionary marriage was meant to shift matrimony from being a means to reproduce inequalities to a means to reproduce social egalitarianism and a shared national identity.[84] These marriages, and the children to which they gave rise, would later stand out to Dhufaris in postrevolutionary times.

Where marriage reforms opened up new pools of conjugal partners to both men and women, other reforms targeted gendered social transformation. Shortly after Hamrin, the Front declared that there should be no more female genital cutting, a practice then prevalent in Dhufar (and still prevalent—though illegal in hospitals—under Sultan Qaboos).[85] Front militants encouraged women to break gendered taboos that, traditionally, had prevented women from milking cattle or bearing arms. They then referred to the lack of adverse consequences resulting from such actions as justification for the principle of women's emancipation.[86] The Front also sought to expand women's freedom of movement and decisions. In addition to being able to request divorce on the same grounds as men, women had new opportunities to attend school, join literacy classes and political discussion groups, join the militia, join the PLA, and to make decisions about their lives. Halliday reported the case of a woman, ʿAziza, whom the Front supported in her defiance of her husband's attempts to control her movements and political activity: "her husband objected to her participation in political activity, but she left home and after walking for several days reached the training camp and volunteered for service in the women's section. Her husband followed her and demanded that his wife be returned to him. PFLOAG refused on the grounds that Aziza had freely decided to join the PLA."[87] Hamran, who spent some of his childhood years in the liberated areas before attending the Front's school in Yemen, recalled to me the scope of gendered changes: "The women gathered together with the men, they participated in battles, they were inspired." He recalled an all-encompassing and enthusiastic women's emancipation.

The Front's efforts at changing gender relations challenged patriarchal relations more broadly, including young men's subordination to senior males. Hamran also recollected that, as fighters, young men received the kind of respect once reserved for senior males: "Women would stand to greet a young man arriving with a Kalashnikov." Nevertheless, it was images of the Dhufar revolution's "inspired" women that caught the attention of international media and solidarity audiences.[88] The most widely circulating images were those of Dhufar's female fighters who had trained in the Revolution Camp military training center in southern Yemen (Figure 3).

Revolution Camp was one of a number of key institutions through which the Front sought to mobilize popular engagement in revolutionary projects for social change. Analysis of these institutions faces challenges of uneven surviving documentation, and the potential postwar reluctance of those who frequented them to discuss their experiences there. This was the case in my conversations with interlocutors. While many questions remain about the workings of popular committees, elections, and political discussion groups, those of the Front's institutions that are better documented in archives, memoirs, and other studies are the Revolution Camp, the primary and intermediate schools, and the hospital and health clinic. All were located in the PDRY at sites split between the vicinity of Hawf, some four miles from the border with Dhufar, and the vicinity of al-Ghaidah, capital of the PDRY governorate of Mahra and fifty kilometers from the border.[89]

Exilic space that results from conflict-induced displacement can prove a fertile setting for social change.[90] Through training, educating, and providing medical care for Dhufaris of all social backgrounds, revolutionary institutions in exile furthered the Front's efforts to promote social egalitarianism.

FIGURE 3. A female combatant at a rally of PFLOAG combatants, 1971, Dhufar. © Jean-Michel Humeau. Reprinted with permission.

Although the military defeat of 1975 eventually led to the Front's demobilization in Yemen, health care services and schooling continued to cater for refugee families and demobilized combatants. In the late 1970s these institutions served some three thousand to five thousand persons across Hawf and al-Ghaidah.[91] The school ceased operation in 1988.[92]

Revolution Camp was one of the first sites to be founded after Hamrin, in 1969.[93] By September 1973, when Revolution Camp was located about a ninety-minute walk northwest of Hawf, it reportedly consisted of "8 or 9 twelve man tents."[94] In line with Hamrin's call to mobilize women, Revolution Camp trained both male and female fighters. The proportion of male to female recruits varied between cohorts, with women reportedly sometimes the majority.[95] Upon recruits' arrival, the trainers stressed the importance of equality between the sexes, as ʿAqil Salim described in his radio broadcast:

> On arrival at the camp, each batch of recruits, both men and women, are given the following articles: a book of Mao Tse Tung's thoughts, a copy of the Communist Party Manifesto, a Chinese rifle and gun belt and a number of articles of clothing. . . . The first talk on the course is given by the Political Guidance officer in the Camp on the subject of embarrassment between the sexes and the necessity of completely ridding oneself of it, so that women and men become exactly equal in dress, training, guard duty and dormitory accommodation and mix with each other completely.[96]

Where recruits reportedly trained for between four and five months, a female graduate recalled that women trained for a year because "they were especially oppressed and consequently needed more education."[97] This graduate recalled that she learned to read and write at Revolution Camp and learned "about the experiences of other revolutions in the socialist and progressive Arab countries."[98]

After training, men and women joined the Front's army, renamed after Hamrin from the Dhufar Liberation Army to the PLA.[99] This new nomenclature chimed with the Front's ambitions to achieve liberation beyond Dhufar. By some accounts, all fighters across ranks and PFLOAG cadres received equal pay.[100] This resonated with the attempt to foster social egalitarianism across Front institutions, such as Revolution Camp and the PLA.

The Front schools likewise sought to promote social, tribal, and gendered equality. The Front had begun to promote education in humble circumstances in 1968. Musallam Said Qatan, whose nom de guerre was

Abu Kamil, pinned a board to a tree and declared: "Here is the martyrs' school."[101] The Front furthered its commitment to education when Bahraini activist and Front member Huda Salim (born Laila Fakhro) founded the Lenin School near Hawf on April 1, 1970.[102] A year later the Front opened the People's School, for intermediate grades, on April 28, 1971.[103] After the counterinsurgency bombed Hawf on May 25–26, 1972, damaging the school and other sites, the schools moved further inland to the relative greater safety of the vicinity of al-Ghaidah. In 1973, a surrendered Front fighter estimated 750–800 pupils across grades one through five.[104] Mona Jabob's sources identified 500 primary school pupils and 320 in the intermediate school by that year.[105]

The schools' physical structure evinced wartime and exilic shortage and pragmatism. The school began as a group of tents that doubled as accommodation at night and classrooms by day.[106] Later, administrators equipped their workspaces with chairs and tables made from the wood of recycled weapons boxes.[107] In May 1971 Soviet visitors to the Front suggested that, so as to avoid reference to a foreign and potentially distant concept, the school should change its name from "Lenin's School." The eventual change of name in April 1972 to the People's School sought to present less of an emphasis on secular Marxism to a forthcoming Libyan delegation. The switch of name did not present much challenge in material terms, as there was no physical sign anywhere with the name of the school. Practically, though, people still continued to call the school by its former name.[108]

In these materially precarious conditions, pupils studied a curriculum covering Arabic, drawing, English, geography, history, mathematics, political instruction, and science.[109] Huda Salim designed and handwrote the school's curriculum herself.[110] The schools encouraged social egalitarianism along gendered and tribal lines. Separated for sleeping arrangements, boys and girls studied alongside one another and shared ancillary tasks of cooking, cleaning, and keeping watch as guards.[111] Work teams mixed children from different tribal backgrounds so as to undermine tribal loyalties.[112] Graduates of the school recalled in a positive light their formation of friendships with members of tribes whom, before the revolution, they had been raised to fear as enemies.[113] Photographer Jean-Michel Humeau captured this sense of pleasure in learning and friendship among revolutionary pupils, amid the movement's emphasis on preparing students for anti-colonial armed struggle (Figure 4).

FIGURE 4. Pupils of one of the revolutionary schools, 1971, Mahra Governorate of PDRY. © Jean-Michel Humeau. Reprinted with permission.

Through interventions in everyday social relations and through revolutionary institutions, then, the Front sought to promote social change along lines of greater social egalitarianism. Yet the question of what socialist, Marxist-Leninist, and Maoist-inspired ideas may mean *in practice* for people living within a particular movement is not so readily forthcoming as stated intentions. Understanding programs' actual meanings in context requires scrutiny of the ways in which different constituencies within vanguards and grassroots engaged with, mobilized, interpreted, and negotiated ideas, values, institutions, and subjectivities.

In Dhufar, there was considerable opportunity for variation in the interpretation of and engagement with Marxist-Leninist and Maoist-inspired ideas. The movement comprised radical left wing thinkers such as ʿAbd al-ʿAziz al-Qadi, Salim al-Ghassani, and Ahmad ʿAbd al-Samad.[114] But wider participation beyond a "few dozen" persons in the movement's ideological turns is open to speculation.[115] Similarly, the revolutionary vanguard was well-versed in Mao's interpretations of Marx, but their familiarity with the writings of Marx is a further area of speculation.[116] Thus, when leaders vernacularized ideas for Dhufaris in speeches and teaching, a "double vernacularization" was at stake from Marx to Mao, and from Mao to Dhufaris.[117] Meanwhile, the extent to which Dhufaris determined their support for the Front on ideological criteria, or nonideological criteria such as the Front's provision of services and welfare, is another topic open to speculation.[118]

Dhufaris' practical experiences of revolutionary policies may also have varied in the light of the absence in Dhufar of a Communist Party. In other contexts, party structures can play significant roles in disciplining populations and imposing policies. These party structures were lacking in Dhufar. Front announcements that targeted specific regions, such as marriage in the western region, perhaps indicate that everyday practices varied from region to region.[119] The Front also operated within the severe material constraints of wartime and/or exile. This made pragmatism (compatible with the Maoist injunction to adapt to local context) all the more important as a survival strategy.[120] To understand the post-1968 Front as a Marxist-Leninist movement that, arising from the intersection of multiple political movements and ideologies, took inspiration from Maoism is not an endpoint, then. Rather, it is a starting point for further questions about the multiple and changing meanings of ideas, policies, and practices.

Contradictions, Problematic Outcomes, and Experiential Gaps

The Front's projects for social change comprised internal contradictions, problematic outcomes, and gaps between the experiences of different constituencies. In the context of supporters' apparent consent and hopes that the revolution promised liberation, the movement made demands that sometimes contradicted emancipatory claims. The presence of twelve-year-old Amina and fifteen-year-old Tufula [*sic*] in Revolution Camp in 1970, and British observations that by 1974 most reinforcement fighters for the Front were "between 14–18 years old," testify to such internal contradictions.[121] Iranian volunteer physician at the revolutionary hospital, Mahboubeh Afraz, bemoaned in her 1975 diary that the Front had imposed nursing training, to be followed by front-line service, on reluctant fifteen-year-old boys and girls who would have preferred to continue their studies.[122] The promise of liberation could contradict lived experiences of those whom the Front mobilized.

At the time, Halliday and Srour did not publicly problematize some of these contradictions.[123] Others did diverge from the Front's official pronouncements. Lebanese Marxist and scholar Fawwaz Trabulsi had traveled to Dhufar in 1970 together with Halliday. Publishing in the early 1970s under a pseudonym, Trabulsi wrote essays about sensitive issues including tribal and class structures. This led the Front's leadership to ban the circulation of the essays in areas under its control. Trabulsi further criticized Front leaders for compromising their values and aims by imposing censorship.[124]

When Dhufaris did not meet the vanguard's expectations for revolutionary commitments and sacrifices, the movement further contradicted its ideals of emancipation by punishing perceived transgressors. In dealing with supporters of the government and opponents of the revolution, the Front used violence. After the mutiny on September 12, 1970, the Front executed dissidents. Records of military trials in the central region in February 1970 offer a glimpse into further executions. Between February 3 and 15, the military court condemned seven men to death after convicting them of high treason. The court claimed that the accused confessed to receiving cash, food, and clothes for activities such as passing on to the counterinsurgency information about the movements, bases, weapons, and numbers of the PLA, the names of Front cadres, the location of an antipersonnel mine, and paths through the *jabal*; passing on information leading the counterinsurgency to arrest Dhufaris; disbursing cash to Dhufaris working for government intelligence; selling weapons and cows to the counterinsurgency; storing weapons belonging to counterinsurgency intelligence networks; and pointing out houses for counterinsurgency forces to burn.[125] It was also Front policy to punish those who refused to sell food to the PLA.[126]

The Front's retribution against perceived traitors fueled accusations of "communist terror" on the part of sympathizers of the counterinsurgency.[127] This internal violence would also feature among the reasons that Dhufaris gave for leaving the Front to join government paramilitaries.[128] Internal violence created lasting postwar memories of trauma.[129] Tensions remained raw decades later. During my fieldwork, some interlocutors warned me not to ask about the Front's executions.

There were further contradictions in the Front's agendas to promote new social relations and identities. Tensions existed within the Front's cultivation of collective identities. These spanned international solidarity and variations of nationalism stretching to all Arabs, only Dhufaris, or an Omani identity encompassing Dhufaris and northern peers.[130]

While each of these nationalisms was meant to supersede tribal loyalties, there were additional contradictions in the Front's attitudes to tribalism.

Although officially the Front condemned tribalism, at times militants worked within and through tribal networks. In a 1980 interview, 'Abd al-Samad, a member of the Front's executive committee, explained that returning migrants from the Gulf had worked within tribal networks to disseminate revolutionary ideas in Dhufar.[131] One former revolutionary also recalled to me that Front leaders had worked to achieve a balance of representation of tribes within certain offices: "The Front depended on the tribal system, we chose someone because he was from a particular tribe and we wanted a contact with that tribe, we looked for someone from a particular tribe with competence." Tribal connections could thus become a means of achieving revolutionary participation.

Similarly, there were contradictions in the Front's efforts to promote gender equality. The Front's agenda to undermine women's subordination did not amount to a promotion of absolute "independence." Looking back from exile in the late 1970s on the Front's emancipation of women, one female activist from the Front's Omani Women's Organization (OWO) suggested that "[w]omen no longer depend on men as they do in capitalistic societies, *since both men and women depend on the revolution*. The result is that new types of relations between men and women are developing" (emphasis added).[132] The Front maintained some forms of gender distinction. At the 1971 Congress, delegates discussed whether there should be mixed political discussion groups for men and women. They decided that while this should be considered for the future, sex-segregated discussion groups could continue (Figure 5).[133]

Ongoing conservative attitudes among some Dhufaris may have held the Front back from fully applying policies of gender emancipation.[134] Revolutions in which women's freedom of movement increases can elicit conservative backlash.[135] Some Dhufaris criticized revolutionary changes in gender relations. 'Aqil Salim complained in his pro-government radio broadcast: "[The women] went off, against the will of their families, if necessary, to join up in military training and do whatever they liked without the knowledge of their relatives. Families were thus broken up, and the young people's first loyalty lay with the Front and not with their kith and kin. Some of these women were then put in charge of watching the movement of people and of accommodation, and innocent people have quite often been maltreated or killed because of the false reports made by these women, who have lost all sense of their old, traditional values."[136] Sultan Said went further, casting Dhufari women as "mountain whores."[137] The desire of some militants

FIGURE 5. "In the Dhofar region: one of the meetings organized by the People's Front for the Liberation of Oman." Photographer unknown, undated. Postcard published by the "Comité de soutien à la révolution en Oman" as a supplement to *Oman en lutte*, Issue 5, 1977. Courtesy of EUL MS 473/5/15, Special Collections, University of Exeter.

to counter such backlash may have influenced some more conservative revolutionary practices.

Besides backlash, ongoing gendered biases among some Front activists may have contributed to persistent gendered distinctions.[138] For instance, when the OWO planned to collectivize childcare among women in exile, activists maintained a gendered division of labor and the responsibility of women for childcare (albeit in a context of a high presence of war widows and potential shortages of adult males).[139] In practice, the Front's claims to promote gender equality could translate into an expectation that women should conform to revolutionary masculinity, rather than a transformation of gender relations into more egalitarian forms.[140] Hamran recalled of his childhood years under the Front: "the women were encouraged not to be feminine. [They] were encouraged to be like men. . . . Women were not encouraged to be weak females, to prepare food . . . no." Even as female revolutionaries faced pressures to conform to masculine norms, they could still face restrictive treatment that the women concerned experienced in gendered ways. Afraz recalled how male revolutionaries monitored the movements of her and her sister while they were in al-Ghaidah. The Front's Aden-based public relations officer, Said Masoud, sent instructions to limit their movements. Revolutionaries justified treating Afraz and her sister differently with reference both to the Iranians' unfamiliarity with the terrain and, specifically, to their gender.[141] Gendered preconceptions did not disappear in the Front.

There were also problematic outcomes of revolutionary agendas. Some were unintended consequences—such as the fact that a movement committed to social egalitarianism also produced new hierarchies between an elevated and enlightened revolutionary vanguard, and those beyond who became the targets of the vanguard's interventions. Some highly educated militants, like Afraz, looked down on "backward" Dhufaris, whom they perceived as having only a limited understanding of the revolutionary program.[142] There were also compromised outcomes whereby militants adapted principles, such as in the 1971 decision to withhold from making mixed-gender discussion groups compulsory. Another problematic outcome, in Afraz's view, was the fallout from the Front's distribution in exile of rations to supporters and its creation of jobs with little practical content. The movement enabled some of its supporters to live off aid without doing productive work themselves, even to the point of hiring Yemenis for cooking, driving, and fishing.[143] A movement in theory committed to upholding working classes created a revolutionary class dependent on others' labor.

Alongside internal contradictions and problematic outcomes were gaps: mismatches between official discourses and Dhufaris' actual experiences of revolutionary social change. Front leaders envisaged the revolution as a mission toward emancipation from exploitation. In practice, however, people had joined the movement for a variety of reasons. Only some of these motivations necessarily evinced sympathy for projects of emancipation and the promotion of social egalitarianism. During Halliday's visits to Front-controlled areas in 1970 and 1973, Front members described their varied motivations for joining the movement. One man explained: "I was exploited [as a wage laborer on government projects]." Another recounted: "I had no food and no clothes. . . . My family was nearly starving." A companion said he had joined "to retrieve pride and honour," another that he had joined "to avoid paying taxes," and another because "I heard of people fighting Said bin Taimur who came from Oman to dominate us."[144] The pathways toward revolutionary participation did not necessarily conform to idealized class consciousness.

Once they had joined the movement, people navigated their own trajectories, embracing some forms of change but rejecting or avoiding others. In the Front's agendas to undermine tribal and gendered hierarchies, there was considerable interest in making "room at the top." Militants expanded the pool of people who could participate in high-status activities, such as bearing arms and fighting, by including previously excluded groups such as enslaved persons and women. But there was less of a "race to the bottom" of more people taking on tasks such as specific categories of manual labor associated with exploited or marginal groups.[145] 'Ali Mohsen, a member of the PFLOAG Central Command, explained to Halliday that "tribesmen" resisted sedentarization, and were attached to cattle ownership as a "sign of honour" and felt "demeaned by physical labour."[146]

Some Dhufaris also rejected outright aspects of the Front's social agendas. One man recalled to me that "in my family we did not let women become fighters." There were also those who took advantage of the Front's social change agenda to pursue personal benefit. One former Front member recalled to me his concerns that the low bride-price allowed some men to marry without a long-term commitment to the relationship. "I knew of more than ten cases," he told me, while also acknowledging that casualties on the battlefield increased the number of short-term marriages. Concerns that marriage had become "too easy" perhaps underpinned the Front's proclamations in 1973 that, after the election of judges to the People's Committee, "any marriage contract taking place in the Western Region without recoursing [sic] to any of the two mentioned Qadhis will be regarded as illegal and unbinding with effect from the issue of this resolution."[147] The Front leadership seems to have battled with its own anxieties about opportunities for lax sexual activity.

These contradictions, problematic outcomes, and gaps in Dhufaris' differential experiences of Front policies may have contributed to some Front supporters becoming disillusioned with the movement. Afraz described in her diary the low morale of her young adult female patients whose husbands "were martyred and who often had one or two small children. They seemed very depressed and often despaired of the revolution."[148] By that time, the Front's ongoing military setbacks likely further contributed to disillusionment. After military defeat, the Front would continue its exilic projects for social change, including the OWO's mobilization of women, the health care centers, and schooling. For Afraz, however, such projects for social change could not erase Dhfuaris' disillusionment with the revolution.

Messiness Strikes: Scales, Negotiation, Choices

Contradictions, problematic outcomes, and experiential gaps in revolutionary social change certainly constrain the reach, impact, and uptake of programs. Yet at the same time they signal the messiness of revolutionary social change—and the opportunities therein for an engagement with social change that anticipates future longer-term legacies.

One indication of the messiness of revolutionary social change in Dhufar is the extended temporalities and scales of Dhufaris' interest therein. Their involvement preceded and at times surpassed the Front's agendas. Before the Front's turn to socialism in 1968, Dhufaris were already engaged in initiatives that questioned tribal privileges and exclusions as well as gendered hierarchies. That engagement went beyond the incubatory effects of migration and colonialism for supra-tribal identities. Dark-skinned Dhufaris of enslaved background had already been organizing in the Gulf as the welfare association "The Black Hand." The emancipation of Dhufar's enslaved persons appealed to Front activists and members of other progressive movements in the Gulf. But emancipation was not a "gift" for these militants to bestow. It followed on from enslaved persons' own initiatives to transform their conditions.[149]

Nor did interest in emancipation among Dhufaris of free origin necessarily originate in the Front or in its Marxist-Leninist incarnation. Dhufaris harbored "religiously motivated sympathy with the notion of abolition."[150] By April 1968—five months before the movement's official socialist turn in September 1968—British intelligence already reported that "the DLF claim to consider [slaves] as free and equal."[151] The Marxist-Leninist declaration of emancipation reiterated and formalized existing trends.

Similarly, efforts toward the emancipation of women preceded the Front's formal adoption of such policies at Hamrin in 1968. Before then, women were already mobilizing with the revolution, as both Front and counterinsurgency sources attest. Women passed on information about counterinsurgency troops.[152] They also set aside food for fighters, nursed the wounded, carried water, and carried arms to battle lines (Figure 6).[153] Some had apparently joined the liberation army by 1967, before the movement's proclamations in 1968 of a Marxist-inspired agenda to emancipate women.[154] Dhufaris had also already taken radical action to pursue educational opportunities before the Front's introduction of schooling, whether through clandestine migration or "smuggling" a pupil into the school at Salalah.

FIGURE 6. A woman and child carrying water to a PFLOAG camp. Photographer unconfirmed but likely Fred Halliday, circa 1970. Courtesy of Alex Halliday and Gulf Committee Archive, EUL MS 473/5/10, Special Collections, University of Exeter.

Initiatives for emancipation and greater social inclusivity thus *preceded* both the Front's formation, and its formal radicalization as a Marxist-Leninist movement.

Moreover, Dhufaris' interest in revolutionary social change could surpass the Front's initiatives. While after 1968 Front cadres pushed for women's emancipation, Dhufari women who were not cadres also pursued their own agendas. Female revolutionaries called for the total abolition of the bride-price—their demands going beyond, and remaining unmet in, the Front's policy of a reduced bride-price.[155] Women in the liberated areas established a rota for childcare so that women could take it in turns to attend other activities. Front organizers later took cues from these initiatives, planning to expand them: "Women are spontaneously organising to solve such problems [as pregnancy, childbirth, and the care of children]; they take turns to look after children collectively. We have to take up these forms of organisation and popularise them. One of our plans is to set up nurseries throughout the liberated areas."[156] In a further instance of vigorous commitment to gender liberation, a female combatant took extremely seriously the task of guarding Lebanese volunteer physician Kamel Mohanna. She insisted on accompanying him—armed with her Kalashnikov—when he retired to bathe. When he questioned this, she informed him that "[t]he revolution has imposed total equality between women and men" and that her presence was to "protect" him. It was an embarrassed Mohanna who turned his back to her before undressing.[157] The commitment of some women to gender emancipation took some male revolutionaries aback.

The existence, timing, and scale of Dhufaris' initiatives for social change qualify revolutionary narratives of the Front as the principal instigator of change, with Hamrin as the Front's version of a watershed date of "before" and "after."[158] (The Front's emphasis on 1968 as a turning point is comparable to the Sultanate's equivalent focus on Qaboos's accession in 1970.) Dhufaris' interest in social change sometimes predated the Front in its initial and later socialist forms, and at times surpassed the Front's official policies. These circumstances call into question any equation of the demise of these projects with the end of the Front's formal activism.

Another sign of the messiness of revolutionary social change was Dhufaris' negotiation of forms of change that were acceptable according to their own concerns. Both cadres and members of the wider public engaged in these negotiations. The former cadre who was anxious about the possibility of men entering into marriages without a long-term commitment improvised a solution: in order to perform a marriage, he wanted "a man who will stay put" (literally, "sit"). He thus added his own criteria to revolutionary transformations of socially acceptable marriages.

Hamran recalled an incident that demonstrated how those not in positions of authority negotiated forms of change that they deemed acceptable and appropriate. He remembered that many women changed their style of clothing and cut their hair short, as images that circulated internationally of Dhufar's revolutionary women showed. "It was incredible to see how quickly women who had been very conservative . . . wore shirts and *wizar* [cloth that men wrap around their lower bodies]," he recollected. But, Hamran recounted, "the women did not want to wear bras, they associated them with camels." Bras reminded mobile pastoralist women of the cloths tied over the udders of lactating camels to prevent calves suckling so that milk would be available for humans. Dhufari women were reflecting on and choosing which forms of change to adopt. They vernacularized revolutionary initiatives and adopted meaningful forms in their own lives.

At times, Front officials and members of the wider population cooperated to find mutually acceptable forms of social change. A health worker in the liberated areas explained in a 1977 interview that Dhufari women were often too shy for male medical personnel from their own tribe to treat them. Patient and medic found solutions, however. The medical teams looked for a (male) nurse who was not from the patient's local area, and shy female patients accepted such a person to treat them.[159] From various subject positions Dhufaris worked to find acceptable forms of social change. This indicates active engagement with the Front's projects for social transformation. That engagement also speaks to the possibilities for continuing interest in those changes, even after the end of the Front's formal activism.

A further manifestation of messy revolutionary social change was the fact that Dhufaris had to make choices about their participation. Women had to make decisions and take actions, such as collectivizing childcare in order to be able to attend Front activities. Dhufaris also made decisions about their participation in education and in religious life—two areas where pro-government sources of anti-communist inclination have often accused the Front of coercing people's behavior. Acknowledgment of Dhufaris' choices in these areas is not only an important qualification of the anti-communist demonization of the Front, the empirical foundations for which deserve scrutiny. Recognition of Dhufaris' acts of choosing also suggests the extent to which revolutionary agendas for social change called upon Dhufaris, like other revolutionary subjects, to cultivate new subjectivities.[160]

A recurring accusation in accounts sympathetic to the counterinsurgency and hostile to the Front is that the movement "abducted" the children who attended the revolutionary schools.[161] This accusation fits with alarmist anti-communist views. Dhufaris' memories, as well as evidence from the time, nevertheless suggest that parental consent preceded and was a condition of school registration. 'Aqil Salim's propaganda broadcast acknowledged that "[t]he people of Dhofar began sending their children voluntarily" to the revolutionary school.[162] In some cases, counterinsurgency violence encouraged parents to make this choice. Some former pupils and parents recounted to Mona Jabob that fear of air strikes and starvation caused some parents to send their children to the school even before they had reached age seven.[163] The school represented a potential, albeit vulnerable, haven from bombing.

The Front actively sought parental consent for pupils' attendance. Heiny Srour recalled that the school put on a play that aimed to persuade the parents of male pupils to send their daughters to attend as well.[164] Hamran, who recounted the circumstances of his joining the school in 1971 when he was eleven years old, also recalled the requirement for parental consent:

Hamran: I decided to join the school. I was there for 18 months.

AW: How did you join the school?

Hamran: I surprised my family. I was a shy child. I did not have many friends. . . . I met a member of the Front. I was looking after my camel. I had a camel who was three or four years old. He was my best friend. I spent all my time with him. I used to drive him along with a stick.

Whenever I was looking after the animals, if I saw a fire, I would go straight to it, because I knew that it meant that I would get good food. So, I met a member of the Front. He told me that they were planning to send a group of children to the school in Yemen. "If you want to go . . ." [he told me]. I told him: "Yes, I want to go." He said: "You have to have the consent of your family." I told him: "You have it." He said: "No, they have to bring you." I said: "They will bring me."

My family were shocked when they learned. They knew that I was shy, that I did not get on with many people. They said: "No, it's not you." I said: "Yes, it's me." My father walked me to the meeting place. We walked [to Yemen].

AW: Did you have any shoes?

Hamran: No, no shoes. There were no shoes in the school.

AW: How long did it take you to walk there?

Hamran: Over a month. There were sixty-two or sixty-three children. About fifteen rebels escorted us. Some joined, some left.

Hamran's account conveyed both the need for parental consent and the formidable efforts to which children and revolutionaries went to enable school attendance.

According to ʿAqil Salim, parental distress arose once "parents found that when their children visited them they had changed from their Arab, Islamic ways, and mocked them and their traditions and values and the things they had held dear and sacred since their own upbringing—like prayer, and fasting." Parents, ʿAqil Salim claimed, were nevertheless "unable to take their children out of the school for fear of incurring punishment."[165] ʿAqil Salim thus accused the Front of coercing parental consent for continued school attendance. This accusation contrasts with Srour's account that at least some parents felt able to refuse to send children to the school.

Where unambiguous evidence has survived of intentions to remove Dhufari children from one location to another without parental consent, it was in fact Sultan Qaboos, and not members of the Front, who suggested such action. In a conversation on April 6, 1974, "[t]he Sultan had ordered CSAF [Commander of the Sultan's Armed Forces] to prepare a plan to attack Al Gheida, bring back the jebali schoolchildren and destroy the town, also to strike Al Gheida from the air if there were further incursions into Oman from the PDRY."[166] However, as British policy did not allow British officers to take part in operations outside the borders of Oman, the ordered attack did not go ahead. The suggested plan reflects the status of the revolutionary school as a symbol of the Front's achievements that Sultan Qaboos wished to destroy as well as the sultan's willingness to attack a civilian site and remove children.

Pro-government sources have accused the Front of suppressing Islam.[167] Such discourses pitch the counterinsurgency as the defender of Dhufaris' religion, as captured in one of the pro-government propaganda slogans: "Islam is our way, Freedom is our aim."[168] The likely appeal, in the eyes of residents of the Front's *jabal* stronghold, of counterinsurgency visions of Islam is nevertheless open to debate. *Jabbali* residents were Muslim, but as mobile pastoralists they did not build or pray in mosques in their *jabal* places of residence. They observed non-Islamic religious beliefs such as food taboos.[169] In a context of frequently experiencing hunger, they ate foods that orthodox Islam did not allow.[170] Some observers have reflected on their distance from, rather than their closeness to, Islamic orthodoxy.[171]

It is the case, though, that in its Marxist-Leninist incarnation, the Front distanced itself from public displays of Islamic religiosity. For instance, prior to Hamrin, in DLF radio broadcasts on the Cairo-based station, Voice of the Arabs, Yusuf bin ʿAlawi had made appeals to God.[172] After Hamrin, public reference to God and religiosity became more sensitive. Interviewees of Abdel Razzaq Takriti recalled that between the post-monsoon seasons of 1969 and 1970, when the Front's military commander of the eastern area increased tolerance for displays of religiosity in order to boost local support, this displeased the central leadership. The Front reasserted tighter control over the area.[173] Further evidence of the avoidance of public religiosity was Soviet journalist Alexei Vasilyev's observation during a visit to Front-controlled areas in 1969 that political discussions began with the formula "In the name of the revolution, in the name of those who died for the revolution."[174] This is a striking departure from the common Islamic phrase for opening formal texts "In the name of God the merciful."

In the context of such measures, when in 1974 the Front announced that mocking religion (alongside attacks on tradition and flirting with women) would "be subject to serious disciplinary measures," leaders signaled both that such mockery took place, and their disapproval of it.[175] Yet the avoidance or restriction of public religiosity is not the same as an official policy of killing those who pray and prohibiting Islam. Counterinsurgency veterans have accused the Front of both.[176] Dhufaris recall such events.[177] Yet there is also contradictory evidence. Dhufaris made choices to engage in religious practice that was neither secret nor punished. Speaking in February 1970 from Revolution Camp—the heart of Front political and military training—Tufula [sic], aged 15, replied to Halliday's inquiry as to whether she prayed that "I live in a society of people who pray and I am one of them."[178] This contradictory evidence raises the question of whether practices may have varied between officials and contexts. It also suggests that the Front's formal position did not prohibit Islam.

Indeed, the Front sometimes called upon religious figures and discourses. When Halliday visited Dhufar in 1970, he met an imam who, after the Front took Rakhyut in 1969, had "made speeches in the town mosque denouncing imperialism and supporting the armed struggle," who "expounded the absence of contradiction between socialism and Islam," and who continued to perform religious duties for the local population.[179] One month before Halliday's visit, the Front had distributed a recruitment leaflet in Salalah that made an appeal to members of the SAF not to fight "against your brothers in faith and nationality."[180] Although Islamic teaching was not part of the curriculum in the Front's primary school, in pupils' memories the schools did not forbid the practice of Islam, as an interlocutor shared with me. Indeed, at its third Congress in 1971, the Front espoused "[t]he freedom of religious belief and affiliation."[181] The notion that the Front had a policy of suppressing Islam, then, certainly reflects anti-communist discourse and prejudice. But it does not adequately reflect the more complex relationship of the Front to Islam. The revolution called upon Dhufaris in new ways to make choices and reflect on their religious practice and its meaning.

Afterlives of Messiness

In a global context of liberation and protest movements demanding social emancipation, Dhufar's Front introduced policies of radical social transformation. The movement sought to counter exploitation by undermining tribal, gendered, and other social inequalities and aimed to increase emancipation by promoting social egalitarianism across new military, educational, and welfare institutions. Contradictions, problematic outcomes, and experiential gaps nevertheless arose, such as the mobilization of adolescent combatants, the production of new hierarchies among militants, and unorthodox motivations for recruitment. These scenarios constrained programs' potential for promoting social emancipation and egalitarianism in line with (some) militants' aspirations. But those very contradictions, problematic outcomes, and experiential gaps foreground the messiness of revolutionary social change. These messy experiences saw Dhufaris engage with different scales, negotiations, and choices of and about revolutionary social change. That messiness is itself revealing.

Messiness brings to light counterhistories of revolution. It grants insight into an expanded notion of revolutionary agency that acknowledges how those not in positions of leadership vernacularized revolutionary social change. Messiness also shifts focus away from polarizing accounts that try to prove or disprove Dhufaris' support for the revolution. These depictions may reveal more about the narrators and their political agendas than they do about revolutionaries' experiences. Indeed, messiness shows the need to qualify straightforward claims of Dhufaris' overwhelming support for or disinterest in the Front's programs. Instead, messiness highlights a diversity of experiences as Dhufaris engaged with different scales, negotiations, and choices of and about revolutionary social change.

Of particular interest to those concerned about understanding revolutionary change and its legacies over time is the potential for messiness to signal engagement in revolutionary social change. Messiness thereby offers a framework for inquiry into how those who once engaged with revolutionary values, such as the promotion of social egalitarianism, may go on—even despite hostile political circumstances—to continue engaging with those values and producing afterlives of revolution. Later chapters examine how some of Dhufar's former revolutionaries found opportunities to do so in kinship, everyday socializing, unofficial commemoration, and occasional extraordinary actions. The next chapter examines another indication of Dhufaris' engagement with revolutionary social change: the intensity of the counterinsurgency's efforts to undermine the Front's programs and to offer alternatives.

3

Patronage, Coercion, and Transformed Spaces

IN OCTOBER 1971, the war between the British-backed sultan and Dhufar's liberation movement was in its seventh year. That month, Donald Hawley, Britain's ambassador in Muscat, visited Dhufar. On the second and last day of his tour, he traveled to the government-held town of Sadah, some 125 kilometers east of Salalah.[1] There was no road linking them. Hawley avoided the arduous and dangerous land journey over mined terrain by taking a helicopter from the RAF base at Salalah. His report described Sadah as "a charming fishing village in a rocky wadi." He noted that Sultan Qaboos's governor for Sadah, Musallam bin Muhammad al-ʿAmri, asked the ambassador for the government's help regarding "a school . . . [m]edical assistance . . . a new well" and "[c]learance of land for new building to house people coming in from the Jebel [mountains.]"[2]

Thus glimpsed, the encounter at Sadah seemingly fits the conventional narrative that the newly enthroned Qaboos brought Omanis the roads, schools, health care, and services that his father, Said, had withheld. On closer examination, however, the meeting at Sadah disrupts that narrative. It was a Dhufari, al-ʿAmri, who was asking for change, and moreover in areas where the Front had already introduced policies. Furthermore, Qaboos's representative was directing requests to a British party. This signaled the colonial backing of the counterinsurgency and Qaboos's rule.

In addition, the discussion highlights that access to government resources was contingent upon Dhufaris' political submission. Hawley noted that al-ʿAmri had been a former supporter of the DLF, for which he had served seven years as a political prisoner. The ambassador recorded that the governor prefaced his requests with assurances that the Sadah area "was now 99% clean" of Front supporters and that "no recent reports of rebels had come in in that area." Government support was conditional upon Dhufaris' submission.

Finally, the British visitors' response to a Dhufari request for civilian development projects indicated the military stakes therein. The highest-ranking British civilian in Oman, Hawley, replied that "these matters were not my concern." Yet Hawley reported that Brigadier John Graham, the officer whom Britain had seconded to hold Oman's highest military position, commander of the Sultan's Armed Forces (CSAF), "took notes."[3] The potential provision of welfare services was in fact a military affair.

The exchange at Sadah thoroughly destabilizes the narrative that Qaboos transformed Oman. Instead, the encounter foregrounds the interplay of revolution and counterinsurgency, anti-colonial aspiration, and colonial intervention. All these were at stake in the transformation of space and social relations.

The meeting highlights Dhufari agency, including Dhufaris' anti-colonial revolutionary agency, as a driver of spatial transformation. The policies of revolutionaries in Dhufar had already set agendas for spatial and social transformation. Dhufaris, including former Front members such as al-'Amri, pressured British and Omani authorities for further policies. The Dhufari agency animating the encounter at Sadah preempts later dynamics. In postwar decades, Dhufaris occupying divergent political positions, including former revolutionaries, continued to shape ongoing spatial and social transformations. As they crafted lasting legacies of revolutionary agency, Dhufaris produced afterlives of revolution.

At the same time, the encounter foregrounds that colonialist counterinsurgency prerogatives also shaped spatial transformations in Dhufar. It was Graham, the British seconded CSAF, who "took notes" about al-'Amri's requests. The encounter furthermore delineates how counterinsurgency-driven spatial transformation in Dhufar worked through the twin dynamics that have helped sustain authoritarian rule in Gulf monarchies: patronage and coercion. The counterinsurgency transformed space through the "carrots" of offering patronage to former revolutionaries such as al-'Amri as well as to the wider population. In parallel, the counterinsurgency transformed space through the "sticks" of coercion. These included the insistence on zero resistance in exchange for access to services and the destruction of *jabal* homes and livelihoods that pushed Dhufaris into government-controlled areas like Sadah. Counterinsurgency patronage and coercion aimed to curb and repress both revolution and the possibility of its afterlives.

That both revolution and counterinsurgency drive spatial and social transformation has implications for inquiry into their intersections. It is necessary to distinguish between the methods and consequences of respective programs for spatial and social transformation. The Front's revolutionary projects for social and economic development were part of an anti-colonial vision of social, political, and economic emancipation from exploitation. As such, these policies not only resisted colonial control and exploitation; their radical reorganization of social relations also went some way, albeit imperfectly, toward undermining social, tribal, ethnic, and gendered inequalities.

In contrast, the government's projects for spatial and social change relied on patronage, a set of relations premised on inherent inequality between patron and clients and between differentiated clients. Meanwhile, the government's reliance on coercion produced new segregated patterns of residence and livelihoods and lasting legacies of ethnicized militarization. In doing so, the patronage and coercion underpinning counterinsurgency spatial and social transformation not only supported colonial agendas but also unavoidably intensified social, tribal, and gendered inequalities while undermining revolutionary social egalitarianism. The Front and Qaboos's government may have overlapped in a modernizing desire to improve welfare and infrastructure, but their respective programs were neither interchangeable nor equivalent.

The transformation of space and society through revolution and counterinsurgency has wider resonance for an analysis of space in contested projects of political control.[4] Recognition of the agency of Dhufaris, including revolutionaries and former revolutionaries, in the region's wartime and postwar spatial transformations advances understandings of how actors who are neither politically nor economically dominant nevertheless shape the spaces in which they live.[5]

Meanwhile, paying attention to counterinsurgency as a driver of spatial transformation advances criticisms of oversimplistic "miracle transformation" narratives about Gulf monarchies. At stake in the government's delivery to Dhufaris of new infrastructure and welfare services was not just the question of regime legitimization that preoccupies all Gulf monarchs. In Dhufar, the sultan's government additionally had to compete with a rival revolutionary state-like authority that had already begun to transform space. Dhufar thus highlights that the drivers of spatial transformation in

Gulf monarchies include counterinsurgency prerogatives. If Qaboos and his British backers—including the avid notetaker Graham—felt this pressure most, so did the Gulf monarchs who gave postwar grants and loans for infrastructure in Dhufar.

Sultan Qaboos and his allies hoped that the wartime and postwar counterinsurgency-driven spatial and social transformation of Dhufar would dispel the possibility of Dhufari resistance. Yet Dhufaris, including former revolutionaries, continued to reshape space and social relations during the war and thereafter.

Spatial Transformations in Gulf Monarchies

The transformation and modernization of space in Gulf monarchies in the second half of the twentieth century has generated nationalist historiographies of dramatic and apparently miraculous change from "rags to riches." In the modest ports and inland oases of the early twentieth century, hardship and hunger were familiar. Within a few decades, these communities morphed into large, economically powerful, and socially heterogeneous cities. Access to government benefits ended Gulf nationals' days of hunger, while nevertheless cultivating socioeconomic differences among them. Shortages of skilled and unskilled labor saw the massive immigration of foreign resident workers. Their living conditions varied between extremes of privilege and exploitation.

Each Gulf country has its own transformation narrative. These narratives generally stress oil as the driver of transformation.[6] The dominant narrative for Omanis, though, as well as for some observers of the Sultanate, stresses that Qaboos authored the country's transformation, commencing the country's "blessed renaissance" (*al-nahdah al-mubarakah*) at his accession in 1970.[7]

In his speech on July 23, 1970, a few days after the coup that secured his accession, Qaboos appealed to the imagery of a "new dawn."[8] In adopting in 1974 the term *al-nahdah* ("renaissance"), Qaboos positioned himself as the author of a moral renewal. This echoed the Ibadhi notion of *al-nahdah* as the return of the just rule of an imam after a period of the imamate being "hidden."[9] The narrative of Oman's "new dawn" under Qaboos charts developments in infrastructure and services in Oman's cities and beyond: the rise toward national coverage of schools, health care, roads, and the electricity grid, the construction of new facilities such as ports and factories, and the development of new housing and neighborhoods.[10]

The personalized nature of Qaboos's style of government, whereby he eschewed sharing power with a ruling family and concentrated key state functions in his own hands, compounds his centrality as the alleged author of Oman's *nahdah*.[11] That narrative was key to legitimizing Qaboos's rule.[12] This task was all the more urgent given the legitimacy deficit under which Qaboos came to power: through a coup against his father, facing an anticolonial revolution, being reliant on British support for survival, and at a time when the UN was scrutinizing the rival claims to the country of the British-backed sultan and the exiled Ibadhi imam.[13]

"Rags to riches" transformation narratives of Gulf monarchies, including the narrative of Qaboos's *nahdah*, are nevertheless problematic. These countries, and their economies, cities, and demographic profiles, have certainly changed. But conventional narratives about these transformations do not adequately account for their causes, character, and consequences. These transformations are not linear.[14] Nor have they been "progressive," since they entrenched systems of political and economic subjugation.[15] They have likewise led to dysfunctional spaces.[16]

Conventional transformation narratives are particularly simplistic regarding the drivers of change. They overemphasize a few factors or one factor as the cause of change: oil wealth or, in the case of Oman, Qaboos himself.[17] While a new economic mode of production—such as the advent in Gulf monarchies of oil production for a global market—leads to new spatial forms, this occurs in the context of political struggles over space.[18] "[O]il alone," then, "cannot explain" the transformation of space in Gulf monarchies."[19] Nor can a sultan-centric narrative explain Oman's transformations. Critical reinterpretations of other relevant political, economic, and historical conditions advance a broader project to de-exceptionalize Gulf economies and cities.[20] Among the multiple factors that have influenced the transformation of space in Gulf monarchies, especially relevant for questioning sultan-centric transformation narratives about Oman, are political factors, as well as the role of actors beyond the ruler and those advising him.

Political factors shaped the oil wealth–era transformation of space in Gulf monarchies. In Kuwait, ruling authorities pursued modernization to legitimize their seizure of unprecedented wealth and political power.[21] Their distribution of material resources was a political project to "weed out" potential dissent.[22] New urban spaces in Gulf cities also enabled greater authoritarian control. In this region, "[t]he infrastructure state aimed at abolishing agency and protest."[23] Urban design here, and elsewhere, presented opportunities for the repressive control of spaces and people.[24]

Ruling authorities were, nevertheless, not the only authors of spatial transformation, nor were theirs the only influential political projects. From divergent positions of influence or marginalization, multiple actors struggle to shape and influence space.[25] Through everyday circulation and other practices, the residents of cities coproduce distinctive spaces, the character of which can contrast with nationalist and official narratives.[26] In Gulf monarchies, other actors beyond ruling authorities shaped spatial transformations.[27] In doing so, they pursued alternative political and economic agendas, including dissent, resistance, anti-colonialism, and the promotion of alternative collective visions.

In Oman, the narrative that Qaboos transformed the country neglects wider political drivers of spatial transformation and the role of multiple actors beyond Qaboos. Qaboos-centric narratives neglect much more than the role of oil revenues in funding the Sultanate's new development programs. Oman's oil revenues began modestly in 1967 with 20.9 million barrels.[28] Production reached 107.9 million and 103.2 million barrels in 1971 and 1972, earning 47.9 million and 49.6 million, respectively, in the new Saidi riyal currency.[29] The 1973 hike in oil prices saw oil revenues in 1974—by which time the new Omani riyal (OR) was pegged to the US dollar—reach OR 281.5 million, equivalent to nearly $815 million.[30] But even these increased oil revenues were not sufficient to fund the country's public spending, which included new infrastructure and the counterinsurgency in Dhufar. Running a deficit from 1972 to 1975, Oman relied on the political and economic support of British subsidies and the donated support of Oman's and Britain's allies, especially Iran and Jordan, for the campaign in Dhufar.[31] The scale on which Omani public funds were available for new infrastructure projects depended on others, including colonial backers, being willing to help pay for the war. To understand the spatial transformation of Oman, and especially Dhufar, therefore requires looking beyond both Qaboos and the country's oil revenues, to wider political agendas and actors.

Those who occupied positions within or close to Oman's government also pushed, to varying degrees, for social and economic development while pursuing diverse political agendas. The rapidity of early change under Qaboos benefited from the fact that Said had already made plans for new infrastructure in anticipation of oil revenues and had begun work on projects. In a rare public speech in 1968, Said had referred to these plans as the country's "new era" and a "bright dawning future."[32] Sultan Qaboos was nevertheless able to claim the credit for these plans.[33]

The British had also been pressuring Said to implement civil development projects.[34] Said and the British espoused two different visions of colonialism: Said favored colonial conservatism, or "maintenance of the status quo and minimal gradual change." The British favored colonial modernism, or "economic transformation and state building."[35] After his accession, Qaboos also favored the latter vision, although British officials expressed their impatience with the pace of development projects in Oman, including in Salalah and in Dhufar's *jabal*.[36] Rather than representing an unprecedented "new dawn," then, policies for socioeconomic development under Qaboos saw one long-standing vision of colonialism take precedence over a rival vision.

New infrastructure projects were a reflection not only of colonial modernism but also of counterinsurgency prerogatives. The British had made the introduction of British-financed infrastructure projects a condition for military intervention to support Said in al-Jabal al-Akhdar in 1957–1959.[37] This reflected the view that infrastructure projects would help prevent the emergence of future unrest. The revised British counterinsurgency plan for Dhufar from September 1970 took a similar approach. It advocated social and economic development to secure Dhufaris' political loyalty.

Beyond the actors and agendas of ruling families, colonial and imperial powers, and elites, however, are other "state makers."[38] They also create and shape space. Dhufaris and other Omanis authored their own initiatives to pressure for social, economic, political, and spatial change. The most extreme form of Dhufaris' pursuit of change was their creation of the Front, and their engagement in its programs for change and its anti-colonial vision of political and economic emancipation. Qaboos was reluctant to introduce political change. He rejected suggestions of autonomy for Dhufaris. With British support, he established an absolute monarchy at the price of sidelining the plans of his uncle, Tariq bin Taimur, for a constitutional monarchy.[39] In the absence of meaningful political reforms, Qaboos's government and the counterinsurgency competed with the initiatives of Dhufaris and the Front for socioeconomic development.

The wartime and postwar spatial transformation of Dhufar, like the transformation of Sadah, was not the "gift" from Qaboos that the *nahdah* narrative suggests. Multiple economic and political factors and multiple actors with divergent agendas, including anti-colonial revolutionaries, shaped and drove spatial transformations in Dhufar, as elsewhere in the Gulf. Dhufar further highlights how counterinsurgency prerogatives drove the transformation of space—even as Dhufaris also shaped those changes. How, then, did spatial transformation become a counterinsurgency priority in Dhufar?

A Revised Counterinsurgency

In early 1970, the war was approaching its sixth year. The military situation was a "stalemate."[40] The Front controlled the mountain areas, and the government controlled Salalah and the surrounding plain. Neither could displace the other. The Front lacked the resources to threaten the government's base. The sultan lacked troops to take hold of the mountains. In addition to being short of personnel, the Sultan's Armed Forces (SAF) faced other challenges.[41] They lacked equipment and intelligence. They also faced issues beyond insufficient manpower, funding, and intelligence.

The very makeup of the army made it unpopular with Dhufaris. At this time, British commentators followed local practice in distinguishing "Dhufaris" from "Omanis" of the northern region from which Dhufar, a dependency of the sultan of Muscat and Oman, was a separate territory.[42] (In the twenty-first century, in everyday speech Dhufaris continue informally to distinguish themselves from "Omanis.")[43] With Said trusting "very few" Dhufaris, the SAF did not recruit among Dhufaris.[44] Prior to 1964, Said had not deployed SAF troops in Dhufar.[45]

SAF rank and file were formed mainly of two groups. The first were Omanis from selected northern tribes known for their loyalty to the sultan.[46] The second were Baluchis. The latter had long-standing connections with the sultans of Muscat and Oman as paid soldiers. Rarely did they speak Arabic. Once the emerging conflict required SAF troops' deployment in Dhufar, "fraternization with the locals" was "forbidden."[47] SAF officers were British, and some lower-ranking officers were Pakistani.[48] Some British officers were loaned service personnel, seconded from British forces to serve the sultan. Others had ceased active service in British forces and worked as mercenaries, or "contract officers," the term that British personnel preferred.[49] Two further elements of the foreign military presence in Dhufar were the air force staff in the Sultan of Oman's Air Force (SOAF), all of whom were British, and the British RAF base in Salalah out of which the SOAF operated.[50]

From a Dhufari perspective, the forces protecting the sultan "looked suspiciously like an army of occupation."[51] Recalling to me his childhood contact with soldiers from both sides, Hamran concurred: "I met the government and the rebels. I met all of them with my animals. With the *jabhah*, they are family. With the Omani troops, it was no such thing, there were Baluchis who didn't speak Arabic, or British [*sic*]. Which was a cause for antagonism. A reason they were hated." The foreign-seeming SAF were ill-placed to win friends in Dhufar.

Moreover, the violence of Said's army and their destruction of the resources essential for Dhufaris' survival made them unpopular. In 1966, the SAF placed the *jabal* under a food blockade, so as to attempt to starve Dhufaris into submission. Blockades are a long-standing technique of counterinsurgency.[52] Earlier sultans had also deployed food blockades against *jabbali* dissidents.[53] Said imposed the blockade in response to the attempt by a clandestine Front cell to assassinate him during an inspection of the DF in 'Ain Razat Camp near Salalah.[54] The blockade took the form of a fence that Dhufaris called the *hisar* ("blockade, siege") and that the British called "the Wire." It separated al-Husn, al-Hafah, al-Dahariz, and Salalah from the plain and mountains.[55] The blockade cut off the mountain population (combatants and civilians) from vital supplies from the coast. These included the dried sardines that were essential for livestock and people to survive pasture shortages during the hot pre-monsoon season and the monsoon. The fence also cut off coastal populations from seasonal supplies of meat, milk, and ghee and further restricted residents' already constrained freedom of movement. Knowing that the fence would worsen conditions on the coast, in the final weeks before its completion many locals voted with their feet. They fled the soon-to-be-enclosed zone in increasing numbers.[56]

By November 1967, the blockade extended to the cutting off of sea trade with Aden.[57] The government also cut off coastal towns such as Mirbat and Sadah for as long as the counterinsurgency feared that contact with the *jabal* would strengthen the Front.[58] To prevent supplies reaching the Front, Said's government rationed food purchases within coastal villages, as a British intelligence report of March 1968 described: "All markets are supposed to run a rationing scheme but this is only really effective in Salalah. Each family is permitted to buy only a small quantity of rice, flour, sugar etc per week. This is registered in the suq and checked by askars [guards] as individuals leave the suq. In the case of weddings etc, Palace permission must be sought to purchase extra quantities. . . . The system is not foolproof.

SAF occasionally carry out food-patrols outside Salalah to check on this system."[59] The counterinsurgency weaponized hunger against the Front and the wider population.

To further deny Dhufaris access to essential resources, the SAF burned wells and homes and destroyed livestock. The commander of the SAF's Muscat Regiment in 1967–1970, Lieutenant Colonel Thwaites, described the violent tactics of Colonel Mike Harvey, commander of the SAF Northern Frontier Regiment: "He instituted a policy of blowing up or 'capping' wells all over the Jebel which certainly inhibited enemy convoys but also denied water to the locals and possibly innocent Jebalis and their herds."[60] With herders needing to water cattle every other day, the denial of water was devastating for the subsistence economy.

While critical of Harvey's methods, Thwaites recalled that he himself ordered the burning of four homes, amounting to one in five of the dwellings in a community where his troops had discovered hidden weapons.[61] Thwaites persuaded himself that the greater cause of the fight against communism justified violence against Dhufaris.[62] Another British veteran, Captain C. Hepworth, nevertheless criticized both the SAF's violence and its colonial context: "[W]e also burnt rebel villages and shot their goats and cows. . . . Any enemy corpses we recovered were propped up in a corner of the Salalah suq (market) as a salutary lesson to any would-be freedom fighters." Hepworth further recounted that after a failed operation to take Dhalkut from the Front, the sultan's forces withdrew after "blowing the village wells." For Hepworth, "[a]part from containing the enemy . . . we were certainly not winning the war." He saw Dhufari combatants as "freedom fighters."[63] While few British veterans followed Hepworth in recognizing Dhufaris' anti-colonialism, others also questioned whether coercion alone could win the war.

Aware of the issues that the SAF faced, including their unpopularity, British advisors suggested revisions to the campaign over the course of 1970. Some elements began to take shape under Sultan Said, and others after the July 1970 coup that saw the accession of Sultan Qaboos. The revised plans increased the number of troops and improved their equipment. Said had agreed in March 1970 to place an order for helicopters and to increase the number of SAF troops available for Dhufar by raising a fourth SAF battalion.[64] Until then, with two of the SAF's three battalions required in the north, only a single battalion had been available for deployment in Dhufar. The plan was for the extra troops on the ground to take control of key areas in the western mountains and block the Front's access to supply routes from the PDRY.[65]

This strategy of increasing military capacity on the ground would continue over the years. The 1973 hike in oil prices increased state revenues. This income, as well as support from Britain, Jordan, and Iran, boosted military spending. The 1975 defense budget was nearly double the entire national budget of 1973.[66] By 1974, the 11,000 pro-government forces in Dhufar comprised 5,000 Omanis (from the north, excluding Dhufaris), 3,000 Iranians, 1,200 Dhufari pro-government paramilitary *firaq*, 1,000 Britons, and 800 Jordanians. (These numbers included combatants as well as support staff, such as British and Jordanian engineers.) They faced an estimated 600 PLA fighters and 1,200 Front militia.[67]

Other revised plans concerned techniques of counterinsurgency: "asymmetrical warfare by a powerful military against irregular combatants supported by a civilian population."[68] In the 1960s there was an emerging body of expertise on counterinsurgency.[69] This addressed both military and political tactics. Military tactics included rounding up populations into controlled "safe zones" to prevent passing on resources and intelligence to insurgents. Another technique was to focus on keeping control of key economic areas even if this meant temporarily giving up other less strategic areas. Political tactics included propaganda campaigns and persuading insurgents that their political and economic interests lay in ceasing resistance. British military forces had gained experience in colonial and anti-communist counterinsurgency campaigns in Kenya (1952–1960) and Malaya (1948–1960). Some Britons serving in Dhufar had previously participated in these campaigns.[70] The prevailing view among British advisors was that the fight against a popular insurgency could not end by military means alone but required political solutions too.[71] The revised plans for Dhufar combined military and political counterinsurgency strategies.

During 1970, British officers developed the political strands of a revised counterinsurgency. In a March 1970 intelligence report, Tim Landon, then Dhufar intelligence officer, suggested a "divide and rule" route to victory that would draw on tribalism. Landon noted long-standing rivalries between cattle-raising Qara tribes in the central mountains and camel-raising Kathiri tribes in the northern desert and Mahra in the eastern and western mountains. Landon suggested that by giving money and weapons to conservative Kathiri and Mahra tribal leaders and building infrastructure such as wells in each tribe's areas, the government could win these tribes' support. The

FIGURE 7. Sultan Qaboos and Tim Landon. Photographer unknown, circa 1970. Courtesy of Papers of John Craven Carter, EUL MS 476/4, Special Collections, University of Exeter.

Qara tribes would then find themselves surrounded. Concerned about accessing the material benefits that other tribes were already enjoying, they would accept a deal from the government to end the conflict.[72] While Sultan Said did not take up these suggestions, Landon's plan contained three elements—"the incitement to tribalism," "the encouragement of collaboration by means of financial leverage," and "the manipulation of existing conflicts over land and resources"—that foreshadowed counterinsurgency measures under Qaboos.[73]

Subsequently, British SAS officers devised political counterparts to the planned military boost. After visiting Dhufar in April 1970, Brigadier Fergie Semple, director of the SAS, suggested that SAS troops should set up civil action teams (CATs) to provide civilian infrastructure and services, such as schooling and health care, in areas of the *jabal* from which SAF troops had removed Front fighters and supporters.[74] In this way—in line with Landon's earlier suggestions—the government's provision of services would persuade Dhufaris of the material advantages of Qaboos's rule. In addition, Semple suggested setting up intelligence cells to gather high-quality information.

In his report based on the same visit, Colonel John Watts, commanding officer of the 2nd SAS Regiment, stressed the importance of disseminating laudatory information about the government and defamatory information about the Front.[75] Watts likewise suggested the recruitment of Dhufaris into pro-government militias. In practice this meant persuading members of the Front to change sides.

Watts's suggestion envisaged that local pro-government combatants would undermine the impression of the SAF as a foreign army.[76] His recommendation also anticipated military gain from the use of locals who knew the terrain and the adversary, advantages that Watts had experienced while working with local recruits in Malaya and Indonesia.[77] Subsequently, *firaq* would indeed point out targets to bombers, a service that British personnel dubbed the "Flying Finger."[78] Nevertheless, Britons would find fault with *firaq* for their perceived lack of discipline.[79] Each *firqah* battalion "mutinied at least once," while paramilitaries "refused to serve in areas or with individuals not of their tribe," and "frequently" passed on intelligence about counterinsurgency movements to the Front.[80] The utility of the *firaq* for military, rather than political, advantage would prove mitigated.

Welfare provision, intelligence, propaganda, and the recruitment of local fighters made up the political dimensions of the revised counterinsurgency campaign. Some commentators, especially veteran British personnel, have foregrounded these factors in casting Dhufar as a "model" counterinsurgency for "winning hearts and minds."[81] Such accounts neglect the importance of conventional warfare strategies for the counterinsurgency victory.[82] They overlook elements that facilitated the counterinsurgency's success that are not replicable, such as the scant global media attention that Britain's ban on press access helped achieve.[83] Crucially, these accounts have neglected the significance of coercive counterinsurgency interventions—bombings, land mines, food and water blockades, and the denial of access to basic resources—for that victory.[84] Indeed, although a conventional "good governance" approach to counterinsurgency proposes that violence against civilians jeopardizes counterinsurgency success, evidence from Dhufar and other campaigns suggests that such violence may be necessary for counterinsurgency victory.[85]

Whether laudatory or revisionist, accounts to date of the Dhufar counterinsurgency, as well as the memories and analyses that interlocutors shared with me, invite deeper consideration of the practice and implications of counterinsurgency strategies. The welfare provision and the recruitment of local pro-government militias contributed to the components of Landon's

Patronage, Coercion, and Transformed Spaces   111

"divide and rule" strategy: increased tribalization, the reliance on patronage to manipulate political loyalties, and the intensification of conflicts over land and resources.

Many Dhufaris understood that tribalization, patronage, and the cultivation of conflicts over resources characterized not only the counterinsurgency but also postwar governance in Dhufar. Commenting on this, one interlocutor, 'Awad, parsed the government's changing styles of wartime and postwar patronage. He identified four "generations" (*ajyal*) of former revolutionaries who left the Front from the 1970s to 1990s. The precise amounts of postwar patronage for former revolutionaries were not usually public knowledge. In this sense, postwar (and some wartime) patronage for former Front members did not assume the formality of disarmament, demobilization, and reintegration programs in vogue from the 1990s.[86] 'Awad and others surmised former revolutionaries' access to patronage from evidence such as jobs in the public or private sector and ownership of houses and other assets. Patronage strategies targeting former revolutionaries, as well as national policies, altered over time while continuing to produce inequalities and to coexist alongside governmental coercion—as 'Awad's analysis foregrounds.

The First Generation: Wartime "Big Opportunities"

"The first generation [of Front supporters to change sides] was between 1970 and 1973. The *jabhah* [Front] was still strong in the *jabal*. The government gave big opportunities." As 'Awad identified this generation, he likely had in mind figures such as Musallam bin Muhammad al-'Amri. The latter had risen from political prisoner in Muscat's notorious Jalali prison to become governor of Sadah. Jalali, located on an island close to Muscat, was formerly a Portuguese fort. Harsh conditions in the jail made P. S. Allfree, a British officer who served as Sultan Said's chief intelligence officer, "physically depressed and mentally sick."[87] Relatives of former prisoners described for me the overcrowded cells. Detainees had to take it in turns to sleep, and even then the person trying to rest could not stretch out fully. Jailers offered salt water to the underfed prisoners who were desperately thirsty, relatives recalled. In March 1969, there were sixty-six Dhufari prisoners in Jalali.[88]

After his accession, Qaboos released many detainees, offering them "big opportunities" if they changed sides. While al-'Amri accepted, others refused. Another Front member, Said Masoud, spent 1965 to 1970 in Jalali.[89] 'Awad mentioned him as an example of those who refused Sultan Qaboos's offer of largesse. After his release, Masoud rejoined the Front in the PDRY. Some visitors in 1975 recalled him as the public relations officer and one of the "old cadres and a member of the Central Committee."[90]

Some who changed sides in the time of "big opportunities" went on to have spectacular political and financial futures. Yusuf bin ʿAlawi was originally a prominent DLF activist and broadcaster in Cairo. Later, though, Front authorities accused him of embezzling the movement's funds in Cairo to buy himself a Mercedes Benz. His critics alleged that, once the Front authorities investigated the accounts and called him for questioning at the Hamrin Congress in 1968, he switched to supporting the government.[91] By 1969, bin ʿAlawi was reportedly offering gifts, in particular watches, to Front members with the aim of persuading them to change sides.[92] He would go on in 1982 to become Qaboos's minister responsible for foreign affairs.[93] He still held this position when Qaboos died in 2020. The three houses that bin ʿAlawi owned in Salalah, on which interlocutors commented to me, were a reminder of the material benefits of securing the sultan's favor.

For many, the opportunities on offer for switching sides were more modest. The government extended an amnesty from September 1, 1970.[94] It gave material support that increased for those who changed sides bringing a weapon.[95] From January 1971, the counterinsurgency offered a place in the *firaq* to surrendered Front fighters.[96] Joining the *firaq* offered access to resources. There was a monthly wage and food.[97] By contrast, the intensifying counterinsurgency blockades would make it increasingly difficult for the Front even to feed its troops, let alone pay them.[98] Paramilitaries received "rewards" for capturing Front fighters' weapons.[99] Additionally, *firaq* members accessed resources for their family members.[100] To join the *firaq* was to engage in government patronage networks.

Patronage during this period also took the form of investments in social and economic development such as al-ʿAmri had requested. SAS personnel, who began to deploy to Dhufar in August 1970, initially led these efforts. The SAS operated in Dhufar as the "British Army Training Team" (BATT), a title that obfuscated British involvement in direct military action. As well as training *firaq* and participating in combat, BATT personnel ran civil aid initiatives. Initially, and while the Front remained strong in the *jabal*, this aid was available in the coastal areas under government control and in sites where the BATT deployed temporarily.

By 1971, every BATT unit included a trained medic, as David Arkless, an RAF crew commander in Dhufar from 1971 to 1972, recalled. Each

BATT deployment set up a room or a tent to provide medical treatment to civilians. Patients' unfamiliarity with Western medicine—sometimes to the point of strapping pills to afflicted parts of the body instead of ingesting them—did not preclude their enthusiastic pursuit of treatment.[101] By 1972, a health clinic operated daily in Salalah, and the SAS was employing a veterinarian.[102] The gradual expansion of the government's positions in the *jabal*—where it held a position through the monsoon in 1972 and remained "in strength" from 1973—required regular delivery by air of supplies, including drinking water.[103] Provisions that sustained military personnel would also have supported Dhufaris living with their *firaq* relatives. While this counterinsurgency medical and other aid reached only those in government-controlled areas, a wider range of blockade-stricken Dhufaris would have learned of those provisions. Dhufaris moved between zones of government and Front strength—despite wartime constraints, and often to the frustration of British personnel suspicious of such mobility.[104] Counterinsurgency aid provisions connected Dhufaris to government patronage and signaled the possibility of such connections to other Dhufari audiences.

The counterinsurgency moved people out of the *jabal* to coastal settlements under government control. Al-'Amri's requests to clear land for new housing in Sadah anticipated migration from the *jabal* to the coast. The 1960s and 1970s were a time when, across the Gulf, rural migrants in search of livelihoods moved to urban settings, often living in slum-like shantytowns.[105] In Dhufar, rural to urban migration was not merely a question of moving closer to new economic opportunities, as became necessary with the decline of the frankincense trade. It was also a question of surviving counterinsurgency bombings and blockades and of government preference to concentrate populations in areas under its control. Well before the 1973 hike in oil prices and the advent of "instant urbanization" in the Gulf, Qaboos was already anxious to increase the rate of resettlement on Dhufar's coast.[106] Sir Geoffrey Arthur, Britain's political resident in the Persian Gulf, observed in September 1971 that "[Qaboos] was determined to improve living conditions in and around Salalah and in places such as Taqah, Mirbat and Sadh. He had this very day assigned a further £100,000 from the privy purse for resettlement in Dhofar. He was dissatisfied at the rate of construction of houses etc."[107] Moving people to the coast was an urgent political priority that deprived the Front of potential supporters.

The impetus toward coastal development saw Salalah become a small boomtown. In February 1972, Brigadier Graham commented that "[a]part from the fact that the towns are wired in and food controls are maintained, life for the civilian population in Salalah and Taqa is normal."[108] By 1972, Dhufar's capital had a new branch of the British Bank of the Middle East.[109] Salalah was open for business. PDO's report on Dhufar in August 1972 commented that "[a]s a result of a severe shortage of both skilled and unskilled labour, an estimated 700 Indians and Pakistanis, labour, craftsmen and clerks, have been brought to Dhofar for employment by the Government and contractors for civilian employment."[110] British firms won lucrative contracts for urban development. Presiding over Salalah's growth was the sultan's new palace, for the building of which he dedicated £2 million in 1971.[111]

The transforming spaces in coastal towns offered new services that rivaled the Front's provisions. Yet the government's and the Front's respective social and infrastructure programs had different effects. Where Front programs had to an extent undermined tribalism, the government's plans and related distribution of patronage encouraged tribalism and related rivalries. This was evident in the operations of the *firaq*. Tony Jeapes recalled of his time as an SAS squadron commander in 1971 how his initial hopes of a pan-tribal paramilitary force proved short-lived. The thirty-two recruits to the first paramilitary group, Firqat Salah al-Din, hailed from multiple tribes. But further recruitment to the paramilitaries followed tribal lines: two Bait Kathir tribal leaders persuaded more recruits to leave the Front and join the paramilitaries, telling Jeapes that they would not fight alongside other tribes. To Jeapes's dismay, the two men anticipated that they could recruit a total of "between 13 and 18 men."[112] As numbers picked up, newly formed *firaq* battalions recruited from specific tribes only. In Firqat Salah al-Din, by April 1971 tensions between the Bait 'Amri and the Bait Qatan put an end to its pan-tribal aspirations.[113] Thereafter, each *firqah* catered to a specific tribe. By the end of the war, there would be twenty-eight *firaq*.[114] With paramilitaries accessing and channeling resources along tribal lines, the *firaq* accelerated (re)tribalization.

Some *firaq* members further profiteered from the counterinsurgency by stealing Front-owned livestock. The prewar *jabal* economy had focused on subsistence production primarily for milk, rather than the sale of meat.[115] Nevertheless, in October 1971 *firaq* members at Jibjat made it a condition of their continuing cooperation that the government provide them with access to fodder and markets on the coast to sell livestock, where the government would be the principal buyer.[116] Counterinsurgency leaders were unwilling to lose the *firaq*, who represented the opportunity of dispelling the SAF's foreign reputation. Accordingly, in Operation Taurus, counterinsurgency forces relocated cattle from the *jabal* to the coast, with families following later.[117] The relocated cattle, however, included livestock belonging to Front members that *firaq* fighters stole during the evacuation: "Most of the animals were owned by firqat families, but many of them also had been owned by men serving in the adoo [enemy] and were 'confiscated' by the firqat during the drive."[118] The colonial backing for the counterinsurgency created opportunities for tribalized accumulation and dispossession, of which some *firaq* recruits took advantage.

Such encouragement of tribalism under Qaboos was not unique to Dhufar. Tribal leaders across Oman received resources through which Qaboos aimed to coopt them.[119] This was a change of policy compared with his father. Said had limited the distribution of resources to some tribal leaders, thereby reducing their political power relative to that of his government.[120] In Dhufar, where tribe members competed to acquire resources from and through the counterinsurgency, Qaboos's policies created new forms of tribalization and conflicts. This undermines the claims of counterinsurgency propaganda that the sultan's government protected Dhufaris' "traditions."[121] Very often, government policies were introducing new conflicts.

Government welfare programs were also more conservative than the Front's as regards gender relations. The cultivation of gendered distinctions and subjectivities is central to counterinsurgency.[122] Dhufar was no exception. Although there were both male and female Front fighters, *firaq* recruitment envisaged male fighters and family dependents. When female members of the PLA wished to leave the Front or became prisoners of war, what were their prospects compared with male peers who would be offered a place in the *firaq*?

Memoirs, archives, and my interlocutors offer only brief answers. When Andrew Higgins, an SAS veterinarian who served in Dhufar in 1974, encountered a recently captured female fighter, a more experienced companion explained that it was "really unusual to capture a bint [woman.]"[123] The price for avoiding capture, though, could be death. David Arkless was surprised to learn that two fighters whom a patrol had killed turned out to be women: "On closer inspection of the bodies it was discovered that both of them were females. . . . The patrol had not realised that they were fighting with two females for they were dressed the same as their male compatriots and fought as well if not better than them."[124] The Front's memorial book of casualties records the names of eleven female PLA fighters and seven female militia members whom counterinsurgency violence killed.[125]

Women fighters could avoid capture via another route, Higgins learned, namely a preference "to surrender to the locals in their own time and place." Higgins's companion had "[n]ever heard of one being captured before." The veterinarian described the female prisoner: "Her face was uncovered and she was very attractive, maybe in her twenties. It was hard to tell. She had a nose ring set with a red carnelian stone. . . . She smiled demurely at us then turned away with a shy laugh." Higgins's orientalizing and sexualizing gaze may be the last extant documentation of this woman. Perhaps captured or surrendered female fighters turned to roles as wives and mothers to build future lives. This was the pattern that Front activists reported of demobilized female fighters in the PDRY after 1975.[126] The *firaq* offered women roles only as wives, mothers, sisters, and dependents.

Government schooling also initially differentiated between boys and girls, in contrast to equivalent revolutionary initiatives. Several Dhufaris recalled to me that early on during his reign Qaboos had founded a school in Salalah for the children of "martyrs" who had died fighting for the government.[127] This school's patronage policies discriminated among Dhufaris in several ways. One interlocutor disagreed that the school was for "martyrs' children," suggesting instead that pupils had not lost a parent but were children of the *firaq* to whom the government gave a stipend and free accommodation. In other words, the school was part of a policy of patronage. A British commentator described in 1974 that a government boarding school in Salalah for *jabbali* students accepted only male pupils.[128] This was a stark contrast to the Front school that catered to both girls and boys, despite operating in circumstances of material shortage likely greater than those of the government's wartime school.

The government school survived as a site of patronage. After the last generations of wartime pupils completed their studies, interlocutors explained, Qaboos dedicated the school to the education of the children of the formerly enslaved. Qaboos had already discussed plans for their education in 1972.[129] Many of these children and/or their parents had been enslaved members of the royal household. Many remained closely linked to Qaboos throughout his reign.[130] In that context, and with the school still catering to *sumur* pupils in the 2010s, *sumur* and non-*sumur* interlocutors commented to me in detail on the perceived signs of the sultan's favor that pupils accessed, such as school buses, a uniform, and a canteen. The school continued to operate as a center of sultan-centric patronage.

The spatial transformation of government-controlled areas of wartime Dhufar was not only the result of patronage. Coercion—food and water blockades, forced resettlement, the destruction of communities and livelihoods, threats against dissidents, bombings, and land mines—also transformed rural and emerging urban spaces. To intensify the long-standing food blockade of the *jabal*, the government timed the introduction of the new Omani riyal currency in April 1971 to coincide with a month-long closure of the food store in Salalah. Dhufaris relied on access to this store for essential supplies. A strict limit on stockpiling preceded the closure. This further reduced the possibilities of food reaching the hunger-stricken *jabal*.[131] A group of Front fighters who changed sides to join the *firaq* in 1971 struck Jeapes as "desperately thin and under-nourished."[132] The blockade was becoming ever tighter.

To intensify the blockade further, from November 1971 the counterinsurgency built several wired and mined defense lines cutting off Front supply routes. While the initial attempt at Operation Leopard failed, later defenses ran north–south from Dhufar's mountains to the coast: the Hornbeam Line (begun September 1972) to al-Mughsail, the Sarfait Line from Sarfait to the coast, and the Damavand Line (from 1975) to Rakhyut.[133] As well as impeding the Front's weapons supplies, these blockades left Front fighters and *jabal* residents all the more hungry.

The mined wires across the *jabal* reinforced the coercive strategy of "resettlement into safe zones." This is a staple of counterinsurgency against rural populations.[134] Resettlement forced Dhufari civilians under threat of attack out of their grazing lands and into government-controlled areas in the *jabal* or coastal towns. A British leaflet dropped on the central mountains in 1973 spelled out the consequences of failure to relocate to the plain: "The arrows in the picture indicate the safe routes which citizens and their families may use if they wish to get to Salala. Citizens must not approach from the forbidden area between the two arrows, as there are field guns in this area always ready to fire, day or night. Keep this warning in mind, for your safety and the safety of your goats, camels and cattle."[135] By designating free-fire zones, the counterinsurgency defined Dhufaris and their livestock there as legitimate targets.

The destruction of Dhufaris' essential resources for survival, already a policy under Colonel Mike Harvey, continued. British officials were of the opinion that the use of napalm bombs would discourage Dhufaris from leaving the Front to support the government. They refused a request from Qaboos in August 1970 to make napalm bombs available, while privately noting the UK's policy of denying possession of napalm.[136] SOAF nevertheless dropped fire bombs—oil drums filled with a mixture containing flammable jet fuel—on Front-held territory, destroying agricultural resources. Arkless recalled one such mission: "We soon arrived over our target. It was a large, deep green field, concealed by low hills, and after circling it a few times to give anyone below a chance to clear the area, the pilot ordered us to prepare the load. . . . We watched [the bombs] fall . . . a cloud of smoke could be seen rising from the first pair of bombs, and after the third pair, the area below was blotted out by thick clouds of black smoke."[137] SOAF continued to target livestock in Front-held areas. Both counterinsurgency and Front sources recorded that air raids destroyed livestock and damaged grazing resources. Camels, which the Front used for transport (alongside donkeys), were a particular target. Cattle numbers dropped too. Seven years into the war, the PDO estimated a decline in cattle by August 1972 of one-fifth, from twenty-five thousand to twenty thousand cows.[138] In a subsistence context, such a drop is especially devastating.

Animals and grazing lands were not the only SOAF targets. SOAF bombed settlements in Dhufar and in the PDRY. Air strikes destroyed Front-held Rakhyut in 1969.[139] Further air strikes hit Hawf on May 25 and 26, 1972.[140] Survivors of the 1972 bombings recounted that these strikes hit the Front's office, the military training camp, and other locations such as the school's kitchen, but not the classrooms.[141] In the respective accounts of these bombings of a former pupil and of British ambassador Hawley, the trauma that counterinsurgency coercion caused for Dhufaris contrasts with British satisfaction with and optimism about the effects of violence.

A former pupil recalled:

> Early in the morning and before we had washed our faces we heard the alarms. The revolutionaries guided us toward the trenches that they had dug especially for us [during air strikes]. We had trained for that several times. Around the trench there were six bags of sand distributed by group. Each group of students knew their trench. We ran with our teacher to the trenches. And in my imagination the school flag fluttered with the three colors, black, red, and white, as a sign of injustice, the martyrs' blood, and education. That's what they told us that the flag symbolizes. And I saw

these three things on that day. I felt injustice. And I saw blood. And we saw our books thrown all over the trench. We dropped them and could not pick them up. The planes could have bombed the school directly but they didn't, and thank God that they didn't. They bombed the school kitchen that was a bit further away. None of us or the teachers got hurt. The main concern for the revolutionaries was taking us to the trench. The bombing was chaotic and everybody was running. We wanted to get out [of the trench] or at least put our heads out of the trench just to watch with child-like curiosity. But the school administrators and our teachers prevented us from going out or even watching. We stayed there until it was dark. We left the trenches during the night and the revolutionaries distributed some biscuits. They took us to Abu Kamil Qatan and we stayed for two or three months in caves until we went to al-Ghaidah and then we went to school there. We had to repeat that academic year.[142]

The trauma of children and teachers running for cover amid bombs, blood, and destruction was not Hawley's primary concern, however. For him, the strikes were "PRETTY SUCCESSFUL." He went on to note that "A CONSIDERABLE AMOUNT OF MATERIAL DAMAGE WAS DONE AND WE KNOW FROM SECRET SOURCES THAT AT LEAST EIGHT MEMBERS OF PFLOAG WERE KILLED IN THEIR HEADQUARTERS." He deemed it "TOO EARLY TO JUDGE WHETHER THERE HAS BEEN ANY SIGNIFICANT EFFECT ON CIVILIAN OR PFLOAG MORALE BUT OMANI MILITARY MORALE HAS RECEIVED SOMETHING OF A BOOST."[143] Hawley valued coercion both for its destruction of people and resources and for its potential to raise the spirits of counterinsurgency fighters.

Might Hawley have been less celebratory had he witnessed scenes of pupils running for their lives? Or scenes of civilian survivors of food and water blockades and air strikes, such as Iranian physician Mahboubeh Afraz later observed? She described women and children who arrived at the Front's clinic in Hawf in late 1975 as "incarnations of . . . absolute deprivation." They had walked for seven days and nights to reach the clinic despite hunger, thirst, and bombs. Their predicament overwhelmed Afraz: "[T]hey fall on the ground in different directions and pass out. You don't know which one to treat first!"[144] Coercion was an ongoing component of the counterinsurgency.

It would be misleading to think of patronage and coercion, carrot and stick, as distinct counterinsurgency methods. Al-ʿAmri had prefaced his request for services with assurances that Sadah residents had ceased support for the Front. The operation of the carrot/patronage depended on the simultaneous presence of the stick/coercion. Coercion disciplined Dhufaris into accepting the government's patronage. As Higgins observed during the war's latter years, counterinsurgency forces made it "clear that if enemy action resumed, the new life-supporting water access supplies and assistance would be cut off."[145] Coercion aimed to make submission the only realistic means of survival.

Coercion exacerbated the inequalities among Dhufaris that counterinsurgency patronage cultivated. This is apparent in Operation Taurus, during which *firaq* took advantage of counterinsurgency backing to enrich themselves and dispossess others. Jeapes defended increasing inequalities between "the luxury of the Sultan's Palace in Salalah with its huge air-conditioned garages and riding stables" and the "one-room hovels . . . built for firqat families in Salalah." He justified them on orientalist grounds, arguing that where a "Westerner" would find in such inequality cause for "disgruntled bitterness," the "Arab mind tended to see quite a different picture."[146] Such orientalism was flawed not only in its essentialism but also in its oversights. Such a view overlooks the role of coercion in forcing Dhufaris into "acquiescing" to these conditions. It also neglects the fact that many Dhufaris took up arms for a movement, the Front, that opposed governance through precisely such inequalities.

Dhufaris certainly resisted counterinsurgency spatial transformations. In 1966, residents ran away from their soon-to-be-blockaded villages. After the fence encircling Salalah and neighboring villages was finished, people fled by sea. Amina, aged 12, recalled her escape in 1969: "[M]y brother got an old car-tyre and we swam in the sea for eight hours till we reached the coastline controlled by the Front. . . . I couldn't swim well, and we got very cold and hungry and thirsty."[147] Dhufaris continued to have clandestine contact despite the blockades. One family recalled to me how female relatives, who were less likely to be searched when they left a coastal town, strapped food to their bodies to smuggle supplies to relatives in the *jabal*. Although Said restricted Dhufaris' access to radios, people inside the fence listened to Front broadcasts.[148] The Front continued to smuggle in recruitment leaflets to Salalah.[149]

Dhufaris not only resisted their enclosure but also, through their activities in the Front, established an agenda for spatial transformation that the government subsequently appropriated. In the era of "big opportunities" for those willing to join the government, it was not only government patronage and coercion that drove Dhufar's spatial transformations. Dhufaris, including those in the Front, created their own spatial transformations and resisted those of the government.

The Second Generation: Early Postwar Dhufar

'Awad characterized the next generation of former Front members to change sides in terms of their unequal access to postwar patronage: "The second generation was [19]75–80. The opportunities that the government gave you depended on your name. The members of the leadership got more." This narrative discreetly passed over the final two years of the war's intense counterinsurgency violence, Front casualties, and refugee desperation, such as Afraz witnessed. During those final years, urban and rural spaces continued to change, shaping the directions of subsequent postwar spatial transformations.

In the wake of the October 1973 hike in oil prices, a construction and infrastructure boom accelerated across Gulf monarchies.[150] In Oman, state revenues increased fivefold, although high military and development expenditure saw deficits persist. Salalah continued to grow. By 1974, a decade after only the palace and adjacent areas had been connected to the electricity grid, a new suq on the outskirts was selling electrical domestic appliances.[151] While some houses in the old quarters were "in varying stages of ancient decay," others were in the middle of "modern rebuild."[152] The high demand for schooling—needed for multiple generations who had lacked educational opportunities under Said—saw Dhufaris, including adults, attending schools in shifts.[153] Yet this boomtown bore the ravages of war.

Increasing numbers of displaced *jabbali* families lived in the city in impoverished conditions. In 1974, in Raysut—a village to the west of Salalah that would later become the city's container port—*jabbali* immigrants lived in precarious improvised homes, as Higgins recalled: "There were three settlements, each containing perhaps ten or twelve dwellings mostly built from *burmails* [oil containers], corrugated iron, salvaged wood and *burusti* [coconut palm fronds]. Shanties were constructed by the very poor from whatever they could find."[154] In addition to drinking milk from animals that they had brought with them, these families also received government support including deliveries of drinking water. Higgins observed women standing in line by the delivery truck.[155] Meanwhile, the immigrant families of some *firaq* members initially lived not in shacks but in the houses of

Salalans who had left to join the Front. A former revolutionary explained to me: "The government brought the families of men who had been in the *jabhah* and left [the Front] to the city, sent the children to school, and gave the families somewhere to live and food to eat. . . . Some of them lived in the houses of people where the family, even the women, had left to go to the Front." Displacement and dispossession stalked Dhufar's boomtown.

In the *jabal*, once the government became dominant over the course of 1974–75, the counterinsurgency increased welfare provisions. A Civil Aid Department (CAD) took over responsibilities for welfare services in Dhufar from the SAS in October 1974. (Retired military personnel nevertheless continued to play leading roles, with former SAS officer Major Martin Robb leading the civilian department.)[156] As *jabal* areas came under government control, new settlements took modest shape as "a few tin huts and sandbag shelters surrounded by a mixed collection of *Bedouin* and army tents," as Higgins observed in 1974.[157] The government distributed food—according to the official directive that "meals" be "cooked and eaten on the spot"—and rations at such centers as a means of attracting locals to switch sympathies from the Front to the government.[158] One of the early priorities at these centers was building wells. These could reach depths of two hundred or three hundred meters, supplying troughs of fifteen to twenty meters in length.[159] These *jabal* development projects bore the marks—and reproduced the effects—of counterinsurgency militarization and tribalization policies. British strategists noted in January 1975 "a desire among the firqat to make sure that they retain control of their tribal areas when the jebel returns to civil control."[160] Once the government took over an area of the *jabal, firaq* leaders seized control of water resources, grazing, and the sale of government-provided goods. For one of Jeapes's colleagues, these leaders became "warlords," with some of them becoming full-time mediators of government patronage to the point of being based not in the *jabal* but mostly in Salalah, close to the centers of resource distribution.[161] Such tribalization of spaces and resources, already a feature in the early 1970s, would continue in the postwar period.

By the early postwar years of 'Awad's second generation, the Front was in exile and militarily defeated. For militants willing to return to Oman and swear loyalty to Qaboos, the government offered a new amnesty in March 1976. It promised those who surrendered within two months, and who cooperated with security forces, a guarantee from arrest.[162] Dhufaris dubbed those who eventually went back to Oman (regardless of their "generation") "returners" (*'aidin*). Interlocutors nevertheless warned me against using the term in conversation with former members of the Front. It had pejorative connotations similar to "defectors." Given these associations, I write of a "return" to Oman only in a physical, rather than political, sense.

Over the following decades, most former Front members would decide to return to Oman. Former secretary general 'Abd al-'Aziz al-Qadi returned as late as 2014. The nature and value of patronage on offer for former Front members varied according to the timing of someone leaving the Front and their previous role in the movement. In general, the weaker the Front's position by the time of return, the less support someone was likely to receive from the Omani government. However, as 'Awad noted, the higher someone's former role in the Front, the greater the benefits that the government was likely to give. Seniority could trump questions of timing. Some interlocutors believed that the government varied the amount of patronage offered to ex-revolutionaries as a strategy of "divide and rule." Differences in payments, Dhufaris suggested to me, could create jealousies between former revolutionaries and undermine the possibility of coordinated political opposition.

One person who returned as part of the second generation and who had "the right kind of name" was Hafidh. He was a former Front member who had returned to Oman in 1979. Other Dhufaris explained that before the revolution Hafidh was one of the sultan's enslaved persons. Hafidh himself did not refer to this in conversation with me, though. He recounted a dramatic reunion scene with Qaboos: "The sultan was waiting for me, looking out for me. [He made the gesture of someone looking out.] When he greeted me, the sultan said to me: 'You did what you had to do as men. Now, put your hand in mine and let us build this country together.'" While "building this country" with the sultan, Hafidh also built up his wealth. His Salalah residence—one of several he owned throughout Oman—was a mansion with palatial aspirations located close to the impressive residences of the sultan's maternal relatives. There was a fountain in the driveway, columns around the entrance, and the high-ceilinged reception room that overlooked this vista was lavishly decorated with furniture in a French eighteenth-century style. A close relationship to the sultan provided a former revolutionary with lasting material benefits.

While some early postwar patronage focused on individuals like Hafidh, policies that targeted broader audiences continued to transform urban and rural Dhufar. Across Oman, the government distributed land to citizens.[163]

Salalah grew as new neighborhoods emerged. In some, the government constructed low-cost public housing (*sha'biyat*) consisting of multifamily prefabricated buildings. This public housing could accommodate incoming *jabbali* families and their peers who had been living in shanty dwellings. The *firaq* families who had been occupying the houses of families who had left for the Front also moved to *sha'biyat*, I learned from an interlocutor. For Jeapes, this public housing amounted to "one-room hovels."[164] In the late 1970s, *sha'biyat* in eastern Salalah had an average of eleven persons per unit.[165] Some residents nevertheless appreciated these homes and objected to later government plans for residents' relocation.[166]

In the *jabal*, the Front's former heartland, some funds for early postwar patronage and spatial transformation came from neighboring rulers concerned about putting an end to communist threat in Dhufar. Kuwait and Saudi Arabia arranged loans and grants in the late 1970s ranging from "a few million dollars" to $26.5 million for roads and community development in Dhufar's interior.[167] New settlements in the *jabal* eventually each included a well, a school, a health care dispensary, a mosque, a shop, and an administrative building.[168] The influx of these new resources further exacerbated tribal tensions. Having worked in Dhufar on development projects from 1975 to 1980, Miranda Morris recalled to me: "[E]ach tribe wanted its own school, health center, *firaq* camp, and water supply, and were unwilling to share with others in the same area, even when they were virtually just across the road."[169] The government's provision of welfare services and infrastructure on the *jabal* propagated tribalism and resulting tensions.

The government's distribution of resources across Dhufar's changing spaces created and reshaped tensions, inequalities, and segregation. When some tribes in the *jabal* were unwilling to share resources with others, this led to the duplication of services and the exacerbation of conflicts over those resources. In Salalah, the emergence of new neighborhoods reflected the residents' relationship with Qaboos. In her account of how residents of prewar villages moved to new neighborhoods, longtime Salalah resident Nada flagged the gains of those who had enjoyed a close relationship with the sultan, either as elite tribes loyal to the ruler or as members of his enslaved retinue. She also emphasized the exclusion at that time from patronage networks of those who had joined the Front. Her account detailed four groups: the Yafa'i tribe who, Nada explained, had traditionally helped guard the palace, the al-Ghassani and Shanfari tribes, prominent members of which had served as Sultan Qaboos's tutor and agent, respectively, and the sultan's enslaved persons.[170] She recounted: "After *al-nahdah*, the Yafaʻi tribe went [from al-Hafah] to New Salalah. They got land and money. The Shanafar went [from al-Hafah] to ʿAwqad. Some of the al-Ghassani [from Salalah village] got land in New Salalah, but the ones fighting in the Front didn't. [The government] knocked down the slaves' houses and gave them new houses."[171] Patronage shaped new kinds of segregated, stratified spaces.

Other early postwar districts accommodated tribes whose leaders had lobbied the government to give land for tribespersons to relocate to the city. Driving me through Salalah one evening, an interlocutor pointed out one such district, saying "the government gave land here to the Kathiri from the *jabal*." Elsewhere he noted that "this is where the government gave land to the Kathiri Bedouin." Another neighborhood was home to many Mahra families, I learned. Sometimes the tribe had settled in the area of the plain and *jabal* foothills where members had built tents during their prewar seasonal transhumance. While sometimes incorporating older histories of connection, the ethnically distinctive early postwar neighborhoods materialized new patronage relations. Dhufaris now accessed land as subjects and dependents of the sultan.[172]

Coercion continued to characterize the government's postwar spatial transformation of Dhufar. SAS personnel remained stationed there until September 1976, Jordanians until May 1977, and Iranians until late 1978.[173] In 1979, government officials debated how to discipline continuing resistance, such as through cutting off water supplies or designating "black" areas in which government forces could shoot anyone out after dark. The final decision was for the sultan to order tribal leaders to remove protection from dissidents, so that their death would not trigger a feud.[174] Such interventions legitimized government-sanctioned violence against dissenting Dhufaris. Enabling this coercion were the enduring colonial dynamics of British military support and training for Oman. These continued in the postwar period.[175]

Ongoing measures of counterinsurgency coercion reflected continuing resistance. Government forces faced outbreaks of armed resistance from isolated groups of Front fighters until at least 1980.[176] Guerrillas were not alone in resisting. The government announced in 1977 that it would destroy public housing in Salalah in order to build a stadium. Some residents, including some to whom the government had distributed land elsewhere in the city, nevertheless refused to leave their housing. The government evicted them by force to tents equipped with a water supply and sanitation. In response, residents "took their revenge by destroying all the sanitary arrangements, removing the tents," and going either to their allotted plot or, in some cases, "[returning] to their traditional territories in the Dhofar range."[177] The *jabal* remained a resource for Dhufaris who resisted government interventions.

Alternatively, resistance to government-led programs of social and spatial change could take subtle forms of nonparticipation. Despite the government's rollout of mosques in *jabal* towns, and despite counterinsurgency claims to have protected Dhufaris from Marxist threats to Islam, early postwar *jabbali* residents were "uninterested in Islam" and "not to be seen praying at the prescribed times," according to a 1982 report. This may have reflected, according to the report, "a nonreligious pre-revolutionary culture rather than the effect of atheist training."[178] Having once made choices about their participation in revolutionary social change, Dhufaris subsequently engaged selectively with governmental agendas.

While some Dhufaris resisted and sidestepped governmental initiatives, others continued to claim responsibility for, and play a role in, postwar transformations. Some *jabbali* people, including former revolutionaries, believed that they were the true winners of the war. Moreover, even after the Front's military defeat some of its former members played significant roles in Oman's development under Qaboos. Erstwhile revolutionaries helped build and deliver new welfare services. Male and female former Front members were among those who returned to Oman with high levels of educational capital, alongside similarly skilled Omanis of Zanzibari and East African origin.[179] They helped staff the schools, medical centers, law courts, and bureaucracies of Qaboos's Oman. In Dhufar, I learned of former militants who had worked as doctors, lawyers, teachers, bankers, and administrators. Former revolutionaries were cocreators of Oman's "renaissance."

Pupils of the revolutionary schools played a significant part in the social and economic development of Dhufar. In the *jabal*, where some residents were unwilling to "share" resources with other tribes, Miranda Morris recalled to me the importance of graduates of the Front's school in rural development projects. These students stood out for their different attitude toward tribalism and their commitment to "the common good" (*al-maslahah al-ʿammah*): "When we started working for the Rural Health Service, all the local employees I worked with, with the exception of three people, were returnees from the Front school in Yemen. The other people would only work for their tribe, but these people would work for everyone, for the common good." Decades later, the discourse of former revolutionaries still stressed their commitment to a common good.[180] Official silence in the Sultanate about the revolution nevertheless neglects former revolutionaries' contributions to the transformation of Oman. In that context, Dhufaris' insistence that they won the war tells a counterhistory. A counterhistory, however, does not necessarily *resist* official narratives.[181] Some former revolutionaries and sympathizers argue for their *inclusion within* national transformation narratives.

In the early postwar period, counterinsurgency strategies of patronage and coercion continued the spatial transformation of Dhufar. This process both reshaped existing inequalities and segregation and introduced and exacerbated new variations. All the while, though, Dhufaris, including former revolutionaries, continued to shape their region's transformations.

The Third and Fourth Generations: The Later Postwar Decades

'Awad characterized the next group of former Front members to return to Oman according to their opportunity to find work: "The third generation was in the 1980s. When someone came back, the government gave them the opportunity to work. These people got jobs and houses." 'Awad depicted more generous openings for those returning in the 1980s than official provisions apparently envisaged. From 1979 the government determined that former Front members who surrendered voluntarily "were to be contained in a special rehabilitation camp where they could be usefully employed on some form of government work projects" but denied a place in the *firaq* or other government organization. Those captured while resisting should face "life imprisonment with hard labour."[182] 'Awad's emphasis on offers of work and housing perhaps reflects Dhufaris' memories of a context in which, with the socialist PDRY still hosting the Front, the government sought to incentivize former revolutionaries to return. The Omani authorities went to considerable efforts to convince some Front members, as one Dhufari explained to me: "The *mukhabarat* [intelligence service] went to the countries where Front students were studying to persuade them to come back. They offered them lots of things to persuade them." Dhufaris recalled an Omani state that strove to win over former revolutionaries.

I heard about several ex-Front members, male and female, who returned in the 1980s and went on to have long careers in the public and private sectors. One person told me about their aunt and uncle, Rim and Naser, who moved from the PDRY to Dhufar in the 1980s. The couple had married in

Hawf, where Naser held a position in the Front's exile political administration. Rim was studying at a university in a country that offered scholarships to Front students. The pair had spent summers together in the PDRY in a simple house that the Front provided for them. In the early 1980s, Rim gave birth to their first child.

Eventually, the couple decided to return to Dhufar. I was not able to learn the reasons behind the decision or the interplay between material factors (the pull of work and housing in Oman versus the material shortages of exile), political factors (the desire to take part in helping Oman develop, even if not in the political circumstances to which they had once aspired), and emotional factors (missing family and home). Naser returned first to Dhufar. Rim followed him, bringing their young child. A year later, with her high levels of education, Rim took a position with a private sector employer where she worked until retirement. Naser took a position in a ministry, and later worked in an entrepreneurial private sector setting. Again, I was not able to learn about the reasons for Naser's change of sector and whether his political background influenced his departure from the ministry.

Rim's employment in one institution until retirement was more stable. The absence from her career of multiple institutions may have reflected social stigma in the 1980s and 1990s concerning the labor force participation of women from high-ranking social backgrounds such as Rim's. Prevailing norms disapproved of the participation of Dhufari women from all but the lowliest social backgrounds in waged labor markets outside the home. The postwar participation in the extra-domestic paid labor force of female former revolutionaries from a historically prestigious tribe stood out. It was one of the more visible legacies in Dhufar of the revolution's former pursuit of gendered emancipation.

A condition for female former revolutionaries' return, though, was their conforming to other conservative gendered norms that once again prevailed in Dhufar. Political backlash against revolution often entails increased control over women's bodies, while female former fighters and militants may have to work hard to counter moral and social suspicion about their past.[183] Dhufar's former female revolutionaries encountered pressures to conform to conservative norms. When the *mukhabarat* persuaded a female graduate of the Front schools, 'Aisha, to return from her studies abroad to Dhufar, they inducted her into new gendered expectations. A relative of 'Aisha told me: "When they found 'Aisha, she was wearing a short skirt and her hair was cut short. When she went back to Oman, they took her to a house in

Muscat before she went to Dhufar. In the room they had laid out a beautiful *'abayah* [loose outer garment that covers the body from the neck down] for her. It was exactly her size. They told her 'Dhufar has changed now. This is what you will wear.'" Some women experienced this backlash as a loss. In 1982, women in regions formerly supportive of the revolution reportedly "resent[ed] the loss of their equality."[184] Miranda Morris also recalled that female former revolutionaries who returned to postwar Dhufar resented the attempts of their husbands and others to impose conservative gender norms. Mourning for the loss of former freedoms marks another legacy of revolutionary gender egalitarianism and feminist consciousness.

'Awad's emphasis on work and housing for Front members returning to Oman in the 1980s reflected a wider national emphasis on Omanis' labor force participation. From 1988, Oman embarked on its policy of "Omanization." The Sultanate was the first of the Gulf Cooperation Council (GCC) monarchies to adopt policies to increase the proportion of nationals working in selected industries.[185] Omanization recalibrated patronage strategies, in that labor force participation became a more important means of accessing resources from the state. The increased emphasis on Omanis' labor force participation also anticipated the future rolling back of patronage. The reduction of patronage was, according to 'Awad, the defining characteristic of the fourth generation of former Front members to leave the Front.

For 'Awad, the fourth generation of those who left the liberation movement to return to Oman dated to 1990, the year that socialist rule ended in the PDRY and the country merged with its northern neighbor. The circumstances under which Front members could continue living in Yemen, or continue studying in socialist countries, became more precarious. By 1992, most of the last cohorts of the Front's students in programs abroad returned to Oman.[186] In the 1990s, 'Awad suggested, the majority of Front members who remained in Yemen returned too. Those who had held a high position in the Front could still expect to receive significant resources. But others missed out. 'Awad explained: "The fourth generation was after 1990. People had to wait five years until they got anything." This period of enforced waiting reflected the movement's weakened position after the loss of material and political support in the PDRY.

One man of whom I heard who belonged to this fourth generation was Bashir. He eventually received a stipend, reportedly after a five-year wait. Bashir apparently did not find paid work during that time, or thereafter. Again, I did not learn of the extent to which his political background may have affected his difficulty in finding work. The stipend that he eventually received was insufficient for living costs, though. Bashir's extended family gave additional support to him and the dependents (a Yemeni wife and children) with whom he had returned.

'Awad did not give a date for the end of this fourth generation of former revolutionaries to return to Oman. Some remained in exile for two decades after the fall of the PDRY. As unrest and violence gripped Yemen in 2015, I heard of a handful of former Front members who were only then leaving Yemen and returning to Dhufar. Former revolutionaries already established in Dhufar collected resources—food, clothes, but, due to government restrictions on fundraising, no cash—to help them. No one mentioned to me whether the government would help recent arrivals from Yemen.

A contrast to the government's material neglect of both the likes of Bashir and those who returned in 2015, however, was its attitude to the Front's former secretary general, 'Abd al-'Aziz al-Qadi. In 2013, veteran revolutionaries believed that the Omani government was still working hard to persuade al-Qadi to return to Oman. A former revolutionary told me then: "This story is not over until he comes." By 2015, al-Qadi was back, and under surveillance. The afterlives of revolution nevertheless call into question whether, even after the return of al-Qadi, the story of the revolution was "over."

The reduced—or nonexistent—"package" available to most former Front members who returned after 1990 resonated with wider patterns that troubled some Dhufaris. On the one hand, some Dhufaris expressed to me their frustration at the perceived slow pace of industrial development in postwar Dhufar. "[L]ong discussions" had preceded the eventual opening of the container port in Raysut in 1998, reportedly "[highlighting] the reluctance to develop the remote region [of Dhufar]."[187] This raises a question: might counterinsurgency prerogatives have *delayed* spatial transformations such as industrial development, because of the government's fears of creating an economic basis for Dhufari independence?

On the other hand, the post-1990 reduction in material offerings to former revolutionaries chimed with shifts in national policies to scale back patronage. Some of this reduction reflected the fact that oil revenues alone could not sustain Oman's economic future. Some citizens in the richer Gulf monarchies live under the impression of "unlimited goods" available to them thanks to oil.[188] In Oman, though, from the late 1990s some lived with growing anxieties that the prosperity they had known "in the time of oil" might disappear very quickly.¹⁸⁹ The government scaled back some spending, for instance, by introducing business taxes in 1994 and health care fees for citizens in 1996.¹⁹⁰

The government also sought to diversify Oman's future economy, such as through developing tourism.¹⁹¹ Government initiatives aimed to reshape space in ways that accommodated heritage preservation and luxury tourism.¹⁹² These agendas made their mark on Salalah. In 2009, an interlocutor explained, the government "restored" (in practice, completely rebuilt) Salalah's oldest mosque, Masjid al-'Aqil, originally built in 1779.¹⁹³ During my fieldwork, in preparation for building luxury tourist facilities on al-Hafah seafront, the government continued to expropriate al-Hafah's predominantly *sumur* population, who had moved to the seafront after al-Hafah's elites, the Shanafar and the Yafa'i, had moved to lands elsewhere that the government had given them. Many Salalans mourned al-Hafah's redevelopment. A pseudonymous blogger asked ruefully: "[D]id they really have to kill the heart of the city?"¹⁹⁴ An older man bemoaned to me: "We have no heritage." Projects for "heritage" and development produced anxieties about the loss of traditions that Salalans shared with Gulf peers.¹⁹⁵

Some of the scaling back of the government's patronage reflected not only finite resources but also the political limitations of its distribution.¹⁹⁶ In 1984, the government scaled back its land distribution by introducing a lottery system, to which women could apply from 2008.¹⁹⁷ By that time, the population in Salalah would soon reach 172,000, including 108,000 Dhufaris (most originally hailing from the *jabal*).¹⁹⁸ Providing land for them was a challenge. Interlocutors explained to me that for several years land distribution in Salalah had been "frozen." They attributed this in part to a political crisis whereby, in a context of wider redevelopment plans in the plain, the government was unwilling to distribute further land there. There was a risk of angering tribes who claimed that land as their own, some members of which, moreover, believed that they had been victorious in a previous conflict against the government.

Tensions over land in Dhufar were all the more fraught because long-standing patronage strategies had increased access to water, fodder, and markets for livestock, leading to rampant inflation, overgrazing, and the depletion of grass and soil in the *jabal*.¹⁹⁹ One of the principles of Landon's plans for the counterinsurgency, namely to encourage competition over resources, bequeathed a legacy of conflicts between growing numbers of people and their animals over ever-depleting resources. These mounting conflicts contributed to a crisis of untenable patronage strategies.

As some patronage scaled back, other forms specific to Dhufar nevertheless continued. The *firaq* remained, providing a "regular stipend" to many male Dhufaris long after the war's end.[200] Interlocutors explained to me that as the original paramilitaries died, sons or relatives took their place in the unit and on the patronage register in return for service as reservists. The *firaq* military bases dotted across Dhufar's landscape were a reminder of the government's ongoing postwar measures of coercion.

Counterinsurgency coercive measures continued long after the ceasefire. The government made former Front members who returned to Oman renounce political opposition, interlocutors explained to me. There were also lasting physical legacies of wartime coercion. The vestiges of the SAF's mined and wired blockades disrupted grazing livelihoods for decades. On a return visit to Dhufar thirty years after the war, British veteran Ian Gardiner, who served between 1973 and 1975 in Dhufar commanding SAF Company A, learned that demining continued and that *jabbali* residents were using wiring from the blockades to build animal pens. He commented that it was "good" that the wire was still "useful."[201] This reaction failed to address how the continuing presence of mines disrupted grazing.

In addition to ongoing measures and legacies of counterinsurgency, Dhufaris, like all Omanis, lived under authoritarian coercion that repressed political opposition. In the arrests in 1994 of Omanis whom the government accused of making an Islamist plot to overthrow it, Dhufaris made up over half of the 125 detainees for whom personal data are available.[202] In the wake of Oman's 2011 protests, coercion intensified for all Omanis as the government embarked on renewed security spending nationwide.[203] The authorities built a new wave of prominent police stations across the country. In 2015, a large new police station was under construction on the site of Salalah's protests.

But just as had been the case during the war and in early postwar years, in the later postwar period Dhufaris shaped the transforming spaces in which they lived. They infused the neighborhoods where tribes had relocated as a group with intimate community ties. Maryam explained to me that women residents of her neighborhood moved between houses without wearing either the *'abayah* overgarment or face covering that, from the 1980s, Dhufari women of historically free status usually wore in public urban spaces: "All the houses near us are family. My father's house is here [pointing in the air], and then [pointing nearby] there is my father's brother's house, then my father's sister's house, and so on. We [women] can go in our house clothes [*thiyab*] between the houses because there is no one foreign [*ghair*]." Using family connections, Dhufaris personalized urban spaces.

In the later postwar districts, the lottery distribution of land had led to more socially mixed neighborhoods. Consequently, women needed to cover their indoor clothing to go between houses. The creation of these neighborhoods also intensified Salalah's ethnic segregation. Low-income foreign residents, most of whom were South Asian, moved into Dhufaris' old, increasingly neglected houses. These included houses of former revolutionaries who were among the different generations of those returning to Oman, as an interlocutor recalled: "When [families who had abandoned their houses to go to the Front] came back to Salalah, they found that their houses were in bad condition [*maksurah*, literally, "broken"]. They bought land elsewhere and then the Indians went to live in them [the old houses]."

Dhufaris still found ways to reclaim the later postwar districts and prewar districts, though. One interlocutor described: "Families still wanted to be near each other [in recent neighborhoods]. People sold their [government-assigned] plots to be near their family. A brother would sell the land he was given to move near his brother." Dhufaris also temporarily reconstituted prewar neighborhoods by holding funeral gatherings in the deceased's community of origin. One Dhufari young man who had moved from the *jabal* to Salalah explained: "People go back to where they are from for a funeral. Mirbat people, even if they have been in Salalah for 30 years, will go back to Mirbat [for burial]." A male mourner from a family from the prewar village of Salalah recalled the strong sense of community recovered during a men's mourning gathering in 2015: "The women's mourning was in a house in 'Awqad, where the family live now. We men were in a tent in [the former prewar village of] Salalah. I saw a lot of people there from the old days. People were greeting me very kindly. We said that we should get together once a month." Dhufaris valued actions and sentiments that reconstituted spaces of long-standing community.

Seasonal movements between the city, plain, mountains, and desert also continued in updated ways. This mobility further personalized Salalah for Dhufaris. Herders moved livestock seasonally, including from the *jabal* to the plain in the monsoon. In addition, many residents of Salalah relocated temporarily during the monsoon to *jabal* houses or tents in the plain, so as to free up their city homes for renting out at lucrative rates to Gulf tourists. The latter sojourned in significant numbers in Salalah during the monsoon to escape the heat elsewhere in the peninsula. The season saw many tents and "thousands of camels" in the plain, Salalans assured me. Some of Salalah's residents also built tents in the plain in the post-monsoon *sarb* season of clear skies and plentiful pastures. They enjoyed what some described as a "change of atmosphere" from life in the city.

Multiple forces shaped the transforming postwar spaces of Dhufar. These included politically and economically hegemonic forces of patronage, coercion, global markets for oil and gas, neoliberalism, international migration, and gender segregation. Throughout, though, Dhufaris themselves shaped these spaces. They included former revolutionaries who continued to play and claim roles in Dhufar's spatial transformations. Veteran militants like Rim and Naser staffed key institutions. More privately, ex-revolutionaries stressed their contributions in setting the very agenda for these changes. One interlocutor assured me that former revolutionaries did not feel remorse for their past. Rather, they considered that they had sacrificed for a greater collective good. More than thirty years after *jabal* residents had asserted that they had won the war, some former revolutionaries still stressed their own role in enabling Oman's transformation. One former revolutionary told me that "Qaboos gave us everything we wanted: roads, schools, hospitals, development . . ." He reproduced the myth of Qaboos's transformation of Oman ("Qaboos gave us"), but credited the prior agency and authorship of change to the revolution ("we wanted").

Spatial Transformation, Revolution, and Counterinsurgency

Dhufar's wartime and postwar spatial and social transformations illuminate the driving roles of revolution and counterinsurgency therein. Dhufar emerges as an arresting case through which to analyze struggles for spatial and political control. On the one hand, Dhufaris' experiences of spatial and social transformation foreground that the nonhegemonic actors and agendas that shape space include revolutionaries in multiple incarnations, from active to former militants. In their heyday, Dhufar's revolutionaries set the very agenda for Dhufar's social and economic development. This recast government programs for spatial transformation as potential evidence supporting Dhufari claims to have "won" the war. As militants shifted to work with the sultan's government, former revolutionaries with their educational capital and, at least in some cases, willingness to work without tribal prejudice, were necessary actors to bring about social and economic development. The agency of revolutionaries and former revolutionaries shaped Dhufar's ongoing spatial and social transformations, contributing to the afterlives of revolution.

On the other hand, Dhufar highlights how counterinsurgency prerogatives also drove wartime and postwar spatial transformations. The revised counterinsurgency in Dhufar from 1970 intensified patronage as a means of persuading Dhufaris to cease political resistance and accept authoritarian rule. Different "packages" of patronage characterized the government's changing policies for former revolutionaries during the war and after. The revised counterinsurgency also prolonged and developed long-standing strategies of coercion.

The significance of counterinsurgency patronage and coercion in driving Dhufar's spatial and social transformation further debunks "miracle transformation narratives" concerning Gulf monarchies. Driving those transformations are many factors beyond oil and a eulogized ruler such as Oman's Qaboos. At stake are not only multiple political agendas—from rulers' legitimization of unaccountable authoritarianism and repression to attempts by (neo)colonial backers and allies to preserve stable global hydrocarbon markets—and the diverse agendas of local residents. In addition, counterinsurgency patronage and coercion that colonial actors backed, planned, and managed drove spatial and social transformation in Gulf monarchies. Dhufar was the stage where these dynamics played out. But this agenda was of wide enough concern for Oman's allies in the peninsula, and beyond, to fund wartime and postwar patronage and coercion through grants, loans, and military assistance. The pattern of counterinsurgency patronage and coercion evident in Dhufar has continued. It resurfaced in the denouement of Oman's and Bahrain's 2011 protests. GCC monarchies endorsed repression, while richer monarchies provided grants and loans to fund patronage that could dispel dissent.[204]

Finally, close scrutiny of counterinsurgency patronage and coercion demonstrates how these strategies cultivated inequalities. In the 1960s and 1970s Dhufaris navigated contrasting visions of spatial and social transformation. The revolutionary vision aimed to promote social egalitarianism, although it only partially achieved this. The counterinsurgency vision of patronage and coercion exacerbated and introduced inequalities and created lasting legacies of tensions and conflicts.

The counterinsurgency vision of spatial and social transformations eventually prevailed, fostering political, economic, tribal, ethnic, racialized, and gendered inequalities. Yet in postwar Dhufar, some ex-revolutionaries continued to challenge those very inequalities. Through practices of kinship, everyday socializing, and unofficial commemoration, as well as occasional extraordinary acts, they reproduced values and networks of the social egalitarianism that militants had once pursued. In doing so, they created afterlives of revolution, as the next chapters explore.

4

Kinship, Values, and Networks

LARGE SOCIAL GATHERINGS on the occasion of weddings and funerals frequently preoccupied my Dhufari interlocutors, male and female alike. They poured hours of energy and resources into planning well-attended celebrations marking these life cycle events. Meanwhile, older Dhufaris remembered impressive kinship festivities from their youth. Among the most elaborate were memories of circumcisions and weddings that took place in the plain during the clear skies and luscious pastures of the post-monsoon *sarb* season. Between ongoing practices and recollections of past impressive gatherings, it would be tempting to imagine that large kinship celebrations had always existed in Dhufar. Yet this was not the case.

The 1965–1976 war disrupted kinship celebrations for all Dhufaris, whether they lived under the Front or the British-backed sultan. In different circumstances, at various points during the war all Dhufaris faced material shortages that constrained survival, let alone the possibility of a wedding feast. Government blockades divided coastal Dhufaris from their relatives in the interior. Landmines across the plain made it impossible to gather there. It was only after the blockades came down that postwar generations of Dhufaris could pour their energies into a *resumption* of kinship celebrations, albeit in changed forms.

Dhufaris are not alone in turning to kinship in the wake of war. Those who have lived through political violence, both victims and perpetrators, can turn toward kinship to reclaim "normal" life. This tendency reflects two wider observations about kinship. First, kinship practices and relations can reproduce dominant social relations, values, and hierarchies—in other words, a dominant, if always contested, social order. Second, though, kinship relations can also lend themselves to resistance against domination and exploitation. In postwar settings, kinship, social reproduction, and resistance intersect when survivors of conflict turn to kinship as a way of reproducing normality and resisting the devastating effects of war.

Dhufari wartime and postwar experiences reflect all these approaches to kinship. Postwar kinship offered many Dhufaris a means of recovering normality. At the same time, postwar kinship often reproduced the dominant social hierarchies that revolutionary kinship had once resisted. But the kinship practices of some former revolutionaries and their relatives invite further probing of the intersections between kinship, postwar contexts, social reproduction, and resistance. What if survivors of conflict seek not to return to a preconflict "normality" but to reproduce relations and values that arose *during* conflict and then became marginal in postwar times? Might postwar kinship reproduce a nondominant social order, even when veteran militants eschew resistance to the authorities that defeated them? What would such counterhistories imply for familiar assumptions that kinship reproduces dominant social values and relations and yet accommodates resistance?

Close examination of Dhufari former revolutionaries and their relatives reveals how kinship can reproduce not so much dominant social hierarchies but different kinds of social relations. Dhufari former revolutionaries maintained family units formed during the revolution that had become socially "unusual" in the postwar context. They named children born during or after the war after revolutionary figures. They forged marriages in postwar generations along lines of revolutionary connection. These practices reproduced social networks: a collectivity of persons connected, in this case, through shared experiences and potentially shared values. These practices also reproduced revolutionary values of social egalitarianism along lines of tribe, status group, ethnicity, race, and gender. Kinship practices were part of the counterhistories through which some former revolutionaries and family members created afterlives of revolution.

The postwar kinship of Dhufari former revolutionaries did not necessarily constitute a form of resistance of concern to the Omani government. Authoritarian rule in Oman allowed no political opposition to the government. Since the Omani government tolerated these kinship practices, it is likely they did not perceive in them cause for concern. Nor is it likely that former revolutionaries engaged with these practices as forms of resistance that threatened the authorities. No Dhufaris described former revolutionaries to me as a source of ongoing resistance of concern to the government. Rather, these practices expand understandings of postwar kinship beyond questions of reclaiming normality and resisting conflict. They push understandings of kinship beyond questions of social reproduction and resistance. Postwar kinship, it emerges, can also reproduce social relations that came into being during the fragile yet innovative context of a conflict such as a revolution. Furthermore, without those who engage in, witness, and surveil these practices experiencing them as resistance that threatens prevailing power relations, or the political authorities who benefit from them, kinship practices can be a means of creating a *counterhegemonic* social order.

If kinship is often a means of reproducing a dominant social order, how specifically might kinship practices come to reproduce a counterhegemonic social order and afterlives of revolution? Maintaining family units, naming children after significant namesakes, and forging new generations of marriages were all conventional activities. As such, they had the potential, in other contexts, to reproduce Dhufar's dominant social hierarchies. Among former revolutionaries, though, such kinship practices reproduced a counterhegemonic social order and afterlives of revolution when they became "out of place" through their shift from a conventional to an unusual social context.[1] This shift to becoming out of place enabled kinship practices of some former revolutionaries to reproduce a counterhegemonic social order and afterlives of revolution, even in the absence of a politically permissive environment.

Rethinking (Postwar) Kinship

Kinship entails the historically specific ways in which people understand themselves to be related to others. These connections can range from sharing biogenetic material to ties through marriage and daily activities such as food preparation or consumption.[2] In postwar contexts, those who have lived through the disruption of war and revolution can turn to kinship as a way of retrieving a sense of normality. Survivors of Partition and communal riots in India found solace from their trauma not in a transcendental experience, but in a "descent into the ordinary" that included the activities and responsibilities of kinship.[3] After years of organized political violence in Sri Lanka, former perpetrators of violence also turned to kinship as a way of recreating normal lives.[4] In the wake of the Algerian revolution, Zora Drif, an icon of Algeria's female militants, observed that some of her fellow veteran female revolutionaries deliberately chose to pursue roles as wives and mothers: "Many women got married, and when you have lived through exceptional moments you are nostalgic for a normal, simple life like everyone else. [Women who remained in the home] made a choice."[5] Turning toward roles as wives, mothers, and sisters in order to retrieve normality was also a path that some Dhufari female veteran revolutionaries pursued. That option may nevertheless be unavailable for female veteran fighters who experience stigma because of their militant past.[6] Where circumstances permit, though, kinship can offer those who have lived, or continue to live, through conflict the promise of a normality that brings some relief from conflict and its legacies.

The phenomenon of postwar kinship as a means of recreating normal life reflects two strands in wider debates about kinship. First, kinship relations and practices can reproduce prevailing social values and relations, that is to say a dominant, if always contested, social order. Replete with notions of authority and dependence, morality and impropriety, connection and distance, that contested social order is always inflected with questions of gender, generation, class, ethnicity, race and sexuality. Second, kinship can facilitate resistance, often in subtle forms, against exploitation and domination.

Both these notions have long histories in analyses of kinship. Disciplinary training encourages social scientists trained in Euro-American social theory to locate these insights in that intellectual tradition. This was my own initial point of departure.[7] Yet kinship's connections with reproduction and resistance span far more diverse traditions of social theory.[8] Long before the emergence of Euro-American social scientific schools of thought, the ideas of fourteenth-century Maghrebi theorist Ibn Khaldun about ʿasabiyyah (the solidarity that fellow members of tribes, and especially mobile pastoralist tribes on the geographical margins of empires and states, felt for one another) addressed the potential of kinship for reproduction and resistance.[9]

For Ibn Khaldun, kinship relations helped reproduce dominant relations and values to the extent that patrilineal membership in tribes made tribe members feel strong solidarity for one another. In practice, kinship was not the only component of this solidarity. The strongest of these tribes were those able to mobilize, in addition, those not related by patrilineal kinship, such as client groups. Such a notion of tribe surpassed kinship and was a more encompassing "sphere of consented solidarity."[10] But to the extent that Ibn Khaldun understood kinship to be a major component of solidarity, his ideas acknowledged a relationship between kinship and the reproduction of a dominant social order.

Yet at the same time, Ibn Khaldun theorized that settled dynastic rulers became vulnerable once sedentary life and its distractions weakened their ʿasabiyyah. Meanwhile, ʿasabiyyah continued to strengthen mobile tribes, giving them an advantage. They periodically swept in from pasturelands to attack dynastic states and empires. In the moment of ʿasabiyyah-strengthened tribes assailing settled dynastic rulers, Ibn Khaldun's ideas also acknowledged the potential of kinship relations to stoke resistance against forces of (weakened) domination. The connections between kinship, reproduction, and resistance that feature in changing revolutionary and postwar kinship relations in Dhufar are implicit in Ibn Khaldun's ideas. They are also apparent in Euro-American social theory.

The notion of kinship as a means of reproducing dominant relations and values flourished in Euro-American social scientific and anthropological approaches in the mid-twentieth century.[11] Schools of thought opposed to one another in other respects converged on the perceived propensity for kinship relations to reproduce dominant social values and relations. From Marx's ideas to later generations of Marxist-inspired scholars, and from structural functionalists to structuralists, the notion recurred that kinship reproduces dominant relations and values in varying forms: class privilege or exploitation, the very notion of society, or the patterns and structures that underpin social life.[12]

In the 1970s and 1980s, feminist and critical revisionist scholarship problematized the emphasis on kinship as reproduction. Such an approach naturalized the exploitation and inequality inherent in kinship relations.[13] Similarly, it normalized Eurocentric assumptions of a universal biogenetic basis for kinship.[14] It also naturalized the alleged self-reproduction of societies on the margins of capitalism and nation states.[15] Kinship studies fell out of fashion. The emergence of "new" kinship studies from the 1990s nevertheless resurrected the theme of reproduction. These studies showed how "new" family forms that questioned some traditional values still reproduced "old" values.[16]

The idea of kinship as a privileged sphere for the reproduction of a dominant social order, with associated hierarchies and distinctions, has thus proven persistent. In Dhufar, many long-standing kinship practices helped reproduce a stratified social order. Consequently, kinship became a key field within revolutionary aspirations for social change. Later, it also became important in some former revolutionaries' strategies for postwar social reintegration.

Further reiterating the links between kinship and social reproduction are analyses of liberation movements and revolutions, such as Dhufar's Front. These movements aim to change social life by targeting family relations. As they seek to disturb the reproduction of an older, now condemned, status quo, these movements disrupt long-standing kinship practices. From Arab liberation movements to Soviet contexts, governing authorities have undermined traditional practices of marriage partner selection, wedding celebrations, and child-rearing arrangements.[17] In parallel, these authorities aim to make kinship into a means of producing, and reproducing across future generations, a new revolutionary social order. From Sri Lanka to Palestine and Western Sahara, kinship interventions have endorsed such aspirations. The language of siblingship has asserted militants' peer-to-peer relationships over generation-based kinship hierarchies.[18] Reworked funeral rituals have emphasized martyrs' glorification over familial ties.[19] Reduced marital gifts and wedding party expenses have encouraged nationalist solidarity.[20] Likewise, Dhufar's militants attempted to disrupt kinship's reproduction of the old status quo and to use kinship to establish an alternative social order.

Although militants intervene in kinship to achieve social transformation, kinship practices in revolutionary and liberation contexts can nevertheless still reproduce elements of the older social order that militants wish to challenge. The expensive weddings that Palestinian and Western Saharan revolutionary authorities opposed in the 1980s reappeared in the 1990s and 2000s, with concomitant markings of social, class-based, and tribal distinctions.[21] In revolutionary Dhufar too, kinship practices that reproduced social stratification sometimes persisted. Dhufari revolutionaries' experiences reflect multiple intersections of kinship and social reproduction.

Euro-American intellectual traditions have linked kinship not only to social reproduction, however, but also to resistance. Kinship, reproduction, and resistance often overlap in practice. In the interventions of liberation movements and revolutions, kinship is a both a means of reproducing a new dominant social order *and* of resisting its predecessor. Similarly, kinship practices of trade unionists in Argentina reproduced militant political subjectivities that resisted capitalist exploitation.[22] The connections between kinship and resistance go further. In resistance movements against colonialism and occupation from Palestine to Northern Ireland, militants have drawn on both metaphorical nationalist kinship and literal kinship to find emotional and physical resources to continue resistance.[23] When militants assume the emotional register of kin in the eyes of marginalized, exploited communities, this can motivate people to join a movement, as was the case for India's Naxalites.[24] In socialist revolutions, kinship relations also facilitated a degree of resistance against the socialist state. Relatives exchanged black market goods.[25] Some people experienced the household, or labor undertaken privately with relatives, as sites of resistance against the socialist state.[26] There is thus a wider context of kinship as a means of resistance in which to situate postwar kinship, in Dhufar and elsewhere, that resists the devastation and trauma of conflict.

When postwar kinship offers a means of reclaiming "normal" life, then, this speaks to diverse intellectual traditions. Each links kinship to the reproduction of a dominant social order as well as to resistance. The component strands—postwar kinship to reclaim normality, kinship to reproduce a dominant social order, and kinship for resistance—all feature in Dhufaris' trajectories through colonialism, war, anti-colonial revolution, and authoritarian postwar times. But other elements of Dhufaris' postwar kinship are at odds with such analyses. They provoke instead questions of how those who have ceased former political activism, and live in conditions that constrain or forbid oppositional mobilization, adapt kinship relations. The latter can become a means of reproducing nondominant values and relations. While counterhegemonic values are at stake, these practices do not necessarily constitute a form of resistance of concern to political authorities. Nor do they necessarily entail resistance of the scale or kind to which former militants once aspired.

These questions resonate far beyond Dhufar. Careful accounts of revolutionary legacies have already hinted at this relevance. Former female revolutionary fighters in late twentieth- and early twenty-first-century Algeria used kinship events such as weddings, circumcisions, and baccalaureate parties as a way of catching up with women whom they knew through militancy or in prison. They thereby kept active connections and histories that official narratives about the Algerian revolution excluded.[27] When the 2011 revolution to depose Egypt's President Mubarak failed to fulfill many participants' ambitions for political and economic change, some participants nevertheless experienced kinship transformations. A daughter questioned her father, a husband and wife found in their political disagreement reason for divorce, and there were "endless other kinds of reconfiguration of family relationships."²⁸ When other goals remain unfulfilled, revolution can still transform kinship and with it, "normal" life.

A focus on the kinship practices of Dhufari former revolutionaries and their relatives exposes that postwar kinship is not necessarily a means of reclaiming the normality that conflict disrupted. Rather, postwar kinship can reinvigorate social relations and values that came into being through conflict. Kinship emerges as a means of reproducing afterlives of revolution and a counterhegemonic social order. This may be so even in the absence of resistance of concern to the political authorities that benefit from the very social hierarchies that counterhegemonic relations and values disrupt. In Dhufar these possibilities exist alongside the long-standing potential of kinship practices to reproduce dominant, hierarchical social relations.

Kinship Reproducing Hierarchy

Kinship practices have long helped reproduce a stratified social order that, outside the context of the revolution, has prevailed in Dhufar in changing forms. Kinship practices have reproduced distinctions between Dhufar's status groups and tribes. They have likewise maintained gendered and generational hierarchies whereby male elders exert authority over women and junior males.

Dhufaris recognize kinship relations through maternal and paternal ties. With the exception of some Mahra matrilineal tribes, it is the (im)possibility of claiming suitable patrilineal descent that situates persons in relation to Dhufar's historically prestigious tribes, its historically lower-status client tribes, and the status groups that were historically excluded from tribal status altogether. Until the 1970s, neither *sumur* nor *bahharah* client fishing families could claim privileges of tribal membership. Nevertheless, in 1981 Sultan Qaboos's government introduced tribalization policies. Omanis who, until then, could not trace suitable ancestry to a tribe now acquired tribal patronyms.²⁹ The government paid salaries to tribal leaders for these "new tribes," as it already did in the case of long-standing tribes.

The advent of these "new tribes" notwithstanding, in everyday interactions Dhufaris continued to acknowledge historical distinctions between stratified status groups. They did so by assessing ancestry and social origins (*asl*). In the context of long-standing interracial mixing between *sumur* women and non-*sumur* men, ancestry determined social classification. Racialized features, though often a topic of observation and commentary among Dhufaris, in and of themselves could not determine someone's status group. Ancestry determined membership in a status group and the social blackness of Dhufar's *sumur*.

The presence or absence of suitable unilineal descent was not the only means through which kinship reproduced Dhufar's hierarchies of status group and tribe. Marriage strategies also marked stratified relations between status groups, tribes, and ethnic groups. Like their peers in the Arabian Peninsula and neighboring regions, Dhufaris idealized "close marriage" (between those sharing social and other ties) and especially patrilateral cousin marriage.[30] In parallel, Dhufaris avoided women marrying below their natal social status. Brides' families expected grooms to make bride-price gifts of suitable value to reflect a bride's social status. Outside the context of the revolutionary disruption of these patterns, the possibility, or perceived impossibility, of certain marriages taking place reproduced stratified hierarchies along lines of tribe, status group, and (sometimes racialized) ethnicity.

Marriage between elites across tribal and ethnic divisions was possible. Sultan Said's marriage to the mother of Sultan Qaboos, Mazoon bint Ahmad 'Ali of Dhufar's Qara Ma'shani tribe, was an example of an interethnic, intra-elite marriage. Another example of intra-elite marriage was a couple whom I encountered where a man of a prestigious mountain Kathiri tribe had married a Qara wife. An alternative pattern, whereby men of high-ranking background married women of lower-ranking background, was historically important as a means of forging hierarchical relations between groups. The marriage of Qara men to *shahrah* women had facilitated the Qara's domination of land and water resources in the *jabal*.[31]

I heard of similarly "asymmetrical" marriages contracted under Sultan Qaboos, such as a man of Qara background marrying a *shahri* woman. Technically, such a union avoided a woman "marrying down." Dhufari interlocutors explained to me that the families concerned could nevertheless still object to such a marriage. Several factors could explain this opposition. Not least, in a context of high financial barriers to matrimony, a marriage with someone "outside" the natal group represented a missed opportunity for a relative of each partner to have secured a spouse. The most controversial marriages, before and after the revolution, were those that saw a man of inferior social status marry a woman of superior social status. Dhufaris associated such a possibility with the revolution's disruption of conventional kinship.

As well as partner choice, marriage celebrations also reproduced (stratified) tribes and status groups. Wedding celebrations before and after the revolution differed from one another. Each also differed from revolutionary weddings. But a common feature of wedding celebrations that preceded and followed the revolution was that they brought together large numbers of persons from the tribes and status groups of the spouses. This helped reproduce those collective identities.

Older Dhufaris recalled for me, as earlier generations of Dhufaris had described for Dhufari anthropologist Salim Tabook, the elaborate postmonsoon wedding celebrations among *jabbali* families. Even more feted were celebrations marking the circumcision of young men.[32] Tabook's account does not specify the influence of tribal status on participation in these celebrations. Of Qara status himself, Tabook did not explain whether these celebrations were limited to those of that background, or whether members of client *shahri* tribes also participated.[33]

For those involved, families moved from caves on the north side of the mountains in which they had been living during the monsoon. They set themselves up on the plain in clusters of huts, which Tabook calls "villages." Celebrations took place at the temporary place of residence of the bride's family or of the tribe organizing circumcisions. Guests established further temporary settlements close to the center of celebrations. In addition to including feasts and poetry recitals, the most elaborate celebrations saw women beautify themselves for competitive moonlit dancing. Men and women watched each other dance and danced together. In some of these dances, women did not cover their hair.[34]

These celebrations enhanced mountain tribes' reputations for honor, poetry, and hospitality. Other styles of kinship celebrations in prerevolutionary Dhufar also marked differences between status groups. The distinctive styles of music and dancing at the funerals of *sumur* enslaved persons of African origin reiterated their differentiated status.[35] Kinship celebrations marked Dhufari forms of social stratification.

After the 1970s, many Dhufaris adopted more conservative Islamic practices as these became popular across SWANA. Revised celebrations favored stricter gender segregation. Dhufar's pre-1970s styles of celebrations, where women of high-ranking tribal backgrounds danced in front of and with men, became "impossible," one male interlocutor explained. The post-1970s gender-segregated wedding celebrations also coincided with greater affluence for many Dhufaris. Those attending kinship celebrations no longer headed out from caves or huts, but from houses of greater material comfort that in some cases were large enough to accommodate multiple generations of an extended household (Figure 8). By the time of my fieldwork in 2013 and

FIGURE 8. A family home in Salalah. Photograph by Alice Wilson, 2015.

2015, women's evening wedding celebrations could see some five hundred women gather in a hired hall for music, dancing, and food. Many female guests kept their black outer robe (*'abayah*) and face covering on as they watched proceedings. But close relatives and friends of the wedding parties showed off spectacular makeup and hairstyles (often stretching to wigs) alongside glistening robes (*thiyab*). These dresses were in the style distinctive to Dhufar, cut at the front to the mid-calf and dropping at the back to a short train. Away from the male gaze, some of these women took it in turns to perform traditional dances on a central stage. Separately, daytime all-male wedding gatherings took place in tents specially erected outside the home of a prospective spouse's family. Male relatives and acquaintances gathered there. They wore impeccable white robes (*dishdashah*), smart head coverings, and some, especially older attendees, proudly sported formal walking sticks.

It was a social duty for a family to send male and female representatives to attend the weddings of relatives and acquaintances. Families planned in advance which brothers and sisters would respectively attend the male and female gatherings of forthcoming nuptials.[36] One Dhufari young man explained to me the expectation that a father should attend with at least one of his sons. On the afternoon in May when he told me this, he and his father had earlier attended three weddings for members of their tribe, as well as three further weddings. Yet this busy wedding schedule did not reflect "peak" wedding season. Our conversation took place several months before the monsoon that had replaced the post-monsoon *sarb* as the most popular wedding season. Dhufaris favored the monsoon because it coincided with many relatives' return from work and study abroad to enjoy the pleasantly cool months of July and August. This young man attributed the high number of weddings on the day of our conversation to a parallel monthly cycle. The first weekend after payday was the most popular weekend for weddings. Male guests' purses were then best able to stretch to the cash gifts, known as *maghbur*, that men gave at wedding parties. Interlocutors proudly described these gifts as distinctive to Dhufar and unknown in northern Oman (even as some men also admitted to finding them financially draining).[37] The highly attended gender-segregated wedding celebrations of the postwar years reproduced stratified tribal and status group identities, as had the contrasting older styles of celebrations.

There was also a national context in which kinship, and especially marriage, was a key means of social reproduction in Sultan Qaboos's Oman. In a series of decrees over the 1980s and 1990s, the Omani government regulated marriage to encourage socially, politically, and economically desirable forms of social reproduction.[38] Governments of other Gulf monarchies made similar interventions.[39] In Oman, Qaboos decreed that, without a special permit, only certain categories of Omani men could marry women from non-GCC countries. Eligibility criteria took into account age and health conditions. There was a further exemption allowing marriages between families living on either side of a non-GCC land border. In practice this functioned as an exemption for Dhufaris to marry Yemenis, a pattern especially common among some Mahra families. The national restrictions aimed to allay alarmist concerns about the marriage of Omani men with women from outside the Arabian Peninsula. Of particular concern were unions with brides from lower-average-income countries, such as India, where families accepted a lower bride-price. Critics feared that such marriages increased foreign cultural influences and reduced opportunities for Omani women to find suitable (Omani) husbands. In Dhufar, then, both local practices outside the context of the revolution and national postwar policies made kinship a means for reproducing a social order stratified along lines of tribe, status group, ethnicity, racialized distinctions, and nationality.

Revolutionary kinship practices, however, had disrupted and challenged kinship's reproduction of such hierarchies.

Revolutionary Kinship

After the Front's Marxist-Leninist turn in 1968, militants sought to rework kinship so as to create new kinds of idealized social relations. The Front encouraged intermarriage across tribes and status groups. To do so, the movement reduced and standardized bride-price. These measures decreased the social barriers to marriage between Dhufaris, regardless of social background. Revolutionary marriage promised greater social egalitarianism, or at least its possibility.

The revolutionary marriages that went furthest in signaling the new ideal of social egalitarianism, beyond questions of tribe and status group, were those between a woman of high-ranking social background and a man of a lower social background. Examples of such marriages of which I heard included that between a man of a client town tribe and a Qara wife, between a man of *sumur* status and a woman of historically free status, and between a *sadah* woman and a man of any other background, no matter how prestigious. These marriages embodied revolutionary ideals of social egalitarianism.

Revolutionary kinship was also meant to take priority over conventional family ties. Huda Salim was "Mama Huda" to her pupils. This nickname situated the bonds among revolutionaries as an alternative kinship that ran alongside, and could replace and surpass, natal kinship arrangements. Long after the last pupils graduated from the school, in postwar Dhufar many still referred to graduates of the revolutionary school as "Huda's children."[40] This nickname located the school's graduates in an alternative filiation to the patrilineal tribes that the revolution had challenged, and that Sultan Qaboos's government cultivated. This nickname also echoed the Front's aspirations to promote gender equality by highlighting filiation through a woman. Filiation through a woman was not unprecedented in Dhufar, as some Mahra tribes are matrilineal. But the nickname challenged dominant conventions of patrilineal filiation, and the stigmatizing suggestion of illegitimacy for those unable to claim patrilineal filiation.

A parallel phenomenon saw militants cultivate new revolutionary subjectivities and loyalties with the potential to surpass traditional kinship ties. Some revolutionaries exalted loyalty to the revolution over personal ties to kin. One who expressed such views was Salim al-Ghassani, a member of the

Front's General Command, chair of the political committee, and head of the Front's Aden office. He told a Yemeni journalist in 1972 that he had left the woman he loved at university in Kuwait in order to join the revolution. He declared: "[M]y love is the Kalashnikov and the homeland."[41] A male medical orderly from northern Oman made similar choices. Reflecting on his work in the liberated territories, and then his time practicing in the Front's clinic and hospital in the PDRY, he observed that "[m]any comrades who are married do not see thir [sic] wives for 2 or 3 years." He himself did not contemplate getting married while his work required him to move regularly between Hawf, al-Ghaidah, and Aden.[42] Militantism prioritized the revolution over family.

Political training taught children to express loyalty to the revolution above kinship. In 1970, Amina was a twelve-year-old female adolescent recruit to the Revolution Camp military training center. When sociologist Fred Halliday asked her whether she missed her parents, Amina replied "I don't think about my parents, I think about the revolution."[43] Halliday did not record his reactions to such a response from one so young. Critics hostile to communism would accuse the Front of indoctrinating young Dhufaris.[44] Those accusations nevertheless discount the potential for politicization to help children to develop resilience while growing up in contexts of organized political violence and occupation.[45] Graduates of the revolutionary school conveyed to Miranda Morris how much they had enjoyed making school friends among members of the very tribes whom, before the revolution, they had been raised to fear as enemies. These friendships were one of the ways that Dhufar's revolutionaries learned to see traditional kinship differently. Kinship ties were distractions that revolutionaries should avoid or de-prioritize, so as to focus on the higher goals of revolution.

In order to lessen the chances of the "wrong" kinds of kinship presenting a distraction from higher revolutionary goals, Front militants also repressed some kinship activities. Hamran spent part of his childhood growing up in areas of the *jabal* under the control of the Front before joining the revolutionary school. He recalled how wedding and circumcision celebrations under the Front changed. In contrast to the exuberant celebrations that Tabook documented, Hamran—who preferred to speak with me in English—recalled austere celebrations under the Front.

AW: What were celebrations like under the Front, such as a wedding or a circumcision?

Hamran: No two boys were circumcised together in a case of a celebration. This was not a time for celebrations anymore. There was no room. We are a nation at war. There is no time for frills.

    There was not any celebration that I remember. There was no song and dance at a wedding. Some food was provided.

AW: Who provided the food?

Hamran: The family of the boy. The dowry [bride-price] became almost nil. The girl got beautification as before. The boy tried to be as handsome as before. There was no change there, but there was no song and dance. I witnessed quite a lot of them [weddings].

Hamran's memory illustrates how revolutionary forms of kinship can (re)produce both a new social order and elements of an older social order.[46] Revolutionary wedding celebrations had transformed long-standing practices while simultaneously retaining certain elements, specifically the responsibility of the groom's party to provide resources for the wedding. Yet where filiation and marriage before the revolution had reproduced Dhufar's stratified status groups, activism with the Front disrupted this. Militancy at least partially reconfigured literal and metaphorical kinship. New kinship forms reproduced alternative social relations, with the latter meant to promote social egalitarianism and shared nationalist commitment to the revolution.

If these were militants' intentions, revolutionary kinship reconfigurations could nevertheless be alienating rather than emancipating. Sources dating from the revolution, and Dhufaris' post hoc memories, describe intrafamilial killings, such as a brother killing a brother in punishment for "unrevolutionary" behavior.[47] Some interlocutors suggested to me that Front militants mandated intrafamilial punishment so as to avoid triggering revenge killings between members of different tribes. How might these violent revolutionary reconfigurations of kinship have led to disenchantment with the revolution and traumatization? Some Dhufaris later recalled how such killings contributed to reasons for switching support from the Front to the government.[48] Once former revolutionaries left the movement, kinship practices offered a means of articulating varied subjectivities and relations in postwar Dhufar.

Postrevolutionary Hierarchies and Reintegration

The revolution in Dhufar had sought for kinship to reproduce new revolutionary subjectivities, rather than influence access to, or exclusion from, economic and political resources. The aftermath of socialist projects can see kinship resume importance in struggles to claim resources.[49] In Dhufar, the military defeat of 1975, and the collapse of the Front's exile activities after the fall of the PDRY, had a similar effect. Kinship relations grew in importance for accessing resources through the government's patronage networks. Kinship also resurged as a means of reproducing the social, political, and economic hierarchies compatible with the Omani government's patronage strategies.

In government-controlled areas during and after the war, tribal leaders turned "warlords" controlled access to government patronage networks.[50] Patrilineal descent and "close" marriage reproduced the very tribes and stratified status groups through which Dhufaris accessed many government resources. Additionally, in Dhufar, and elsewhere in Oman, kinship connections facilitated crony capitalist patronage relations. Relatives of government protégés accessed lucrative business opportunities, as did members of the family of Yusuf bin 'Alawi.[51] Kinship also reproduced hierarchical political, economic, and social relations in ways that were particular to Dhufar's wartime and postwar history.

British counterinsurgency officers had founded Dhufari pro-government paramilitaries, the *firaq*, in 1971. Underlying British hopes of some *firaq* developing into highly trained Dhufari troops never materialized, however.[52] A highly trained Dhufari force did emerge in time, the Sultan's Special Forces (SSF) (modeled on the British SAS who played an important part in the Dhufar counterinsurgency). The emergence of the SSF might suggest the redundancy of the *firaq*. After all, the government declared victory over the Front in December 1975 and dated the last counterinsurgency and Front casualties to 1979 and 1980, respectively.[53] Yet despite these indications of the end of a military need for the *firaq*, the paramilitaries became a permanent fixture of Dhufar's landscapes and security personnel. As the original recruits died out, the government sourced new recruits among their relatives. As one Dhufari man explained to me: "Places in the *quwat al-firqah* are inherited. The man who retires can name his successor, or when a man dies it goes to his son or another close relative." The *firaq* persisted as a channel of patronage, with kinship replenishing its ranks.

Kinship discourses further reproduced dominant postwar hierarchies. Many Dhufaris, like other Omanis, explicitly and strategically identified with a discourse that situated them as the children of the ultimate patriarch,

Sultan Qaboos. Some dubbed him "Baba ('father') Qaboos."[54] Even those critical of the government could claim Qaboos as their father. A young Dhufari who spoke to me about the protestors in Salalah in 2011 voiced the words of demonstrators who located themselves within this national patriotic kinship: "[Protestors said:] 'We are not against the Sultan. We are *his children*. We ask from him because he is *our father*. We are against the government corruption'" (emphasis added). This notion of all Omanis as the children of Sultan Qaboos contrasts with Dhufaris' informal dubbing of pupils of the revolutionary school as "Huda's children." The metaphorical national kinship of Qaboos as the patriarchal father of all Omanis resonates with the intersections of kinship with tribalism, crony capitalism, and hereditary paramilitary service. Across them all, Dhufaris experienced daily the potential of kinship to reproduce a dominant social, political, and economic—and in this case inherently hierarchical—social order.

Against this backdrop, kinship relations also offered some of Dhufar's former revolutionaries pathways toward recovering a sense of "normal" life. Kinship promised a means of reintegration into the stratified social order that the revolution had sought, at least officially, to undermine. Female activists in the OWO operating in exile in the PDRY after the military defeat noted regretfully that some of the Front's demobilized female former fighters drifted away from militancy, turning to domestic roles as wives and mothers: "[M]any women in the border area were demobilized. They left the People's Army and the Schools of Revolution to get married and then relapsed into their traditional role."[55] OWO activists attributed this "relapse" to women's "lack of skills in reading and writing, political knowledge and experience" relative to their male peers.[56] Nevertheless, Iranian volunteer physician Mahboubeh Afraz had privately noted in her diary that some women in exile were depressed and disappointed in the revolution.[57] For those women who did seek lives as wives and mothers, the tribal loyalties against which Front militants had once mobilized may have facilitated transitions from military to domestic lives. One former revolutionary, Khalfan, explained to me that women returning to Oman from exile or education abroad did not usually struggle to find a marital partner upon their return. A patrilateral male cousin was usually willing to marry such a woman. Once former revolutionaries returned to Oman, kinship relations nevertheless also presented other possibilities for some—but not all—to reproduce revolutionary networks and values.

Kinship Out of Place

Dhufar's former revolutionaries were not homogeneous. They followed different pathways to join or leave the Front and had contrasting postwar experiences of economic and political favor—or marginalization. Across their diverse lives, however, a point of commonality among many was their participation in kinship practices familiar to all Dhufaris. "Close" marriage, Khalfan had explained, had offered a means of social reintegration for some former revolutionaries on their return to Oman. Former militants also attended weddings and funerals, like any other Dhufaris. But the finer details of the kinship practices of some—but not all—former revolutionaries were distinctive. The ways that some of them maintained family units, named children after significant namesakes, and celebrated weddings among the next generation became remarkable when they shared qualities of being out of place.

When things—and, we might add, persons and relationships—become out of place, they have moved from their conventional social setting to a socially transgressive context.[58] Dirt is "matter out of place."[59] It stands out as "dirt" because it has moved out of context and transgressed its socially expected place. Food on a dish is food, but when it has fallen from a dish to the floor it is no longer food. It has become dirt. That which has shifted context to become out of place becomes hypervisible as a marker of the very distinction between norm (being, we might say, "in place") and transgression (being "out of place.") The notion of "out of place" thus assumes underlying categories of a "correct" social order when things are "in place." Being out of place references the very possibility of having once been in place. The transformation of becoming out of place has both temporal and spatial dimensions.

An adapted notion of being out of place can track how, when kinship practices move from a conventional to an unusual social setting, they can shift from reproducing not a dominant but a counterhegemonic social order. In conventional settings, kinship practices can reproduce dominant social, gendered, generational, class-based, ethnicized, and racialized values, relations, and hierarchies. By contrast, kinship practices that move to an unusual social context, and thereby become out of place, can reproduce dissonant values. Among Dhufari ex-revolutionaries, kinship practices such as maintaining family units, naming children after significant namesakes, and forging marriages in the next generation became out of place when they moved context to occur in the unusual setting of connection between former Front members who, outside the revolution, might not have been linked. Once out of place, these practices preserved connections between exmilitants that cut across prevailing social, gendered, ethnicized, and racialized hierarchies. Out of place kinship challenged a dominant social order and reproduced a counterhegemonic social order.

One particular form of kinship out of place probably stood out the most for Dhufaris, whether they were closely connected to the revolution or not. This was former militants' maintenance of kinship relations that had arisen through nontraditional revolutionary marriages. These marriages had once again become unusual in the postwar resurgence of a stratified social order of differentiated tribes and status groups. Even when revolutionary marriages had ended in divorce or widowhood, the children of these marriages were living instances in the next generation of kinship out of place.

My first encounter with such a revolutionary family unit was with a marriage that transgressed the taboo against the union of a *sumur* husband and a wife of historically free status. Among relationships that flaunted the expectation that a woman should not marry a man of "lower" status, the most controversial were perhaps such instances of interracial marriage where the man occupied the stigmatized position of blackness. In revolutionary societies with histories of the import and ownership of enslaved persons of African descent, whether through the Atlantic Ocean, Indian Ocean, or trans-Saharan slaving routes, marriages between militants that transgress locally stigmatized forms of interracial unions become one of the most iconic symbols of idealized revolutionary egalitarianism.[60] In Dhufar—where marriage between a non-*sumur* husband and a *sumur* wife lacked comparable historical stigma—iconic revolutionary interracial unions concerned marriages between a *sumur* husband and non-*sumur* wife. On separate occasions in 2013 and in 2015, different interlocutors pointed out one such marriage to me.

These conversations took place when the members of the marriage in question were not themselves present. Interlocutors stressed both the differences between the spouses' ancestry and those distinctions between their physical appearances that were significant in the Dhufari context. The husband, interlocutors explained, had been born to enslaved persons whom Sultan Said owned, whereas the wife was born to a family of free status. Dhufaris stressed to me the light skin tone of the wife, describing her as "white." Their emphasis left implicit the contrast with the husband's darker skin tone and with other physical features that Dhufaris associated with African heritage. This couple had met and married under the auspices of the revolution, had lived together in exile in Yemen, and had made new lives together in Sultan Qaboos's Oman, where they raised their children. Their contrasting ancestries and appearances made their marriage appear out of place to Dhufari observers.

It is possible that the frequency of Dhufaris' comments to me about this kind of marriage increased from my first visit in 2013 to my longer fieldwork in 2015. By then, interlocutors were aware of my own relationship: also a marriage between a light-skinned woman and a man whose ancestry encompassed enslaved persons of sub-Saharan African heritage. The concerned comments to me about my marriage on the part of some non-*sumur* interlocutors further underlined the remarkable nature, in a Dhufari context, of revolutionary couples who transgressed Dhufari taboos surrounding interracial marriage.

Beyond interlocutors' reactions to my marriage, the possibility (that had become a reality during the revolution) of a marriage between a *sumur* man and a woman of free origin fascinated Dhufaris. Such out of place marriages were hypervisible in contexts where Dhufaris did not necessarily know the couple in question. They had opportunities to observe such unions during the casual encounters with unknown persons in mixed-gender groups that arose during hospital visits. In Dhufar and elsewhere in SWANA, illness, like death, necessitates visits from a wide circle of relatives and acquaintances. Until the advent in November 2013 of the "Gardens Mall" shopping mall in Salalah, hospital visiting was virtually the only acceptable form of extra-domestic socializing for many women in Salalah beyond formal occasions such as weddings and funerals.[61] As such, hospital visits were a morally acceptable and popular social activity. A visit to a ward, I learned, could expose former revolutionaries' out of place kinship relations.

Having enjoyed a wonderful welcome and dinner in a family's home, I was chatting one evening with several female members of the extended household. I was fortunate that the generation of women whose parents had been young adults during the war encouraged me to ask "anything" about what they had heard of that period. The women avoided the more usual shrouding of this topic in silence and discretion. When I asked if they knew of any couples who had married under the Front in a way that flaunted traditional hierarchies, the women paused to reflect. One woman, Tuful, then replied that she had heard a story from friends about such a marriage. These friends had been visiting a sick relative in the hospital. Nearby was a female patient who, like Tuful, hailed from a high-ranking mountain tribe, which Tuful named for me. Yet the husband who visited this woman was black. The observant hospital visitors later asked the patient's sister why her sibling was married to a black man. The sister explained that the husband treated his wife well. Tuful commented to me that this interracial marriage must have occurred under the Front. Notably, the response reported from the sister in the hospital not only eschewed mention of the revolution (as was politically prudent) but also subtly defended the legitimacy of a marriage in which a black husband treated his nonblack wife of historically free status "well." When former revolutionaries maintained interracial marriages, and when either they or their relatives defended such marriages, they reproduced a counterhegemonic social order of enduring connections between those whom prevailing social hierarchies would normally separate.

Unexpected encounters in a hospital ward could also expose the offspring of revolutionary marriages. These children's unusual family ties meant that otherwise conventional kinship activities, such as visiting a sick relative, became instances of kinship out of place. This opened up possibilities for former revolutionaries to reproduce networks and values that contravened Dhufar's everyday hierarchies. One evening in 2015, when I was in Gardens Mall with some male undergraduate students from Dhufar University, one of them recounted to me, and to the group, how an encounter during a hospital visit exposed his own kinship out of place.

'Ali explained that under the auspices of the Front his parents had formed a marriage that, outside that context, would have been unusual. His father was from a mountain tribe in western Dhufar but his mother was from the *sadah*. Usually, these religious elites who claim descent from the Prophet do not give their daughters in marriage to non-*sadah* families. 'Ali's parents had married in the revolutionary base in the PDRY, and his three elder siblings had been born there. Eventually the family returned to Salalah, where his father took a government position. 'Ali was born in the early 1980s, and his father died a few years later. At the time of our conversation, the family continued to benefit from the father's government pension. Raised by his Arabophone mother and her family in Salalah, 'Ali spoke his father's mountain language with an unusual accent.

As a young adult, 'Ali had once been making a hospital visit and was with a group speaking his father's language. A man at a nearby bedside overheard him speaking with a strange accent for the context. What could a young man who spoke like that be doing with those companions? 'Ali explained what happened: "The man saw me, noticed how I spoke, also how I looked, and asked me whose son I was. I gave a first answer, and then the man asked whose son exactly [I was], and I gave my father's full name. The man—I didn't know him at all—came and hugged me and said that he was with my father in the Front, that he had named his eldest daughter after my sister." 'Ali continued: "[The man] asked about my mother. He had to ask about her." The significance of this clarification is that Dhufaris would normally consider it an inappropriate suggestion of intimacy for a man to ask about a woman to whom he was not related by kinship.[62] Yet by saying that the man "had" to ask about his mother, in this instance 'Ali implied otherwise. He suggested that the apparent transgression of ordinary, here gendered, social boundaries was justified. The camaraderie between former revolutionaries and their family members transformed the man's inquiry from offensive to appropriate.

'Ali's parents' former companion had spotted him in the hospital ward because the way 'Ali spoke stood out in that context. But I belatedly realized that 'Ali's revolutionary parentage also made him out of place on the night that I met him. It was in fact the exposure of him being out of place in the mall that led to him sharing the story of his family's connection to the revolution.

On the evening in question, a young male Dhufari interlocutor from a high-ranking town tribe had taken me to Gardens Mall, where we joined a group of his friends at a café. Dhufaris usually socialized informally with those who shared a background of the same status group. All in the group that evening, except 'Ali, hailed on their father's side from a high-ranking town background. 'Ali's maternal family, who had brought him up, was from a comparably high-ranking town tribe. Outside the revolution, 'Ali's mother would most likely never have married his father. The group's shared background, and 'Ali's exclusion from it in patrilineal terms, came to the fore when I began to ask each of the young men where they voted. I was also conducting research about how electoral leagues in Dhufar were reconfiguring tribal connections to achieve sometimes innovative outcomes.[63] Each young man had answered that he voted in a district of Salalah's urban area. As Omanis typically voted in their place of patrilineal origin, these answers all fitted the common pattern whereby members of an informal social gathering shared a status group background, in this case that of elite town tribes. When it was 'Ali's turn to answer, however, he replied that he voted in the mountains.

My host and his peers would have immediately recognized that this answer was *odd*. For any Dhufari used to socializing with peers from the same status group, and used to seeing other Dhufaris do so, ʿAli's answer had exposed a situation that *needed* explaining: why was a young man from a mountain background socializing with young men of elite town background? In the hospital ward, ʿAli's accent had exposed something that needed explaining. In the mall, the revelation of his voter registration had a similar effect. My host that evening quickly intervened to explain: "[ʿAli] votes in the mountains because his father was in the Front." This interjection implicitly acknowledged that ʿAli's parents' revolutionary marriage had set him up for a lifetime of being the "odd one out." Having grown up in one social context, his patrilineal heritage tied him to a different social world in a way that, but for the revolution, Dhufaris would not expect to encounter. The way he spoke, where he voted, and other details signaled ʿAli's social oddness and underlying revolutionary ancestry. Other Dhufaris, like the man in the hospital ward and my host in Gardens Mall, were alert to such clues.

As we sat in the mall, my focus was instead on what seemed a lucky break: my host's willingness to voice an explanation that referenced the revolution. Rarely did interlocutors raise the sensitive topic of the revolution outside a one-on-one conversation with me. The break just seemed to get luckier when ʿAli himself responded to my host's interjection with a smile and affirmation. Rather than seeking to avoid or change the topic, ʿAli followed up by telling me, and the group, the story of his parents' marriage and how his parents' former companion had identified him. That both my host and ʿAli spoke of the revolution in front of a group of peers reflected the relative greater preparedness of those born after the revolution to mention this sensitive topic compared with the older generations who had lived firsthand through the government's repression of the movement. As ʿAli spoke, and as I later wrote up my notes, I was too focused on the discussion of the revolution and its legacies to reflect on how the "lucky break" arose. Only on returning to my notes did I understand ʿAli's exposure as out of place both in the mall and in the hospital ward.

Years after the revolution's formal defeat and later formal dissolution, some former revolutionaries maintained unusual family units. The children of revolutionary marriages were a living legacy of these unions. The very acts of maintaining family units, visiting sick relatives, asking after a namesake, and voting in the community of one's patrilineal heritage were not in and of themselves extraordinary. In other contexts they would ordinarily reproduce Dhufar's everyday social hierarchies. In the context of families with revolutionary backgrounds, however, these kinship practices were out of place. They linked persons who outside the revolution would not usually have been thus connected. Such kinship out of place created opportunities for former revolutionaries and family members to reproduce a counterhegemonic social order. In that alternative sphere, women and men could marry, stay married to spouses, and assert ongoing connections of friendship with persons with whom such contact, for reasons of tribe, status group, ethnicity, race, and gender, would ordinarily be avoided.

Revolutionary marriages and the children of such marriages could become hypervisible to Dhufaris even without prior acquaintance. By contrast, a second form of kinship out of place was primarily visible to former Front families. Some veteran Front families adapted the common practice of naming children after those whom one wished to respect and honor. They made it into a means of projecting connections from the time of the Front onto ensuing generations.

Dhufaris frequently explained cases to me where a child was named in honor of a significant person. Naming children is loaded with moral force.[64] Names are a powerful means of generating relationships, while giving a particular name to a child can reveal the name-givers' relations to that child.[65] Naming patterns in Dhufar often reproduced conventional kinship ties. A family might give a baby the name of a relative such as a grandparent or a parent's sibling. The case of 'Ali's sister, and her namesake who honored her parents' revolutionary connections, shows how former revolutionaries reworked the practice of naming a child after a significant person. Their naming practices shifted to become out of place when, instead of referencing conventional kin, they honored revolutionary figures. These names projected onto a new generation counterhegemonic histories and connections.

I learned of a further instance of revolutionary namesakes as I was telling a former militant, Rajab, that the father of a Dhufari female friend of mine had worked for the Front. Rajab immediately asked about the names of the children. I listed the names of the three girls, abbreviated here to X, Y, and Z. He repeated and checked each name with me. Then he exclaimed: "He [the father] has named them after the women who were with us [in the revolution]. X is my father's brother's daughter, so is Y, and Z is the name of the president of the women's association. They [former revolutionaries] do this. . . . Ask them why he named his daughters this way." He seemed confident that the family would acknowledge the names' revolutionary connections.

Rajab then offered another example of such naming in honor of former Front members: "I called my oldest daughter Narjes [changed here, and a word meaning a type of plant]. No one was called Narjes. But then I started hearing about lots of daughters called Narjes—I would ask, and they would say that they were called after her. I called her after [Polish/German Marxist theorist and revolutionary] Rosa Luxemburg." Rajab had made the connection between Narjes, a name meaning the flower narcissus, and Rosa, a name similarly derived from a flower. Significantly, X, Y, and Z, as well as Narjes and her namesakes, were born after the end of the war. Some of these daughters were born after their parents' return from exile to Oman. Long after they had ceased formal revolutionary mobilization, some parents still sought opportunities to cultivate revolutionary connections. Naming is a strategy of visibilization: the imposition of fixed surnames made individuals visible to states for purposes such as taxation.[66] Among Dhufari former revolutionaries, the passing on of first names with revolutionary associations made former militants legible to other members of the erstwhile revolutionary community.

These naming practices were all the more significant given the politics of public nomenclature under Sultan Qaboos. Salalah, like Oman more broadly, was saturated with street names and monuments that commemorated Sultan Qaboos and his renaissance. There were no monuments or street names to recognize revolutionaries. As the imprisonment of journalist 'Abdullah Habib showed, public discussion in Oman of the unmarked graves of revolutionaries whom government forces executed risked serious punishment. Official silence about the revolution contrasted with the choice of former revolutionaries to name children after figures important to the revolution either as historical inspiration or in the parents' personal experiences. Naming practices that shifted focus toward honoring the revolution became out of place. They were an alternative means of revealing relations, as well as passing on a collective memory to a future generation. In acknowledging these namesakes in conversation with me, despite government surveillance, Dhufar's former revolutionaries implied that these naming strategies did not entail political resistance that would be of concern to the Omani government (as might be the case in the naming strategies of other politically repressed groups).[67] But in Dhufar these naming strategies did reproduce, in a future generation, the possibility of knowing a counterhegemonic social order that contravened traditional distinctions along lines of tribe, status group, and gender.

A third kinship strategy that helped ex-revolutionaries to reproduce a counterhegemonic social order concerned the forging of marriages in the next generation. No Dhufaris ever suggested to me that, once they had formally left the revolution, former revolutionaries or their children urged or received encouragement to forge new marriages that transgressed traditional social hierarchies, as had been the case during the revolution. On the contrary, Khalfan recalled that "close marriage" between cousins had provided opportunities for female former revolutionaries to regain elements of a socially conventional position. Yet conforming to a dominant marriage pattern such as "close marriage" does not preclude other parallel connections between spouses and their families.

Some Dhufari ex-revolutionary families formed marriages in the next generation that acknowledged closeness on the basis of previous generations' erstwhile Front connections.[68] Najat, the daughter of a veteran revolutionary couple, informed me that her older sister had married about a year before our conversation. "She married a man whose father was in the Front," she related. After a short pause, Najat added that the groom was also the bride's patrilineal cousin. The family's marriage strategy simultaneously conformed to the dominant ideal of patrilineal marriage and projected connection between former Front families into a new generation. This marriage between the children of former revolutionaries thus reproduced networks between former revolutionaries *as* former revolutionaries in addition to their connections as kin.

Wedding celebrations, as well as funerals, for members of former Front families presented further opportunities to reassert revolutionary social values. These included egalitarian leanings to socialize beyond conventional tribal, ethnic, and racialized hierarchies. One former revolutionary commented on this, drawing on language that expressed Dhufaris' familiarity with social segregation based on questions of ethnicity and race. He told me: "We don't care whether someone is black or white, red or yellow." He flagged former revolutionaries' willingness to embrace social mixing at weddings of members of Front families.

Making marriages in the next generation into a means of maintaining connection between former Front families was perhaps the most subtle form of ex-revolutionaries' kinship out of place. These marriages also blended with convention: Najat's sister's wedding was a marriage between patrilineal cousins (even though Najat stressed first the connection through former militancy). Similarly, large wedding parties usually already entailed social mixing based on educational, professional, and residential connections. Yet for those participating who hailed from former revolutionary families, these kinship practices had shifted from conventional to unconventional contexts, becoming another form of kinship out of place. Instead of merely reproducing convention, these practices simultaneously reproduced revolutionary social networks and a counterhegemonic social order. Kinship practices embodied former Front members' social connections that contravened Dhufar's everyday hierarchies.

Questions of Intentions

A common feature of kinship out of place was that these practices harbored a degree of choice or intentionality. This was still the case even when they were subtle to the extent of blending with conventional kinship practices. To clarify, that intentionality entailed, at least, making connections with other former revolutionaries or their children. It is my own interpretation and argument that, even if Dhufaris did not explicitly intend so, in addition those kinship practices maintained social legacies and afterlives of revolution, and specifically revolutionary networks and values.

The intentionality of some former revolutionaries at least to make connections with other veteran revolutionaries was also reflected in their alertness to clues about another Dhufari's potential revolutionary background. It was not merely that erstwhile militants were attuned to strange accents overheard in a hospital ward. Former revolutionaries sometimes frequented places where they might encounter other veteran revolutionaries, or even their children. For example, one ex-revolutionary, Suhail, explained to me that he had once come across the son of a former revolutionary comrade—a son whom previously he had never met—while they were both visiting the public library that opened in Salalah in 2015. Suhail told me: "I recognized the son because he looks so much like the father." Suhail went on to strike up a conversation with the young man. I was not able to learn whether the young man had visited the library knowing that he might be likely to encounter his father's former revolutionary comrades there. But the older man at least had been alert to that possibility.

The purposefulness of kinship out of place distinguishes these practices from other disruptions to wartime and postwar kinship that originated in the revolution. Militants and former militants intentionally turned to kinship during and after the revolution to create and maintain relationships that contravened ordinary hierarchies and distinctions. In contrast, Dhufaris who were not revolutionaries, and who did not seek out revolutionary disruptions to kinship, could nevertheless unwillingly experience such disruption, both during and after the revolution.

When I interviewed Salim Tabook (who died in 2019) at his home in Muscat in 2015, he discussed with me that socially transgressive marriages resulting from the revolution did not always take place between revolutionaries. He drew my attention to a woman whose marriage ended after her husband left to join the revolution. She eventually remarried a man of lower social status than hers, contravening the usual taboo against such a union. Tabook suggested that this socially unusual remarriage was a "post-1970s thing." This remarriage was not an instance of intentional kinship out of place that reproduced revolutionary networks or values. Rather, the remarriage reflected the disruption of the revolution for those whom militants left behind. It likewise highlighted the postwar kinship compromises that offered a pathway toward recovering a "normal" life—for this woman, as a wife and mother.

Another instance of revolutionary kinship disruption also differed from kinship out of place and its purposefulness. This was the possibility of revolutionary legacies producing an unusual marriage in a later generation, without the spouses or families having intended this at the outset. One postwar marriage of which I heard took place between a couple whose social backgrounds would normally have led one of the families to oppose the marriage. Dhufaris described this marriage to me as so unusual as to be "impossible" (*mustahil*). For the sake of this couple's privacy, in addition to modifying some biographical details I do not specify here the tribal, ethnic, and racial dimensions that made the marriage controversial for many Dhufaris. At first sight, this unusual marriage between people born after the revolution and who married decades after the Front's defeat seemed unconnected to the revolution. Although one party to the marriage was the child of a deceased former revolutionary, no close relatives of the other spouse had been revolutionaries. On closer examination, however, the marriage indeed arose from revolutionary connections and their afterlives.

Specifically, the "impossible" marriage arose because some former Front members socialized in socially heterogeneous groups that transgressed informal everyday social segregation between status groups. The husband, who had no close relatives in the revolution, had a male relative, Tahir, whose parent was a former revolutionary. Tahir did interact with ex-militants. He socialized with his parent's former revolutionary comrades at the nightly all-male evening gatherings that took place in outdoor spaces such as the sidewalk tables of a café. At such gatherings, regular attendees occasionally brought a friend or relative. Tahir sometimes brought along his relative who had no close relations in the revolution himself. While women did not participate in such gatherings, there was a possibility—however small—of catching sight of a female relative, for instance if she were in a car that stopped to bring someone to the gathering. It was a chance encounter in the periphery of one of these gatherings that led Tahir's relative to catch sight of the child of a deceased revolutionary. That sighting eventually led to an "impossible" marriage. The element of chance makes this case different from kinship out place and its degree of intentional connection-making. Yet, as this case shows, the fact that some former revolutionaries and their relatives reproduced revolutionary networks created novel opportunities. Future generations of Dhufaris could make connections, including marriages, that constituted further afterlives of Dhufar's revolution.

Although some former revolutionaries and their relatives purposefully used kinship to make connections with one another, not all of them did so. Some former militants moved in distinct spheres around Salalah, meeting only occasionally and some not doing so for years. Some even deliberately avoided the possibilities of kinship for marking revolutionary connections. Their concern was not how to continue acknowledgment of the revolution (through kinship or other means) but rather how to "cut the network" of connections.[69] For Muhad, a young professional in his thirties and the child of a former revolutionary, his decisions regarding the presentation of his patronym became a means through which he distanced himself from the father who linked him to the revolution.

Muhad explained to me that his father had been absent in his childhood because, as far as he understood, he was one of the underground guerrilla fighters still attacking government positions into the 1980s. "Actually, I don't know what he was doing," Muhad hastily clarified. He went on to recall how his father's absence had placed his mother under great financial and emotional strain as she raised their children in his absence. The fallout of revolution for this family was painful.

I considered mentioning Muhad's father's name to another interlocutor who had served in the revolution, to see if I could learn more about the father's story. Dhufaris habitually listed the names of fathers and grandfathers on business cards. I later consulted the card that Muhad had given me. But most unusually, Muhad's card omitted his father's and grandfather's names and featured only his first name and the name of his tribe. It was as if Muhad had excised from his public self the father and former fighter from whom he had distanced himself in our conversation. This echoes the way that children of political activists can distance themselves from a parent absent because of their militancy.[70] For those living in the wake of revolution, kinship offered a potential means to forge and maintain connections with the revolutionary past—but some directed their efforts at curtailing, rather than pursuing, those possibilities.

Kinship and Revolutionary Afterlives

The intersections of kinship with Dhufar's revolution and its afterlives are complex. In part, these intersections reflect three familiar strands within analyses of kinship. Postwar kinship offered a means for people to reconnect with "normal" life in the wake of organized political violence. For some former revolutionaries who returned to Oman, and for a wife abandoned when her husband left for the revolution, kinship promised a resumption of normality.

In addition, kinship helped reproduce a dominant stratified, albeit contested, social order. Outside the context of the revolution, Dhufaris' kinship arrangements—from patrilineal tribal affiliation to "close marriage" and the avoidance of women marrying "down"—reproduced hierarchies of status group, tribe, ethnicity, race, gender, and generation. Kinship also helped reproduce the prevailing social, political, and economic hierarchies of patronage networks that flourished through the government's channeling of resources through tribes, crony capitalism, and hereditary paramilitary service.

Moreover, kinship accommodated resistance against domination and exploitation. The Front's interventions in kinship supported militants' resistance against colonialism and imperialism. A different kind of research project from my own might have considered how in Qaboos's Oman, kinship practices in Dhufar, such as the distinctive *maghbur* wedding gifts, provided Dhufaris with a means of resisting the homogenizing national identity of Omaniness. This national identity neglected Dhufari cultural specificities that were an uncomfortable reminder of Dhufaris' histories of insurrection against the al-Busaid sultans. Whether kinship practices like *maghbur* resist official discursive erasures merits further exploration.

But other postwar kinship practices of some former revolutionaries in Dhufar did not easily fit these familiar analyses. Through kinship practices such as maintaining revolutionary family units, naming children after revolutionary namesakes, and arranging marriages in the next generation that connected former revolutionary families across generations, some former revolutionaries knowingly and intentionally maintained connections with other erstwhile militants. Not all former revolutionaries engaged in such practices, with some avoiding these possibilities altogether. But the implications of these practices for understanding the intersections of kinship, postwar contexts, social reproduction, and resistance are significant.

First, postwar kinship relations may reproduce not so much a sense of the normality that conflict disturbed but the social relations that came into being in a context of conflict such as revolution. In Dhufar, it is difficult on the basis of extant records, or interlocutors' memories, to resolve whether or not kinship that transgressed traditional social hierarchies during the revolution ever became "normal" for militants. Times of conflict, and their aftermath, can blur the distinction between normality and abnormality.[71] But at least in the postwar context of Dhufar, some kinship relations of former revolutionaries and their relatives, as well as the underlying values, were not "normal." Postwar kinship, then, does not necessarily reproduce normality, and in Dhufar it has reproduced unusual relations and values.

Second, to interpret these practices as resistance may miss the crux of what was at stake for the Dhufaris involved, as well as for the authorities who surveilled them. Dhufari former revolutionaries engaged in conventional kinship practices such as "close marriage." They were not necessarily "resisting" the wider potential of kinship to reproduce dominant relations and values. Nor is it clear that those who engaged in these practices did so as a form of resistance of concern to the Omani state. State authorities proved their willingness to punish perceived infringements, but they did not identify these practices as threatening.

Third, and most significantly with regard to the long-standing and intellectually diverse tendencies to link kinship with the reproduction of a (contested) social order, kinship can help reproduce a counterhegemonic social order. This can be so even in the absence of either clear dynamics of resistance or a permissive political context that tolerates oppositional mobilization. The Dhufari case suggests that kinship helps reproduce a counterhegemonic social order when kinship practices become out of place, having shifted from a conventional to an unusual social context. Once out of place, kinship practices that otherwise might have reproduced dominant values and relations—such as maintaining a family unit, naming children after significant namesakes, and forging a new generation of marriages—can instead reproduce a counterhegemonic social order. Through their kinship out of place, some Dhufari former revolutionaries reproduced a counterhegemonic social order of revolutionary networks and values of social egalitarianism—and afterlives of an officially silenced revolution.

These complex intersections of kinship with Dhufar's revolution and its afterlives are significant beyond questions of kinship's significance for postwar contexts, social reproduction, and resistance. They invite fresh reflection on the stakes of kinship for former insurgents and former revolutionaries. Kinship connections have provided means for militants, and former combatants, to relate to the insurgencies in which they serve or that they once supported. In particular, female supporters of insurgencies have often related to and recalled their connections to insurgencies through kinship, such as the coincidence of life cycle events with revolutionary events.[72] The experiences of Dhufari revolutionaries suggest how kinship may have much broader implications for former combatants and former revolutionaries, both male and female. This may be especially relevant for those who live in conditions of political repression that preclude formal mobilization as a movement referencing past militancy. Former combatants and former revolutionaries may find in kinship a way of reproducing legacies and afterlives of erstwhile revolutionary mobilization and insurgency. At stake is the refocusing of peoples' engagement with networks and values associated with a past revolution or insurgency. The emphasis of that engagement can shift from the realm of political mobilization, such as that which was possible in the past, to the realm of the intimate, including kinship relations. The refocusing of revolutionary values and networks onto intimacy such as kinship counters official narratives of revolutionary defeat and failure. This points instead to a more open-ended experience of ongoing revolutionary afterlives.

The next chapter examines how everyday socializing in Dhufar also provided a means for some former revolutionaries to reproduce revolutionary social values of social egalitarianism. But when everyday interactions did not go far enough, an extraordinary action, such as one woman's unusual electoral candidacy, could create reverberations of revolutionary social values.

5

Everyday and Extraordinary Interactions

EVERY EVENING, AT THE OUTDOORS table of a café in a quiet suburb of Salalah, a group of men aged for the most part in their sixties or older met to drink tea and talk. Theirs was just one of many such all-male informal evening gatherings across the city. What brought these particular men together was that they were former revolutionaries. In their youth most had been members of the Front. After the movement's formal defeat in 1975, several of these men had continued as militants in exile in the PDRY. At various points, each had returned to Oman on the condition of professing loyalty to Sultan Qaboos, the ruler against whom they had once fought.

One warm evening in 2015, I joined this gathering as a guest. Soon after my arrival, one of the men asked me to explain my research interests. I began to describe my wish to understand the long-term effects of revolutionary social policies aimed at challenging Dhufar's long-standing social inequalities. I mentioned as an example the revolutionary encouragement of marriages that contravened traditional social hierarchies. Another man interjected to clarify: "The important thing was to encourage the idea that people had equality (*al-musawah*). Marriage was a small part of that, the more important thing was the idea of equality." He went on to mention other means of the Front marking equality, such as giving pastoralists equal access to water resources. He could have added more examples, such as opening up education to girls, boys, women, and men alike, and emancipating enslaved persons.

When this man highlighted the importance of social egalitarianism, or *al-musawah*, during the revolution, he left unspoken a broader question. To what extent had this value and its enactment remained important and possible for former revolutionaries living in Qaboos's Oman? Elsewhere, when revolutionaries have failed to achieve goals of political and economic transformation, revolutionary values such as egalitarianism have the potential to survive in institutions such as workers' councils.[1] In Oman, government repression obliged former revolutionaries to renounce past values of antiimperialism, republicanism, socialist economic organization, and democratic participation. Nor did Oman's postrevolutionary political environment allow them to participate in any kind of formal organization such as a workers' council. But there were opportunities to reproduce revolutionary values of social egalitarianism. One such possibility was everyday socializing, such as the gathering that I witnessed that evening.

Everyday interactions have been an important sphere for revolutionary movements to achieve social transformation.[2] Yet the everyday is also important for creating revolutionary afterlives. Through everyday socializing and other quotidian interactions, some Dhufari former revolutionaries reproduced values of social egalitarianism. These values continued to challenge Dhufar's gendered, tribal, status group, ethnic, and racialized hierarchies, as had earlier revolutionary policies.

The everyday may be especially significant for creating revolutionary afterlives in politically constrained conditions such as those that pertain in Oman. The Sultanate not only forbade the formation of a political party or veterans' association but also omitted mention of the revolution (and other episodes of dissent) from official historiography and routinely banned the sale of books on such topics. Amid such constraints, mundane everyday interactions that blended with "normality" provided opportunities for creating revolutionary afterlives. Given the ubiquity of daily interactions, Oman's intelligence service could observe such relations. Their regularity perhaps even facilitated surveillance of former dissidents' networks. The fact that the intelligence service tolerated these interactions suggests that the authorities did not find in them cause for concern. This provided me with some reassurance when making the decision to write about them. A focus on everyday interactions illuminates the conditions and possibilities of revolutionary afterlives and counterhistories.

First, an examination of the quotidian brings to light both the possibilities *and* the limitations of the everyday for reproducing afterlives of revolution. Daily interactions such as an all-male evening gathering could only go so far to reproduce values of social egalitarianism. Sometimes it instead took an extraordinary act to reproduce revolutionary values. This was the case for one woman who took the unusual action of running for election, despite facing backlash because of her background. She ran in order to publicly endorse gender equality. That message echoed the gendered egalitarianism that revolutionaries had earlier pioneered. Both everyday and extraordinary actions can reproduce afterlives of revolution, with the extraordinary offering possibilities where the everyday cannot.

Second, the turn to the everyday, and to the extraordinary as a supplement to the everyday, foregrounds the intersectional dimensions of the afterlives of revolution. From revolution to modernization and transnationalism, experiences of social, economic, and political transformations intersect with gender, generation, class, ethnicity, and race, among other social distinctions.[3] Similarly, experiences of the afterlives of revolution are intersectional. In Dhufar, gender, generation, and social status encompassing tribe, ethnicity, and race all affected dominant views about socially acceptable interactions and public visibility. They also shaped access to political and economic resources. Consequently, everyday or extraordinary actions that reproduced revolutionary social values, and created revolutionary afterlives, were not equally available or necessary for all Dhufaris.

Men had the privilege of circulating in public without stigma. It was more feasible for male former revolutionaries to draw on everyday socializing in nightly café gatherings to reproduce revolutionary social values. Women faced potentially high costs of stigma if they transgressed the conventional expectations of public (in)visibility that corresponded to their social status. It was more feasible for a woman with privileged access to independent income and other social, political, and economic resources to undertake extraordinary action that chimed with revolutionary values.

Gendered and class-inflected "privilege of revolution" has facilitated participation in revolution.[4] The aftermath of Dhufar's revolution highlights how privilege can similarly underpin the afterlives of revolution—even as former revolutionaries' privileges nevertheless overlapped with their vulnerabilities as surveilled and politically repressed former dissidents. Whether taking extraordinary or everyday forms, the afterlives of revolution relied on intersectional privilege. They also often depended on social camouflage.

An examination of the everyday during and after revolution not only offers insight into revolutionary afterlives but also foregrounds complexities and tensions inherent within the notion of the everyday.

The Everyday: Reproduction, Creativity, Contradiction, and Subversion

Daily socializing encompasses the informal, casual social interactions that take place on a regular basis among people who frequently meet, whether for planned or unplanned encounters, in homes, workplaces, leisure venues, and public spaces. Everyday socializing includes quotidian gestures, choices of words, and ways of greeting, interacting with, or avoiding others. Such interactions exist on a spectrum of degrees of (in)formality of social interaction. Informal interactions can overlap with and be part of more formal social occasions (such as life cycle events, religious rituals, ceremonies of state, etc.).

Everyday interactions are important means for normalizing and reinforcing dominant values, power relations, and incumbent hierarchies. Generations of anthropologists have followed the pioneers of the discipline in taking part in and observing everyday social interactions (as well as extraordinary events) in order to analyze wider social phenomena.[5] In the latter decades of the twentieth century, social theorists probed the everyday and the specific ways in which cumulative small gestures produced persons, subjects, and social relations. Daily practices including socializing help create habitus. This is the structured social environment with its attendant power dynamics and distinctions that shape the choices people make, with these choices further reinforcing their habitus.[6] Through daily interactions, among other "techniques of the self," persons cultivate dispositions and subjectivities and signal these to those around them.[7] Daily repetitions of everyday gestures produce and normalize the nuts and bolts of social life, such as gendered identities.[8] The mundanity of everyday interactions helps normalize and legitimize social differences, hierarchies, and associated values. They may make them seem so ordinary to those involved as to appear almost unquestionable.

These capacities of the everyday for social reproduction are apparent in many Gulf settings. Since the influx of oil and gas wealth and of the leisure opportunities that associated incomes have afforded Gulf nationals, new forms of gender-segregated quotidian socializing have arisen in the region. Kuwaiti men gather in out-of-town villas on the first evening of the weekend, and northern Omani women meet in daily neighborhood gatherings to drink coffee.[9] Such informal socializing marks gendered and national identities. In Salalah, ubiquitous all-male evening outdoor gatherings were one of the forms of informal socializing that reproduced, signaled, and reinforced social distinctions along lines of gender, generation, tribe, status group, racialized identities, and ethnicity.

The everyday is far more than a vehicle of social reproduction, however. It is also potentially a site of creativity, contradiction, and subversion. Ethnographers, other social scientists, social theorists, and historians have explored these qualities across many areas of social life, including the projects for radical social change of revolutionaries and insurgents.

The creative qualities of the everyday emerge in their potential for cultivating transformation. With daily practices' capacity to be constitutive of social identities and worlds comes their potential to create new social horizons. Everyday practices, such as modes of bodily deportment and dress, are techniques through which people seek to fashion themselves into the subjects they aspire to be.[10] Accordingly, revolutions and armed insurgencies intent upon achieving radical social change focus on everyday interactions, including socializing, as a means of marking or achieving the transformation to which they aspire. Changes in everyday gestures, ways of dressing, greeting, socializing, organizing families, working, and setting up neighborhoods have helped create new identities, subjectivities, and relationships. This recurs from the socialist revolutions of the early twentieth century to the anti-colonial revolutions of the 1960s and 1970s and the revolutionary movements of the early twenty-first century.[11]

Everyday interactions also provide insurgents with opportunities to foment change. Underground Maoist guerilla fighters in India's Jharkhand region cultivated respectful everyday interactions with the socially marginalized Adivasi tribal populations. They sat on the floor with them and ate with them. This legitimized militants in the eyes of local civilians and inspired new recruits.[12] Reflecting these capacities of the everyday to create new revolutionary social relations, militants in the mountain strongholds and PDRY bases of the Front aimed to transform daily life. They adopted new forms of address, clothing, and daily schedules. They formed socially mixed armed battalions, schools, work projects, and families. All of this was part of the effort to engender revolutionary social change.

Quotidian interactions are also the site of contradiction. It is not merely that the everyday may be a realm of literal contradiction. Those interacting on a daily basis may, of course, be in disagreement about values and assumptions that underpin those interactions. In addition, everyday interactions may fundamentally problematize prevailing narratives about the societies in question, such as their being "revolutionary," "egalitarian," "postwar," etc. It is a familiar predicament for those living through and studying revolutions that proclamations of gendered and social equality clash with flawed lived realities of ongoing and new gender and class distinctions and hierarchies.[13] In societies living in the aftermath of organized political violence, everyday practices of social stigmatization and segregation can problematize the very notion of being "postwar."[14] In Dhufar, both during and after the revolution, everyday experiences exposed contradictions that official narratives occluded. During the revolution some militants strayed from official anti-tribalist rhetoric by boasting of the absence from their tribe of deserters.[15] In the aftermath of the revolution, everyday interactions of former militants reproduced revolutionary social egalitarianism. They thereby contradicted official narratives of the revolution's demise.

Everyday interactions also facilitate subversion, ranging from subtle to overt resistance. By virtue of their very ubiquity, everyday interactions must fall at least partially beyond the scope of domination. They thereby offer potential for resistance.[16] In situations where overt resistance against extreme exploitation risks punishment, marginalized groups can use everyday interactions to articulate "hidden transcripts" of subtle subversion only intelligible to other marginalized persons.[17] Accordingly, the realm of the everyday has facilitated varying degrees of subtle or overt resistance against exploitation and marginalization. In socialist Poland, rural domestic life became a space of anti-state resistance.[18] Meanwhile, those facing current or recent political violence have drawn on everyday interactions to resist the ravages of violence and its legacies.[19] From their kinship configurations to their linguistic choices, Palestinians, Tibetans, Kashmiris, and others have resisted occupation.[20] For marginalized former revolutionaries who have abandoned overt activism but cannot simply "cast away" the new identities that they had cultivated as revolutionaries, the everyday offers opportunities for continued subversion of social convention.[21] For instance, male veterans of Bengal's 1970s Maoist militancy continued to resist the conventional masculine roles of providing for a household or being a religious renouncer.[22] Similarly, in postrevolutionary Dhufar everyday interactions allowed some former militants to continue subverting dominant social hierarchies.

The trajectories of politically marginalized former revolutionaries, such as some of the men and women whom I met in Dhufar, foreground how the everyday encompasses reproduction, creativity, contradiction, and subversion. Everyday interactions helped *reproduce* the long-standing social hierarchies that revolutionaries then went on to contest. During the revolution, militants drew on the everyday to *create* new identities intended to embody revolutionary values of social egalitarianism. Militants' everyday experiences with the Front could nevertheless *contradict* revolutionary values, while the afterlives of revolution *contradicted* official governmental narratives of the revolution's collapse. By maintaining revolutionary social values, some former revolutionaries *subverted* Dhufar's dominant hierarchies. These afterlives of revolution were subversive precisely because so much of Dhufaris' everyday socializing and other quotidian interactions reproduced dominant hierarchies.

Everyday Socializing in Salalah

Most forms of everyday socializing in Salalah reproduced social distinction and stratification along lines of gender, tribe, social status, ethnicity, and racialized identities. This happened in varied ways according to different generations of Dhufaris' preferences for quotidian, usually gender-segregated, socializing.

Male and female younger adult Salalans liked to socialize, separately, in the city's mall. Many Dhufaris had greatly anticipated the opening of Gardens Mall in 2013. They considered its arrival as evidence of the city's economic and social development. At the mall, groups of women tended to visit shops, ending their visit at the food court. They usually chose to eat in the upstairs family area where most customers were women and children (although sometimes a male adult accompanied them). Some of these women felt distant enough from the male gaze to take off their face coverings to eat.

Young men visiting the mall tended to walk around the main paths, eventually settling at one of the onlooking cafés to order a (nonalcoholic) drink. The friends of a young man who spent too long walking around the mall might tease him: "He likes to come here to look at women," one young man joked to me of his friend, whom he judged to be overly interested in watching women at the mall.

The mall was a cosmopolitan environment, in that Dhufari (young) men and women from diverse backgrounds socialized there, as did families from the Arab, Indian subcontinent, North American, and European migrant communities in Salalah. Walking around the mall, one would overhear different strains of Dhufari Arabic (from Salalah's different urban communities as well as Bedouin accents), Modern South Arabian languages, Palestinian and North African dialects of Arabic, as well as English, Hindi, and Malayalam, among other languages.[23] Nevertheless, these groups tended to move through the mall avoiding or minimalizing direct interaction across gendered, ethnic, and national distinctions. Everyday socializing in the mall thus reproduced a range of social, ethnic, gendered, generational, and national distinctions.

Similarly, everyday socializing among older generations of Salalans reproduced social differences. Older women who had many family responsibilities favored evening socializing in domestic spaces with female adult relatives and children. Staged around kinship, these gatherings reiterated connections that kin shared along lines of tribe, status group, ethnicity, and racialized identities.

For older generations of men, gatherings focused on friendship encompassed such connections. Married men's gatherings were the most publicly visible kind of everyday socializing in Salalah. These men tended to socialize outside in the street.[24] In the late afternoon and evening, men, and especially those of middle age or older, gathered in groups that ranged from two or three to twenty or so (Figure 9). Sometimes they sat on plastic chairs by the side of the street; others lounged on sofas under the awning of a café's outside space. Typically, a man of middle age or older would be out of the marital home every evening between sunset and around ten or eleven p.m. He would meet his habitual group of friends at their regular spot to drink tea and talk.[25] Men referred to these gatherings (in local pronunciation) as their *galsah* (literally, "sitting"). The ex-revolutionaries who gathered every evening were taking part in one such *galsah*.

At the core of each *galsah* was a network of male friendship. Typically, a man had a regular *galsah* that he attended. Men might also occasionally visit other gatherings as an invited guest, dropping in on known acquaintances. But a man's presence at his regular *galsah* was expected. When he was absent, his companions would notice this. Common interests could motivate a man to choose to join a particular *galsah*. One man explained to me that members of his *galsah* all shared high levels of education and common interests of intellectual conversation. Men also expected a certain level of integrity, commitment, and availability from fellow members. One man explained what he expected of a companion at his nightly *galsah*: "I sit with him; he is supposed to be frank with me." Another man summed up the special quality of his gathering to him. One evening, after we had

FIGURE 9. An informal social gathering of men in Salalah. Photograph by Alice Wilson, 2015.

visited his home and greeted a wide array of relatives, once we arrived at his *galsah*, he gestured toward the men seated there and said: "This is your family." He modified the common trope of offering hospitality to an outsider via assurances that the guest should feel as if they were among their own family. He chose instead to emphasize members of his *galsah*, rather than his literal family, as key givers of hospitality.

The characteristics of *galsah* gatherings marked social difference and hierarchy just as much as did other forms of everyday socializing in Salalah. The *galsah*'s most immediately noticeable characteristic was its gender segregation. Dhufaris highlighted and appreciated this feature when I questioned them about it. Separately, I asked a group of female relatives spending their evening together at home, and a group of men at a *galsah*, and about men's habitual evening absence from domestic spaces. Both groups found my question amusing. One woman explained, with a gentle laugh: "Normally the woman is with her mother or her sisters." One of the men, similarly bemused, went further as he replied: "This is normal, a woman is usually with her mother or her sisters. Do you think that if a woman has seven or eight children to look after, she wants her husband to look after too?" The implication was not merely that men's evening gatherings outside the home freed up domestic spaces for women to socialize. Dhufaris also understood that men lightened women's domestic burden by absenting themselves.

A *galsah* reproduced further forms of social distinction that encompassed and went beyond the immediately visible gendered segregation. Men's presence at a *galsah* not only relied on the gendered division of labor that assigned most childcare to women but also rested on an ethnicized division of labor. The men's opportunity to relax and talk together benefited from the oil wealth economy of Omani men's privileged access to disposable income generated from public and private sector employment, and from cheap migrant labor servicing families and workplaces. Those spaces included the commercialized sites of consumption and service like the cafés where *galsah* gatherings often took place. Similarly, Dhufari women's leisure-time gatherings relied on the labor of migrant workers to perform domestic tasks.

In addition, groups of men sitting outdoors marked the ethnicized, racialized, and tribal distinctions of Salalah. Dhufaris were familiar with the city's social geography. Tribal and ethnic groups were associated with the old prewar districts and the early postwar neighborhoods for which the government had distributed land to groups rather than to individuals. If a male interlocutor was driving me across the city to drop me off somewhere, along our way he might refer to these distinctions by pointing out groups of men sitting outside in their *galsah*. "This is where the Somalis sit," an interlocutor told me one evening, gesturing to the groups of men sitting outside in that neighborhood.

The specific location of a *galsah* could relate to a particular tribe or family. One gathering that I visited took place in an area of prewar Salalah that was associated with a prestigious high-ranking family. The man who took me to this gathering, and who crossed the city to get there on an almost nightly basis, came from a similarly high-ranking town background. He had maternal relatives among the specific tribe associated with the *galsah*'s location. Another *galsah* of which I knew took place in a postwar district of Salalah outside a multistory residential block that one of the *galsah* members owned and rented out. The neighborhood and even the street of a *galsah* often marked participants' social connections and positioning. A *galsah* in Salalah—like other all-male social gatherings in Arab contexts—represented a zone of sociability associated with a specific tribal, ethnic, or racialized group.[26]

In fact, a typical *galsah* brought together regular members from only one of Salalah's traditional social groupings. In multiple visits to a *galsah* of town elites, for instance, the regular members I met there spanned various prestigious town tribe backgrounds. I only once met a man of mountain background at this *galsah*. But he was a guest whom a regular member of the gathering had invited specifically for me to meet him. Although as a foreign woman I was a clear outlier at the *galsah*, this guest was also an outsider. He had entered a zone of sociability, protection, and hospitality associated with men of an elite town tribe background that differed from his own. Styles of dress signaled these differences of insiders and outsider. The regular attendees of this *galsah* wore a long (usually white) robe. In contrast, the visitor wore instead a shirt paired with the colorful wraparound cloth (*wizar*) that men of mountain background favored.[27]

In its tribal, ethnic, and racialized configurations, a *galsah* was somewhat distinctive among other regional forms of gender-segregated socializing. In Kuwait, before oil wealth, the hosting of a *diwaniyyah* implied political prestige. Since oil wealth, the "average Kuwaiti" has been able afford to build a home accommodating a suitable space to host a *diwaniyyah*. Thus, in both older and contemporary forms a *diwaniyyah* functions as a space of social and political connection for men hailing from different backgrounds to network.[28] In contrast, in the Oman of Sultan Qaboos, Salalans of all backgrounds hosted *galsah* gatherings in which the presence of persons from different social backgrounds was exceptional rather than routine.

The homogeneity of *galsah* members' tribal, ethnic, and racialized background also differed from the heterogeneity observed in women's informal daily gatherings based on neighborhood in northern Oman.[29] In those settings, it was common for the backgrounds of women mixing on a daily basis to span socially prestigious families and women of lowly background. In one case, neighbors continued to socialize with a woman whom they believed transgressed conventional propriety by being a sex worker.[30] But in Dhufar, only occasionally did I encounter informal socializing that approached heterogeneity of tribe, racialized identity, and social prestige. One such exception was gender-segregated socializing among groups of young people of university age or who had recently graduated.[31] I once joined a gathering of male college-age students in the mountains near Salalah and a gathering of female graduates on the beach in a town beyond Salalah. On both occasions, young people of mixed backgrounds ate together, talked, and laughed. Notably, these groups staged their heterogeneous socializing *outside* the city and its habitual informal segregation.

The avoidance of socially heterogeneous informal gatherings may be more pronounced in Salalah than in other parts of Oman and the Gulf.[32]

In separate instances of "offstage" conversations when no third person was present, some *sumur* commented to me on their experience of Dhufar's pronounced informal social segregation and their corresponding marginalization. One *sumur* woman, Amira, explained that she wished to migrate to northern Oman where she believed that there was less racialized discrimination than in Dhufar. Amira also recounted the surprise of a black Kuwaiti friend of hers, Khulud, who was living in Salalah and asked: "Why are the blacks always with blacks and the whites with whites?" This struck Khulud as different from the greater degrees of mixing with which she was familiar in Kuwait. Amira had replied: "That's what it is like here, the blacks [sit] with the blacks and the whites with the whites. They don't mix."[33] Salalans' preference for social homogeneity in daily interactions likewise underpinned one interlocutor's suggestion that if my husband visited, he could "sit with his own people," meaning the *sumur*, whom Dhufaris associated with my husband because of their blackness. In Salalah, from the mall to homes and *galsah* gatherings, social homogeneity of background characterized most informal socializing.

Within a *galsah*'s homogeneity of social background, there was nevertheless internal distinction among members. At the *galsah* that took place next to a building owned by one of the members, the owner of the apartment building, Omar, was a patron figure to the *galsah* in additional material ways. Other members of the *galsah* had explained to me that Omar was extremely rich. Like his peers at this *galsah*, he hailed from a prestigious town tribe: one of the high-ranking Dhufari tribes that northerner Omanis would name to me when they spoke of famous tribes from Dhufar. In addition to owning this and other buildings in the center of town, Omar owned businesses and livestock. He generously drew on this wealth to treat his *galsah* companions.

Usually, food was not the focus of a *galsah*. Men ordered something (nonalcoholic) to drink but typically ate at home on their return from the *galsah*. Every few weeks, though, Omar would order a generous delivery of Lebanese-style grilled meats and side dishes. On these occasions, he treated everyone at the *galsah* (including me when I was present) to dinner.

I eventually learned that it was unusual for another person to take on the role of sponsoring a meal for everyone at this *galsah*. One evening, Omar arrived to find that everyone at the *galsah* was tucking into a hearty meal of freshly slaughtered meat. Surprised, Omar stopped in his tracks and asked: "Where is this from?" One of his companions explained. Another member of the group had opened a new business and had brought for his companions a share in the meat that he and his associates had provided to celebrate the opening. Omar's surprise underscored that the *galsah* had a patron figure—a microcosm of the relationship familiar to all Omanis in their role as protégés of the sultan's patronage.

Galsah gatherings encapsulated dynamics of social connection, distinction, and hierarchy that were familiar to Dhufaris: gendered segregation, male solidarity, citizens' privileges that rested on government patronage and the exploitation of migrant labor, social and physical separation between hierarchically ranked tribal, ethnic, and racialized status groups, and the distribution of resources along lines of patronage. Other kinds of everyday socializing in the city, from the mall to private homes, similarly reproduced gendered, tribal, racialized, and status group distinctions. These were precisely the dynamics that the everyday socializing and interactions of some former revolutionaries challenged.

Revolutionary Social Values in the Everyday

I learned by chance that some ex-revolutionaries met each evening. An interlocutor happened to mention to me that "of course" former revolutionaries had a *galsah*. The casual tone implied that the existence of these men's regular social gatherings was common knowledge among Dhufaris and inevitably, therefore, the state's intelligence service.

Having heard of this *galsah* of former revolutionaries, I made inquiries through acquaintances, and someone arranged for me to visit this nightly gathering. A few weeks later, I found myself the guest of these ex-revolutionaries. When I approached, I walked the length of the whole group greeting each of the men by hand. At this close proximity I saw how some of these men physically embodied a history of armed revolutionary struggle. One man was only able to move and greet with his left hand. Someone later explained to me that his disabled right hand was the result of a war wound. Another man had several fingers missing. I learned that this was also a war injury. One man rested a pair of crutches by his chair, his swollen legs leaning on an improvised footstool under the table. Age as well as war had weathered these men.

The incidence of injuries that hinted at histories of armed combat was likely higher in this *galsah* than in most others taking place across the city. But in many other respects the ex-revolutionaries' *galsah* would have looked ordinary to the casual observer. Some dozen men sat together around plastic tables forming an elongated circular group. A migrant worker from the

Indian subcontinent waited on them, moving back and forth between the tables and the nearby café as he supplied the group with tea. As was typical, the men were immaculately dressed in freshly laundered and pressed white robes. Not far away, several had parked the shiny cars in which they would return to their homes. The casual observer might also notice, on looking more closely, that the skin tone of those gathered ranged in darkness and lightness. This was not necessarily unusual in Dhufar. Social gatherings focused on a single status group or tribe were indeed the norm. But interracial marriage between dark-skinned enslaved women of African origin and men of free tribes of varying skin tones has a long history in Dhufar. Accordingly, those hailing from the same status group did not necessarily share a skin tone.

The observer who lingered would also see that, just as was the case for other gatherings, during the course of an evening other men dropped by to greet the group. Some stayed till the gathering broke up while others stayed only briefly. Two middle-aged men who arrived separately joined the group when I was there. One was a former student at the revolutionary school and later in the USSR. The other man turned out to have no connection to the Front, but explained that he enjoyed the company and intellectual quality of the conversation. During the course of the evening, a young relative of an acquaintance of the group pulled up in a smart four-wheel drive car to bring greetings and some fresh camel milk. Such visits signaled how this *galsah*, like others where I also saw younger men drop by over the course of an evening, was embedded in intergenerational networks of social connection. The café sidewalk scene that I witnessed in Salalah was far from the social abjection and isolation of the gathering of defeated and coopted former dissidents in Orwell's Chestnut Tree Café.[34]

For an observer who knew the men's revolutionary and anti-colonial past, their sidewalk gathering in Qaboos's authoritarian Oman indicated their distance from that history. The gulf that separated them from their past became acutely palpable during my visit. One man questioned me about my previous research with the liberation movement for Western Sahara, Polisario Front. When serving as diplomats for Dhufar's exiled Front in the late 1970s and 1980s, two men at this gathering had visited Polisario Front's refugee camps in Southwest Algeria. With curiosity and almost as if puzzled, one of them asked me: "Are they [Polisario] still there?" Polisario Front and the refugees were indeed "still there," pursuing national liberation for Western Sahara as well as broader goals of social emancipation and revolution.[35]

In contrast, the men seated around the table that evening had ceased anti-colonial revolution. They lived as coopted subjects of an authoritarian security state. A major axis of political, economic, and social life there was the hierarchy of an absolutist sultan ruling over subjects allowed few freedoms of expression or association. One of the men at the *galsah* reminded me of our respective places and vulnerabilities in those hierarchies as ex-revolutionaries and a foreign researcher. He warned me with a wink that had a chilling effect on me that I should "stay away from politics."

Distant though these men were from their anti-colonial revolutionary past, and much as their *galsah* bore resemblances to many taking place across the city, this gathering was nevertheless extraordinary. The fact of its mere existence was remarkable in the context of the government's repression of the Front and official silencing of that history. In addition, this was the only *galsah* in Salalah that I encountered, or that Dhufaris described to me, where the regular members hailed from heterogeneous social backgrounds. Other Dhufaris explained to me afterwards that those present at the ex-revolutionaries' *galsah* spanned town elites, mountain elites, former enslaved persons, members of client fishing families, town non-elites, and mountain non-elites. This was a stark contrast to the homogeneity of social background among the habitual attendees of other gatherings where "the blacks [sit] with the blacks and the whites with the whites."

This *galsah*'s egalitarian ethic furthermore extended to the group's internal dynamics. Absent from this gathering was the patronage present in other groups, with the inherent hierarchy between a patron (such as Omar) and those who benefited from his largesse. By contrast, in the *galsah* of the ex-revolutionaries, as one of them explained, "[e]very two weeks, one of us invites everyone for dinner, and then the next time it is someone else—last night it was him, next time it will be someone else." Instead of a regular patron figure distributing largesse, everyone took turns to share the responsibility of providing food. That reciprocity again signaled an egalitarian dynamic.

This group contrasted sharply with the typical characteristics of other *galsah* gatherings in Salalah, then. Other gatherings reproduced everyday tribal, ethnic, and racialized hierarchies and distinctions, as well as patronage dynamics. The membership and internal dynamics of the ex-revolutionaries' *galsah*, however, reproduced social egalitarianism that had once animated revolutionary projects from classrooms to mixed battalions, work groups, and families.

Admittedly, the *galsah* brought together a small number of people. But it was one of several kinds of everyday socializing through which some (but not all) ex-revolutionaries reproduced social egalitarianism. Male ex-revolutionaries hailing from a similarly diverse range of social backgrounds also dropped in on one another on a regular basis in spaces where they knew they were likely to meet other ex-revolutionaries. These spaces included a library that opened in 2015, and, before then, a bookshop that by 2015 had closed.[36] Such spaces of intellectual exchange and learning reverberated with the revolutionary promotion of education. Salalah, a city of informal segregation, hosted unofficial spaces where former revolutionaries sought out and staged socially inclusive mixing.

In addition to their socially inclusive informal interactions, former revolutionaries' choices of words and greetings implied an ongoing interest in social egalitarianism that challenged Dhufar's everyday distinctions. One veteran berated me for having adopted the common local word for "woman," *harim*. He chided me that since this word derived from the root meaning "forbid," it associated women with restrictions. His correction of my vocabulary echoed the Front's attempts to promote gender egalitarianism by banning the word *harim*.[37] This former militant was not alone in continuing to challenge Dhufaris' predominant tendency to associate (socially prestigious) womanhood with seclusion. Male former revolutionaries who inquired after female former revolutionaries to whom they were unrelated by kinship, such as the man in the hospital ward who inquired after 'Ali's mother and the taxi driver who greeted Khiyar, also challenged conventional gendered barriers to social interaction. Beyond the *galsah* that I visited, then, other kinds of everyday interactions among ex-revolutionaries reproduced social egalitarianism.

What were the wider impacts of ex-revolutionaries' socially egalitarian practices? Did they affect interactions with peers who had not participated in the revolution and with younger generations of ex-revolutionary and nonrevolutionary families? Did female ex-revolutionaries also socialize on a daily basis? The constraints of politically sensitive fieldwork prevented me from pursuing these questions with the depth that they merit. The few female ex-revolutionaries whom I met avoided discussing their revolutionary past with me. No one with whom I spoke, male or female, mentioned regular social gatherings for female veterans.

Although aspects of ex-revolutionaries' interest in social egalitarianism remained beyond the scope of this research, some limitations of their engagement did become apparent. Access to forums of everyday socializing such as *galsah* gatherings and leisurely visits to a library or bookshop relied on the privilege of Dhufari men to circulate in public spaces without the risk of the varying degrees of social stigma that women faced. Moreover, not all ex-revolutionaries wanted to participate in egalitarian socializing. Returnee ex-Front members had divergent postwar trajectories. Some—among them some of the men I encountered in Salalah—lived in economic precarity as they struggled to secure long-term employment. At the other end of the spectrum, Yusuf bin ʿAlawi and ʿAbd al-ʿAziz al-Rawwas held ministerial portfolios. Meanwhile, the former revolutionary turned businessman, Hafidh, lived in opulence across several countries and cities, including a Salalah mansion next to the grandiose residences of Sultan Qaboos's maternal relatives. To my knowledge, those ex-revolutionaries who enjoyed the sultan's close political and economic favor did not partake in the egalitarian-oriented everyday socializing that I observed among other former revolutionaries.

Even when they reproduced social egalitarianism in their everyday socializing, ex-militants might pursue other goals in parallel. Some former revolutionaries networked among themselves (and presumably with others) to seek material benefit for themselves or for their family. When one veteran got to know of my acquaintance with the economically privileged Hafidh, he used this renewed connection to speak on the telephone with Hafidh and ask for help in seeking work for his unemployed son. Veterans of the Front could also resemble nonveterans in reproducing hierarchical social relations. When I saw ex-revolutionaries interact with servants from the Indian subcontinent, their manner could be as distant as that of the majority of Dhufaris whom I observed in such situations. Despite the Front's international renown for the promotion of gender egalitarianism, postwar female veterans regretted lost equality.[38] Some complained that male veterans' long-term commitment to gender equality failed to extend to them taking on their share of women's domestic burdens.[39] Where the lives of some of Dhufar's ex-revolutionaries evinced lasting legacies of revolutionary values of social egalitarianism, this impact was partial, patchy, and incomplete. Indeed, even when a revolution achieves anti-colonial and liberation goals, it can still strike its supporters as "unfinished."[40]

To what extent were daily enactments of social egalitarianism distinctive to veterans of Dhufar's revolution? In the Oman of Sultan Qaboos, in theory all Omanis were equal with respect to being citizens and subjects of the state (with some exceptions, though).[41] Social mixing did occur in school and university, student dormitories, and places of employment. Nevertheless, in Salalah, as elsewhere in Oman and in the Gulf monarchies more broadly, both official claims of formal equality and practical experiences of cooperation in places of work and study existed in tension with hierarchies in everyday lived experience.[42] Hierarchical patronage networks encompassed Omanis. This patronage was particularly prominent in Dhufar as the target of extensive counterinsurgency redistributive patronage. Front veterans participated in those very patronage networks.

In this context, the socially egalitarian values of veteran revolutionaries stood out. Dhufari observers, as well as former members of the Front, acknowledged this. In the words of one middle-aged male interlocutor, Nabil, who spoke from a position of feeling no close ties to the Front but with a tone of kindness: "Their culture is different" (*Thaqafat-hum ghair*). Mutual cautiousness during my conversations with former members of the Front meant that I had limited opportunity to ask them directly about the reproduction of social egalitarianism. But when I broached this theme during a one-on-one conversation with one former revolutionary, he confirmed that, as he put it, "we [the people from the Front] don't care if someone is black or white, red or yellow."

Afterlives of revolution, then, emerge from the everyday with its conflicting potential for reproduction, creativity, contradiction, and subversion. Decades after the Front's efforts to *create* new kinds of socially inclusive everyday interactions, the egalitarian-leaning spirit of the Front lived on in former militants' inclusive everyday socializing and other daily interactions. By *reproducing* social egalitarianism, these acts *subverted* Dhufar's prevalent tribal, status group, ethnic, racialized, and, to an extent, gendered distinctions and hierarchies. These everyday interactions *contradicted* official narratives that the story of the revolution was long finished.

In the Dhufari context, men had privileged access to unstigmatized circulation in public spaces. As such, all-male everyday interactions in a *galsah*, library, or bookshop had limited potential for enacting the gendered egalitarianism for which the Dhufar revolution was once famed. Instead, that task might require extraordinary action.

Extraordinary Acts: "It is a woman's right to go anywhere"

Vestiges of the erstwhile revolutionary promotion of radical gender equality could be initially hard to see in postwar Salalah, despite official proclamations of the equality of all Omanis. In practice, everyday gendered inequalities in Dhufar restricted the unstigmatized circulation of women's faces, names, and identities to a greater degree than was the case in parts of Oman such as Muscat.

In early twenty-first-century Salalah, it was rare to see a woman circulate in public with her face uncovered or sitting at the steering wheel of a car. Both sights were common among Omani women in Muscat, however. In fact, like some *sumur*, some Dhufari women experienced northern Oman as a space where they could avoid some of the constraints that they faced on a daily basis in Dhufar. Some women I met who covered their faces in public in Dhufar chose not to do so when in Muscat or further afield.[43] But Dhufari women might face consequences from family members or strangers if, when in Dhufar, they failed to adhere to local protocol regarding the public circulation expected of their social status. One young male interlocutor advised me that if I were circulating alone in Salalah, I should not wear an *'abayah* and head scarf but should dress in a (modest) way that nevertheless showed I was a (white) westerner. This way, he reasoned, I could avoid the hostile reactions that he anticipated could befall a figure whom passersby might perceive to be an unaccompanied, and therefore morally suspect, local woman.

The extent to which a Dhufari woman's reputation for propriety rested on her seclusion from public circulation varied according to a woman's tribe, ethnicity, racialized identity, and generation. Women of prestigious social status from both town and mountain backgrounds faced greater expectations of seclusion from public circulation in the city. Nevertheless, families of mountain backgrounds considered it socially acceptable for female relatives to drive. Dhufaris understood their greater mobility as an extension of mountain tribes' more permissive gender norms in specific areas of social life.[44] Racialized stigma against *sumur* women meant that they lacked the social privilege that made public circulation so stigmatizing for higher-ranking women. Thus, the few women driving around Salalah were usually of either *sumur* or mountain background. The few women circulating with their faces uncovered were usually *sumur*.[45] The anxieties around the public circulation of socially privileged women shaped the gendered division of labor in Salalah. Women may have borne most of the care responsibilities in the home while men socialized outside at night, but public-facing care activities, such as the school run and the weekly food shop, were male-dominated.

TABLE 5. Female Labor Force Participation (FLP) in Dhufar and in Oman, 2014–19

Year	% FLP in Dhufar	% FLP in Oman
2014	33.59	31.53
2015	34.61	33.75
2016	32.62	32.51
2017	33.07	32.85
2018	32.87	32.94
2019	33.14	33.36

Source: National Centre for Statistics and Information, Sultanate of Oman.

Anxieties around women's public circulation did not preclude Dhufari women who had acquired suitable educational experience, either in revolutionary schools or under Sultan Qaboos, from participating in waged labor outside the home. By the time of my fieldwork, their rates of labor force participation were comparable to, and sometimes higher than, those among their northern peers (see Table 5). But the manner of these generations' growing incorporation into the labor force nonetheless reiterated rather than undermined gendered and racialized inequalities.[46] Dhufari women of non-*sumur* background tended to work in sectors with a strong female presence such as teaching, banking, and government work. These women avoided female-dominated but stigmatized sectors such as nursing and retail, where many of their *sumur* peers worked. Female wages could also end up subsidizing male relatives. Some married and unmarried female workers of non-*sumur* status explained to me that it was common for them to pay a portion of their salary directly to their father or a brother, every month.[47] Amid such evidence of women's gendered and racialized positionings and vulnerabilities, where were the legacies in Dhufar of the erstwhile revolutionary agenda for gender equality?

Female former revolutionaries had returned to Qaboos's Oman with high levels of educational attainment. Their education—and, perhaps, their broader revolutionary experiences—equipped them to challenge early postwar restrictions around women's circulation in public life. In the 1970s and 1980s waged female labor force participation outside the home was stigmatized for Dhufari women except for those of *sumur* or similarly low status. Despite this stigma, women graduates of revolutionary educational programs who hailed from diverse backgrounds helped meet shortages of skilled labor. They worked as teachers, doctors, engineers, and administrators.

Nevertheless, female former militants and participants in insurgencies often face higher barriers than their male counterparts in gaining social acceptance in postwar civilian life.[48] Female graduates of Dhufar's revolution were no exception. One male former revolutionary commented to me that female former militants had faced painful stigma on their return because of their revolutionary histories. After meeting many veteran revolutionaries, Mona Jabob concluded that "the female graduates of Revolution Camp who exemplified women's liberation in the Dhufar revolution are currently some of the women in Dhufar who adhere most to traditions, customs, and signs of religiosity. . . . They consider that they were under the hammer of blurred vision and the anvil of encouragement and intimidation."[49] This conservatism, Jabob concedes, did not prevent these women from working in selected fields. But Dhufari female veteran revolutionaries, it seems, addressed potential stigma by turning to a familiar compromise. They compensated for a behavior that might elicit controversy (here, working outside the home) with visible adherence to conservative gender norms.[50]

Conformity with gendered religious conservatism did not just provide spiritual rewards; it was also a means of claiming the social respectability that these women's revolutionary antecedents and unusual labor force participation otherwise jeopardized in the eyes of Dhufari critics. Female revolutionary graduates' precocious labor force participation therefore pioneered more than female waged labor. By combining waged labor with religious conservatism, former female revolutionaries also advanced a legitimization of female labor force incorporation conditional upon making spaces of female labor complicit with conservative gender norms. The gendered afterlives of Dhufar's revolution entailed not only the progressivism of former female revolutionaries' pioneering labor force participation. Gendered afterlives also encompassed these women's compromises and the conservatism of their meticulous piety.

Gender-segregated everyday socializing, the stigmatization of women's public circulation, and the conservative compromises of ex-revolutionary women were rife in postwar Dhufar. This situation might seem to offer limited opportunities for promoting a bold feminist position that chimed either with revolutionary gender equality programs or with the letter of Qaboos's law. To promote a feminist position could require turning to extraordinary action. Dhufari journalist Susan Al Shahri did exactly that. She pioneered advocacy for the cessation of female genital cutting that, while illegal in hospitals, is still common in Dhufar.[51] Another Dhufari woman who was intent upon sending the feminist message that, in her own words, "it is a woman's right to go anywhere," was Fahima. She took the extraordinary action of running for election to national office.

Since the revolution, very few women in Dhufar have run for election to national office. At the time of writing so far none from Dhufar have won a seat. Women from Muscat have achieved some electoral success, though.[52] It is hard to anonymize the story of any of Dhufar's trailblazing female electoral candidates. Not only are there very few of them, but also the very act of candidacy by default circulates a name in public. Fahima stood out all the more because her social background was unique among the already small pool of women candidates. As the only interlocutor in this book for whom I discuss an extraordinary action that was already part of Dhufar's public domain, I cannot anonymize Fahima for those already familiar with postwar Dhufari society and politics. Those readers already have access to Dhufaris' networks of information and to knowledge about electoral candidates and their backgrounds. For such readers, the book reveals no hitherto unavailable information about this woman's identity, background, and action. I refer to her through a pseudonym in an effort to offer her anonymity in the eyes of readers less familiar with Dhufar.

The impossibility of full anonymity for Fahima made the decision as to whether to include her story in this book weigh especially heavily on me. I was mindful that Fahima had consented to tell me her story—and that she flagged to me that she enjoyed the sultan's protection. I also considered how to avoid risk to interlocutors by including only information that was already available to concerned parties in Oman. On that basis, I decided to include her story along with some of Dhufaris' additional context. But I omit some details of that context that were sensitive for Fahima and her family for personal or political reasons. In making this decision, I found some reassurance in the eventual intervention of the sultan in Fahima's favor. His involvement allows those who are so inclined to locate Fahima's story in an alternative narrative. Differently contextualized, her story conforms with official government silence about the revolution and its afterlives, as well as with praise for Qaboos. Such an alternative narrative would focus on how Fahima's story demonstrates the support of Sultan Qaboos and the Omani state for all citizens, whatever their background.

In 1994, Sultan Qaboos extended candidacy for Oman's National Council (*majlis al-shura*) to women across the country.⁵³ The first pioneering women to run for election in Dhufar in 1997 and in 2000 were *sumur* women. The very exclusion of *sumur* women from significant forms of social and economic privilege meant that they did not face the pressures of a tribe that opposed the circulation of their names and faces in public. Such tribal pressures made the candidacy of women from non-*sumur* backgrounds all the rarer.⁵⁴ The candidacy of women from elite town or mountain backgrounds—the tribes placing greatest pressure on women to avoid circulating in public—was particularly elusive.⁵⁵ When we met in 2015, Fahima remained the only Dhufari woman candidate hailing from a high-ranking tribe (whether town or mountain) to have run in a mixed-gender contest for election to national office.

I learned of Fahima's candidacy through my interest in contextualizing revolutionary legacies within wider postrevolutionary platforms for progressive politics. Eager to meet Fahima, I sought mutual contacts to request an introduction and interview. An interlocutor, Zaid, turned out to be her relative. He gained her permission for me to accompany him at a meeting with her. Zaid remained with us throughout the meeting.

Fahima was the founder and director of a successful and growing business. Zaid arranged for us to meet at her workplace. Zaid and I arrived on the premises a little before Fahima. A senior manager, of Egyptian nationality, welcomed us and settled us into comfortable padded leather-style armchairs in a spacious reception area. A Dhufari female employee dressed in a fashionably patterned *'abayah* brought us some refreshments before retiring. After a short while Fahima arrived, clad in a black *'abayah*. Her face was uncovered. I noted that her head scarf was neatly fixed with pins, preventing the possibility of any slippage. It was difficult to surmise her age, but in the course of the conversation I learned that she was a grandmother and that her professional career spanned four decades.

We settled into a two-hour discussion. We spoke in Arabic, with occasional interjections from Zaid to me in English when he wanted to elaborate on Fahima's words or to stress his own interpretation. At first Fahima and Zaid discussed Fahima's business. She had founded it in the early 1990s. The company had recently moved to the current premises. Zaid asked about the rent, and Fahima discussed the costs and how much she had borrowed from the bank to secure the move. She explained what made her business distinctive among competitors. For such an evidently accomplished business owner and developer, the beginnings of her career had nevertheless not been smooth.

In the 1980s she had worked for the government ministry active in the field in which she would later found her company. At that time, her husband received some visitors: "Men from my tribe came to my husband and told him that they would give him the money for my salary, so that I would stop working." She refused to stop working and objected to such attempts to control her movements. "I go anywhere. I don't fear anyone," she insisted. She repeated these phrases over the course of the interview. Once Fahima decided to set up her own business, she encountered a further obstacle. "When I went [to the government office] to get the permit to start the business, they did not want to give the permit to a woman." This reaction foreshadowed some of the difficulties that she would encounter when setting out to become an electoral candidate. Regarding levels of acceptance of women in the workplace Fahima nevertheless added: "Things are much better now. There are women working everywhere now."

When conversation turned to the elections, Fahima set my expectations for the interview. She told me: "I don't remember much about the elections—I've been focused on the business for the past years." The crux of her candidacy was nevertheless clear. She repeatedly stressed her support for women's emancipation and participation in public life, including in the National Council. "I ran for election to send a message to girls [*banat*] that nothing is impossible for us, that it is a woman's right to go anywhere.... We [women] are humans [*bashar*], we should have a presence in the Parliament [National Council]."[56]

But just as conservative Dhufaris had earlier opposed her professional career, so they opposed her candidacy for election. When Fahima went to register as a candidate, the government official responsible for registering candidates turned out to be a kinsman. When she presented herself in his office, he at first told her the name of their tribe's candidate, that is, the candidate whom tribal leaders had agreed to field as their internally approved candidate. Fahima replied that she knew that the tribal leaders had selected this man, but that she was there to register her name. The official initially refused to write down her name as a candidate. She did not waver, telling him: "I'm in the governor's office and it is your job to write my name down."

Fahima told me that she directed her message "that it is a woman's right to go anywhere" to "girls" (*banat*). But she found little support from the Dhufari branch of the Women's League. She explained: "I went to the Women's League and they said no [we won't support you], we are with are tribes [a reference to the predominance of tribe-based electoral leagues]." In the year she ran—2007—Salalah's tribe-based electoral leagues had acquired renewed importance. The leagues of prestigious tribes faced competition from a coalition representing non-elite tribes. The latter ultimately successfully supported the first popularly elected black Omani of enslaved descent to become a member of the National Council.[57] Fahima recalled how this intense mobilization of tribal networks across elites and non-elites affected her: "We didn't win. I knew I wouldn't win. No one supported me."

Her resistance to the marginalization of women in Dhufar's public life did not end with her defeat in the polls, however. After the election she appeared in a television interview in which she argued that "the tribal leagues are against us women. Women will never win [while these leagues operate]." She went on to describe how many people in Dhufar criticized her for making these comments. Amid this ongoing criticism, in 2009, Sultan Qaboos sent her an invitation to meet him. Zaid intervened to explain: "The Sultan invited her because he knows what goes on here, he knows that people were against her."

At first Fahima delayed meeting the sultan on the grounds of family commitments. But the sultan repeated his invitation. In her words: "They told me: 'It's your duty to the country [*al-watan*] to go.' And so I went." At the meeting, she and Sultan Qaboos discussed ways to encourage women's participation in political life. After the meeting with the sultan, when she returned to Dhufar, "no one said a word," Fahima told us, dramatically drawing her fingers across her lips in a gesture imitating the way her critics had suddenly turned silent.

Fahima had clearly already demonstrated in her professional life the sentiment "I don't fear anyone. I go anywhere." Why, then, had she opted to reiterate this message by running for election? Hoping to broach this question, I first asked her about the women candidates who had run before her. Fahima acknowledged that previously Salalah had seen two female candidates. Turning to Zaid, rather than addressing me, she added that these women were black, and immediately acknowledged the sensitivity of calling out this racialized identity by telling him "I say things frankly." Seizing this opportunity to broach the sensitive question of social hierarchies, I replied that, speaking frankly for my part, I wanted to ask if she was the first woman from a "strong" tribe to run for election. Fahima confirmed that this was the case. This led me to ask more about the barriers for these women to run, and why she was different in overcoming them.

AW: In your view, why don't women from "strong" tribes run for election?
Fahima: In the past, these women were dominated [being controlled, *yusaytirun 'alaihim*]. But now, I don't know why they don't run.
Zaid: There are two reasons: Basically, women follow their husbands. The second reason is that these tribes, because they have an electoral league, have already chosen their candidates—so even if a woman wanted to run, the tribes will have chosen a man.
AW: But why haven't other women from this background done like you, to send a message to girls?

Both Fahima and Zaid paused at this question. When Fahima spoke, she reflected on the importance of the support that she received from her husband and male kin. "I went to my husband when I wanted to run and told him that I wanted to run. My husband said to me: 'If you can face the consequences, go ahead.' I went to my brothers and asked the same thing, and they also said, 'If you can face the consequences, go ahead.'" She continued, explaining that, once she ran, many people criticized her, in addition to criticizing her husband and her brothers. "Many people came to me and said 'You don't have any men [to protect you]. If you had men [who cared about you], they would stop you.' I told them: 'I have men, and the best men. They trust me and have confidence in me.'" She went on to describe the context for that confidence. In general, she and her husband consulted with one another. She sought her husband's opinion, and he gave her advice. Also, she used her freedom judiciously: "I come to the office, I sit with the manager alone for two hours. At the end of the afternoon, I am at home, I read." She stressed the balance between her busy professional life and the irreproachability of her personal life.

Still struck by the extraordinary nature of her actions in the Dhufari context, and as the interview drew to a close, I asked again:

AW: Why are you different? Where did your openness come from?
Fahima: From my father, from his culture. He brought me up that way.
AW: Where did this openness come from in your husband?
Fahima: He is my father's brother's son, he was brought up the same way.

AW: Has this openness affected your daughters?
Fahima: Two are teachers and one is a doctor.

Fahima's was an extraordinary story. Demonstrating that she feared no one, she embraced an explicitly feminist message that "it is a woman's right to go anywhere." Her explanation for her determination to convey this message—namely that her father brought her up that way and that her husband was raised in the same way—nevertheless left unanswered questions. The contrast with other families of similarly elite background was unmissable. In families of comparable elite background, it was more common for me to hear views about women's roles that reflected deep conservatism. For instance, one young man of such background once told me: "[I]f my sister drives, I will kill her." And an older man recounted to me: "I told my wife [who was from a different tribe] that if she didn't vote for my tribe, it would be as if she had gone back to her family [i.e., that I would divorce her]." What made Fahima's upbringing and the men in her family so different?

Hers was in fact no ordinary upbringing. As I had been talking to interlocutors to try and find a way to meet Fahima, some had shared with me further information about her family. Other Dhufaris placed Fahima and key members of her family in the context of a revolutionary past in which different generations of the family had taken part in the Front, its leadership, its armed forces, and its revolutionary schools. As Fahima did not mention a connection to the revolution to me, I refrained from introducing this sensitive topic to our conversation. For the same reason, I have omitted here the details that others shared with me about the relationship of specific family members, including Fahima, to the Front. More important for the present discussion is to stress how the revolutionary past in which Dhufaris placed this family helps address the otherwise unanswered questions as to why this family was so different from many peers.

With concision and political discretion, Fahima attributed her openness to her upbringing. Other Dhufaris contextualized her family within a revolutionary past. The two explanations are not contradictory, but compatible. Her pioneering career across the public and private sector had begun forty years earlier. At that time, virtually the only Dhufari women who had accessed the formal education necessary for such professional activity were graduates from revolutionary educational programs. She carefully flagged her personal propriety, from her carefully pinned hijab to her evenings spent at home reading. She also avoided mentioning the Front. Both strategies echoed wider patterns of discretion and compromise in the carefully negotiated postwar lives of Dhufari women who traced family or personal histories in the revolution.

By her own admission, Fahima's determination to "send a message that it is a woman's right to go anywhere" sprang from her family background. Her family had cultivated feminist consciousness in her, her brothers, and her husband. Yet if, like other Dhufaris, we locate Fahima in a context of her family's revolutionary past, her story also brings to the fore the intersectionality at stake in the afterlives of revolution. Men could reproduce revolutionary values of tribal, ethnic, and racialized social egalitarianism through everyday socializing. By contrast, the promotion of gendered egalitarianism was most visible when women and men undertook or supported extraordinary action. At the same time, privilege underpinned the afterlives of revolution in an extraordinary act such as Fahima's electoral candidacy, just as was the case in everyday *galsah* gatherings. Fahima was a woman with high educational capital and independent income from her own business. Neither a public nor private sector employer could dismiss her. She hailed from a family enjoying sufficiently close personal connections to the sultan for him to learn that she faced backlash and intervene in her favor. Privileges placed Fahima in a stronger position than many to "face the consequences" of challenging Dhufar's everyday hierarchies and inequalities.

Intersectionality, Privilege, and Ambiguity

Everyday interactions have been a crucial sphere for attempts to create and experience revolutionary change and the enactment of related values. When revolutionaries have eventually failed to achieve the political and economic transformation to which they aspired, their values have the potential to survive in contexts such as workers' forums. Bringing these insights to bear on the analysis of Dhufar's former revolutionaries sheds further light on revolution and its afterlives.

The everyday plays a key role in the afterlives of revolution. Politically marginalized and repressed former revolutionaries can draw on everyday interactions to reproduce revolutionary values of social egalitarianism. In Dhufar, some former revolutionaries met nightly in a socially diverse group, dropped in on one another in spaces such as a bookshop or library, and made linguistic and social choices that reflected support for gender equality.

They thereby drew on the everyday to create afterlives of revolution in the form of ongoing values of social egalitarianism.

It follows that quotidian interactions are not always the means for restoring a social world that has been threatened by political violence. The everyday can also help continue legacies of a social world that came into being through revolutionary activism. This was the case in Dhufar.

Such possibilities arise because of the conflicting complexities of the everyday as a crucible for reproduction, creativity, contradiction, and subversion. These contrasting possibilities foreground the potential of the ordinary to acquire extraordinary effects. The lines between the ordinary and the extraordinary, the normal and the abnormal, often blur in contexts of political violence and its aftermath.[58] In retrospect, it is hard to gauge the changing meanings over time of everyday interactions in Dhufar's revolutionary schools, military training, battalions, and workplaces. To what extent did Dhufaris continue to experience interactions there as novel? Or did those everyday interactions eventually come to feel "normal" during the revolution? In the postwar context, it is certain that the distinction between the ordinary and extraordinary was blurred. The ordinary everyday socializing of former revolutionaries became the means for reproducing what in the Dhufari context were extraordinary values of social egalitarianism.

Yet the potential of the everyday is specific to a given historical context. Socioeconomic status, gender, ethnicity, race, generation, and sexuality, among other social differences, inflect and constrain the experiences of the everyday. It follows that the experience of not only revolution but also its afterlives is intersectional. Dhufar's former revolutionaries and their relatives were positioned differently according to gender, generation, status group, tribe, ethnicity, and racialized identity. This affected their scope to create and participate in revolutionary afterlives. Predominant expectations in Dhufar stipulated that women should not circulate in public without facing stigma that varied in line with their status group, ethnicity, and racialized identity. Accordingly, those wishing to enact values of gendered egalitarianism sometimes had to go beyond everyday interactions and instead undertake extraordinary acts. Female former revolutionaries who pioneered labor force participation in the 1970s and 1980s, and Fahima who ran for election, undertook such extraordinary acts. Their actions stood out to Dhufaris, who called my attention to them. Through divergent means, women and men created different kinds of afterlives of revolution that reflect gendered and other intersectional subjectivities.

The intersectionality of the afterlives of revolution is a reminder that in the aftermath of the "privilege of revolution" comes the privilege of revolutionary afterlives.[59] Privilege can underpin the very possibility of creating and participating in afterlives of revolution, whether in everyday interactions or extraordinary acts. In Dhufar such privilege ranged from male access to public spaces to high socio-educational capital, independent income, and family connections within the sultan's sphere of protection. These privileges existed alongside the wider political vulnerability and marginalization of many former revolutionaries.

Whatever privileges underpinned them, afterlives of revolution in this context of political repression harbored ambiguity. Everyday and extraordinary actions that reproduced revolutionary values of social egalitarianism often blended with nonrevolutionary discourses or conventions. Male ex-revolutionaries' inclusive daily socializing transgressed Dhufar's everyday tribal, ethnic, and racialized hierarchies. Yet it also overlapped with men's quotidian evening gatherings. Fahima's defiance of social pressure to exclude women, and especially those of high-ranking tribal backgrounds, from public life reflected a family background that other Dhufaris identified as revolutionary. But it also mirrored official sultan-approved rhetoric of gender equality. Ex-revolutionaries' "different culture" of ordinary and extraordinary actions that reproduced social egalitarianism could often pass as part of wider, less politically controversial phenomena.

It was difficult to discern whether former revolutionaries intentionally created social camouflage for everyday and extraordinary actions that disrupted Dhufar's everyday hierarchies and reproduced revolutionary values. Political constraints hung over all my conversations with veteran militants. In the context of surveillance and repression, in practical terms a degree of social camouflage may have been inevitable. Ambiguity may also have been a contributing factor to the authorities' tolerance for these actions.

Social camouflage might make the afterlives of revolution not immediately apparent. So indeed might their subtlety. Vestiges of Dhufar's revolutionary feminism might initially seem elusive. Female graduates of Revolution Camp recalled that they had been under pressure and adopted conservative postwar behaviors. Male peers apparently disappointed their wives with their lack of participation in everyday domestic tasks. But alongside resurgent conservatism, feminist consciousness did survive among both men and women. Fahima's narrative acknowledged the enabling support of her husband and her brothers for her own feminist actions. Their support was a feminist act in its own right. Men as well as women with revolutionary histories undertook extraordinary action that evinced feminist consciousness. These feminist afterlives of revolution took place in homes as well as in the public gaze.

Finally, the ongoing investment of some former militants in revolutionary social values foregrounds counterhistories of Dhufar's revolution and its aftermath. Official narratives in Oman, and the analyses of some scholars and British veterans, have asserted that the revolution's socialist program had little appeal for Dhufaris. Yet the everyday and extraordinary actions of Dhufaris who hailed from revolutionary histories suggest otherwise. As their choices demonstrated, enacting values of social egalitarianism that the revolution had earlier pioneered remained both important and possible. The Conclusion addresses the wider ongoing appeal of these values for Dhufaris and other Omanis who discussed and pursued them in diverse social and political forums. Before that, the next chapter examines the lasting influence of the revolution as this manifested in the unofficial commemoration of the revolutionary past.

6

Resources of Unofficial Commemoration

"THEY SAY OF THEMSELVES: 'We sacrificed for our people.'" This was how one interlocutor described former Front members' beliefs that, as revolutionaries, they had sacrificed for a cause that they understood in terms of a greater collective good. Yet what opportunity was there in postwar Oman to remember and commemorate revolutionaries' claimed sacrifices? Government narratives offered no acknowledgment whatsoever. Wartime official narratives had cast revolutionaries as communist terrorists who threatened stability and morality—hardly national heroes. Postwar official narratives cloaked the revolution in silence, even eschewing to dwell on the government's victory. Instead, postwar official commemoration celebrated Sultan Qaboos as the putative author of Oman's modernization. Dhufaris convinced of former revolutionaries' sacrifices and contributions thus faced a dilemma: what is to be done with the dead and those who have sacrificed, but who do not fit dominant national narratives?

This dilemma hangs over the fraught commemorative landscapes of societies living in the aftermath of organized political violence. How does one live with "political ghosts," the dead who are absent in public discourse but who leave traces in intimate lives?[1] How do people claim and debate martyrdom for those of "disputed grievability?"[2] Such dilemmas, which former revolutionaries in Oman faced, raise wider questions. In politically hostile circumstances, what are the possibilities *for* commemoration (what can people do) and what are the possibilities *of* commemoration (what effects do those acts have)? When no *official* commemoration is possible, what resources are available for *unofficial* commemoration, and to what ends?

It is not straightforward to seek answers to such questions in any postwar or authoritarian setting, including in Oman. Interlocutors did not speak to me explicitly about commemorating the revolutionary past. Such reticence was prudent in the context of the government's repression of the Front and its surveillance of all Omanis. The imprisonment of 'Abdullah Habib, who had called for private mourning at the graves of executed revolutionaries, provided a stark reminder of the risks of advocating in Oman for the commemoration of former revolutionaries. Yet Dhufaris found ways to improvise an unofficial commemoration of the revolutionary past. When Oman's authorities tolerated such acts, they apparently did not find in them cause for concern. Yet for those seeking to understand revolution and its afterlives, as well as the possibilities for and of commemoration, these acts are of great interest indeed.

First, an exploration of the historical and political contexts for unofficial commemoration helps retrieve marginalized counterhistories. Postwar unofficial commemoration in Dhufar arose in the wake of prior histories of the Front's official revolutionary commemoration in its liberated and exilic spaces. The shift in revolution-focused commemoration from official to unofficial raises questions: what happens to cultures of commemoration when hostile governing authorities silence them? Can a past official commemoration that a subsequent government has repressed go on to have legacies in unofficial forms? Acknowledgment of previous official commemoration and of subsequent unofficial commemoration challenges conventional historical narratives. Official postwar commemoration lauds Sultan Qaboos while marginalizing the revolution. But in practice, many Dhufaris' experiences of national commemoration (as well as of other activities of statecraft) began not with Qaboos, but with the Front. Furthermore, explanations of the rise of Oman's sultan-focused commemorative culture should address not only the strategies and preferences of Qaboos and his British advisors. The Front's thriving commemoration culture was also a contributing pressure. A focus on unofficial commemoration foregrounds multiple counterhistories.

Second, by challenging a chain of absences regarding the revolution in postwar commemoration, unofficial commemoration creates afterlives of revolution. Official revolutionary commemoration declined and finally ceased with the end of the Front's formal activities in exile in 1992. Meanwhile, alternative commemorative fields became prominent. But, to different degrees, each of these fields neglects, misrepresents, or underrepresents the experiences of revolutionaries in Dhufar. Official commemoration in

Oman silenced the revolution. Counterinsurgency memoirs orientalized Front members. Sympathizers of the revolution, including some former members of the Front, published novels, memoirs, and studies that engaged more closely with experiences of revolutionaries. But at the time of writing, no Dhufari former member of the Front who was in Dhufar during the revolution has published such work under his or her name. Unofficial commemoration challenges this chain of absences. Finding a way around the obstacles that blocked official commemoration of the revolutionary past, former revolutionaries and other Dhufaris in Oman drew on "cultural resources" to perform unofficial commemoration.[3] This repertoire included the everyday social experience of space, the circulation of written and oral texts, and circumlocutory activities such as jokes and euphemisms that stood in lieu of more conventional commemoration. There were also more recognizable commemorative acts, such as funerals and ritual hosting to mark former revolutionaries' return to Dhufar. This unofficial commemoration created afterlives of revolution.

Third, the Dhufari case calls for greater acknowledgment of the unofficial within commemoration studies. Much analysis to date concerns commemoration that is not subject to official prohibition, often in contexts of increased recognition or urgency for commemoration. These contexts have influenced expectations of the effects and qualities of commemoration for cultivating collective identities, loyalties, and resistances. Unofficial commemoration in contexts of political repression, however, challenges such expectations. In unofficial commemoration, the elaboration of identities, loyalties, or resistances may be ambiguous, and perhaps purposefully or unavoidably so. Yet acknowledging unofficial commemoration—however "uncommemorative" it sometimes appears—is vital for understanding not just the afterlives of revolution. It also illuminates the broader possibilities for transmitting to future generations knowledge about an officially silenced past. Attention to the unofficial helps decolonize commemoration.

Locating Unofficial Commemoration

Acts of commemoration are "ritual performances that evoke and reenact the past."[4] These acts often have distinctive effects and qualities. Commemoration helps transmit collective or social memory, that is, memories about the past that persons cocreate through social interaction.[5] Durkheimian interpretations have highlighted that in producing, legitimizing, and disseminating hegemonic narratives about the past, present, and future, commemoration fosters collective identities, communities, and solidarities.[6] These effects typically rest on commemoration's qualities as public, performative, and ritual. Commemoration concerns "*public* performances, rituals, and narratives."[7] Acts of commemoration "prove to be commemorative (only) in so far as they are performative."[8] Rituals, such as those embedded in religion or social relations that outlast an individual lifespan, institutionalize these public performances. In addition, there is usually explicit clarity around the subject of commemoration, such as the persons or events at stake. Differences in the interpretation or selection of subjects may make commemoration "multivocal" (when different audiences attribute diverse meanings to a shared commemorative context) or "fragmented" (when different commemorative contexts arise about the past, addressing disparate audiences).[9] Beyond such disparities, the underlying principles still hold of commemoration as a public performative ritual with the potential to foster social memory and collective identity.

These effects and qualities have made commemoration especially important for ethnic, religious, and political groups for whom collective identity and solidarity is strategic for ongoing legitimacy. Prominent among these are nation-state projects, with their cultivation of national identities and narratives. Beyond differences of democratic or authoritarian style, existing or anticipated international recognition, and the sincerity or cynicism of audience participation, actual or aspiring state authorities invest heavily in commemoration.[10] State authorities enjoy privileged opportunities to institutionalize commemoration in "*lieux de mémoire*"—sites such as history books, museums, and monuments that construct public and collective memories of the past.[11] These sites function through strategies of inclusion and exclusion. In anti-colonial and postcolonial contexts, official commemoration and *lieux de mémoire* often glorify liberation warfare and key figures of liberation and socialism such as Lenin and Mao.[12] But once governing authorities have defeated an armed opposition, vanquished veteran fighters occupy a sensitive place in national postwar narratives.[13] Some governments marginalize and exclude such veterans from national narratives altogether.[14] In Oman, official commemorative narratives omit histories of dissent, such as the imamate opposition to the Muscat-based Sultans.[15] In Dhufar in particular, the Front had institutionalized public performances and rituals to commemorate its liberation struggle. But after the counterinsurgency victory, Dhufar's revolution joined the list of episodes of dissent that government authorities excluded from official commemorative narratives.[16]

The effects and qualities of commemoration, and its consequent significance for collective identities and narratives, have shaped the centers of gravity within commemoration studies. There is usually some degree of official tolerance, or at least a lack of efficacious official prohibition, for the commemoration under study. In addition, recognition for that commemoration has often become politically or historically urgent. The threatened loss of a generation or of a group's very existence brings urgency to commemoration, often with the injunction "not to forget" past atrocities. This was the case in the creation in the 1990s of new memorials and museums addressing the Holocaust and WWII atrocities.[17] But urgency may arise from the advent of greater freedoms of expression and association during political transitions. These invite new forms of commemoration, such as in the wake of perestroika, apartheid, and dictatorship.[18] Such political opening can encourage ethnic, religious, or sexual minorities to engage in commemorative acts such as public protests or the opening of a new museum. These actions aim to overcome these groups' marginalization from official narratives.[19] The urgency of commemoration in some postwar environments, though, is not necessarily a sign of political aperture. Rather, it may signal state authorities' need to legitimize postwar power relations and reconciliation narratives.[20] In Oman, most analysis of commemoration has focused on the sultan-centric corpus that the government encourages. This commemoration was politically urgent as a means of generating legitimacy for Qaboos and of imposing the postwar narrative of national unity under his rule.

A focus on historically or politically urgent commemoration that state authorities either encourage, or have no choice but to tolerate, is incomplete, however. It does not allow for a full account of how people enact the meanings of the past—or refuse to do so. Other scenarios and questions demand attention.

We cannot assume that potential participants in and audiences for commemorative initiatives want to remember or commemorate the past in question. When it is too painful or dangerous to remember the past, people can refuse to remember. They may engage instead in "active forgetting."[21] In postwar Lebanon, a former member of a communist faction who found it too painful to acknowledge the contrast between the past and the present made efforts to forget not just "a simple memory of the past" but also "past ideals one held, . . . the type of person one was during the war, and the type of person one turned into, or was forced to become after the war."[22] In Peru, rural survivors of political violence during the Shining Path uprising judged it too dangerous to narrate fellow villagers' involvement to researchers from the National Truth and Reconciliation Committee. They insisted instead that "[w]e just want to forget."[23] In Dhufar, the evasive statements of some former revolutionaries in conversation with me hinted at the potential appeal of actively forgetting a sensitive past that might be painful or dangerous to remember.

Although active forgetting may sometimes prove appealing, official silence does not necessarily succeed in mandating forgetting. Even in totalitarian contexts where state authorities attempt to colonize public and private narratives, "official histories, whilst plentiful, never precluded the active construction and transmission of unofficial pasts."[24] Accordingly, those who experience public, official commemoration as frustrating or incomplete may create "dominated" *lieux de mémoire* that contrast with dominant, officially institutionalized *lieux de mémoire*.[25] A notion of "dominated" *lieux de mémoire* as "places of refuge, sanctuaries of spontaneous devotion and silent pilgrimage, where one finds the living heart of memory," is nevertheless problematic.[26] It risks romanticization and neglects the possibility of deep attachment to official commemorative ceremonies.[27] It is striking that many Omanis, including Dhufaris, passionately engaged with official sultan-centric commemoration. At the same time, though, many in the Sultanate also remembered the past in ways that fell beyond the scope of government-approved official narratives, silences, and omissions.[28] These alternative memories do not necessarily cultivate opposition to the sultan's rule. Some Omanis mourn the imamate past not for its political dissent, but for its perceived community and reciprocity such as they found lacking in their experiences of modernization.[29] The question emerges in Dhufar, and beyond, of how people may combine participation in official commemoration with the unofficial commemoration of multifarious interpretations of a revolutionary past.

The remembrance and commemoration of an officially silenced past raises an issue: "[w]hat cultural resources make it possible for ordinary people to counter official amnesia and so remember the forgotten, unmourned dead that such amnesia produces?"[30] In the context of authoritarian socialist China's silences about victims of the state's persecution, people countered official silences and commemorative omissions by drawing on available cultural resources. In Tiananmen Square in 1976 and in 1989, Chinese workers, students, and others drew on funeral commemorations as a means of expressing remembrance and, eventually, dissent.[31] Such repurposing of funeral commemorations to challenge official silences invites a wider rethinking of commemorative repertoires, with a view to exploring the breadth of cultural resources that challenge official silences. Such rethinking can expand commemoration studies into scenarios where political aperture is lacking, but where people nevertheless evoke the meaning of an officially silenced past.

Among the cultural resources of commemoration is the very experience of social space. Especially in conflict settings, "historical memory" can be "mass-produced" in ways that span not merely the official commemoration of "place names, memorials" and "almost every calendrical observance," but also "people's choice of residence and spouse."[32] When people relive aspects of past conflict in their daily lives, their "entire social space" can become "sites of memory."[33] The potential of social space for commemoration invites inquiry into its provision of cultural resources for the unofficial commemoration of an officially silenced past.

Where official commemoration disappoints popular aspirations, and where there is a sufficiently permissive political environment, grassroots initiatives can promote alternative written, oral, and visual texts that supplement official commemoration. Grassroots memory books and film choices can celebrate a nationalism that encompasses identities and aspirations that diverge from those of national leadership.[34] Published personal memoirs commemorate political activism that is marginal within hegemonic national narratives.[35] Storytelling at family gatherings rehearses private memories of wartime "good old days" that belie official national insistence that war produces "no winners."[36] Such grassroots initiatives prompt consideration of practices among those without access to a permissive political environment. How might people discreetly circulate alternative written and oral texts that engage with an officially marginalized past?

In the absence of a permissive political environment, commemoration may rely on circumlocution. In the 1980s in China, an official event in honor of a philosopher that stressed his survival allowed mourners to use those discussions as a way of addressing their own survival of Mao's Cultural Revolution.[37] How, then, might jokes, suggestive omissions, and euphemisms, among Dhufaris and others, evoke the commemoration by circumlocution of an officially silenced past?

Alongside space, text, and circumlocution are more directly commemorative acts that provide resources for countering or supplementing official memories and narratives. In the Bosnian diaspora, survivors of genocide organized alternative commemorations that questioned rather than reinforced the nationalism of official commemoration.[38] Among former militants of the Liberation Tigers of Tamil Eelam, émigrés organized informal get-togethers on the movement's official commemorative dates.[39] In the context of Vietnamese state authorities' neglect of "political ghosts" (those whose civilian and anti-communist combatant deaths did not fit the category of having died fighting for national liberation), Vietnamese families commemorated these ghosts by inviting them into the space of domestic worship that ordinarily honored ancestors.[40] For these mourners, as in Tiananmen Square, existing commemoration for the deceased provided cultural resources for alternative commemoration. How might Dhufaris, alongside peers elsewhere, repurpose existing rituals to commemorate an officially silenced past?

This rereading of commemoration studies with attention to space, text, circumlocution, and ritual repurposing outlines a provisional arc for investigating the cultural resources of unofficial commemoration. The present preliminary exploration is also an invitation for future investigation of unofficial commemoration. Only by developing a theoretical sensitivity to such resources is it possible to foreground unofficial commemoration, and by extension its rich possibilities for challenging both official histories and expectations of commemoration itself. In Dhufar it was, nevertheless, not only wide-ranging cultural resources that enabled unofficial commemoration of the revolutionary past but also former revolutionaries who brought ample experience from the Front's own official commemorative program.

Revolutionary Commemoration under the Front

Dhufaris' commemorative repertoires predate the agendas of rival projects of state power in the region. The rich histories of poetry and song in MSAL include commemorative genres that mark events, deceased persons, and significant events.[41] Ritual attendance and hosting at funerals has commemorated individual persons as well as the collective identity of the community of mourners.[42] But prior to the Front, Dhufaris had little experience of commemoration focused on legitimizing state power or national (or other supra-tribal) identities. Sultan Said's statecraft in Dhufar focused on exploitation, taxation, and coercion, rather than on commemoration. The closest available experience in prerevolutionary Dhufar of commemoration linked to state power was perhaps the school that Said founded and named after himself, Salalah's al-Saidiyyah school. This establishment nevertheless was only accessible to male pupils close to the sultan's town-based entourage. As an exclusive space, the school had limited commemorative potential in the lives of most Dhufaris. The advent of the Front transformed commemorative landscapes in Dhufar.

The Front introduced Dhufaris to new forms of commemoration. Some of this repertoire reworked existing practices, such as poetry and funeral attendance, for the purposes of revolutionary commemoration.[43] Other commemorative forms drew on techniques of statecraft that had little precedent in Dhufar, such as the creation of nationally significant space and calendrical events. The movement institutionalized commemoration in both long-standing social institutions and new state-focused political institutions. Across these broad institutional forms, the Front's commemoration aimed to cultivate nationalist, anti-colonial, revolutionary, and socialist values and identities.

A survey of the Front's commemoration is lacking to date. It is beyond the scope of the present purposes to attempt a full investigation. This preliminary account of the movement's commemorative repertoire can nevertheless begin to address its historical and political significance. The movement's commemorative activities are important in their own right as a marker and frontier of decolonization efforts. They also impacted subsequent official national commemorative culture and charted possibilities for the unofficial commemoration of the revolutionary past.

The Front's commemoration was public in multiple ways. Commemoration filled public spaces. The movement gave commemorative names to strategic places. It named the military zone supply corridor that connected Dhufar's western and central mountains "Ho Chi Minh."[44] Militants originally named the revolutionary primary school after Lenin. The hospital in al-Ghaidah was named after Dhufari martyr Fatma Ghanana, and the clinic in Hawf after Dhufari martyr Habkook. Commemoration was also public in its eliciting of audience participation in events such as parades. Kamel Mohanna, who worked in the Front's clinic in Hawf in 1973, recalled a public meeting to discuss revolutionary policy. The gathering ended in a parade in which "participants held up their rifles and at which people brandished weapons in the air and chanted revolutionary songs."[45] Commemoration helped create the public spaces and audiences of revolutionary identities.

Parades also spoke to the ritual qualities of revolutionary commemoration. Commemorative ritual was woven into regular events, such as the minute's silence to honor martyrs at the beginning of a political meeting.[46] The Front further cemented commemorative ritual by establishing a revolutionary calendar. A key date was June 9, the date of the first armed action that Front discourses designated as the start of the revolution. This date not only filled public spaces, for instance in becoming the name of the intermediate school and the monthly magazine; it was also a yearly event. For the occasion, the Front doubled the broadcasting time of *Revolution Radio*.[47] The military leadership even planned military attacks to mark the date. In June 1971, a British counterintelligence report recorded: "UPSURGE OF REBEL ACTIVITY COUNCIDES [sic] WITH SIXTH ANNIVERSARY OF DHOFAR WAR ON 9 JUN."[48] Commemorative ritual linked the revolutionary past with projected futures.

The creation of revolutionary space and time were part of the Front's statecraft that helped institutionalize commemoration. National resources such as schools and health centers bore revolutionary names, but so did military battalions in the PLA. The Western and Eastern Units were initially named after Ho Chi Minh and Lenin, respectively. In November 1972, these and the Central Unit were named after Dhufari martyrs Said Giah, Said Addhahab, and 'Ali Masoud.[49] A further technique of institutionalization was the Front's use of mass media: its daily 6 p.m. to 8 p.m. *Revolution Radio* broadcast from Aden, its *9 Yunyu* monthly magazine, and *Saut al-Thawra* weekly newspaper.[50] The 1971 commemoration of June 9 saw "SPECIAL POSTAGE STAMP ISSUES IN ADEN DEPICTING PFLOAG IN ACTION."[51] This institutionalization in mass media allowed the Front to target an international audience through its newspaper *Saut al-Thawra* and magazine *9 Yunyu*, published in both Arabic and English editions (the latter under the title of *9 June*), as well as other bilingual publications.[52] The Front embraced the languages of state-led institutionalized commemoration.

In parallel, the Front institutionalized revolutionary commemoration in ways more specific to Dhufar. Revolutionary songs and poetry flourished, reworking indigenous traditions for the purposes of the revolution.[53] Revolutionary poetry served many purposes. The ambiguities of poetry and song in MSAL, replete with oblique meanings, lent themselves to Dhufaris adapting poetry for resistance. A popular form of poetry in the MSAL Shahri is *nana*.[54] Dhufaris adapted *nana* to share intelligence about counterinsurgency troop movements.[55] Poetry also became part of the corpus of commemoration. Poems in Modern Standard Arabic in Front publications glorified revolution and anti-colonialism.[56] Yet the tone of commemorative revolutionary poetry could also be playful. Revolutionary poet Abu Arif composed lines to seek forgiveness from a martyr. Unable to see clearly on a dark night, the poet had unwittingly urinated on the fallen fighter's grave.[57]

Across different varieties of Arabic and MSAL, poetry helped commemorate revolutionary persons and values.

The Front's commemorative corpus was explicit about events and people, such as June 9, Dhufari martyrs, Lenin, and Ho Chi Minh. More contested was the question of the collective identities at stake in commemorative acts. The underlying reference points spanned anti-colonial revolutionary culture and local loyalties. Discussions about the name of the primary school, the eventual official change from the Lenin School to the People's School, and ongoing informal use of the earlier name, reflected a potential tension. The parallel names spoke to the multiple collective identities at stake in the Front's commemoration. Indeed, over the course of the Front's formal activities, its commemorative and wider ambitions engaged with collective identities that spanned Dhufari, Omani, Gulf-wide, Arab, and supra-ethnicized revolutionary identities. The changes in name of the movement itself reflected the potential for overlap and tension within these identities. Having begun as the *Dhufar* Liberation Front in 1965, the movement became the Popular Front for the Liberation of the *Occupied Arabian Gulf* in 1968, and then in 1971 the Popular Front for the Liberation of *Oman and the Arabian Gulf*, and finally in 1974 the Popular Front for the Liberation of *Oman* (emphases added). The first decade of resistance and revolutionary discourse saw Dhufaris *become* Omanis. Revolutionary commemoration cultivated collective identities that changed over time.

The historical urgency of the Front's official commemoration also evolved. Initially, this commemoration was urgent in the context of the Front's need to mobilize people to fight for anti-colonial liberation—of Dhufar, then of the occupied Arabian Gulf, then of Oman. After the Front's military defeat, formal commemoration continued in exile, especially for the June 9 anniversary.[58] A large commemorative celebration event took place for the twentieth anniversary in 1985.[59] The urgency by then had shifted to the cultivation of the movement's very survival.

In such changing circumstances, reception and participation in commemoration must have varied across time and between persons. Eyewitness accounts and memoirs indicate some of the difficulties in gauging commemorative participation. On the one hand, Mohanna recalled scenes from 1973 of sociable participation in informal acts of commemoration. At night, the wounded fighters' tent at Hawf clinic became a social hub where Mohanna passed his "best evenings" as people "recorded revolutionary songs" and shared jokes.[60] The doctor also recalled a moonlit evening spent with other revolutionaries by the cave that was home to Dhufari revolutionary poet Salem al-Attar, his wife Fatma, and their son Ahmad. The poet "sang some popular songs." His audience "repeated in chorus," and the party "stayed up singing under the moonlight until late."[61] On the other hand, in his memoirs of the parade that he had observed, Mohanna recalled feeling "bitterness" at what he considered to be "signs of exaggerated collective enthusiasm."[62] In a diary entry from late 1975, when the military situation had turned against the Front, Iranian volunteer doctor Mahboubeh Afraz bemoaned that Dhufari patients and their nursing staff were not interested in listening to revolutionary broadcasts.[63] Glimpses into commemorative participation indicate its variability.

Whatever the changing reception of the Front's commemorative efforts, its leadership harbored anxieties about how to maintain Dhufaris' support for the revolution. The context for such anxieties was not simply the question of the appeal of a socialist revolution for Dhufaris, on which commentators sympathetic to the sultan's rule and the counterinsurgency have often cast doubt. In addition, counterinsurgency forces were destroying the homes and livelihoods of Dhufaris in areas of Front influence, while offering, from 1970, material benefits to Dhufaris who abandoned the Front in order to support the sultan.

Against this tense backdrop, one corollary of the Front's commemorative culture was its repression of threats to its own narratives. The parade that Mohanna recalled followed a public meeting in which leadership figures sought to justify the Front's severe punishment, including the death penalty, of those whom revolutionary authorities judged to be traitors.[64] The movement suppressed the essays of Fawwaz Trabulsi about the revolution that it deemed controversial.[65] Official commemoration went hand in hand with the Front's repression of (perceived) threats to survival and legitimacy.

The struggle between the Front and the counterinsurgency for Dhufaris' support also saw counterinsurgency actors impede the commemoration of Front casualties. A British fighter explained to Andrew Higgins the usual procedure through which counterinsurgency troops dealt with the corpses of Front fighters. "They get shipped down to Salalah for identification unless one of the *firqat* [pro-government paramilitaries] recognizes them. They often do—somebody's cousin's wife's brother. That helps as they can be buried at once out on the hill, which the Moslems prefer. So do we, actually."[66] These corpses buried on the hill were nevertheless vulnerable. Higgins noted that honey badgers living in the mountains "will even dig up carcasses, including human remains, of which there was no shortage on the *jebal*."⁶⁷ Moreover, burial was not guaranteed.

The counterinsurgency publicly displayed corpses of Front fighters as a means of discouraging resistance. British veteran C. Hepworth recalled this of his service in 1970–1971.⁶⁸ After the Front's heavy losses during its failed attempt to capture Mirbat in 1972, the counterinsurgency displayed the corpses of Front casualties in Salalah for several days.⁶⁹ Ian Gardiner recalled the progressive dehumanization of an unburied corpse on the mined *jabal*: "It seemed imprudent to rescue an enemy corpse from a dangerous minefield at risk to oneself. Besides, the sight of his corpse might be a disincentive for others. So he became something of a tourist attraction for patrols operating in that area. Photographs were taken. Soon the foxes had a go at him. He had once been an individual with his own name. Now he was the disarranged detritus of a sudden and desperate action in the night. He was rubbish."⁷⁰ The counterinsurgency's denial of burial rites for Front corpses made the movement's later efforts in exile to name and commemorate Dhufari casualties all the more important as an act of resistance and recuperation.⁷¹

The corpse who became "rubbish" on the *jabal* was not the only instance in which counterinsurgency authorities impeded burial for a revolutionary killed by state violence. The novelist Sonallah Ibrahim addresses historical events of July 18, 1973, when the authorities tortured and killed Dhufari revolutionary Mubarak Hamad. They buried his body in a secret place and forbade his relatives from receiving condolences.⁷² Such wartime repression of potential revolutionary commemoration prefigured the eventual suppression of the Front's very existence, including its official commemoration.

The recovery of revolutionary commemoration from official silence is important in its own right. It is an act of retrieval of the "lost archive of Arab Marxism" and of the region's "vexed archives of decolonization."⁷³ That act of recovery also challenges conventional narratives about twentieth-century Oman. First, the Front's commemorative culture challenges predominant historical narratives that associate Qaboos with the emergence in Oman of official commemoration culture. It advances critical evaluations of those narratives' disproportionate focus on the sultan. For Dhufaris in Front-controlled areas, their first encounters with nationalist commemoration took place in the context of the Front, rather than under Qaboos.

Second, the existence of the Front's thriving commemoration culture requires a rethinking of explanations for the swift emergence of Qaboos-focused commemoration. Those explanations must go beyond a focus on the predicaments and preferences of the sultan himself. It is certainly important to recognize Qaboos's urgent political need to create legitimacy, as well as his partiality for pageantry such as he encountered while training as an officer in the British armed forces at Sandhurst.[74] An explanation that looks beyond Qaboos must also acknowledge the British counterinsurgency authorship and swift dissemination of the "myth of Qaboos."[75] But a more comprehensive account of the emergence of Oman's official commemoration culture must acknowledge, too, revolutionary agency and influence in the form of the Front's flourishing revolutionary commemoration. Its existence made the creation of an alternative commemoration culture all the more urgent.

Counterinsurgency actors were conscious of the Front's investment in commemoration. This awareness stretched beyond British military intelligence bulletins that tracked stamps and commemorative field attacks. Gardiner noted that the Front "were very keen on anniversaries. They named their regiments after special dates—a conference, the start of the revolution, or some other such inspiring event."[76] This sensitivity to the Front's commemoration translated into an impetus to create rival commemoration. For instance, the counterinsurgency emulated the Front's use of commemorative names for fighting units. Dhufari Salim Mubarak first proposed this (as well as the initiative to have Dhufaris who had joined the counterinsurgency speak on the radio to disseminate their experience).[77] Mubarak had previously served as second-in-command of the Front's eastern military area before joining the counterinsurgency in September 1970. Familiar with the Front's commemoration, he suggested calling the first *firqah* unit after Salah al-Din. The counterinsurgency went on to name *firaq* battalions after military heroes from Arab and Islamic history, such as Gamal 'Abd al-Naser. These names aimed to boost the counterinsurgency's credentials as a defender of Islam, even as they saw British personnel run fighting units named after military leaders renowned for resisting British and European forces.[78]

Third, taking the Front's commemorative culture seriously raises questions that Oman's subsequent official silences about the revolution have quashed. When hostile political authorities repress prior rival official commemoration, does the commemoration of that past simply disappear? Do only new official commemorations follow in the wake of such repression? Seeking answers to these questions requires decentering Oman's official Qaboos-focused commemoration, despite its apparent omnipresence.

A Chain of Absences

In postwar Dhufar, as across the rest of the country, official sultan-centric commemoration filled public spaces. It marked Sultan Qaboos as the author of the country's modernization, progress, and renaissance (*al-nahdah*). The scope and ubiquity of this official commemoration narrative is well-rehearsed.[79] An examination of Dhufaris' familiarity with and participation in that official commemoration can establish the context for the chain of absences concerning the revolutionary past and its commemoration.

Moving through Salalah, Dhufaris encountered many reminders of *al-nahdah* and Qaboos's central role therein. The city boasted its share of *lieux de mémoire*. The Renaissance tower and roundabout were well-known landmarks. The Sultan Qaboos Mosque was completed in 2009. In 1977, 1981, 1997, and 2010, the city had hosted the high point of the national calendar: National Day, on November 18, with its parade and a speech by Sultan Qaboos.[80] Salalah bore other marks of the sultan, including Qaboos's multiple palaces in the city. These official *lieux de mémoire* and commemorative events emphasized the incorporation of Salalah and Dhufar into a sultan-centric iteration of the Omani nation.

This official narrative overlooked Dhufar's regional specificity, such as its speakers of MSAL and its Sunni connections with the Hadhramawt. Salalah's "Museum of the Frankincense Land" at al-Baleed Archaeological Park placed Dhufar's frankincense production and trade in a mainstream national narrative that overlooked ethnic and political specificities. Given the dearth of official commemoration and recognition for Dhufar's distinctive heritage, some Dhufaris found alternative means of marking that heritage. In an initial publication about the linguistic and cultural heritage of the *jabal*, Dhufari researcher and MSAL speaker ʿAli al-Shahri had to opt for publication outside Oman.[81] Interlocutors encouraged me to visit an unofficial museum of MSAL and culture that al-Shahri had curated in his home in Salalah. In contrast to such private initiatives, official commemorative spaces neglected Dhufari specificities.

The oversight of Dhufari particularity within national commemoration did not prevent Dhufaris from appreciating and participating in official commemoration alongside other Omanis.[82] When I observed interlocutors watch rebroadcasts of previous National Day parades and speeches, several spontaneously recognized a particular parade as the "*n*th" National Day, where the first was the celebration of 1971.[83] They thereby conveyed their familiarity with a "national timeline" that normalized 1970 as the inauguration of Oman's new national life and calendar.

Interlocutors also personalized sultan-centric commemoration in private spaces and habits. It was commonplace for Sultan Qaboos's portrait to hang in homes and offices. Dhufaris also took their commemorative enthusiasm to the street, both around the time of my fieldwork and for other key events.[84] A few months prior to my fieldwork, while Sultan Qaboos was receiving medical treatment in Germany, he made his first public appearance in months in a televised address on November 5, 2014. Recalling their joy at seeing him, interlocutors proudly shared with me images and stories of how they had danced in the streets to celebrate this event and decorated their clothes with Omani flags to embody their national loyalty. On the occasion of Sultan Qaboos's return on March 23 to Oman, one interlocutor commissioned specially labeled plastic water bottles showing the national colors and flag. Such personalized and vigorous participation in official commemoration was all the more poignant in the context of the anxieties of Dhufaris, and other Omanis, about the sultan's ailing health and the country's post-Qaboos future.[85]

The official commemoration of Sultan Qaboos and of his *nahdah* that flourished in Dhufar omitted events that contradicted official narratives of Omanis' unwavering loyalty to Qaboos and the al-Busaid dynasty. Official history, museum displays, and textbooks excluded the period between the 1920 Treaty of Seeb and Qaboos's accession in 1970, missing out the insurrections in al-Jabal al-Akhdar and Dhufar.[86] In his 1974 National Day speech, Sultan Qaboos confirmed his determination to silence such past events. He stated that "Oman loves all her sons, and the principle we have declared is to forget the past. We shall adhere to this code."[87] Government policy aimed to enjoin that silence on Omanis.

As far as Dhufar was concerned, official histories also imposed silences on sensitive events prior to the Treaty of Seeb. A conversation that took place a few weeks into my fieldwork in 2015 highlighted the multiple silences about Dhufar in official history. One evening, as I waited at a café to meet an interlocutor, I was reading a Muscat-published historical and statistical guide to Oman. In due course Hamza arrived. He was born and raised in the city, middle aged, and hailed from a prestigious Salalah family. He had just emerged from his long day of juggling a government job, a private trading business, care responsibilities for aging and young family members, and his all-male evening gathering. He showed no sign of fatigue as he immediately picked up the book and searched for the pages on Dhufar's history. He wanted to see how the study represented his tribe and its prominent members.

As Hamza scanned the pages on Dhufar, he provided his own commentary on how the author had presented its history. As the narrative approached the late nineteenth century, however, Hamza paused. "But there is a gap here. It does not say how the al-Busaid dynasty came here," he exclaimed. Putting the book to one side, and occasionally gesturing to it authoritatively with my pen as he spoke, Hamza filled in the "gap" that he perceived in the narrative of the power struggle following the expulsion of Sayyid Fadhl bin ʿAlawi in 1879. Hamza explained: "A Shanfari and a Kathiri [members of two prominent town-based tribes] went to Muscat to ask the sultan to come and rule. Because there was instability in Dhufar." Having clarified this, Hamza then considered why the book had omitted these events. He turned to the cover of the book to check the author's name and thus his tribal and regional background. He concluded: "The man who wrote this, he is not from here [Dhufar], so maybe he doesn't know. But he did his best." Unlike Hamza, I was not surprised that the book missed out evidence of the contingency of the al-Busaid dynasty's claims to Dhufar. But I was struck that an avid reader keen to correct lacunae did not even comment on the book's omission of the revolution. Official silence about the Dhufar revolution was so much the norm that, for Hamza, it did not even merit commentary.

Indeed, *lieux de mémoire* in Oman that explicitly mentioned the Dhufar war, even in the context of government victory, were elusive.[88] Veiled or occasional public reference to the war surfaced in some official communications. In some National Day speeches Sultan Qaboos thanked the *firaq*, while avoiding or minimizing acknowledgment of their history in fighting against fellow Dhufaris.[89] If a public media discussion required mentioning the war, the focus was on a disembodied government victory against "rebellion." Accordingly, a national newspaper report covering the 2016 screening of a documentary film about British troops serving in the war avoided mentioning that Dhufaris and other Omanis had been fighting against Sultan Qaboos.[90] Those interlocutors who learned that at a book fair in Salalah I had been able to buy a copy of Dhufari researcher Muhammad al-ʿAmri's Beirut-published study about the Dhufar revolution considered this to be an exception to the Ministry of Information's habitual ban on the sale in Oman of books about the Dhufar war.[91] This was the only book on that topic that I encountered on sale in Oman. Outside veiled or occasional references, the war was as absent from public discourses as were the missing graves of revolutionaries. Those who contested these silences risked imprisonment, as befell ʿAbdullah Habib.

Outside official Sultanate narratives, however, material and discursive commemoration of the conflict emerged from the point of view of sympathizers of both the counterinsurgency and the revolution. But in different ways and to different degrees, the absence of Dhufari revolutionaries still haunted these commemorative fields.

Sympathizers of the counterinsurgency created *lieux de mémoire* and other commemorations of counterinsurgency victory and heroism. A monument in the UK and another in Fiji (the latter inaugurated in 2019) commemorate the counterinsurgency victory at the Battle of Mirbat on July 19, 1972, and the deaths there of counterinsurgency personnel, including Fijian Talaiasi Labalaba.[92] These memorials outside the Sultanate contrast with the elusiveness of *lieux de mémoire* within Oman that explicitly refer to the war, even in the context of counterinsurgency victory.

Additionally, two bodies of writing sympathetic to the counterinsurgency further commemorate the conflict. First, a body of writing that spans military studies, history, and memoir mythologizes the Dhufar campaign as successful in winning local "hearts and minds."[93] Recent historiography, though, contests this myth by underscoring the role of coercion in the counterinsurgency that the "hearts and minds" myth neglects.[94] Second, the memoirs of pro-government veterans commemorate counterinsurgency action and heroism.

The corpus of counterinsurgency memoirs is more extensive than is possible to review here.[95] These memoirs span ranks and class backgrounds.[96] The most popular volumes have run to multiple editions.[97] With the UK government initially seeking to conceal the deployment of British troops in Dhufar from public knowledge, scant awareness of the war among Anglophone audiences added to some writers' motivation to record their experiences.[98] A corresponding interest for some audiences in retrieving experiences from earlier British official silence may have contributed to the genre's popular appeal among some Anglophone audiences.

The existence of this corpus speaks to the enduring popularity for specific audiences of anti-communist white savior narratives that map onto a wider glorification of colonial violence. In a contrasting political environment claiming to denounce colonial violence, the Islamic Republic of Iran condemned the shah's intervention in Dhufar. This made Iranian counterinsurgency personnel who died in Dhufar into "political ghosts" who became problematic to commemorate.[99] Memoirs of British personnel have not faced such hostile reception, however. In addition to praising British intervention, the accounts of British counterinsurgency personnel orientalize Dhufaris. Descriptions infantilize the *firaq*, naturalize Dhufaris' "preference" for despotism, reduce locals to wailing victims, and make Dhufari women into objects of erotic fantasy.[100] In its various material and discursive guises, counterinsurgency commemoration neglects the experiences of revolutionaries.

Challenging the marginalization of revolutionary experience in pro-government and counterinsurgency commemoration are works that, published outside the confines of Oman's censors, address the revolution and revolutionaries.[101] These include fiction, published eyewitness accounts, memoirs, and historical and social scientific research, as well as writing that blends these genres. The authors include non-Omani sympathizers, former members of the Front hailing originally from northern Oman and Bahrain, and Dhufaris in exile during the revolution. This "upsurge" in memory work has emerged at the historical distance of several years after the Front's last formal activity in 1992.[102] This memory work is ongoing. Its emergence, evolution, and reception, especially in Oman, merit further research beyond the scope possible to attempt in an exploratory discussion.

Fiction is the genre of an early landmark of the retrieval of and reflection on revolutionary experiences. In *Wardah*, published in 2000, Egyptian novelist Sonallah Ibrahim interweaves the fictional revolution-era diary of the eponymous Omani heroine and female combatant for the Front, the visit of the Egyptian narrator to Sultan Qaboos's Oman in 1992, and extracts from historical documents.[103] Fiction and history further intersect as diary entries refer to events from eyewitness accounts, such as ʿAziza's marital dispute concerning her support for the revolution.[104] The book reached audiences in Oman, other Arab-majority countries, and non-Arabophone contexts through translations into French in 2005 and into English in 2021.[105] Some veterans of the revolution found the novel "controversial."[106] On the one hand, the novel brought the story of the revolution to wide and potentially new audiences. On the other hand, its portrayal of a sexually liberated heroine risked fueling misleading stereotypes about the sexuality of Dhufar's revolutionary women, whom Sultan Said had branded as "whores."[107] Fiction is also the genre through which Dhufari novelist Ahmed al-Zubaidi (1945–2018) reflected on the revolution in a trilogy published in Beirut between 2008 and 2013.[108] Al-Zubaidi was a student activist abroad during the years of the revolution.[109] Omani novelist Bushra Khalfan also revisits Dhufar's revolution in her 2018 novel *Al-Bagh*.[110] Memory work about the revolution through fiction is long-standing and flourishing.

Memoirs have also commemorated the experiences of revolutionaries. Published memoirs emerged first from Front sympathizers, such as Fawwaz Trabulsi, and volunteers, such as Kamel Mohanna and Mahboubeh Afraz.[111] The latter's medical memoirs shed light on the trials of revolutionary health care, morale, and the possibility that revolutionary activists echoed counterinsurgency personnel in essentializing "backward" Dhufaris. Around the time of my fieldwork and thereafter, former Front members also published memoirs: Bahraini 'Abd al-Nabi 'Ikri in 2015, and Omani Zahran al-Sarimi in 2020.[112] The publication of novels and memoirs by Omanis outside the Sultanate reflects official censorship in the Sultanate. Al-Sarimi's decision to publish, while living in Oman, memoirs of his activism in exile is unprecedented. His resolve to do so perhaps signals that ongoing memory work may have shifted the Omani government's perception of the need to take disciplinary actions against former dissidents.

Further commemorating Dhufar's revolutionary past is the historical and social scientific research of Dhufaris too young to have fought during the revolution. They hail from diverse backgrounds of generation, gender, ethnicity, and family and historical connections to the revolution.[113]

In this memory work about Dhufar's revolutionaries, a notable absence nevertheless persists. At the time of my fieldwork, no Omani from the Front had published memoirs of the revolution. Since then, al-Sarimi's memoir has broken this silence. But at the time of writing, it is still the case that no former revolutionary *from Dhufar* who was *in Dhufar* during the revolution has published memoirs. When they were formally active in exile in southern Yemen, Front members wrote autocritiques about the revolution.[114] But after the Front's formal cessation, published memory work on the part of Dhufaris who fought with the Front was elusive. Dhufaris themselves drew my attention to this absence. One interlocutor attributed this absence to a desire to avoid causing local controversy: "Everyone sees [the Front] from his point of view. Whatever he writes, someone might say, 'No it wasn't like that.'" This interlocutor anticipated that any Dhufari writing about the revolution would provoke local controversy. This, various interlocutors explained to me, had already occurred for existing studies.

A further and arguably greater obstacle to former revolutionaries' published memory work, and even Dhufaris' informal memory work, was government censorship and the threat of repression. When I felt able to ask some interlocutors about revolutionary poetry, they assured me that they had forgotten any poems. This hinted at "active forgetting" and the internalization of government censorship, at least in certain settings. By contrast, in a context where self-censorship did not have the same political importance, and where the narrator had been able to continue a life of activism, Mohanna recalled details of revolutionary poems.[115] Former revolutionaries who had returned from physical exile abroad might continue to inhabit the "inner exile" of those who live estranged from their officially repressed political past.[116] Such self-silencing was another link in the chain of absences regarding the commemoration of revolutionary experiences. Unofficial commemoration nevertheless challenged that chain of absences.

Space, Text, and Circumlocution

With sensitivity surrounding the transmission in Oman of knowledge about the revolutionary past, the insights that I gained into unofficial commemoration were partial. Elsewhere, research participants who share stories of a previously silenced past can experience catharsis and relief.[117] Given the concerns about surveillance that interlocutors and I shared, I did not attempt such in-depth interviews. No one volunteered to show me commemorative objects that spoke to revolutionary experiences, such as stamps, photographs, or official documents from that time.[118] Some interlocutors did broach the highly sensitive topics of trauma and mental ill-health among former revolutionaries. Rather than attempt to address those experiences here, my hope is for Dhufaris to choose as part of their own memory work the terms on which to address the trauma that some experienced as a result of living with a revolutionary past.

Those experiences that I have included here arose in conversation with Dhufaris of different backgrounds, genders, generations, and histories. For the sake of protecting interlocutors' anonymity, I present these discussions as if they were the words of one person: "Ahmad." The reader can imagine Ahmad as a Salalan born to one of the postwar generations that, having not personally experienced the government's repression of the Front during the war, was often more willing than some of the ex-revolutionaries themselves to share stories with a foreign researcher about legacies of the movement. Of the fields of experience that I have interpreted as unofficial commemoration, three were subtly commemorative: the experiences of socially inflected space, the circulation of written and oral texts, and circumlocutions that stood in lieu of conventional commemoration.

Dhufaris' experiences of social space unofficially commemorated the government's repression of the revolution as well as the revolutionary past. The mountain hinterland and coastal urban spaces functioned as unofficial *lieux de mémoire* for the counterinsurgency. In the *jabal*, every few kilometers there was a military base for the local *firqah* unit. These bases bore witness not just to the counterinsurgency war, but also to the government's ongoing postwar investment in counterinsurgency. The bases conveyed a message "not to forget" that pro-government armed forces continued to surveil the *jabal*.

In the city, the very demographic makeup of Salalah's urban districts reflected counterinsurgency land distribution policies aimed at relocating people out of the hinterlands into the more easily controlled urban coast. For those who had lived through the war in Salalah, memories lingered on of the fence with which the government had surrounded the then villages of Salalah, al-Husn, al-Hafah, and al-Dahariz, in order to cut off food supplies to the *jabbali* population. Driving through the city, older Dhufaris pointed out to me landmarks that for them still traced the fence, telling me "this was as far as we could go," or "we couldn't come here during the war, it was outside the blockade." The lingering specter of a fence that no longer physically existed echoed ongoing government control over space.

Social space could nevertheless also reflect experiences of revolutionary space. The fact that some revolutionary spaces, like the school, had lacked physical signs could facilitate this. While this meant that it was unnecessary to remove signs, it also meant that it was impossible to do so. By extension, signless spaces could retain revolutionary associations long after the counterinsurgency would have destroyed any formal evidence of those histories. The Front's erstwhile supply corridor retained in popular usage the name "Ho Chi."[119] The *jabal* also encompassed other everyday reminders of the revolutionary past. Driving through the hills and across the plateaus, one could catch sight of men seated by the roadside playing chess. This game was not popular in the *jabal* before the revolution, interlocutors explained to me. At the revolutionary schools, however, students and teachers played chess, including friendly matches with the Cuban medical personnel.[120] Chess became so popular in the *jabal*, including among generations born after the revolution, that chess games became a common sight there. Chess players, by the roadside or in more private spaces, were an unofficial testimony to the *jabal*'s revolutionary past.

It was also possible that particular landscapes encapsulated memories of revolutionary experiences for individual Dhufaris. Hafidh, the affluent ex-revolutionary who had a home in Salalah near Qaboos's maternal relatives, drove me around his *jabal* haunts one day. As we traversed the plateau, he recalled the sites of battles in which he had participated as a member of the Front. A tree reminded him of one that had allowed him to hide from counterinsurgency forces, he explained. It was perhaps Hafidh's postwar closeness and unquestioned loyalty to the sultan that allowed him to narrate these memories to me. Ex-revolutionaries who did not enjoy such postwar royal favor shared no such battle memories with me. Within the constraints of each person's political positioning, everyday experiences of social space contributed to the unofficial commemoration of the revolutionary past.

Dhufaris consumed books that, published outside the constraints of Oman's official censorship, addressed the revolutionary past. Their circulation further contributed to the unofficial commemoration of the revolution. Interlocutors frequently asked me about which of the books by Dhufari authors al-'Amri, bin 'Aqil, and Jabob I had read. In some cases they gave me copies, along with assurances that government prohibition of the sale of these books did not extend to a prohibition of their informal circulation. (These assurances did not fully dispel my apprehensions at having such books in my possession in Oman.) They advised me how to purchase books and asked how they could access Takriti's study of the revolution, which at the time was not yet available in Arabic. Some older Dhufaris especially appreciated the intergenerational interest of younger Dhufaris in the revolution. One interlocutor who had lived through the revolution told me: "It is good that young people like [Mona] Jabob, Draibi [al-'Amri], and Salim 'Aqil write about it. Because we want people to know what the *jabhah* did, how it tried to change society, its ideas, its experience in education." This reaction indicated local support for and interest in research about the revolution.

Dhufaris authored, circulated, and consumed information about the revolution in oral and, over time, digital forms. When Jeapes returned to visit Dhufar in 1991, his Dhufari guide told him: "The tribesman [*sic*] still meet of an evening around the fire and tell stories of the war. You are all part of our history now. These people and the battles they fought; we know of them. They live on."[121] Since the guide was addressing a British veteran, it is likely that he referred to stories in which tribesmen's role in the *firaq* positioned them as allies of British fighters. These were the kinds of stories that one Dhufari family found easier to tell me. Several members of that family directed my attention during conversation toward their memories of a relative who had died fighting for the *firaq*. They moved discussion swiftly away from relatives who had died fighting for the Front.

But undoubtedly in other contexts Dhufaris shared stories about revolutionaries. One Dhufari female college student wrote an essay recounting how a poem reminded her "of my grandmother, that at the past in Oman, she fights with soldiers [in the Dhofar War] to protect her father and her brothers."[122] No women fought for the *firaq*, so this grandmother was undoubtedly a veteran revolutionary. As one interlocutor told me: "We [Dhufaris] are a revolutionary society. All Dhufari young people hear from their parents about the revolution, and they hear stories of heroism, and they all want to be heroes." This person positioned the revolution as an incontrovertible part of Dhufaris' past, present, and future.

The circulation of revolutionary poems and songs was another possibility. No Dhufaris indicated to me that they recalled revolutionary poetry. But the fact that some recalled revolutionary poets hinted at a familiarity that may have extended beyond what interlocutors were prepared to discuss with me. Some Dhufaris did encourage me to look up revolutionary songs on YouTube. They also referred to material that they had seen shared through social media platforms such as WhatsApp. Those who mentioned sites and messages to me nevertheless deferred sharing them with me directly, usually telling me that they no longer had access. Concerns about surveillance may have influenced this restraint. Indeed, some interlocutors preferred to share with me their tips about how to diminish the likelihood of Omani intelligence services collecting information from my cell phone. Their comments about sources that they had seen alerted me to a transformation. The unofficial commemoration of the revolution that had flourished in oral spheres—such as family stories, as well as poetry in MSAL (to which I had no access)—had extended to include the digital.

Internet sites commemorating the revolution multiplied in the wake of Salalah's protests in 2011. This was a political moment in which many in SWANA spoke of having "lost their fear" of authoritarian repression. Signed and anonymous posts about sensitive topics, including Dhufar's revolution, grew in numbers. In 2012, Dhufari journalist Muhammad al-Shahri interviewed Fawwaz Trabulsi in Lebanon.[123] Others chose anonymity. A post on one site, published on August 21, 2011, showed the pictures and names of eleven male and one female revolutionary "martyrs," in the words of the post's author, attracting by February 2021 103,928 views, 318 likes, and 71 dislikes.[124] Another post, from 2009, also showing pictures of revolutionaries had by February 2021 attracted 162,578 views, 354 likes, and 70 dislikes.[125] A significant audience for these sites indicated that they "liked" this alternative commemoration of the revolutionary past.

Memory work about the revolution in cyberspace has increased in recent years, tracking memoirs, novels, and studies. Internet users in Oman and beyond have discussed Khalfan's *Al-Bagh*, the much-awaited 2019 Arabic translation of Takriti's *Monsoon Revolution*, and al-Sarimi's memoirs.[126] Some debates proved heated. Former revolutionary al-Sarimi sparred with government sympathizer Said bin Masoud al-Maʿshani over the disputed significance of the revolution. The essays circulated over WhatsApp, with part of the discussion appearing online.[127] Exchanges and memory work that have long taken place through southern Arabians' poetry now also thrive in internet controversies. These digital spaces are familiar to Omanis skirting (even if only temporarily) censorship.[128] Alongside books, stories, songs, and poems, cyberspace has nourished unofficial commemoration of the revolution.

A third field of unofficial commemoration consisted of acts that, in the context of official silence about the revolution, stood in lieu of more conventional commemorative acts. The nightly evening gatherings at which some male former revolutionaries engaged in socially egalitarian friendships, and the pioneering labor force participation of some female former revolutionaries in the 1970s and 1980s, were in a sense alternative daily commemorations of revolutionary networks and values.

Jokes also provided a circumlocutory means of acknowledging the revolutionary past. Humor occupies conveniently ambiguous grounds in social commentary, allowing the dismissal of reference to sensitive topics as "only a joke."[129] Humor allowed Dhufaris to mention the revolutionary past without this seeming to threaten the usual official avoidance of the topic. One day, I was talking with two male interlocutors who had known each other for many years. We were in a place where they could be confident that no one overheard us. The elder man, Marhun, had been a member of the Front, whereas the immediate relatives of the younger man, Firas, had not been members of the Front. I explained to Marhun, whose daughter was studying English at university, that I would like to give her some books to help in her studies. Marhun joked: "We take anything from the British." Firas immediately quipped: "He will take anything, he's a communist." They both laughed, enjoying the jokes that had taken me somewhat by surprise. Firas had not previously acknowledged Marhun's past in front of me. Under the ambiguity of comments that were "only jokes," Dhufaris acknowledged how the revolution had shaped and affected them.

Another circumlocutory form of unofficial commemoration was suggestive avoidance. This could take the form of euphemism. A conversation with Ahmad as we drove across the city one afternoon hinted at euphemistic commemoration, or a desire for it. Gesturing toward the hills in the distance along the edge of the plain, he told me: "There was a big battle here in the days when the Portuguese were here. A big battle. There are many bodies in the hills. We don't know how many, or where they are. They are there." The Portuguese presence in the area dated back to the sixteenth and seventeenth centuries. I wondered: what had made him think of these bodies in the hills in unmarked graves?

In the year after my fieldwork, journalist ʿAbdullah Habib, having posted on Facebook that the "Popular Front is finished and no longer represents a political or military threat to the government," went on to make the following plea: "The Omani government has a simple and moral obligation, and that is to disclose the locations of the burial grounds of martyrs that were executed. . . . We're waiting for the government's brave decision to announce where, which will contribute to the national reform/reconciliation. . . . The mass graves will not be transformed into revolutionary shrines; on the contrary, it is the right of a mother to visit her son's grave on Eid."[130] Habib's subsequent arrest and imprisonment indicated the high price of open advocacy for the commemoration of those whom the counterinsurgency killed.

I cannot be sure if Ahmad's intention was to draw a parallel between the unmarked graves from the Portuguese incursion and those resulting from the counterinsurgency over which official silence hung. In the context of repercussions for direct advocacy, as befell Habib, euphemism may have appealed as a means of voicing yearning for commemoration of missing dead bodies.

An alternative to euphemism was another suggestive avoidance: nonparticipation in official commemoration. A subtle gesture such as not displaying a picture of Sultan Qaboos in a place where other Omanis might expect to see it was perhaps a form of "silent disagreement" with official commemoration.[131] Like jokes and euphemism, the avoidance of saying or doing certain things might be an ambiguous, circumlocutory means of signaling an interest in the unofficial commemoration of the revolutionary past. The resonances of space, text, and circumlocution as part of a spectrum of cultural resources for unofficial commemoration become all the clearer in the light of repurposed ritual acts that were more explicitly commemorative.

Ritual Repurposing

Some Dhufaris repurposed existing rituals in order to incorporate unofficial commemoration of the revolutionary past. Kinship rituals at birth and death provided such opportunities. In addition to some former revolutionaries naming children after revolutionary namesakes, postwar funeral attendance commemorated the revolutionary past.

Formal mourning rituals (*'azza'*) are an important social obligation across Arabia, including in Dhufar. Waʻd, a grandmother, explained typical funeral arrangements for Dhufaris: "In the past all the funerals used to be three days. This is very expensive and now when someone dies, they announce how many days the *'azza'* will be. If it is someone very important it will be three days. A tent will be set up outside for the men, and they sit in rows. The women are in the house. . . . There will be about 5, 6 rooms, all with a different relative [such as the mother, the sister]. . . . In the past the older women used to wail at the funerals. . . . Now this doesn't happen so much anymore because the younger women refuse to wail." Attendance at an *'azza'* was a social obligation for those with connections to the deceased. I soon became accustomed to interlocutors' frequent attendance at formal mourning gatherings. For men who, like Hamza, cultivated large circles of acquaintances, driving across the city and the governorate to attend *'azza'* seemed to be an almost constant obligation, fitted in on top of everything else.

Younger relatives attended the funerals of older relatives, even if they had not met them. One young man explained: "My brother and I went to a funeral in the *jabal* yesterday. We didn't know the old woman, but she is from the tribe, so we went." Funeral attendance could involve considerable adjustment to one's social routine. Bereaved women and their visitors refrained from wearing the usual fine clothes and makeup donned for other visits, Waʻd explained.[132] I also observed that the otherwise physically infirm who rarely left the house for other social visits made efforts to offer condolences in person. Mourners converged on the place where the family had chosen to organize the ʿ*azza*ʾ. This was usually the historical place of residence of the deceased's family—even if the deceased had long moved away to a new district or to government-distributed land. Mourning rituals commemorated not just a deceased person, then. They also commemorated the collective identities with which the deceased identified as well as the prewar communities that had dispersed following government land distributions and the city's expansion.

Given Dhufaris' social obligations to attend funerals, former Front members' attendance at mourning events for peers was in a sense unexceptional. But as was the case for ex-revolutionaries' kinship practices and nightly all-male gatherings, some *details* of ex-revolutionaries' funeral attendance were socially distinctive. These details would not necessarily be immediately visible amid the wider context of large gatherings for mourning rituals. But they would be clear to ex-revolutionaries and others attending the events. These details imbued the funerals of ex-revolutionaries with the *potential* for unofficial commemoration. Mourners could unofficially commemorate the deceased as a former revolutionary, the networks and values of social inclusivity associated with the revolution, and the collective identities and communities of the revolutionary past.

Ahmad had attended several ʿ*azza*ʾ of former Front members. He explained to me: "When someone from the Front dies, everyone goes to the funeral." His recollections stressed the breadth of participation in funerals through which former Front members reconvened revolutionary networks. Ahmad recalled attending the funeral in 2014 of a former Front leader, Rahul. By the time of Rahul's death, the Front's former secretary general al-Qadi had returned to Oman and was in Muscat. Ahmad explained to me: "ʿAbd al-ʿAziz came to the funeral. Many people from Muscat came to the funeral." Ahmad also described how al-Qadi sent condolences for the funeral of Naʿma, a well-known female former supporter of the Front who was an old woman and great-grandmother when she passed away. Ahmad explained to me that al-Qadi had not traveled from Muscat to attend Naʿma's funeral in Dhufar in person but had telephoned Naʿma's family from Muscat to express his condolences. In addition to former revolutionaries participating in each other's funerals in Dhufar, Ahmad explained that after the death in 2006 of Laila Fakhro, "some ex-revolutionaries traveled to Bahrain for the yearly memorials. It's a custom they have in Bahrain that we don't have in

Dhufar." Unofficial commemoration through funeral attendance surpassed national and confessional differences, echoing the Front's ambitions for social inclusivity.

The breadth of participation in the funerals of former revolutionaries reiterated egalitarian-leaning revolutionary values. Typically, mourning rituals in Arabia emphasize social distinctions. In late twentieth-century Zabid, Yemen, members of a socially prestigious family restricted their mourning for the death of one of their servants, compared with the mourning that they would conduct for a social equal. They thereby marked social hierarchy between elites and low-ranking persons.[133] In late twentieth-century northern Oman, formerly enslaved women mourned in a separate room from those of more prestigious social background.[134] By contrast, since the Front had comprised Dhufaris of all social backgrounds, former members' funerals accommodated a distinctive social inclusivity. It was not only that "everyone goes to the funeral," as Ahmad had stressed. There was also an unusual degree of social connection between genders given the Dhufari context where, as one male interlocutor put it, "[i]t is not ok here [for a man] to have a friendship with a woman." Male former revolutionaries with no kinship relationship to a deceased female former revolutionary participated in their funerals, as was the case for the commemorations for Naʿma and Laila Fakhro. In a Dhufari context, this was an extraordinary acknowledgment of men and women as equal companions. Mourning rituals for former Front members commemorated not just deceased persons and their relationships, but also revolutionary values of social and gendered egalitarianism.

No one spoke to me about whether security officers policed the possibilities for al-Qadi to attend Rahul's funeral but not Naʿma's, or more generally policed the limits of funeral celebrations for former revolutionaries. Ritual repurposing to mark the return of former revolutionaries to Dhufar, however, did cause Dhufaris to reflect on the government policing of these events.

Dhufaris typically celebrated the return of a fellow Dhufari after an absence, such as travel abroad, with ritual acts of reception and hosting. Large groups at Salalah airport, awaiting an arrival, were a sign of the beginnings of such ritual hosting. Later, the returned traveler's kin, friends, and acquaintances would host one or more celebratory gatherings and feasts. In a similar spirit, when former revolutionaries returned to Dhufar, relatives and peers organized gatherings to mark their return. Ahmad had participated in such events on several occasions. His experiences underscored the ambiguity of these events. On the one hand, such gatherings celebrated the incorporation of a former Front member into the fold of Dhufaris who had made lives under Qaboos, as well as indicating government success in winning over a former opponent. On the other hand, however, these gatherings could stray into celebration of former revolutionaries and their ongoing connections. In that case, Dhufaris suspected that they could attract government sanction.

In the 1990s, Ahmad attended the celebrations marking the return of Wafiq. This man had been a high-ranking member of the Front in the 1980s and early 1990s, involved during exile in the movement's diplomatic representation in Syria, Yemen, and Libya. Ahmad's account of the gatherings to mark Wafiq's return to Dhufar highlights the potential of such events to mark government victory, the power of the security forces over former Front members, and the incorporation of former revolutionaries into networks of political patronage.

Ahmad: After the fall of the Soviet Union, the support for the Front went down. Also, [Wafiq] was getting old. And there was his attachment (*irtibat*) to the region. He returned with his wife and their children. She was originally from Dhufar. The children were still young. In the first year of coming back, Wafiq was in Muscat for about two months for security [police] measures. An "investigation" [Ahmad switched languages to use the English word]. Then after two months he came to Dhufar. His father and his brother organized a celebration for him. His father was a shaikh. Half of Salalah was there. We built tents. We made food for five hundred or six hundred people. His father organized the first celebration, and then maybe three days later his brother organized a celebration.

AW: Do you have any photos?

Ahmad: No. Well, we haven't kept them. The early celebrations were the biggest, the ones after were a bit smaller. The father's celebration is bigger than the eldest brother's party, and so on. The celebrations went on for about one month.

AW: Were there women at the celebrations?

Ahmad: Yes, but there were more men there. In our habits in Salalah, if it is a celebration for a woman, then there are more women there. If it is a celebration for a man, then there are more men there. We have food for the men and women separately. After that, the sultan gave him a gift (*makramah*) of 150,000 Omani riyals [circa $390,000], and very expensive gifts—he gave him a watch that cost 20,000 Omani riyals [circa $52,000].[135] They gave him a government job with a very good salary, similar to a director. The government rented a house for him in Muscat for two years, and after that they said they would buy him a house [in Muscat], this house or another house. . . . They agreed [on a house and] with the owner and bought that one, maybe it was 100,000 to 150,000 Omani riyals [circa $260,000–$390,000]. He settled in Muscat for a while. Then in [the early 2000s] they [the government] asked him to go to Salalah. I don't know why. Maybe for security reasons. They gave him a gift to buy a house. He stayed in Salalah for about ten years. He didn't work anymore.

This narrative of Wafiq's return celebrations, which had taken place over twenty years earlier, stressed the government's control over Wafiq's movements, and the royal largesse that marked Wafiq's cooptation.

By contrast, Ahmad's account of the return celebrations for former secretary general 'Abd al-'Aziz al-Qadi cast a more nuanced light. The celebrations had taken place a little under a year before our conversation. Ahmad's narrative revealed the potential red lines in these celebrations, and his belief that the government policed those who crossed them.

Ahmad: When 'Abd al-'Aziz came back, first he was in Muscat. For security reasons. Questioning. Then he came to Dhufar.
AW: Was there anything in the news when 'Abd al-'Aziz returned?
Ahmad: Yes. Well, I mean, just "Whats"[App], on the internet. You can probably find videos on YouTube.
AW: How long was he in Dhufar for?
Ahmad: About ten days.
AW: Since then has he been back?
Ahmad: Yes, he came for the *'azza'* of [Rahul]. Then he went back to Muscat. The government has given him a big house there. When he came [to Dhufar], it was September or October 2014, I think. People made big celebrations for him—his brothers, his maternal relatives, and the people from the Front all made a celebration for him. They went to the big square [*midan al-ihtifalat*], where people have weddings, and they did a big celebration there. They built tents to receive him.

As had been the case for Wafiq, Dhufaris who gathered to celebrate the return of 'Abd al-'Aziz marked connections through kinship, friendship, as well as past membership in the Front.

I was eager to learn more of the celebrations that former members of the Front had organized for al-Qadi. Ahmad explained: "[One of the former members of the Front] made a special celebration, with a select group of people—maybe 15 people were invited. That was the first time I met him." Another celebration that former Front members arranged for their former secretary general did not go to plan, however, as Ahmad recounted:

> After the celebration by his [paternal] family, and then by his mother's family, there was a big celebration by the people in the Front. But on the day, 'Abd al-'Aziz sent some people to the organizers to say that he was not coming because he was ill. That's what he said. But some people think that the security services told him that he could not go. We can't know for sure. He sent his brothers [to the celebration] instead of him. He said that he had diarrhea. It's true that there was a virus going around at the time. At the end he was tired of the celebrations. Maybe he is ill, maybe he has cancer. Maybe this is why he doesn't come [to Dhufar] anymore.

Al-Qadi's absence from the principal celebration that former Front members staged for him was, for some Dhufaris, a sign. It showed the government drawing a line at ex-revolutionaries celebrating the presence of their former leader, even in the context of all of them being fellow subjects of cooptation. Ahmad also tactfully provided an alternative, politically neutral narrative of al-Qadi's absence due to illness.

That ex-revolutionaries' return celebrations might nevertheless cross a red line was apparent in Ahmad's account of a third instance: videos that had circulated of a celebration for al-Qadi in the *jabal*.

Ahmad: They also made a celebration for him in the *jabal*. He did go to this. At the celebration, they used some strong words. I saw some WhatsApp videos. There were people saying "Welcome, comrade" (*ahlan ya rafiq*). These are the kind of words that they used in the days of the Front.
AW: Were there any problems because they used these words?
Ahmad: No, no.

Ahmad quickly went on to assure me that he did not have access to these videos.

The absent but remembered photographs of the celebrations for Wafiq, and videos of those for al-Qadi, had nevertheless captured Dhufaris attending these events, remembering a revolutionary past, and unofficially commemorating it. In this ritual repurposing, unofficial commemoration took one of its more explicitly commemorative forms. This greater clarity of form only highlights all the more how unofficial commemoration can nevertheless lack the clarity of subject and effects of more official commemoration. It is difficult to say whether these celebrations commemorated events, persons, values, or collective identities. Ahmad both acknowledged and dismissed the possibility that they were indicative of political sentiment of concern to Oman's government. What remains is the possibility of unofficial commemoration, with all its ambiguities.

Ambiguous Commemorations

Dhufaris living in postwar Oman under the rule of Sultan Qaboos (and, later, that of his successor Haitham) faced a similar dilemma to peers in Vietnam, Sisi's Egypt, and post-Mao authoritarian China. How can one commemorate the figures and events of the past that do not fit official and hegemonic narratives? The proposition that Dhufaris and others have met that dilemma with a resourcefulness that challenges official silence has wider implications.

Unofficial commemoration of an officially silenced past challenges the neglect and biases of official history by retrieving counterhistories. In Dhufar, probing the wider context for commemorating the revolutionary past brings to attention the earlier histories of the Front's official revolutionary commemoration. That history challenges official narratives of Qaboos as the initiator of a new kind of statecraft. Instead, it emerges that Dhufaris' experiences of statecraft-led commemoration, and other aspects of state practice, began with the Front. Acknowledgment of that counterhistory furthermore prompts revision of the factors that influenced the emergence of Qaboos-focused commemoration. Those factors included revolutionary agency and related commemoration.

Additionally, unofficial commemoration contributes to a decolonization of commemoration that challenges the omissions and distortions of colonial and colonialist narratives. In Oman, a decolonizing approach to commemoration counters the chain of absences surrounding the commemoration of Dhufar's anti-colonial and revolutionary past. The unofficial commemoration of that past challenges both the Sultanate's official silence about decolonization efforts in the days of the Front and the orientalism of counterinsurgency commemoration that celebrates colonial violence.

Unofficial commemoration of Dhufar's revolutionary past furthermore exposes the limitations of authoritarian censorship and self-censorship.

Omanis found ways around that censorship in cyberspace. Censorship also had limitations as a means of excluding former revolutionaries and others in Dhufar from memory work about the revolutionary past. Despite their exclusion from published memory work, Dhufari former revolutionaries in Oman engaged in alternative, unofficial memory work. Their experiences, alongside those of other Dhufaris, of space, text, circumlocution, and ritual repurposing evoked and enacted meanings of the revolutionary past. A researcher in a position different from mine would likely identify further cultural resources for their doing so. This unofficial commemoration produced legacies of the revolutionary past by offering possibilities for maintaining networks and values of revolution. Unofficial commemoration was part of the afterlives of revolution.

The study of new kinds of commemoration requires new concepts.[136] In particular, unofficial commemoration in hostile political circumstances, such as the commemoration of the revolutionary past in postwar Dhufar, raises new questions. Such unofficial commemoration prompts reconsideration of common expectations of the possibilities for and of commemoration. It flags uncertainties about the very form, subject, and effects of commemoration. Those uncertainties may resist any straightforward resolution. Unofficial commemoration may take obscure forms, sometimes looking as "uncommemorative" as a joke or euphemism. There may be a lack of clarity around the subject(s) of commemoration. Did Dhufaris commemorate persons, events, or values connected to the revolutionary past?

The intended and actual effects of unofficial commemoration may also remain unclear. When Dhufaris and other Omanis evoked the revolutionary past, did they seek to undermine conventional narratives of Sultan Qaboos's program of modernization? Or did they instead demand *inclusion* therein on grounds such as revolutionaries' prior establishment of a modernization agenda and their sacrifices in order to achieve it? Unofficial commemoration challenged the official marginalization of the revolution, but it could still be partially compatible with official narratives. It was also unclear how much unofficial commemoration cultivated resistance or, alternatively, loyalty to Qaboos through the claiming of a place for former revolutionaries *within* his polity. In this respect, the circumstances of Dhufaris' dilemma of how to commemorate those falling outside hegemonic narratives differs from the predicament of Antigone. Her decision to bury the brother for whom their uncle forbade funeral rites has attracted comparison with similar commemorative dilemmas.[137] Antigone rebelled against her uncle. But in Dhufar, it is not clear to what extent acts of resistance were at stake in unofficial commemoration. Quite possibly, unofficial commemoration in Dhufar was both multivocal and fragmented, as former revolutionaries varied in their interpretation of, and selection of subjects for, commemoration.

Some of these ambiguities within unofficial commemoration may have been purposeful. The overlaps with conventional funeral attendance, and between the celebration of a return to the national fold and that of the revolutionary past, provided unofficial commemoration with social camouflage. This may have protected against government sanction (up to a point). More broadly, the possibility of semi-hidden meanings in acts of unofficial commemoration fitted wider qualities of layered social life in Dhufar. Strong social pressure to demonstrate conformity with dominant norms meant that even when Dhufaris outwardly displayed conformity, they sometimes engaged more privately in other kinds of social relations. Given the political context of government surveillance and repression of perceived or actual opposition, ambiguities of unofficial commemoration were likely unavoidable.

The many ambiguities of unofficial commemoration demand a readiness to relinquish expectations of clarity of form, subject, and effect for commemoration. The alternative of insisting on conformity with the qualities of more conventional commemoration risks failure to recognize unofficial commemoration at all. This only jeopardizes its promises of counterhistories and decolonization. By contrast, a preparedness to relinquish conventional expectations of commemoration offers the prospect of knowing more, rather than less, about the possibilities for and of commemoration in politically hostile circumstances.

Against the uncertainties and ambiguities of unofficial commemoration stands the certainty that it created possibilities for transmitting knowledge about an officially silenced past, including to future generations. In Dhufar those audiences included the children and grandchildren who grew up hearing "about the revolution, and . . . stories of heroism" and about combatant grandmothers who defended fathers and brothers. The transmission of that knowledge raises the further question of the influence of the remembered past on the emergence of future political aspirations. The protests in Salalah in 2011 make it as timely to ask of Dhufaris as it is to ask of Yemenis, Libyans, and Kurds how memories of past anti-colonial institutions and projects have helped mobilize later political forms.[138] It is to this aspect of the afterlives of revolution that the Conclusion turns.

Conclusion

Postrevolutionary Platforms for Progressive Politics

FROM LATE 2010, WAVES of protest spread in SWANA from Western Sahara to Bahrain. Omanis across the Sultanate demonstrated too.[1] In Salalah, from February 25 to May 12, 2011, protestors occupied the parking lot in front of the office of the governor of Dhufar. They numbered at times up to ten thousand and made demands for political, economic, and social reform.[2] Demonstrators chanted: "The one who forgets the 1970s should think of the grandchildren of the free men."[3] Mirroring this chant's injunction, this book has looked both to Dhufar's revolution and to the experiences of Dhufaris living in its wake. Such inquiry into revolutionary afterlives has invited analysis of revolution through expanded temporalities and spatialities.

Recognition of the afterlives of revolution, and especially those of an officially silenced revolution, destabilizes polarizing accounts about the aftermaths of both revolution and counterinsurgency. Conventional narratives posit putatively definitive endings, either of success or of failure/defeat. As concerns Dhufar, there are rival, but similarly polarizing, accounts. Government and counterinsurgency actors, as well as some commentators, have drawn selectively on the reach of the counterinsurgency to stress, on the one hand, counterinsurgency victory over "hearts and minds" and, on the other hand, revolutionary defeat. Failure and defeat were undoubtedly very real for many of Dhufar's revolutionaries who experienced depression and disappointment in the late wartime and postwar years. Just as real, though, have been the persistent convictions of many Dhufaris that they in fact won the war. They perceived that they forced both the coup deposing Sultan

Said and the state's subsequent modernization agenda. The afterlives of revolution nevertheless disrupt these polarizing narratives.

Accounts of counterinsurgency victory and corresponding revolutionary defeat, and even the alternative interpretation of Dhufari victory, occlude counterhistories. These counterhistories take both everyday and, more occasionally, extraordinary forms. Some former revolutionaries in Dhufar, and their family members, drew on kinship, everyday socializing, and unofficial commemoration, as well as occasional extraordinary acts, to reproduce revolutionary social values and networks. In enacting these counterhistories, former militants created afterlives of revolution.

These counterhistories and afterlives challenge widely circulating narratives of counterinsurgency victory/revolutionary defeat and the related "winning hearts and minds" thesis. To the extent that conventional narratives occlude counterhistories, their claims about revolutionary failure risk becoming self-fulfilling. Attention to lasting legacies of revolution disrupts that possibility by showing how revolutionary values and networks continued to be important in postwar Oman. The notion that Dhufar's revolution ended in defeat and failure is, at the very least, an incomplete account.

A focus on afterlives also radically surpasses the narrow narrative that Dhufaris won the war because they changed Said's rule and government policies. Rather, afterlives bring into view a broader vision of revolutionary ideals and values. As Omani veteran revolutionary Zahran al-Sarimi has argued, a revolution's "goals, principles, values, and ambitions" persist beyond questions of military outcomes and run through society like "wildfire."[4] Such goals include the aspiration to create different, more egalitarian kinds of social relations. Former revolutionaries in Dhufar have continued to achieve small victories in that respect, long after the demise of armed insurgency and of formal exilic political opposition. As a result, the afterlives of revolution prompt a wholesale rethinking of the contested meanings of wartime and postwar political, social, and economic life. Such rethinking must avoid polarizing discourses of victory versus defeat and instead inquire how specific and diverse social interactions see legacies persist and transform.

The afterlives of revolution require not just reconsideration, from the perspective of what-survives-of-revolution, of the putative endings of revolution and counterinsurgency. They also demand reevaluation of revolutionary contexts and times of revolution-in-progress. The persistence of afterlives of revolution among former militants in Dhufar belies conventional accounts that few Dhufaris ever really supported Marxist-inspired programs. Such skepticism is inadequate. It cannot account for Dhufari wartime revolutionary resistance to counterinsurgency. Nor can it account for how and why former revolutionaries in postwar Dhufar reproduced values of social egalitarianism. These were values that Dhufaris had most fully embraced during the revolution and especially its Marxist-influenced incarnation.

Ongoing legacies of revolution prompt reconsideration of revolution-in-progress such as the Front's governance in Front-controlled Dhufar and in exile in southern Yemen. Dhufaris encountered contradictions, problematic outcomes, and gaps within programs for revolutionary social change. They nevertheless engaged with those programs. Activists exceeded the temporalities and scales of official programs, negotiated acceptable forms of change, and made choices about their engagement. This engagement made their experiences of revolutionary social change "messy," far from a neat fit with official revolutionary plans and narratives. This very engagement, rather than its putative absence, offers a framework for understanding lasting legacies resulting from that engagement. Moreover, this engagement did not end with the revolution. In postwar times, graduates of the revolutionary schools proved willing to work with Dhufaris of any tribal background and pioneered women's labor force participation. Though conventional histories have neglected revolutionary impacts, Dhufaris' revolutionary agency proved an enabling condition for later social and spatial transformation in postwar Dhufar.

The scope and form of the afterlives of revolution in Dhufar highlight the need to broaden the scales through which we apprehend revolutions and their outcomes. Some of the afterlives of revolution in Dhufar might seem hard to see. Those seeking legacies of the radical gender egalitarianism and feminism that made the revolution famous, and that Dhufar's women fighters seemed to embody, may initially be surprised—and perhaps disappointed. In postwar times, Dhufaris themselves acknowledged the social and religious conservatism of female former revolutionaries. Further probing nevertheless highlights other legacies of revolutionary gender emancipation. The pioneering labor force participation of female revolutionary graduates in the 1980s and 1990s helped normalize extra-domestic labor for later generations of women. Men and women tracing family histories to the revolution undertook feminist actions, such as supporting female electoral candidacy despite facing backlash for doing so. Some of the afterlives of revolution in Dhufar, such as a telephone conversation between a male cab driver and a woman with whom he shared revolutionary histories, or a gathering of old men among hundreds of such gatherings taking place across Salalah each evening, may seem so small in scale that some might discount them altogether. Yet in the context of Dhufar's predominant social conventions and hierarchies along lines of gender, tribe, ethnicity, race, and social status, all these afterlives, however apparently small-scale, were significant. They stood out to other Dhufaris, who acknowledged of former revolutionaries that "their culture is different."

Consequently, when thinking of the legacies that arise from revolutions that fail to achieve many of the goals for which militants struggled, we should not confine ourselves to thinking of grand scales of tangible legacies, such as the emergence of western European welfare states in the wake of the 1848 revolutions.[5] We should also recognize how revolutionary "actions produce dreams and ideas" both for participants and for future generations, with revolutions creating a "*horizon of expectations*" (italics in the original) outlasting the difficulties of a given historical moment.[6] One of the horizons where those expectations can play out, despite inauspicious circumstances of political repression, is in militants' sense that even if they did not transform society as they had hoped, they have nevertheless achieved personal transformation.[7]

The afterlives of revolution in Dhufar highlight the *social* dimensions of such personal transformation. Lasting personal transformations affected the ways former revolutionaries interacted with one another, with relatives, and with peers, and stood out to Dhufari observers. Small-scale, then, does not preclude social and, in specific contexts, other kinds of significance. Indeed, to the extent that "minor gestures and tendencies" constitute the means of people sustaining an interest in achieving different kinds of social relations, they "may be just as significant as major events" when it comes to creating and sustaining social change.[8]

Where anthropological studies of revolution have focused on the liminality of revolutionary experience and its social dimensions, the afterlives of revolution offer insight into how liminality can survive over time. Social relations that arose during revolutionary liminality, and its suspension of ordinary hierarchies, can persist. They endure in the longer-term alternative liminality of living under the surveillance of an authoritarian state. In Dhufar, friendships and affinities that began in the revolutionary liminal context survived in the postwar liminal context of a repressed political minority. These postwar friendships and affinities transgressed dominant social hierarchies along lines of gender, tribe, social status, ethnicity, and race.

At least in Dhufar, the means for the survival of liminality often lay in the sphere of the quotidian social interactions of kinship, everyday socializing, and subtle unofficial commemoration. The social camouflaging of these actions, arising from their overlapping with ordinary activities and interactions, also bestowed these actions with qualities of ambiguity. This further facilitated the survival of liminality in a context of absolutist authoritarian repression and surveillance.

The afterlives of revolution, then, radically extend the spatial and temporal horizons of revolutionary experiences, processes, outcomes, and legacies. Consequently, there is opportunity to rethink how Dhufar's revolution has gone on to have lasting effects. When it comes to the Front's most ambitious goals of establishing popular democratic rule and republicanism and achieving social, political, and economic emancipation from capitalist, colonial, and imperial oppression, "the revolution sustained by [the Front's] fighters" may well be "[l]ike the monsoon" with its "profound, if *temporary*, impact on their homeland" (emphasis added), with the revolution "rendering [Dhufar's] striking mountains and coasts more fertile with ideas, events, and possibilities than before or after."[9] When it comes to wider questions, however, of creating and sustaining appetites for enacting different kinds of social relations, for imagining a different kind of society and polity, and for taking action to show one's attachment to and willingness to enact related values and goals, then the afterlives of Dhufar's revolution suggest a different kind of resemblance to the monsoon. The similarity would lie not in the *temporariness* of effects but in the creation of conditions for long-term, recurring growth that continues and survives beyond vicissitudes. The fertility of Dhufar's revolution for "ideas, events, and possibilities" has in fact persisted beyond the exceptional catalyzing context of its anti-colonial liberation movement. There continue to be new roots and branches of the metaphorical tree of afterlives of revolution. They flourish in Dhufar, Oman more broadly, and further afield.

Dhufaris have created multiple postrevolutionary platforms for progressive politics. They have forged inclusive connections across traditional social hierarchies. These are the kinds of connections that revolutionaries once made, and which former revolutionaries have continued to cultivate in postwar everyday interactions. Forging and participating in these progressive initiatives, postwar generations of Dhufaris demonstrated the continuing appeal of the socially inclusive values of Dhufar's revolution. The ongoing appetite for such connections among younger generations suggests that their appeal may persist, even beyond the approaching day when those who experienced the revolution firsthand will no longer be there to reproduce revolutionary values through their own actions. Former militants' recreation of revolutionary social values in everyday interactions did not, in the view of my interlocutors, represent a cause of political concern to the Omani authorities. This was not necessarily the case, however, for the reemergence of Dhufaris' inclusive connections in postwar progressive politics. There, socially inclusive connections not only attracted the attention of Dhufari publics but also drew the attention, and sometimes the restrictive intervention, of Oman's authorities.

In the years since the Front's last formal activity as an exile political opposition in 1992, Dhufaris have created alternative platforms for progressive politics within Oman. In doing so, on most but not all occasions they triggered repression. In 1994, Dhufaris numbered over half of a group of religiously and socially diverse Omanis, many of whom were highly educated, whom the government accused of forging a political opposition that was amassing foreign support and illegal arms with the aim of overthrowing the government. Independent reports cast doubt upon these accusations. Dhufaris among the accused had formed a "charitable association" (*al-jam'iyyah al-khairiyyah*), strikingly taking up the same name as the association founded in 1962 that had preceded the DLF. The government arrested 430 Omanis, eventually trying (in closed courts, without legal representation for the accused) 160, and issuing sentences ranging from three to twenty years of imprisonment and three death sentences. The government reduced all these sentences to a pardon a year later. It sent a strong message that it "authorised no interference in the decision-making process" of the state.[10]

A few years later, a different political initiative in Dhufar sought to expand the terms of participation in public office. Under Qaboos, for many years the Dhufaris who occupied appointed and, eventually, elected government positions hailed from elite backgrounds. From the 1990s, the range of Omanis allowed to vote in elections to Oman's Consultative Council expanded, reaching universal suffrage in 2003. In the early 2000s, Dhufaris whose traditionally low-ranking social backgrounds had until then excluded them from appointed and elected government positions used broadened suffrage to challenge elites' domination of these roles.

Dhufaris hailing from backgrounds that, traditionally, attracted different degrees of stigma and marginality forged socially diverse voting leagues.

They pursued electoral success and inclusion in political office. The alliances brought together former urban client tribes, *shahrah* former mountain client tribes, *bahharah* client fishing families, and *sumur* formerly enslaved and their descendants. In 2003, these leagues elected to Oman's Consultative Council Said al-Shahri. He considered himself to be the first *shahri* to hold government office under Sultan Qaboos. In the 2007 Consultative Council elections, the leagues successfully supported al-Rashid al-Safi. He was the first Omani who traced family origins to enslaved status to achieve office through a popular vote. Al-Safi's election so disrupted traditional hierarchies that some Dhufaris nicknamed the league *al-gono*, after the cyclone that had devastated Oman's agricultural sector that year. The electoral leagues achieved forms of political inclusion previously unknown in the context of the Sultanate, but that nevertheless had precedents in the revolution. These alliances were exceptional among postwar progressive platforms in continuing to operate without attracting government sanction.[11]

Government repression would nonetheless befall subsequent initiatives for progressive politics. In Salalah's 2011 protests, some demonstrators echoed peers elsewhere in SWANA, as well as the earlier generations of Front activists in Dhufar. They celebrated the eclipsing of tribal identities, distinctions, and hierarchies in what Dhufaris dubbed their "Freedom Square."[12] The chant warning the government not to forget the 1970s and to "think of the grandchildren of the free men" suggested how some protestors took inspiration from Dhufar's revolution. After Salalah's became the longest-lasting of the 2011 protests in Oman, the government sent in tanks and troops from May 12 to 29.[13] They arrested "hundreds" of demonstrators.[14] Nevertheless, some Dhufaris continued to celebrate the detained protestors. One person explained to me their conviction that Dhufari popular support for the prisoners influenced the government decision to postpone the flight that had been scheduled to take released prisoners back from Muscat to Dhufar. In this person's understanding, the delay arose when the government learned that "there was a big reception (*istiqbal*) for [the released prisoners] at the airport, and the government didn't want them to arrive to that, and so they changed the time of the journey." Despite these tactics, many Dhufaris greeted the prisoners upon their eventual release on July 5, 2011.[15] The 2011 protests sparked further waves of the celebration of Dhufari oppositional dissent. In August that year, someone posted a video on YouTube celebrating the Front's revolution and its martyrs that would attract over one hundred thousand viewers.[16]

The 2011 protests constituted a liminal space in which supra-tribal identities arose, to the delight of some protestors. Two years later, Dhufaris from diverse social categories—elites, non-elites, city-dwellers, mountain-dwellers, *sumur*, and those hailing from client fishing backgrounds—sought to give such socially inclusive connections an institutional home in the form of a newly founded Council of Dhufar. The Council aimed to promote and celebrate Dhufar's rich cultural life.[17] Someone familiar with the initiative explained to me that the then advisor to the sultan on cultural affairs, ʿAbd al-ʿAziz al-Rawwas—himself a former member of the Front associated with those dissatisfied with the turn toward Marxism-Leninism—nevertheless shut down the Council, forbidding it from further activity. The government would not tolerate the existence of a formal organization enacting and promoting social inclusivity.

Why did the government repress the Council of Dhufar? The revolutionary social values of egalitarianism and inclusivity that underpinned ex-revolutionaries' everyday interactions apparently lacked political threat in that context. The government allowed highly surveilled persons to continue those interactions. But this perceived lack of threat did not necessarily hold in other settings. The very social values formerly associated with Dhufar's revolution could and did in other contexts have political implications. Values of social inclusivity animated and helped create platforms for progressive politics. Oman's government interpreted some of these platforms as resistance of actual or potential concern and repressed them accordingly.

It is not only social values of inclusivity and egalitarianism, once associated with the revolution, that Oman's government has repressed; Dhufari nationalism featured in the Front's early incarnation as the DLF and continues to attract punishment in postwar Oman. This may have been an even more sensitive topic for my interlocutors than ongoing revolutionary networks, relationships, values, and unofficial commemoration. No Dhufaris discussed with me the government's punishment of a Dhufari nationalist, the poet, writer, and activist Said al-Darodi, a few months before my fieldwork. On October 7, 2014, al-Darodi wrote on Facebook "I'm not Omani. . . . I'm Dhofari." He was detained incommunicado from October 10 to November 5, 2014, sentenced in absentia on March 18, 2015, to one year of prison on the accusation of "disturbing public order," and also sentenced to six months in prison and a fine of 1000 Omani riyals (circa $2,600) for "spreading sedition and hatred."[18] The potential connections between contemporary

Dhufari nationalism and its revolutionary precedents are a story that Dhufaris themselves are best placed to tell.

Dhufaris who lived through revolutionary governance and counterinsurgency violence have a distinctive experience of both, as well as their afterlives. But with revolutionaries having aspired to liberation for Oman and the Arabian Gulf, their history remains significant, and much debated, across Oman and beyond. Former Front member (and northerner) Zahran al-Sarimi writes not of Dhufar's revolution, but of "Oman's revolution."[19] In such memory work that skirts official censorship, Omanis locate this revolution within national history. They revisit sensitive episodes in Oman's past, including this revolution, as formative for Omani identity and futures. Undertaking such a task, Omani novelist Bushra Khalfan makes the case for including revolutionaries as contributors to national history. She both pleads that "[Dhufar's revolutionaries] loved Oman" and warns that when a "wound" remains "covered," it will be "always present and deep."[20] Beyond the Sultanate, the revolution continues to appeal to Arabophone and other audiences eager to engage with its protagonists and ideas through film screenings, books, and debates.[21] Such engagement is not mere retrospection. Responding to the 2019 Arabic edition of Takriti's *Monsoon Revolution*, the Bahraini former Front member Qasim Hadad argues that unless they learn about the lessons of the revolutionary past, "the new generations of militants and activists seeking a future of political change . . . will not be able to identify the prospects of our struggle."[22] Engagement with the revolution that gripped Dhufar remains an inspiration for multiple future projects of liberation.

In novel forms that emerge among new generations of Dhufaris, other Omanis, and wider audiences, the afterlives of Dhufar's revolution seem to be growing, and not decreasing, in political salience. This suggests that the significance of afterlives of revolution is likely to continue, rather than disappear, with the passing of time as long as new generations position themselves as "the grandchildren of the free men." Seeing themselves in this light, they warn the government—and themselves—not to forget the 1970s. Yet the terms on which Dhufaris can make claims on the government are undoubtedly changing. During my fieldwork, Dhufaris voiced anxieties about perceived uncertain economic futures. These concerns also preoccupy their northern neighbors.[23] Omanis were anxious in 2015 for new generations, many of whom struggled to find jobs. They feared for the country as a whole as the price of a barrel of crude oil dropped, hitting less than $30 in January 2016. Since then, amid COVID-19 curfews, global oil industry uncertainties and volatility, and greater transparency than in many years previously around Oman's deep-seated economic vulnerabilities, these anxieties can only have only multiplied.[24]

As Dhufaris and other Omanis face these uncertain times, in May 2021 some took to the streets of Salalah and other cities in protest.[25] They and their peers must look to futures beyond economies and political life dependent on oil and patronage. In that context, the afterlives of revolution continue to reissue invitations to imagine, for Oman and elsewhere, alternative horizons and futures.

Notes

Introduction

1. Alhassen, "Please."
2. See in anthropology e.g., Armbrust, *Martyrs*; Boutieri, "Bastardy"; Boutieri, "Events"; Dahlgren *Contesting*; Donham, *Marxist*; Hafez, *Women*; Hegland, *Days*; Montoya, *Gendered*; Rosendahl, *Inside*; Shah, *Nightmarch*; Wilson, *Sovereignty*.
3. E.g., Halliday, *Arabia*; Trabulsi, *Dhufar*.
4. Jabob, *Qiyadat*.
5. Takriti, *Monsoon*.
6. E.g., Bayat, *Revolution*; Behrooz, *Rebels*; La Botz, *What*.
7. E.g., Al-Khalili, *Waiting*; Babb, *After*; Silber, *Everyday*; Sprenkels, *After*; West, "Girls"; Wolin, *Wind*.
8. E.g., Donner, "Radical"; Thiranagama, *Mother's*.
9. E.g., Bayat, *Revolutionary*; Vacchiano and Afailal, "'Nothing.'"
10. E.g., see Makram-Ebeid, "'Old.'"
11. Takriti, *Monsoon*, 254–56, 48–49, 63–64, 69.
12. See e.g., bin Said, *Royal*, 16, 26–28, 33, 43–44, 48–49, 63–64, 69.
13. E.g., Fiennes, *Soldiers*, 168, 173, 178; Gardiner, *Service*, 73; Higgins, *SAS*, 8, 193; Jeapes, *SAS*, 27; Thwaites, *Muscat*, 73; Hughes, "'Model,'" 291; Peterson, *Oman's*, 253.
14. E.g., Arkless, *Secret*; Fiennes, *Soldiers*; Jeapes, *SAS*; Gardiner, *Service*; Higgins, *SAS*; Ladwig, "Supporting"; Peterson, *Oman's*, 393–94.
15. DeVore, "Complex"; Hazelton, *Bullets*, 81–105; Hughes, "Demythologising"; Newsinger, *British*, 136–56.
16. Spivak, "Subaltern."
17. See e.g., Maldonado-Torres, "Coloniality."
18. Thompson, *Making*.
19. Hazelton, "'Hearts'"; Hazelton, *Bullets*, 81–105; Jabob, *Qiyadat*; Newsinger, *British*, 136–56; Takriti, *Monsoon*.

20. See Donham, *Marxist*, 1–2. On terms in other languages, some with different associations, see Wilson, "Revolution."

21. Clapham, *Transformation*, 1.

22. Thomassen, "Notes," 683.

23. Skocpol, *States*, 4–5.

24. Cherstich et al., *Anthropologies*.

25. E.g., Foran, "Theories"; Allinson, "Fifth?" On typological approaches that seek to distinguish revolution "from all other processes of historical transformation" see Goodale, *Revolution*, 27.

26. Tilly, *Mobilization*, 189–222.

27. Badiou, *Event*. For anthropological interrogation of revolution as an event, see Boutieri, "Events"; Lazar, "Historical."

28. Mauss, "Sociological," 336.

29. E.g., Bayat, *Revolutionary*; Dahlgren, *Contesting*; Rosendahl, *Inside*; Humphrey, *Karl*; Armbrust, *Martyrs*; Donham, *Marxist*; Hegland, *Days*; Winegar, "Privilege"; Cherstich et al., *Anthropologies*; Thomassen, "Notes"; Wilson, "Revolution"; Starn, "Missing."

30. Donham, *Marxist*, 35.

31. E.g., Bayat, *Revolutionary*; Dahlgren, *Contesting*; Goodale, *Revolution*; Hafez, *Women*; Hasso and Salime, *Freedom*; Schielke, *Egypt*; Vince, *Fighting*; Winegar, "Privilege"; Winegar, "Civilized."

32. E.g., Al-Khalili, "*Halaqas*"; Bayat, *Revolutionary*; Hegland, *Days*; Wilson, *Sovereignty*.

33. Gennep, *Rites*; Thomassen, "Notes"; Turner, *Anthropology*.

34. Armbrust, *Martyrs*; Thomassen, "Notes."

35. Holbraad, "Revolución."

36. Al-Khalili, "Rethinking"; Bayat, *Revolutionary*, 235–48; Foucault, "Useless," 264–66; Ghamari-Tabrizi, *Foucault*, 72.

37. Ahram, *Break*; Dahlgren, "Making"; Lazreg, "French." On temporal connections in revolutionary time, see Lazar, "Historical." On revolutionary networks as resources for migratory emancipatory projects, see Enriquez, *Children*.

38. Valéri, "Qaboos," 5.

39. Silber, *Everyday*; Sprenkels, *After*; Traverso, *Left-wing*; West, "Girls." See also Frederiksen and Gotfredsen, *Georgian*.

40. Babb, *After*; Wolin, *Wind*, 234; ʿIkri, *Dhakirat*.

41. Babb, *After*, 15–16.

42. See e.g., Said al-Hashemi's review of Zahran al-Sarimi's memoir and ʿAbdullah Habib's Facebook posts about graves of executed revolutionaries. Al-Hashemi, "al-Umani"; Abroughi, "Omani."

43. *Merriam-Webster.com Dictionary*, s.v. "afterlife," accessed September 9, 2022, https://www.merriam-webster.com/dictionary/afterlife https://www.merriam-webster.com/dictionary/afterlife.

44. Scheffler, *Death*.

45. Salem, *Anticolonial*; Schäfers, "Afterlives."

46. Goodale, *Revolution*.
47. E.g., Behrooz, *Rebels*; Ghamari-Tabrizi, *Remembering*.
48. Behrooz, *Rebels*, xi. The focus of Behrooz's study is not afterlives, though, but the failures of leftist activism.
49. Donner, "Radical."
50. Thiranagama, *Mother's*, 219.
51. Worrall, *Statebuilding*, 289.
52. Abrougui, "Omani"; Donaghy, "Oman."
53. Al-Azri *Social*, xv; Matthiesen, *Sectarian*, 20–21; Ottaway and Ottaway, *Tale*; Worrall, "Oman."
54. E.g., Diamond, "Why," 98.
55. See Piliavsky, *Patronage*.
56. See Auyero and Benzecry, "Practical."
57. See e.g., Beblawi, "Rentier"; Beblawi and Luciani, *Rentier*; Gengler, *Group*; Mahdavy, "Patterns."
58. Shehabi, "Uncovering," 43.
59. See e.g., AlShehabi, *Contested*; Fuccaro, *Histories*; Matthiesen, *Other*; Takriti, *Monsoon*.
60. Hobbes, *Leviathan*.
61. Arkless, *Secret*, 64, 76, 143, 189; Jeapes, *SAS*, 133, 141–43.
62. Peterson, *Oman's*, 416.
63. Janzen, *Nomads*, 200.
64. E.g., Le Renard, *Society*; Ménoret, *Joyriding*.
65. I use "postwar" rather than "postconflict" in recognition of the fact that the boundaries between times of armed conflict and supposedly "postconflict" times can be unclear as similar tensions, social divisions, and ideologies continue.
66. Das, *Life*.
67. Hughes, "'Retired.'"
68. Kelly, "Attractions."
69. Johnson et al., "Weddings," 20.
70. See Chapters 4 and 5.
71. See Al-Azri, *Social*; Sachedina, *Cultivating*.
72. Scott, *Weapons*; Scott, *Domination*.
73. Freedom House, *Freedom*, 523. The website of Freedom House lists reports for years before and since my fieldwork of 2015.
74. E.g., al-'Amri, *Dhufar*; 'Aqil, *Uman*; Jabob, *Qiyadat*; Takriti, *Monsoon*.
75. Al-Shahri, "Madrasat"; Singh, "Award."
76. Al-Azri, *Social*, xiv.
77. Link, "China." I thank an interlocutor for explaining another element of ambiguity in Oman. Security agents may seek to create the impression of the efficiency and broad reach of their surveillance. In practice, though, surveillance may not be ubiquitous. The *impression* of efficiency nevertheless encourages people to surmise that they are under surveillance.
78. For similar implications in Cuba, see Shayne, *Revolution*.

79. See Wilson, "Oman's."
80. Coulter, *Bush Wives*.
81. On similar warnings, see Peutz, *Islands*, 22.
82. E.g., al-Sarimi, "Ma'athir."
83. Sachedina, *Cultivating*, 178.
84. Al-Azri, *Social*; Sachedina, *Cultivating*, 185–88.
85. E.g., Fanon, *Black*; Powell, *Tell*; Vaziri, "'Saidiya'"; Wright, *Physics*.
86. See e.g., Gross-Wyrtzen, "'There'"; Mahajan, "Remembering."
87. Powell, *Different*, 4.
88. Scaglioni, *Becoming*, 17.
89. Sachedina, *Cultivating*, 179–80.
90. See e.g., Aidi et al., "Racial"; al-Azraki, "Uncovering."
91. Link, "China."
92. E.g., al-'Amri, *Dhufar*; Halliday, *Arabia*; Jabob, *Qiyadat*; Takriti, *Monsoon*; Worrall, *Statebuilding*.
93. E.g., Afraz and Afraz, *Hamrah*; Rafeh, *Mohanna*; Srour, *Sa'at*; Trabulsi, *Surat;* Trabsulsi, *Dhufar*. Unfortunately I was not able to obtain a copy of al-Sarimi, *al-Bahth*.
94. Akehurst, *Won*; Fiennes, *Where*; Gardiner, *Service*; Higgins, *SAS*; Jeapes, *SAS*; Thwaites, *Muscat*.
95. Phillips and Hunt, "'Without,'" 657; "Oman: Defence Attaché's Report for 1973," stamped January 24, 1974, pp. 17–18, in FCO 8/2233, https://www.agda.ae/en/catalogue/tna/fco/8/2233/n/87.
96. Habib was convicted of "using the Internet in what would prejudice the state public order" under Article 19 of the 2011 Cyber Crimes Law. Abrougui, "Omani."
97. E.g., Dhofari Gucci, "Remaining"; Sachedina, *Cultivating*, 240n14.
98. I am grateful to Abdel Razzaq Takriti for sharing relevant sources with me.
99. I thank Miranda Morris for drawing my attention to unpublished MSAL poetry addressing Dhufar's revolution and counterinsurgency. On oblique meanings and the expression of rivalries in MSAL poetry, see Morris, "Thoughts," 23; Morris, *Oral*, 1090–105, 1675–712. For MSAL poetry addressing political violence in Soqotra, Yemen, see Peutz, *Islands*, 221–24.
100. Al-Azri, *Social*, xv.
101. E.g., Mockaitis, *British*, 72–95; Peterson, *Oman's*; Fiennes, *Where*; Gardiner, *Service*; Jeapes, *SAS*; Ministry of Defence, "Countering."
102. Mockaitis, *British*, 89.
103. Both the counterinsurgency and the Front laid land mines.
104. See e.g., Maldonado-Torres, "Coloniality."
105. Janzen, *Nomads*, 180n18.
106. E.g., al-Sarimi, "Ma'athir"; Trabulsi, *Dhufar*, 32–33.
107. Peterson, *Oman's*, 399.
108. Valéri, *Oman*, 231.
109. Gardiner, *Service*, 173.
110. Jones, "Military," 641.

111. Akehurst, *Won*, 71; Jeapes, *SAS*, 174–78, 240.
112. Hughes, "'Model,'" 291.
113. Dhufaris did not raise such accusations with me. Miranda Morris did not hear of such accusations from Dhufaris (personal communication).
114. Fiennes, *Soldiers*, 64–65.
115. Jabob, *Qiyadat*, 194.
116. Takriti, *Monsoon*, 272–73.
117. See e.g., Maldonado-Torres, "Coloniality."
118. Fiennes, *Soldiers*, 87; Jeapes, *SAS*, 239; Peterson, *Oman's*, 407.
119. DeVore, "Complex," 163.
120. Takriti, *Monsoon*, 84.
121. Hughes, "'Model,'" 283–84.
122. Higgins, *SAS*, 8; Ladwig, "Supporting," 77.
123. Ladwig, "Supporting," 76–77.
124. E.g., Akehurst, *Won*, 16; Ladwig, "Supporting."
125. Takriti, *Monsoon*.
126. Fuccaro, *Histories*.

Chapter 1

1. Rafeh, *Mohanna*, 94.
2. E.g., DeVore, "Complex"; Hazelton, "'Hearts'"; Hazelton, *Bullets*, 81–105; Hughes, "Demythologising"; Newsinger, *British*, 136–56; Takriti, *Monsoon*; Worrall, *Statebuilding*.
3. Government of Oman, *Census*.
4. Morris, "Dhofar," 54.
5. Crone, *Meccan*, 12–29.
6. See e.g, Morris, "Harvesting." Frankincense also grows in parts of southern Yemen, in the Soqotra archipelago, and in parts of the Horn of Africa.
7. Tabook, "Tribal," 12.
8. Ibn Battuta, *Travels*, 2:382–91.
9. See Costa, "Study"; Zarins, "Aspects."
10. Morris, "Dhofar," 67.
11. See e.g., Janzen, *Nomads*, 161; Morris, "Thoughts"; Tabook, "Tribal," 2–3.
12. On Dhufar's tribal hierarchies, see Tabook, "Tribal," 43, 276–86.
13. The plain is named after a type of grass on the foothills. Morris, "Dhofar," 63.
14. On the prewar suq, see al-Ghassani, *al-Tariq*, 13–15.
15. Unless writing explicitly of Salalah village, I use Salalah to mean the post-1970s agglomeration of historically separate villages.
16. *Sadah* families tracing descent from the prophet Muhammad first moved from Yemen's Hadhramawt to Dhufar in the twelfth century. Tabook, "Tribal," 75. Some interlocutors attributed the presence in Dhufar of families of Somali origin to historical ties with Somali traders of frankincense.
17. Bent, *Southern*, 233–34; Janzen, *Nomads*, 149–50; Thomas, *Arabia*, 9.

18. Tabook, "Tribal," 108.
19. Morris, "Dhofar," 66.
20. On the distinction between Kathir al-jabal and Bedouin Kathir, see Tabook, "Tribal," 49–51.
21. Tabook, "Tribal," 61–66.
22. Janzen, "Modern," 291.
23. Janzen, *Nomads*, 56–57, 66–68, 72–73, 85–86, 113–17, 132, 155; Tabook, "Tribal," 17, 25–27, 61–70.
24. Tabook, "Tribal," 14.
25. Morris, "Dhofar," 68.
26. "Possible effects in RAF Salalah arising from threats to the Sultan in Dhofar" (hereafter, "Possible"), January 20, 1969, p. 22, in FO 1016/804, https://www.agda.ae/en/catalogue/tna/fo/1016/804/n/183; Burdett, *Records*, 4:116.
27. Morris, "Dhofar," 56.
28. Morris, "Dhofar," 56.
29. There are long-standing Sunni, Shiʿa, and Hindu minorities in present-day northern Oman. See Valéri, *Oman*, 19–22.
30. On Ibadhi beliefs in Oman, see Hoffman, *Essentials*, 5–26; Wilkinson, *Ibâḍism*; Wilkinson, *Imamate*.
31. Tabook, "Tribal," 75.
32. Morris, "Thoughts," 19.
33. Takriti, *Monsoon*, 26.
34. Jones and Ridout, *History*, 54.
35. Jacob, *God*.
36. Takriti, *Monsoon*, 28, 31.
37. Owtram, *Modern*. British advisors did not always succeed in persuading Sultan Said to take their advice regarding internal governance affairs. Worrall, *Statebuilding*, 131.
38. Jones and Ridout, *History*, 64–96; Owtram, *Modern*; Valéri, *Oman*, 24–26.
39. Townsend, *Oman*, 43.
40. Valéri, *Oman*, 28.
41. Boustead, *Wind*, 223.
42. "Report by Major R. J. F. Brown on Dhofar" (hereafter, "Report,") March 31, 1968, p. 5, in FCO 8/572, https://www.agda.ae/en/catalogue/tna/fco/8/572/n/21.
43. Atheer, *Sultanate*.
44. "Report," March 31, 1968, p. 5, in FCO 8/572, https://www.agda.ae/en/catalogue/tna/fco/8/572/n/21.
45. Pridham, "Oman," 135; Anonymous, "Notes," Appendix A.
46. Takriti, *Monsoon*, 232; Valéri, *Oman*, 62. For an argument that observers have exaggerated Said's restrictions, see Pridham, "Oman," 133–35.
47. "The Russian's Technology in the Service of Sultan Qabous," by Salim al-Lawzi, published in Hawadith March 17, 1972, p. 3, translated in FCO 8/1844, https://www.agda.ae/en/catalogue/tna/fco/8/1844/n/60.

48. Peterson, *Oman's*, 418.
49. Martin, "Dhufar."
50. Burdett, *Records*, 1:57.
51. Halliday, *Arabia*, 314; Takriti, *Monsoon*, 36; Townsend, *Oman*, 97.
52. For reinterpretations of Said, see Chatty, "Rituals"; Jones and Ridout, *History*; Rabi, *Emergence*; Valéri, *Oman*, 34–38.
53. E.g., Arkless, *Secret*.
54. E.g., Halliday, *Arabia*.
55. Takriti, *Monsoon*, 155.
56. Said diminished his financial dependence on British subsidies in the 1930s and benefited from British military subsidies during WWII, but British subsidies became more important again from the 1950s. Owtram, *Modern*, 82.
57. See e.g., Jones and Ridout, *History*, 115–31; Newsinger, *British*, 139–44; Peterson, *Oman's*, 63–183.
58. E.g., Ta'i, *Mala'ikat*. On the (de)colonial implications of using or avoiding "revolution," see e.g., Lazreg, "French."
59. The Iraq Petroleum Company (IPC) created a subsidiary, originally Petroleum Development (Oman and Dhofar), in 1937. The shareholders were Anglo-Persian (the predecessor of British Petroleum, BP), 23.75%; Shell, 23.75%; Compagnie Française des Pétroles (CFP, the predecessor of Total), 23.75%; Near East Development Company (NEDCO, a predecessor of ExxonMobil), 23.75%, and Calouste S. Gulbenkian, 5%. Between late 1959 and early 1960, Shell became the major shareholder. By 1967, Shell owned 85%. As of 1980, and at the time of writing, the shareholders of PDO are the Omani government, 60%; Shell, 34%; Total (formerly CFP), 4%; and Partex (a holding company of Gulbenkian), 2%. Clark, *Underground*, 14, 32, 50, 93.
60. Owtram, *Modern*.
61. Townsend, *Oman*, 63–64.
62. Development Department materials do not discuss projects in Dhufar. E.g., "Review of Progress of the Development Department of the Sultanate of Muscat and Oman covering July 1959 to December 1960," n.d., in FO 371/156787, https://www.agda.ae/en/catalogue/tna/fo/371/156787/n/74.
63. Burdett, *Records*, 4:136.
64. "RAF Salalah," October 16, 1969, FO 1016/804, p. 1, https://www.agda.ae/en/catalogue/tna/fo/1016/804/n/51.
65. Anonymous, "Notes," 6; "Appointment of Major Chauncy as Administrative Deputy to the Sultan of Muscat and Oman," August 17, 1960, in FO 371/148907, https://www.agda.ae/en/catalogue/tna/fo/371/148907/n/73.
66. This discussion of historical context draws on Takriti, *Monsoon*.
67. See e.g., Takriti, *Monsoon*, 81; Worrall, *Statebuilding*, 49–50.
68. Valéri, *Oman*, 61.
69. Worrall, *Statebuilding*, 49–50.
70. United Nations Ad Hoc Committee on Oman, "Report"; Takriti, *Monsoon*, 79–81.

Notes to Chapter 1

71. Anonymous, "Notes," 7. John Craven Wilkinson archive, EUL MS 119/3/29. Courtesy of Special Collections, University of Exeter.
72. Chalcraft, "Migration."
73. Takriti, *Monsoon*, 55.
74. Takriti, *Monsoon*, 55.
75. "Report," March 31, 1968, p. 4, in FCO 8/572, https://www.agda.ae/en/catalogue/tna/fco/8/572/n/20; Jabob, *Qiyadat*, 274.
76. Jabob, "Inha'."
77. Saudi Arabia and the exiled imam of Oman supplied bin Nufl and his supporters with weapons for the 1964 attacks. Takriti, *Monsoon*, 62–64.
78. Takriti, *Monsoon*, 71.
79. "Voice of the Arabs," December 26, 1967, in FCO 8/571, https://www.agda.ae/en/catalogue/tna/fco/8/571/n/89.
80. Takriti, *Monsoon*, 72.
81. "Dawn at Arab Gulf" (hereafter, "Dawn") in *The Baghdad Observer*, April 27, 1971, in FCO 8/1678, https://www.agda.ae/en/catalogue/tna/fco/8/1678/n/11.
82. Burdett, *Records*, 1:218.
83. Ladwig, "Supporting," 67.
84. "Report," March 31, 1968, pp. 3–4, in FCO 8/572, https://www.agda.ae/en/catalogue/tna/fco/8/572/n/19.
85. Gulf Committee, *Women*, 23; Thwaites, *Muscat*, 116.
86. Srour, *Sa'at*.
87. Takriti, *Monsoon*, 103–4.
88. Takriti, *Monsoon*, 85.
89. "Sultanate balance sheet, second quarter 1968," June 27, 1968, p. 2, in FCO 8/589, https://www.agda.ae/en/catalogue/tna/fco/8/589/n/162.
90. Takriti, *Monsoon*, 108–11.
91. Takriti, *Monsoon*, 113.
92. Takriti, *Monsoon*, 109.
93. Lovell, *Maosim*.
94. See Mampilly, *Rebel*, 217–18.
95. Lovell, *Maoism*, 39.
96. Takriti *Monsoon*, 266.
97. Jabob, "Inha'."
98. "Possible effects on RAF Salalah," January 20, 1969, p. 27, in FO 1016/804, https://www.agda.ae/en/catalogue/tna/fo/1016/804/n/188.
99. E.g., see PFLO, *Sijil*, 144, 170, 191–92.
100. Al-Sarimi, "al-Qawl." On links between leftist movements in the Gulf, see Matthiesen, "Arabia."
101. Afraz and Afraz, *Hamrah*; Jabob, *Qiyadat*; Takriti, *Monsoon*, 103–5, 116, 128–29, 131, 280, 294–98, 302–3, 307. Relations between the Front and China declined early in 1972. Worrall, *Statebuilding*, 215, 283.

102. Afraz and Afraz, *Hamrah*; Bayat, *Revolution*, 31; Rafeh, *Mohanna*. The parties to the conflict did not map onto clear-cut national divisions. There were, eventually, Dhufaris and Iranians fighting for both sides.
103. DeVore, "Complex," 163.
104. DeVore, "Complex," 163.
105. Townsend, *Oman*, 120, 175.
106. Newsinger, *British*, 152.
107. Clark, *Underground*, 17; de la Grandville, "Marmul."
108. Hurewitz, "Persian," 107.
109. "Consequences of the Sultan's Sudden Death," January 25, 1968, Attachment B. FCO 8/574, https://www.agda.ae/en/catalogue/tna/fco/8/574/n/52.
110. Iran initially preferred secrecy too. Goode, "Assisting," 452.
111. E.g., Arkless, *Secret*, 153; Higgins, *SAS*, 1, 3, 6; Jeapes, *SAS*.
112. Arkless, *Secret*, 30.
113. Akehurst, *Won*, 3, 76.
114. Phillips and Hunt, "'Without,'" 657.
115. Takriti, *Monsoon*, 2013: 160–93.
116. Takriti, "Colonial."
117. Takriti, *Monsoon*, 199–200, 253–54.
118. "Bombs for SOAF," August 17, 1971, in FCO 8/1687, https://www.agda.ae/en/catalogue/tna/fco/8/1687/n/12.
119. For discussions see e.g., DeVore, "Complex"; Hazelton, *Bullets*, 81–105; Hughes, "Demythologising"; Jones, "Military"; Newsinger, *British*, 136–56.
120. Hazelton, *Bullets*, 84, 89, 99, 102–4.
121. Hazelton, *Bullets*.
122. Hazelton, *Bullets*, 100.
123. Jeapes, *SAS*, 131–32.
124. Ladwig, "Supporting," 76.
125. Ladwig, "Supporting," 76.
126. "The Principles Governing British Military Assistance in Oman," pp. A6–A8, May 14, 1974, in FCO 8/2229, https://www.agda.ae/en/catalogue/tna/fco/8/2229/n/25.
127. Halliday, *Arabia*, 334; Peterson, *Oman's*, 286.
128. E.g., see Embassy of the Sultanate of the Oman in London 1973, "Erroneous."
129. The British recovered thirty-eight Front corpses but suspected more losses. Newsinger, *British*, 151. In a later compilation of casualties (which it recognized as incomplete), the Front included biographies of eighteen combatants who died at Mirbat. PFLO, *Sijil*, 101–11.
130. Fitchett, "End," 5; Graham, *Iran*, 6.
131. PFLO, *Sijil*, 7.
132. PFLO, *Sijil*.
133. Fitchett, "End," 5.
134. Graham, "Iran," 6.
135. Ministry of Defence, *UK*, 4.

136. Akehurst, *Won*, ix–x.
137. PFLO, "Annual," 30.
138. Mockaitis, *British*.
139. Miranda Morris, personal communication.
140. See Chapter 6.
141. I interpret the report's use of the term "Caviar" to refer to Iranian forces. The first Iranian supplies to the counterinsurgency were dubbed "Operation Caviar." Peterson, *Oman's*, 290.

Chapter 2

1. Srour, *Saʿat*.
2. Halliday, *Arabia*, 378; Srour, "Visit," 7.
3. PFLO, *Sijil*, 130.
4. Lal, *African*, 232.
5. E.g., Fiennes, *Soldiers*, 87; Jeapes, *SAS*, 239; Peterson, *Oman's*, 407.
6. Takriti, *Monsoon*, 269.
7. Hafez, *Women*; Matthiesen, *Sectarian*; Mahfaif, "Min Fawaʾid"; Mahdavi, *Passionate*.
8. Bayat, *Revolution*.
9. Al-Khalili, "Rethinking"; Bayat, *Revolutionary*, 15; Fernández-Savater et al., "Life," 146–47; Vacchiano and Afailal, "'Nothing.'"
10. E.g., Donham, *Marxist*; Humphrey, *Karl Marx*; Kim, *Everyday*; Lackner, *P. D. R. Yemen*; Lal, *African*; Luong, *Revolution*; Mauss, "Sociological"; Montoya, *Gendered*; Nugent, *Spent*; Rosendahl, *Inside*; Verdery, *Socialism*; Yan, *Private*.
11. E.g., Peteet, *Landscape*; Shah, *Nightmarch*; Thiranagama, *Mother's*; West, "Girls"; Wilson, *Sovereignty*.
12. Mampilly, *Rebel*, 78, 217–20.
13. Srour, *Saʿat*; Takriti, *Monsoon*, 262; Trabulsi, *Dhufar*, 141.
14. See e.g., Lal, *African*; Montoya, *Gendered*; Wilson, *Sovereignty*.
15. E.g., Kim, *Everyday*; Montoya, *Gendered*; Thiranagama, *Mother's*; Wilson, *Sovereignty*.
16. Vince, *Fighting*, 34.
17. Wilson, *Sovereignty*, 191.
18. Molyneux, "Mobilization."
19. E.g., Scott, "Revolution"; Stoll, *Between*; Vince, *Fighting*, 47.
20. Shah, "Intimacy," 503n12; Stoll, *Between*, 28, 42–57; Schielke, *Egypt*, 215.
21. Shah, "Intimacy."
22. Winegar, "Privilege"; Wolf, *Peasant*.
23. Scott, "Revolution."
24. Kim, *Everyday*, 12.
25. Donham, *Marxist*, 59–81.
26. Verdery, *What*, 65; Vince, *Fighting*, 129–30.
27. Montoya, *Gendered*, 190.
28. E.g., Ledeneva, *Russia's*.

29. Scott, *Conscripts*.
30. Bardawil, *Revolution*, xiv.
31. E.g., Bardawil, *Revolution*; Silber, *Everyday*; Sprenkels, *After*; Traverso, *Left-wing*; West. "Girls"; Wilson, *Sovereignty*, 243.
32. Lal, *African*, 10, 15, 232; Wilson, *Sovereignty*, 3.
33. Bardawil, *Revolution*, 22; Lal, *African*, 239; Scott, *Conscripts*, 55.
34. Montoya, *Gendered*, 195–96. See also Babb, *After*; Sprenkels, *After*.
35. Thiranagama, *Mother's*, 12.
36. On similar distinctions elsewhere in northern Oman and SWANA see e.g., Limbert, *Time*; Abu Lughod, *Veiled*.
37. Liebhaber, "Society."
38. Thomas, *Arabia*, 19.
39. Thomas, *Arabia*, 32.
40. Al-Nakib, *Kuwait*, 80.
41. On interpretations in Oman of Islamic precedent for the avoidance of women marrying "below" their social status, see Al-Azri, *Social*.
42. Janzen, *Nomads*, 149.
43. Thomas, *Arabia*, 31.
44. Janzen, *Nomads*, 149.
45. "Report," March 31, 1968, pp. 4–8, in FCO 8/572, https://www.agda.ae/en/catalogue/tna/fco/8/572/n/20.
"Possible," January 20, 1969, p. 22, in FO 1016/804, https://www.agda.ae/en/catalogue/tna/fo/1016/804/n/191.
46. "Character of the Sultan," July 18, 1972, in FCO 8/1845, https://www.agda.ae/en/catalogue/tna/fco/8/1845/n/122; Halliday, *Arabia*, 277; Martin, "Dhufar."
47. Takriti, *Monsoon*, 36.
48. Janzen, *Nomads*, 150.
49. Takriti, *Monsoon*, 192–93.
50. Martin, "Dhufar."
51. Gulf Committee, *Women*, 32.
52. Sichel, "Sultanate," 12.
53. "Report," March 31, 1968, p. 5, in FCO 8/572, https://www.agda.ae/en/catalogue/tna/fco/8/572/n/21; Janzen, *Nomads*, 196.
54. "Report," March 31, 1968, pp. 3–5, in FCO 8/572, https://www.agda.ae/en/catalogue/tna/fco/8/572/n/20; Burdett, *Records*, 5:201. On the "colonial gaze" and the construction of ethnic distinctions in Arabia, see AlShehabi, *Contested*.
55. Burdett, *Records*, 4:116.
56. Takriti, *Monsoon*, 27.
57. United Nations Ad Hoc Committee on Oman, "Report," 163.
58. Gulf Committee, *Women*, 9.
59. See e.g., Lackner, *P. D. R. Yemen*; West, "Girls;" Wilson, *Sovereignty*.
60. KROAG, "Interview with Hudda," 48.

61. Takriti, *Monsoon*, 118–19.
62. Halliday, *Arabia*, 382.
63. Halliday, *Arabia*, 383.
64. Tabook, "Tribal," 72–73.
65. Halliday, *Arabia*, 383.
66. The fourth region existed by 1970. Takriti, *Monsoon*, 115.
67. PFLOAG 1972 in Gulf Committee 1974: 54–56.
68. KROAG, "Interview with Hudda," 48.
69. Halliday 1974: 382; Takriti 2013: 119.
70. Halliday 1974: 382.
71. "Dawn," April 27, 1971, in FCO 8/1678, https://www.agda.ae/en/catalogue/tna/fco/8/1678/n/11; Halliday, *Arabia*, 382.
72. "The Truth About the Communists in Dhofar" (hereafter, "Truth"), February 19, 1973, p. 4, in FCO 8/2031, https://www.agda.ae/en/catalogue/tna/fco/8/2031/n/114.
73. "Truth," February 19, 1973, p. 4, in FCO 8/2031, https://www.agda.ae/en/catalogue/tna/fco/8/2031/n/114.
74. PFLOAG National Charter of 1968, cited in Trabulsi, *Dhufar*, 246.
75. Takriti, *Monsoon*, 122.
76. Takriti, *Monsoon*, 123
77. E.g., Allan, *Silenced*; Shayne, *Revolution*; Montoya, *Gendered*; West, "Girls"; Vince, *Fighting*.
78. Takriti, *Monsoon*, 119–20.
79. Halliday, *Arabia*, 376. See also KROAG 1980, "Traditional," 22; Srour, *Sa'at*.
80. Halliday, *Arabia*, 380; Takriti, *Monsoon*, 122.
81. "Truth," February 19, 1973, p. 4, in FCO 8/2031, https://www.agda.ae/en/catalogue/tna/fco/8/2031/n/114; Halliday, *Arabia*, 380.
82. Halliday, *Arabia*, 380.
83. Gulf Committee, *Women*, 15.
84. Wilson, *Sovereignty*, 147–79.
85. Takriti, *Monsoon*, 122; Al Shahri, "Issue."
86. KROAG "Second," 34–35.
87. Halliday, *Arabia*, 378.
88. E.g., see Afraz and Afraz, *Hamrah*; Hennebelle and Martineau Henebelle, "Hour"; Ibrahim, *Warda* (trans. Jacquemond); Liberation Support Movement, "New"; PFLO, *Uman*. On the ongoing problematic appeal of contemporary equivalent images of Kurdish female combatants, see Schäfers, *Voices*.
89. Halliday, *Arabia*, 374–75; "Oman Intelligence Report 48," August 26–September 8, 1973, p. 8, in FCO 8/2022, https://www.agda.ae/en/catalogue/tna/fco/8/2022/n/79; Jabob, *Qiyadat*; KROAG, "Experiences"; Rafeh, *Mohanna*; Afraz and Afraz, *Hamrah*. For film footage, see Srour, *Sa'at*.
90. E.g., Malkki, *Purity*; Wilson, *Sovereignty*.

91. KROAG, *Revolution*, 23.
92. Jabob, *Qiyadat*, 200.
93. PFLO, "9th June," 5; "Truth," February 19, 1973, p. 2, in FCO 8/2031, https://www.agda.ae/en/catalogue/tna/fco/8/2031/n/112.
94. "Oman Intelligence Report 48," August 26–September 8, 1973, p. 8, in FCO 8/2022, https://www.agda.ae/en/catalogue/tna/fco/8/2022/n/79.
95. A surrendered Front fighter recalled seventy male and thirty female recruits. A female recruit recalled from her time there eighty-four women and seventy men. Overall estimates of the proportion of women fighters in the Front range from 5 percent to 30 percent. "Oman Intelligence Report 48," August 26–September 8, 1973, p. 8, in FCO 8/2022, https://www.agda.ae/en/catalogue/tna/fco/8/2022/n/79; KROAG, "Hudda," 49; Takriti, *Monsoon*, 122.
96. "Truth," February 19, 1973, p. 2, in FCO 8/2031, https://www.agda.ae/en/catalogue/tna/fco/8/2031/n/112.
97. "Truth," February 19, 1973, p. 2, in FCO 8/2031, https://www.agda.ae/en/catalogue/tna/fco/8/2031/n/112; KROAG, "Hudda," 49.
98. KROAG, "Hudda," 49.
99. Takriti, *Monsoon*, 114.
100. Takriti, *Monsoon*, 115. Nevertheless, a surrendered Front fighter described to the British that "High Command members are paid the equivalent of RO 40 pm," but "[o]rdinary fighters get nothing—only the sick, who receive RP 4 pm." "Oman Intelligence Report 59," January 27–February 9, 1974, p. 3, in FCO 8/2233, https://www.agda.ae/en/catalogue/tna/fco/8/2233/n/50.
101. Jabob, *Qiyadat*, 175.
102. Takriti, *Monsoon*, 124.
103. Jabob, *Qiyadat*, 211–12.
104. "Oman intelligence report 51," October 7–20, 1973, p. 3, in FCO 8/2022, https://www.agda.ae/en/catalogue/tna/fco/8/2022/n/43.
105. Jabob, *Qiyadat*, 183–84.
106. Jabob, *Qiyadat*, 181.
107. Jabob, *Qiyadat*, 192.
108. Jabob, *Qiyadat*, 207.
109. "Oman intelligence report 51," October 7–20, 1973, p. 3, in FCO 8/2022, https://www.agda.ae/en/catalogue/tna/fco/8/2022/n/43; Jabob, *Qiyadat*, 197, 216.
110. Jabob, *Qiyadat*, 178; Takriti, *Monsoon*, 124.
111. Halliday, *Arabia*, 374.
112. Srour, *Saʿat*.
113. Miranda Morris, personal communication.
114. Takriti, *Monsoon*, 105.
115. Takriti, *Monsoon*, 112.
116. Takriti suggests that few had read Marx. Soviet journalist Alexei Vasilyev reported seeing Front fighters reading translations of Lenin in Arabic. The curriculum in Revolution

Camp reportedly included works by Marx, Engels, and Mao Tse Tung. Takriti, *Monsoon*, 213; "Soviet interest in Dhofar," August 11, 1971, in FCO 8/1667, https://www.agda.ae/en/catalogue/tna/fco/8/1667/n/64; "Truth," February 19, 1973, p. 2, in FCO 8/2031, https://www.agda.ae/en/catalogue/tna/fco/8/2031/n/112.

117. Takriti, *Monsoon*, 112–13.
118. Takriti, *Monsoon*, 112.
119. PFLOAG, "Liberated," 2.
120. Lovell, *Maoism*, 36.
121. Halliday, *Arabia*, 378; "Oman Intelligence Report 60," February 10–23, 1974, p. 2, in FCO 8/2233, https://www.agda.ae/en/catalogue/tna/fco/8/2233/n/40.
122. Afraz and Afraz, *Hamrah*, 55.
123. Halliday later published critical reflections. Halliday, "Arabia."
124. Trabulsi, *Dhufar*, 11.
125. PFLOAG, *al-Mahkamah al-'askariyyah*, 3, 5, and 15 February 1970, in OMA 409535 JAB SHA, Special Collections, Old Library, Exeter University.
126. Takriti, *Monsoon*, 273.
127. E.g., Arkless, *Secret*, 215; Fiennes, *Soldiers*, 35, 37–39, 145–47; Gardiner, *Service*, 21, 73; Higgins, *SAS*, 8; Jeapes, *SAS*, 27.
128. Embassy of Oman in London, "Communist," 7.
129. Risse, *Community*, 43.
130. On revolutionary collective identities and the contrast between the Front's and the sultan's understandings of Arabization and Omanization, see Takriti, *Monsoon*, 252–53, 300–1.
131. KROAG, "Abdel," 28.
132. KROAG. "Role . . . Third," 35.
133. Takriti, *Monsoon*, 264.
134. Takriti, *Monsoon*, 121–22.
135. E.g., see Hafez, *Women*, 133–81.
136. "Truth," February 19, 1973, p. 4, in FCO 8/2031, https://www.agda.ae/en/catalogue/tna/fco/8/2031/n/114.
137. Takriti, *Monsoon*, 88, drawing on a 1969 source.
138. See also Montoya, *Gendered*.
139. Gulf Committee, *Women*, 26.
140. See also Bernal, "Equality"; Montoya, *Gendered*.
141. Afraz and Afraz, *Hamrah*, 83–84.
142. Afraz and Afraz, *Hamrah*, 42–43.
143. Afraz and Afraz, *Hamrah*, 94.
144. Halliday, *Arabia*, 331.
145. Manual labor necessary for livestock-raising did not necessarily hold stigma for historically free Dhufaris. Miranda Morris, personal communication.
146. Halliday, *Arabia*, 382.
147. PFLOAG, "Liberated," 2.
148. Afraz and Afraz, *Hamrah*, 82.

149. On self-emancipation prior to abolition in Atlantic enslavement, see e.g., Helg, *Slave*.
150. Takriti, *Monsoon*, 123.
151. "Report," March 31, 1968, p. 4, in FCO 8/572, https://www.agda.ae/en/catalogue/tna/fco/8/572/n/21.
152. Gulf Committee, *Women*, 34; Thwaites 1995: 116.
153. Gulf Committee, *Women*, 11, 34.
154. PFLO, *Sijil*, 17, 22.
155. Takriti, *Monsoon*, 122.
156. Gulf Committee, *Women*, 26.
157. Rafeh, *Mohanna*, 112.
158. E.g., PFLO, "Astar."
159. KROAG, "Experiences," 22.
160. Kim, *Everyday*.
161. E.g., Fiennes, *Soldiers*, 146; Gardiner, *Service*, 73; Jeapes, *SAS*, 27.
162. "Truth," February 19, 1973, p. 1, in FCO 8/2031, https://www.agda.ae/en/catalogue/tna/fco/8/2031/n/111.
163. Jabob, *Qiyadat*, 194.
164. Takriti, *Monsoon*, 238.
165. "Truth," February 19, 1973, p. 1, in FCO 8/2031, https://www.agda.ae/en/catalogue/tna/fco/8/2031/n/111.
166. "Record of a Conversation Between HM Ambassador, Muscat . . .," April 9, 1974, p. A1, in FCO 8/2241, https://www.agda.ae/en/catalogue/tna/fco/8/2241/n/133.
167. E.g., "Truth," February 19, 1973, p. 1, in FCO 8/2031, https://www.agda.ae/en/catalogue/tna/fco/8/2031/n/111; Arkless, *Secret*, 215; Fiennes, *Soldiers*, 31–32, 168; Jeapes, *SAS*, 38.
168. Jeapes, *SAS*, 60.
169. Halliday, *Arabia*, 307; Thomas, *Arabia*, 51.
170. Miranda Morris, personal communication.
171. Trabulsi, *Surat*.
172. E.g., bin 'Alawi, "Arabian Gulf," Voice of the Arabs, December 12, 1967, in FCO 8/95, https://www.agda.ae/en/catalogue/tna/fco/8/95/n/55.
173. Takriti, *Monsoon*, 263.
174. Vasilyev, "Rebels against slavery," in *New Times* 38, n.d. 1971, p. 27, in FCO 8/1668, https://www.agda.ae/en/catalogue/tna/fco/8/1668/n/57.
175. Takriti, *Monsoon*, 301.
176. Fiennes, *Soldiers*, 168; Jeapes, *SAS*, 38.
177. Miranda Morris, personal communication.
178. Halliday, *Arabia*, 380.
179. Halliday, *Arabia*, 384. When the Front took Rakhyut in August 1969, the western region came under the movement's control. The government reclaimed Rakhhut on January 9, 1975, and the wider western region over the course of 1975. Worrall, *Statebuilding*, 281, 286–87.

180. Takriti, *Monsoon*, 137.
181. PFLOAG, "National," 29.

Chapter 3

1. Government forces recaptured Sadah from the Front on February 23, 1971. Worrall, *Statebuilding*, 283.
2. "Visit to Dhofar, 17-18 October 1971," p. 3, in FCO 8/1668, https://www.agda.ae/en/catalogue/tna/fco/8/1668/n/44. I have modified the spelling of Musallam.
3. "Visit to Dhofar, 17-18 October 1971," p. 3, in FCO 8/1668, https://www.agda.ae/en/catalogue/tna/fco/8/1668/n/44.
4. Lefebvre, *Production*.
5. De Certeau, *Practice*; Fuccaro, *Histories*.
6. E.g., Al-Nakib, "Kuwait's"; Al-Nakib, *Kuwait*; Bristol-Rhys, *Emirati*.
7. For a discussion see e.g., Valéri, *Oman*, 121–22. Oman's dominant narrative pairs transformation under Qaboos with claims of ancient national heritage. Sachedina, *Cultivating*.
8. In his July 23, 1970, accession speech, Qaboos said: "Yesterday it was complete darkness and with the help of God, tomorrow will be a new dawn on Muscat, Oman and its people." Bin Said, *Royal*, 7.
9. Qaboos first used *"nahdah"* in the National Day speech on November 18, 1974. Bin Said 2015: 31. While the adoption of the term *nahdah* echoed Ibadhi discourse, Ibadhism, which supports the appointment of an imam on the grounds of merit, has an uneasy relationship with hereditary monarchy.
10. See e.g., Valéri, *Oman*, 77–80.
11. Valéri, *Oman*, 101.
12. Phillips and Hunt, "'Without.'"
13. See Valéri, *Oman*.
14. Fuccaro, *Histories*, 11.
15. Gardner, "Rumour"; Gardner, "Transforming"; Beaugrand, "Urban"; Ménoret, *Joyriding*.
16. Al-Nakib, "Kuwait's"; Al-Nakib, *Kuwait*, 14.
17. Philips and Hunt, "'Without.'"
18. Lefebvre, *Production*.
19. Fuccaro, *Histories*, 221.
20. Abu-Lughod, "Islamic"; Fuccaro, *Histories*.
21. Al-Nakib, "Kuwait's," 9.
22. Al-Nakib, *Kuwait*, 6
23. Ménoret, *Joyriding*, 8.
24. Scott, *Seeing*, 61.
25. Lefebvre, *Production*.
26. De Certeau, *Practice*.
27. Fuccaro, *Histories*.
28. Halliday, *Arabia*, 290. Halliday's figures value Oman's 1967 oil output at £1 million.

29. Townsend, *Oman*, 151. Before 1970, Oman used the Indian rupee and the Maria Theresa dollar. In 1970, Oman adopted the Riyal Saidi, pegged to the British pound. From 1973 the currency became the Omani riyal.

30. Townsend, *Oman*, 151.

31. On Oman's deficits, see Townsend, *Oman*, 151. In August 1972 Britain waived fees worth £850,000 that the Sultanate owed. Britain's Treasury agreed to use public funds for up to £500,000 of the costs of deploying British Loan Service Personnel in Oman in 1973–74. From 1971, Britain encouraged the Sultanate to establish relations with neighboring states who could donate military aid. Jordan, Iran, Saudi Arabia, the UAE, India, Pakistan, and Qatar provided military aid to Oman. Worrall, *Statebuilding*, 176, 181–92.

32. "The word of Sultan Said bin Taimur," January 1968, pp. 10, 13, in FCO 8/574, https://www.agda.ae/en/catalogue/tna/fco/8/574/n/42.

33. See e.g., Philips and Hunt, "'Without,'" 652–53.

34. Rabi, *Emergence*; Townsend, *Oman*, 62.

35. Takriti, *Monsoon*, 155.

36. Worrall, *Statebuilding*, 110.

37. Townsend, *Oman*, 63–64; UNGA, "Question," 44.

38. Fuccaro, *Histories*, 220.

39. Takriti, *Monsoon*, 194–229.

40. DeVore, "'Complex,'" 151.

41. See e.g., Ladwig, "Supporting."

42. E.g., "Report," March 31, 1968, p. 5, in FCO 8/572, https://www.agda.ae/en/catalogue/tna/fco/8/572/n/21; Gardiner, *Service*, 14; Jeapes, *SAS*, 49.

43. Valéri, *Oman*, 207.

44. "Report," March 31, 1968, p. 9, in FCO 8/572, https://www.agda.ae/en/catalogue/tna/fco/8/572/n/25.

45. "Report," March 31, 1968, p. 10, in FCO 8/572, https://www.agda.ae/en/catalogue/tna/fco/8/572/n/27.

46. Takriti, *Monsoon*, 135. See also Wilkinson, "Notes," 10–11, 26.

47. "Report," March 31, 1968, p. 7, in FCO 8/572, https://www.agda.ae/en/catalogue/tna/fco/8/572/n/24.

48. Takriti, *Monsoon*, 81.

49. Arkless, *Secret*, 25.

50. Takriti, *Monsoon*, 134.

51. Gardiner, *Service*, 159.

52. Khalili, *Time*, 194–96.

53. Janzen, *Nomads*, 49; Takriti, *Monsoon*, 42; Thomas, *Arabia*, 13.

54. Takriti, *Mosoon*, 77–78.

55. Al-Ghassani, *al-Tariq*, 19; Higgins, *SAS*, 14, 55.

56. Al-Ghassani, *al-Tariq*, 18.

57. Bin ʾAlawi, "Arabian Gulf," Voice of the Arabs, November 28, 1967, in FCO 8/95, https://www.agda.ae/en/catalogue/tna/fco/8/95/n/66.

58. E.g., in August 1971, following five weeks without Front activities close to Sadah, the governor of Dhufar allowed food exports from Sadah to the nearby *jabal*. "To Routine Cabinet Office," August 31, 1971, in FCO 8/1667, https://www.agda.ae/en/catalogue/tna/fco/8/1667/n/40.

59. "Report," March 31, 1968, p. 6, in FCO 8/572, https://www.agda.ae/en/catalogue/tna/fco/8/572/n/23.

60. Thwaites, *Muscat*, 76.
61. Thwaites, *Muscat*, 7–8.
62. Thwaites, *Muscat*, 73.
63. Trabulsi, "Liberation," 9.
64. Takriti, *Monsoon*, 158.
65. DeVore, "Complex," 151.
66. DeVore, "Complex," 162.
67. DeVore, "Complex," 163.
68. Khalili, "Gendered," 1471.
69. E.g., Thompson, *Defeating*.
70. Akehurst, *Won*, 2; DeVore, "Complex," 152; Takriti, *Monsoon*, 133–34, 211.
71. DeVore, "Complex," 151–52; Takriti, *Monsoon*, 81.
72. Takriti, *Monsoon*, 139–42.
73. Burdett, *Records*, 5:201–4; Takriti, *Monsoon*, 142.
74. DeVore, "Complex," 152.
75. Jeapes, *SAS*, 32.
76. DeVore, "Complex," 152; Gardiner, *Service*, 159; Jeapes, *SAS*, 142.
77. DeVore, "Complex," 152.
78. Jeapes, *SAS*, 68–69.
79. E.g., Jeapes, *SAS*, 102.
80. De Vore, "Complex," 166. See also Hughes, "Demythologising," 441–43.
81. E.g., Ministry of Defence, "Countering"; Gardiner, *Service*; Higgins, *SAS*; Jeapes, *SAS*; Peterson, *Oman's*. For a critical review, see Hughes, "Demythologising."
82. DeVore, "Complex"; Hughes, "Demythologising"; Newsinger, *British*, 136–56.
83. Hughes, "'Model;'"; Hughes, "Demythologising."
84. Hazelton, "'Hearts'"; Hazelton, *Bullets*, 81–105; Takriti, *Monsoon*.
85. Hazelton, *Bullets*.
86. See e.g., McMullin, *Ex-Combatants*.
87. Allfree, *Warlords*, 164.
88. Takriti, *Monsoon*, 73.
89. Halliday, *Arabia*, 277.
90. Afraz and Afraz, *Hamrah*, 4n19, 83.
91. PFLO, "Al-Alawi," 14–15.
92. Takriti, *Monsoon*, 263.
93. Valéri, *Oman*, 72–73.
94. Takriti, *Monsoon*, 264.

95. Al-'Amri, *Dhufar*, 160; Peterson, *Oman's*, 238.

96. Worrall, *Statebuilding*, 283.

97. On cash payments for *firaq* during 1971–72, see Arkless, *Secret*, 143. Jeapes, who served in 1971 and 1974, notes a *firaq* wage of 50 Omani riyals by 1974. Jeapes, *SAS*, 173.

98. On food shortages among Front combatants in 1972, see Jones, "Military," 636. On the difficulties that, from November 1973, the Front faced in paying combatants, see "Oman Intelligence Report 59," January 27–February 9, 1974, p. 3, in FCO 8/2233, https://www.agda.ae/en/catalogue/tna/fco/8/2233/n/50.

99. Jeapes, *SAS*, 61.

100. On access to such resources during 1971–72, see Arkless, *Secret*, 76, 143, 189.

101. Arkless, *Secret*, 64–65; Jeapes, *SAS*, 44.

102. Arkless, *Secret*, 83, 143.

103. Worrall, *Statebuilding*, 284–85; see also Akehurst, *Won*, 20; Arkless, *Secret*, 30, 78; Gardiner, *Service*, 81–82. Gardiner began his deployment in Dhufar in November 1973.

104. Arkless, *Secret*, 57.

105. Al-Nakib, "Revisiting"; Ménoret, *Joyriding*.

106. Abu-Lughod, "Urbanization," 287.

107. "Dhofar," communication to Geoffrey Arthur, received September 29, 1971, in FCO 8/1668, https://www.agda.ae/en/catalogue/tna/fco/8/1668/n/76.

108. "CSAF's Military Assessment of the Situation in Dhofar as at 14 February 1972," p. 3, in FCO 8/1856, https://www.agda.ae/en/catalogue/tna/fco/8/1856/n/70.

109. Arkless, *Secret*, 138.

110. "Some Facts and Figures on Dhofar" (hereafter, "Facts"), August 1972, p. 3, in FCO 8/1846, https://www.agda.ae/en/catalogue/tna/fco/8/1846/n/11.

111. Takriti, *Monsoon*, 218.

112. Jeapes, *SAS*, 58–59.

113. Jeapes, *SAS*, 111–13.

114. Peterson, *Oman's*, 430–31.

115. Morris, "Dhofar," 67.

116. Jeapes, *SAS*, 142.

117. P 300830Z, received December 2, 1971, in FCO 8/1668, https://www.agda.ae/en/catalogue/tna/fco/8/1668/n/13.

118. Jeapes, *SAS*, 143.

119. See e.g., Valéri, *Oman*, 136–39.

120. Razi, *Emergence*, 143–44.

121. "Truth," February 19, 1973, p. 1, in FCO 8/2031, https://www.agda.ae/en/catalogue/tna/fco/8/2031/n/111.

122. Khalili, "Gendered."

123. Higgins, *SAS*, 102.

124. Arkless, *Secret*, 196.

125. PFLO, *Sijil*. The list also includes a female pupil and a woman without a stated military role.

126. KROAG, "Role . . . Third," 39.
127. See also Ibrahim, *Warda* (trans. Aboul-Ela), 195.
128. "The Principles Governing British Military Assistance to Oman," May 14, 1974, p. A7, in FCO 8/2229, https://www.agda.ae/en/catalogue/tna/fco/8/2229/n/26.
129. Letter from Donald Hawley to Patrick Wright, July 18, 1972, in FCO 8/1845, https://www.agda.ae/en/catalogue/tna/fco/8/1845/n/122.
130. See e.g., Dhofari Gucci, "Festival."
131. Jones, "Military," 636.
132. Jeapes, *SAS*, 70.
133. DeVore, "Complex"; Worrall, *Statebuilding*, xxxii.
134. Khalili, *Time*, 173–83.
135. Halliday, *Arabia*, 349–50. I have modified the translation to "goats," in keeping with livestock practices in Dhufar.
136. "Bombs for SAF," August 18, 1971, in FCO 8/1687, https://www.agda.ae/en/catalogue/tna/fco/8/1687/n/14; "Oman: Napalm," August 20, 1971, in FCO 8/1687, https://www.agda.ae/en/catalogue/tna/fco/8/1687/n/9. On alleged use of napalm in Dhufar, see Valéri, *Oman*: 255n30.
137. Arkless, *Secret*, 82.
138. "Facts," August 1972, pp. 5–6, in FCO 8/1846, https://www.agda.ae/en/catalogue/tna/fco/8/1846/n/13.
139. Takriti, *Monsoon*, 146.
140. "Lord Brockway's Parliamentary Question," June 2, 1972, p. 3, in FCO 8/1862, https://www.agda.ae/en/catalogue/tna/fco/8/1862/n/53.
141. Jabob, *Qiyadat*: 167, 187.
142. Jabob, *Qiyadat* 187–88.
143. FM Muscat 311100Z, received June 1, 1972, p. 1, in FCO 8/1862, https://www.agda.ae/en/catalogue/tna/fco/8/1862/n/128.
144. Afraz and Afraz, *Hamrah*, 113.
145. Higgins, *SAS*, 8. See also Gardiner, *Service*, 74. The counterinsurgency monitored cattle brands to track whether people were using livestock watered at government wells to assist the Front. Halliday, *Arabia*, 54.
146. Jeapes, *SAS*, 238.
147. Halliday, *Arabia*, 378–79.
148. Takriti, *Monsoon*, 232, 239.
149. Takriti, *Monsoon*, 137.
150. Abu-Lughod, "Urbanization," 287.
151. "Report," March 31, 1968, p. 5, in FCO 8/572, https://www.agda.ae/en/catalogue/tna/fco/8/572/n/22; Higgins, *SAS*, 59.
152. Higgins, *SAS*, 58.
153. Higgins, *SAS*, 56.
154. Higgins, *SAS*, 65.
155. Higgins, *SAS*, 65.

156. See "Notes on the Progress of Civil Development . . ." (hereafter, "Notes"), May 11, 1975, p. 2, in FCO 8/2456, https://www.agda.ae/en/catalogue/tna/fco/8/2456/n/161.

157. Higgins, *SAS*, 75.

158. "Notes," May 11, 1975, p. 7, in FCO 8/2456, https://www.agda.ae/en/catalogue/tna/fco/8/2456/n/166.

159. Higgins, *SAS*, 77.

160. "The Progress of Operations in Oman," February 26, 1975, p. 3, in FCO 8/2477, https://www.agda.ae/en/catalogue/tna/fco/8/2477/n/36.

161. Jeapes, *SAS*, 167.

162. Peterson, *Oman's*, 383.

163. The Omani government envisaged in 1972 that "each Omani" had the right to four lots of land for housing, agriculture, business, and industry. Allen and Rigsbee, *Oman*, 162. Interlocutors' emphasis to me that women only began to receive land from 2008 suggests that the original policy envisaged male citizens.

164. Jeapes, *SAS*, 238.

165. Janzen, *Nomads*, 210.

166. Janzen, *Nomads*, 212.

167. US Embassy Muscat, "Contractor's"; "(U) FMS"; "Saudi."

168. "Notes," May 11, 1975, pp. 5–6, in FCO 8/2456, https://www.agda.ae/en/catalogue/tna/fco/8/2456/n/164.

169. Miranda Morris worked for the Civil Aid Department in the office of the Governor of Dhufar, and later for the Rural Health Service in the Ministry of Health.

170. Members of the Shanfari tribe administered Sultan Said's affairs in Dhufar. Said al-Shanfari was a "fixer" and later minister for petroleum for Sultan Qaboos. Hafidh Salim al-Ghassani was personal tutor to Qaboos, and later press advisor to Sultan Qaboos. Allen and Rigsbee, *Oman*, 22; Takriti, *Monsoon*, 268; Beasant and Ling, *Sultan*, 35; 170455Z, received October 18, 1971, in FCO 8/1677, https://www.agda.ae/en/catalogue/tna/fco/8/1677/n/10.

171. See also Higgins, *SAS*, 91.

172. The early postwar government did not always encourage *jabbali* families to settle on the coast, however, since people were arriving in great numbers, and many were armed. Miranda Morris, personal communication.

173. Goode, "Assisting," 461; Worrall, *Statebuilding*, 288.

174. Peterson, *Oman's*, 398.

175. Owtram, *Modern*.

176. Worrall, *Statebuilding*, 289.

177. Janzen, *Nomads*, 212.

178. Labour Party International Department, "Dhofar," 6–7.

179. See e.g., Al Rasheed, "Transnational"; Valéri, *Oman*, 18.

180. Al-Sarimi, "Ma'athir."

181. Sachedina, *Cultivating*, 142–71.

182. Peterson, *Oman's*, 397.

183. See e.g., El Said et al., *Rethinking*; Wiegink, *Former*.

184. Labour Party International Department, "Dhofar," 6.
185. See e.g., Valéri, *Oman*, 178–89.
186. Jabob, *Qiyadat*, 42.
187. Wippel, "Globalized," 18.
188. Khalaf, "Gulf."
189. Limbert, *Time*.
190. Valéri, *Oman*, 80, 194.
191. Valéri, *Oman*, 192–93.
192. Sachedina, *Cultivating*; Wippel, "'Paradise.'"
193. This Sunni mosque manifested Dhufar's cultural distinctiveness from northern Ibadhism. The mosque that now dominates Salalah's landscape is the Sultan Qaboos Mosque, completed in 2009.
194. Dhofari Gucci, "Salalah."
195. E.g., Bristol-Rhys, *Emirati*; Dresch, "Foreign," 414; Sachedina, *Cultivating*.
196. Al-Nakib, "Revisiting."
197. Heim et al., "Process."
198. Sultanate of Oman, *Statistical*.
199. Janzen, "Destruction"; Jeapes, *SAS*, 173.
200. Peterson, *Oman's*, 416.
201. Gardiner, *Service*, 80.
202. Valéri, *Oman*, 166.
203. Oman's estimated military spending as a proportion of GDP is among the highest in the Gulf and the world. Valéri, *Oman*, 235, 274n21.
204. Toumi, "GCC."

Chapter 4

1. Parts of Chapter 4 draw on, extensively revise, and develop material in Alice Wilson, "Invisible Veterans: Defeated Militants and Enduring Revolutionary Social Values in Dhufar, Oman," *Conflict and Society: Advances in Research* 5, no. 1 (June 2019): 132–49, and Wilson, "Kinship and a Counter-hegemonic Social Order: Former Revolutionaries in Southern Oman," *Journal of the Royal Anthropological Institute* 26, no. 2 (March 2020): 302–20.
Douglas, *Purity*.
2. Sahlins, "Kinship."
3. Das, *Life*.
4. Hughes, "'Retired.'"
5. Vince, *Fighting*, 170.
6. See e.g., West, "Girls"; Wiegink, *Former*.
7. Wilson, "Kinship."
8. I am grateful to a Dhufari interlocutor, who wishes to remain anonymous, for discussions about Ibn Khaldun's ideas in relation to solidarity ties in Dhufar. These discussions led me to revisit kinship, reproduction, and resistance through the lens of Ibn Khaldun's ideas.
9. Ibn Khaldun, *Muqaddimah*.
10. Wilson, *Sovereignty*, 48.

11. For a discussion, see Wilson, "Kinship."
12. E.g., Engels, *Origin*; Chayanov, *Theory*; Radcliffe-Brown, *Structure*; Levi-Strauss, *Elementary*.
13. Yanagisako, "Family."
14. Schneider, "Kinship."
15. Kuper, *Invention*.
16. See e.g., Clarke, *Islam*; Goodfellow, *Gay*; Hayden, *Gender*: 47–48; Ragoné, "Surrogate"; Rivers, *Radical*; Strathern, *Reproducing*; Weston, *Families*. For a discussion, see Wilson, "Kinship."
17. E.g., Goldman, *Women*; Wilson, *Sovereignty*; Wood, *Baba*.
18. Thiranagama, *Mother's*, 32.
19. Thiranagama, *Mother's*, 215.
20. Johnson et al., "Weddings"; Wilson, *Sovereignty*, 154–59.
21. Johnson et al., "Weddings"; Wilson, *Sovereignty*, 159–75
22. Lazar, *Social*.
23. Peteet, *Landscape*, 162; Rolston, *Children*, 23.
24. Shah, "'Muck.'"
25. Ledeneva, *Russia's*.
26. Pine, "Naming"; Szalai, "Aspects," 161. A local discourse of the family as a site of resistance against socialism nevertheless deflects attention away from the family's reliance on the socialist state and its resources. Gal and Kligman, *Politics*, 70.
27. Vince, *Fighting*, 235–36.
28. Fernández-Savater et al., "Life," 146–47.
29. This official tribalization affected not only *bahharah* and *sumur* in Dhufar but also other communities in the north of Oman, such as those tracing ancestry to enslaved persons and immigrant communities such as Baluchis. Valéri, *Oman*, 140.
30. See e.g., Clarke, "Closeness."
31. Morris, "Thoughts," 24; Janzen, *Nomads*, 136–37.
32. In the *jabal* the traditional age for circumcision was shortly before marriage. See Tabook, "Tribal," 107–9, 169–200. Families considered a boy ready for circumcision "when hairs started to grow properly on their chin and upper lip." Miranda Morris, personal communication.
33. When he names preferred geographical areas for kinship celebrations, Tabook mentions only Qara tribes. Tabook, "Tribal," 200. *Shahrah* clients would have been associated with particular Qara tribes.
34. Tabook, "Tribal," 179–85.
35. Thomas, *Arabia*, 29–31.
36. Risse, *Community*, 60, 110.
37. Already by the 1990s, Tabook notes the expectation that those (men) formally invited to a wedding, such as tribal leaders and the heads of militias, should make contributions to wedding celebrations. Tabook, "Tribal," 174.
38. Limbert, "Marriage."
39. Dresch, "Debates."

40. Takriti, *Monsoon*, 124.
41. Takriti, *Monsoon*, 127.
42. KROAG, "Experiences," 23.
43. Halliday, *Arabia*, 379.
44. E.g., Fiennes, *Soldiers*, 135; Gardiner, *Service*, 73; Higgins, *SAS*, 193; Jeapes, *SAS*, 27; Thwaites, *Muscat*, 73; Anxieties about indoctrination are a common feature of anti-Maoist sentiment. Lovell, *Maoism*.
45. Punamäki, "Ideological"; Rolston, *Children*.
46. Wilson, *Sovereignty*, 147–79; Wilson, "Gifts."
47. "The Gulf Revolution," *The Baghdad Observer* IV, 1163, November 22, 1971, in FCO 8/1846, https://www.agda.ae/en/catalogue/tna/fco/8/1846/n/99; Risse, *Community*, 43.
48. Risse, *Community*, 43.
49. Peutz, *Islands*, 169–72; Verdery, *Socialism*, 163–64.
50. Jeapes, *SAS*, 167.
51. Valéri, *Oman*, 139.
52. Jeapes, *SAS*, 215.
53. Front fighters killed a government Southern Regiment soldier on October 21, 1979. The Southern Regiment killed one Front fighter, and probably wounded another, on March 28, 1980. Worrall, *Statebuilding*, 288–89.
54. Risse, *Community*, 48.
55. KROAG, *Revolution*, 39.
56. KROAG, *Revolution*, 39.
57. Afraz and Afraz, *Hamrah*, 57, 82.
58. Douglas, *Purity*.
59. Douglas, *Purity*, 40.
60. See e.g., Fernandez, *Romancing*; Wilson, *Sovereignty*, 176.
61. Miranda Morris, personal communication.
62. See e.g., Risse, *Community*, 11.
63. Wilson, "Oman's."
64. Bodenhorn and vom Bruck, "'Entangled,'" 11.
65. Bodenhorn and vom Bruck, "'Entangled,'" 3.
66. Scott, *Seeing*, 71.
67. See e.g., Shelley, *Endgame*, 105.
68. See also Johnson et al., "Weddings," 16.
69. Strathern, "Cutting."
70. Rolston, *Children*, 58.
71. E.g., Agamben, *Homo*; Das, *Life*; Rolston, *Children*, 51, 68, 147.
72. Vince, *Fighting*, 39.

Chapter 5

1. Parts of Chapter 5 draw on, extensively revise, and develop material in Alice Wilson, "Invisible Veterans: Defeated Militants and Enduring Revolutionary Social Values in Dhufar,

Oman," *Conflict and Society: Advances in Research* 5, no. 1 (June 2019): 132–49, and Wilson, "Kinship and a Counter-hegemonic Social Order: Former Revolutionaries in Southern Oman," *Journal of the Royal Anthropological Institute* 26, no. 2 (March 2020): 302–20.

Makram-Ebeid, "'Old.'"

2. Kim, *Everyday*.
3. See e.g., Campbell, *Interpreters*; Montoya, *Gendered*; Rofel, *Other*.
4. Winegar, "Privilege."
5. E.g., Malinowski, *Argonauts*. In contexts of capitalist modernity, the notion of the everyday facilitates submission to capitalist discipline. Lefebvre, *Everyday*. Anthropological interest in the potential of the everyday for reproducing dominant social norms and relationships extends beyond contexts of capitalist modernity.
6. Bourdieu, *Outline*.
7. Foucault, *Essential*.
8. Butler, *Gender*.
9. Knowles, *Flip-flop*, 31–32; Limbert, *Time*, 46–81.
10. Mahmood, *Politics*.
11. E.g., Dahlgren, "Making"; Hafez, *Women*, 84; Kim, *Everyday*; Wilson, "Revolution"; Wilson, *Sovereignty*.
12. Shah, *Nightmarch*, 137.
13. E.g., West, "Girls"; Montoya, *Gendered*; Thiranagama, *Mother's*.
14. E.g., Coulter, *Bush*; Hughes, "'Retired'"; Stefansson, "Coffee"; Wiegink, *Former*.
15. Afraz and Afraz, *Hamrah*, 84.
16. De Certeau, *Practice*.
17. Scott, *Domination*.
18. Pine, "Naming."
19. Das, *Life*; Hughes, "'Retired'"; Kelly, "Attractions."
20. See e.g., Duschinski et al., *Resisting*; McConnell, "Contextualizing," 122; Peteet, *Landscape*, 162.
21. Thiranagama, *Mother's*, 12.
22. Donner, "Radical."
23. A distinctive accent was one of the distinguishing features of Salalah's *sumur*, compared with non-*sumur* urban Arabophones.
24. Within the bounds of social etiquette, Salalans of various ages and backgrounds enjoyed socializing outdoors. Outside the monsoon season, in the late afternoon it was common to see nuclear or extended family groups sitting together on the beach. But given young people's preference for the mall, and (varying levels of) social pressure on women to refrain from circulating their face in public spaces, it was men who were a common sight socializing on the streets of Salalah. Typically, a Dhufari man made sure to have a rolled-up plastic mat in the trunk of his car, along with one or two folding plastic chairs, so as to be readily equipped for outdoor socializing.
25. Dhufaris pointed out to me that among the differences that they perceived between Dhufar and northern regions of Oman were the typical items for hospitality. In contrast to

Dhufar, in Muscat and northern Oman it is common at informal gatherings for people to consume coffee and dates. E.g., Eickelman, *Women*, 2; Limbert, *Time*, 46–81.

26. For locals as well as a visiting researcher, approaching one of these spaces can feel like crossing a social border as one moves into a sphere of protection, or from one sphere of protection to another. See e.g., Wilson, *Sovereignty*, 189–90.

27. The use of the *wizar* was not exclusive to men of mountain background. But interlocutors associated a man's attachment to the *wizar* to the point of wearing it in the street, beyond the comfort of his own home, with hailing from a mountain background. Historically, the use of a *wizar* was common in other parts of Oman. E.g., Eickelman, *Women*, 3. Several interlocutors suggested to me that the Omani government no longer allowed men to wear a *wizar* in public but had made an exception to allow its ongoing use in public in Dhufar.

28. Chay, "Dīwāniyya," 15–16.

29. Wikan, *Behind*; Limbert, *Time*, 135.

30. Wikan, *Behind*, 116.

31. University campuses in the Gulf create opportunities for social mixing among nationals. E.g., Le Renard, *Society*, 88.

32. Interlocutors did not articulate to me perceived reasons for social differentiation to be more pronounced in Salalah than in other parts of Oman and the Gulf. No interlocutors discussed with me the potential influence of Ibadhism, the dominant sect in the north, which idealizes the equality of all regardless of birth. In Ibadhi settings, everyday interactions can nevertheless vary in the degree to which they articulate notions of social equality. See Eickelman, *Women*, 50; Sachedina, *Cultivating*, 74.

33. Non-*sumur* Dhufaris sometimes also experienced the north of Oman as a more socially permissive space than Dhufar.

34. Orwell, *Nineteen*.

35. Wilson, *Sovereignty*.

36. Wilson, "Invisible," 140.

37. Al-'Amri, *Dhufar*, 140.

38. Labour Party International Committee, "Dhofar."

39. Miranda Morris, personal communication.

40. Vince, *Fighting*, 174.

41. Al-Azri, *Social*.

42. E.g., Al-Azri, *Social*; Limbert, *Time*, 135; Sachedina, *Cultivating*, 172–97.

43. On complex dynamics of veiling, see e.g., El Guindi, *Veil*.

44. Historically, mountain women enjoyed greater possibilities than their town-based counterparts to circulate and to interact with unrelated males. By the 1990s, the greater seclusion of women, including those of mountain background, was more common. Tabook, "Tribal," 40, 179, 192, 226–28.

45. In Salalah, Dhufaris have long associated face covering with social respectability. Historically, the socially marginal status of enslaved women and women from *bahharah* client fishing families excluded them from the privilege of seclusion and face covering. Thomas, *Arabia*, 12, 17. At the time of my fieldwork older *sumur* women did not usually cover their faces in public. But I observed some younger-generation *sumur* women donning a face

covering when leaving a home or removing one after leaving the street. Their adoption of face covering reflects its historical and ongoing role in Salalah for Dhufari women wishing to claim social respectability.

46. Kar, "Securitizing."

47. I did not hear about instances of *sumur* women passing on portions of wages to male relatives. Indeed, the economic practices of *sumur* women could resemble those of Dhufari men, with *sumur* women reporting that they gave wedding gifts (*maghbur*) that were normally exclusively male contributions.

48. E.g., Coulter, *Bush*; West, "Girls."

49. Jabob, *Qiyadat*, 279.

50. See e.g., Macleod, *Accommodating*; Gilbertson, "Balance."

51. Al Shahri, "Genital"; Al Shahri, "Issue."

52. See e.g., Al Subhi, "Women's."

53. Women candidates were allowed to run for election to Oman's National Consultative Council in Muscat in 1991.

54. One woman from a historically subordinate town tribe ran in the 2011 elections. Her bold step spoke to the unprecedented participation that year of candidates and voters in the charged atmosphere and optimism for political aperture of the first elections after the protests earlier that year.

55. In 2011, a woman candidate registered herself as an electoral candidate under the name of a prestigious town tribe. This caused controversy because, in the view of that tribe's senior figures, she hailed from a client tribe and was not herself a member of the prestigious tribe. As an interlocutor explained: "she was a client" [*tabi'ah*, literally, "following [them]"]. Dhufaris reported to me that the leaders of the tribe in question requested the removal of the tribe's name from the candidate's listing.

56. Omanis commonly referred to the National Council in conversation with me as the "Parliament" [*barlaman*].

57. Wilson, "Oman's."

58. E.g., Agamben, *Homo*; Das, *Life*; Rolston, *Children*, 51, 68, 147.

59. Winegar, "Privilege."

Chapter 6

1. Kwon, *Ghosts*.
2. Armbrust, *Martyrs*.
3. Watson, "Making."
4. Watson, "Making," 71.
5. Connerton, *Societies*, 4.
6. Connerton, *Societies*; Halbwachs, *Collective*.
7. Khalili, *Heroes*, 4.
8. Connerton, *Societies*, 71.
9. Wagner-Pacifici and Schwartz, "Vietnam"; Vinitzky-Seroussi, "Commemorating."
10. E.g., Deeb, *Enchanted*, 137–40; Khalili, *Heroes*; Wagner-Pacifici and Schwartz, "Vietnam"; Wedeen, *Ambiguities*.

11. Nora, "Between."
12. Wiegink, *Former*, 182.
13. Schafer, *Soldiers*.
14. Metsola, "Struggle."
15. Sachedina, *Cultivating*.
16. E.g., Sachedina, *Cultivating*, 156.
17. E.g., Linenthal, *Preserving*.
18. Nora, "Reasons"; see also e.g., Bouvard, *Revolutionizing*; Wanner, *Burden*.
19. E.g., Peutz, *Islands*, 230–34; Uehling, *Beyond*.
20. E.g., Hermez, *War*.
21. Hermez, *War*, 146–47.
22. Hermez, *War*, 144.
23. Theidon, "Gender," 462.
24. Watson, "Memory," 2, 14.
25. Nora, "Between," 23.
26. Nora, "Between," 23.
27. E.g., Navaro-Yashin, *Faces*.
28. Limbert, *Time*, 12.
29. Sachedina, *Cultivating*, 145, 157–60.
30. Watson, "Making," 65.
31. Watson, "Making."
32. Feldman, "Political," 60.
33. Hermez, *War*, 50.
34. Allan, *Refugees*, 59–60; Khalili, *Heroes*.
35. E.g., Trabulsi, *Surat*.
36. Hermez, *War*, 144.
37. Schwarcz, "Memory."
38. Halilovich, *Places*.
39. Mantovan, "Adieu."
40. Kwon, *Ghosts*.
41. Tabook, "Tribal," 254–57, 262–63, 265–66.
42. Tabook, "Tribal," 112–15.
43. The Front's promotion of revolutionary values could also repress existing rituals. The Front disapproved of women's beautification rituals, judging them a distraction from women's emancipation. For Tabook, this repression may have contributed to their post-1970s decline. Tabook, "Tribal," 186.
44. Takriti, *Monsoon*, 115.
45. Rafeh, *Mohanna*, 137.
46. Takriti, *Monsoon*, 276.
47. Takriti, *Monsoon*, 238.
48. 1505557 JUN, received June 16, 1971, p. 2, in FCO 8/1667, https://www.agda.ae/en/catalogue/tna/fco/8/1667/n/102.

49. Takriti, *Monsoon*, 301. As early as 1965 the Front commemorated Dhufari martyrs. Takriti, *Monsoon*, 73, 76.

50. Takriti, *Monsoon*, 238–39.

51. 1505557 JUN, received June 16, 1971, p. 2, in FCO 8/1667, https://www.agda.ae/en/catalogue/tna/fco/8/1667/n/102.

52. E.g., PFLO, *Uman*.

53. See e.g., MENA Vinyl Project, "Chants"; Rafeh, *Mohanna*, 133, 195, 202; Tabook, "Tribal," 227.

54. See Tabook, "Tribal," 234.

55. Takriti, *Monsoon*, 252.

56. Takriti, *Monsoon*, 251.

57. Rafeh, *Mohanna*, 133.

58. PFLO, *Path*.

59. PFLO, "[Special]," 460.

60. Rafeh, *Mohanna*, 133.

61. Rafeh, *Mohanna*, 195.

62. Rafeh, *Mohanna*, 138.

63. Afraz and Afraz, *Hamrah*, 59.

64. Rafeh, *Mohanna*, 136.

65. Trabulsi, *Dhufar*, 10.

66. Higgins, *SAS*, 103.

67. Higgins, *SAS*, 144.

68. Trabulsi, "Liberation," 9.

69. Arkless, *Secret*, 211.

70. Gardiner, *Service*, 126.

71. PFLO, *Sijil*.

72. Ibrahim, *Warda* (trans. Aboul-Ela), 257–58.

73. El Shakry, "'History,'" 930.

74. Chatty, "Rituals"; Valéri, *Oman*.

75. Takriti, *Monsoon*, 199–200, 253–54.

76. Gardiner, *Service*, 71.

77. Jeapes, *SAS*, 40–41.

78. Takriti, *Monsoon*, 270.

79. E.g., Limbert, *Time*; Phillips and Hunt, "'Without'"; Valéri, *Oman*.

80. Bin Said, *Royal*.

81. Al-Shahri, *Kayfa*. He later published a bilingual volume in Oman. Al-Shahri, *Lughat*.

82. See e.g., Limbert, *Time*; Phillips and Hunt, "'Without.'"

83. On memorable National Day celebrations, see Chatty, "Rituals," 48.

84. E.g., Dhufaris participated vigorously in the nationwide mourning rituals upon the death in 1992 of Qaboos's Dhufari mother, Mayzoon bint al-Maʿshani. Miranda Morris, personal communication.

85. Limbert, *Time*.

86. On official omissions, see Valéri, *Oman*, 119–20; Sachedina, *Cultivating*, 10, 142, 156.

87. Bin Said, *Royal*, 36.

88. A *lieu de mémoire* that merits further research is the "tomb of the unknown soldier" at the palace in Rabat, Salalah. Government sympathizer Said al-Maʿshani mentions this site in an online essay that circulated on WhatsApp circa 2020. It is unclear from the essay if the site makes explicit mention of casualties of the Dhufar counterinsurgency. The site is apparently located in a private royal residence, rather than in a site that all Omanis could easily access. Al-Maʿshani expresses the hope that the authorities will broadcast on public television a memorial ceremony that takes place at the site. This suggests that this ceremony was not ordinarily readily accessible for a wide Omani audience. I thank Abdel Razzaq Takriti for sharing this unpublished essay with me.

89. Bin Said, *Royal*, 26, 42–43, 49, 63, 69, 77, 101, 108.

90. El Haremi, "Documentary."

91. Al-ʿAmri, *Dhufar*.

92. Imperial War Museum, "Battle"; Low, "Prince." Some commentators narrate the Front's heavy losses at the Battle of Mirbat as a military turning point in the war. Nevertheless, there are counterarguments. The counterinsurgency's intelligence breakthrough in December 1972 was arguably more significant in undermining the Front. The designation of Mirbat (when Front forces outnumbered counterinsurgency forces) as a military turning point serves an ideological function: it reverses the direction of the wider "David and Goliath" material inequalities between the Front and the counterinsurgency. Newsinger, *British*, 151–52.

93. E.g., Ministry of Defence, "Countering"; Gardiner, *Service*; Jeapes, *SAS*; Peterson, *Oman's*.

94. E.g., DeVore, "More Complex"; Hazelton, "'Hearts and Minds'"; Hazelton, *Bullets*, 81–105; Hughes, "Demythologising"; Takriti, *Monsoon*.

95. See Hughes, "Demythologising."

96. E.g., Akehurst, *Won*; Arkless, *Secret*; Jeapes, *SAS*.

97. E.g., Gardiner's *Service* ran to eight editions from 2006 to 2017.

98. The British press exposed British military intervention in the war in January 1971. Cobain, "Britain's." On the war's low profile among nonspecialist (Anglophone) audiences, see Gardiner, *Service*, 1. Higgins found the initial secrecy of his mission "exciting." Higgins, *SAS*, 3.

99. Personal communication, Ahmad Moradi and Anahita Hosseini-Lewis. I am grateful to them for drawing my attention to Islamic Republic discourses about Iranian intervention in Dhufar.

100. E.g., Fiennes, *Where*, 132; Gardiner, *Service*, 15, 157; Jeapes, *SAS*, 214, 238; Thwaites, *Muscat*, 7–9.

101. Most of these books are published outside Oman. However, ʿAqil published his book in a private, nongovernmental publishing house in Salalah. ʿAqil, *Uman*. Dhufaris told me that the Ministry of Information did not grant a permit for the sale of this book in Oman.

102. Nora, "Reasons."

103. Ibrahim, *Wardah*.

104. Halliday, *Arabia*, 378; Ibrahim, *Warda* (trans. Aboul-Ela), 162.
105. Ibrahim, *Warda* (trans. Jocquemond); Ibrahim, *Warda* (trans. Aboul-Ela).
106. Al-Sarimi, "Ma'athir."
107. Takriti, *Monsoon*, 88.
108. Al-Zubaidi, *Ahwal*; *Sanawat*; *Imra'ah*.
109. See Mu'ammari and al-Hashemi, *Ubayd*.
110. Khalfan, *Al-Bagh*.
111. Afraz and Afraz, *Hamrah*; Rafeh, *Mohanna*; Trabulsi, *Surat*.
112. Al-Sarimi, *al-Bahth*; 'Ikri, *Dhakirat*.
113. 'Aqil, *Uman*; al-'Amri, *Dhufar*; Jabob, *Qiyadat*.
114. E.g., PFLO, *al-Qabilah*.
115. Rafeh, *Mohanna*, 113, 202.
116. Rahal, "Fused," 135.
117. Uehling, *Beyond*, 112–13.
118. By contrast, photographs of the imamate circulate privately in northern Oman. Sachedina, *Cultivating*, 157.
119. Takriti, *Monsoon*, 115n31.
120. Afraz and Afraz, *Hamrah*, 66.
121. Jeapes, *SAS*, 243.
122. Risse, *Community*, 71.
123. Al-Shahri, "Bidayat."
124. RMC-MENA, "Aghani."
125. Binbkhait, "Thawrat."
126. Khalfan, "Munaqashat"; Ahmad and Khalfan, "Jalsat"; al-Sarimi, "al-Qawl."
127. Al-Sarimi, "al-Qawl." I thank Abdel Razzaq Takriti for sharing unpublished parts of this exchange with me.
128. E.g., Sachedina, *Cultivating*, 240n14.
129. Apte, *Humor*.
130. Donaghy, "Oman."
131. Havel, *The Power*.
132. See also Meneley, *Tournaments*, 134.
133. Meneley, *Tournaments*, 137–40.
134. Eickelman, *Women*, 64.
135. The dating of Ahmad's valuation was unspecified. Since 1986 the Omani riyal has been pegged to a value of US$2.6008.
136. Watson, "Memory," 19.
137. Kwon, *Ghosts*, 158–63.
138. Ahram, *Break*.

Conclusion

1. See al-Hashemi, *al-Rabi'*.
2. Worrall, "Oman," 101.

3. Valéri, "Qaboos-State," 5.
4. Al-Sarimi, "Ma'athir."
5. Clark, "Why."
6. Ross, *Communal*, 7; Beverley, *Failure*, xvii.
7. Thiranagama, *Mother's*.
8. Pedwell, *Revolutionary*, 6.
9. Takriti, *Monsoon*, 2.
10. Valéri, *Oman*, 167. See also Valéri, *Oman*, 166–67; Jones and Ridout, *History*, 219–21.
11. Wilson, "Oman's."
12. Mahfaif, "25 Fibrayir"; Mahfaif, "Min fawa'id"; Al Shahri, "Protests."
13. Dhofari Gucci, "Tension"; Dhofari Gucci, "URGENT"; Worrall, "Oman."
14. Dhofari Gucci, "URGENT."
15. Dhofari Gucci, "Remaining."
16. RMC-MENA, "Aghani."
17. Jabob, "Majlis."
18. GCHR, "Oman."
19. Al-Sarimi, "Ma'athir."
20. Khalfan, "Munaqashat."
21. E.g., Ahmad and Khalfan, "Jalsat"; Arif, "Heiny"; Saba, "Heiny."
22. Hadad, "Dhufar."
23. Limbert, *Time*.
24. Barbuscia, "Oman"; Jalabi, "Oman."
25. Jalabi, "Omanis."

Bibliography

Archival Collections
Middle East Documentation Unit, Durham University Library, Durham University
Arab World Documentation Unit and Special Collections, Old Library, University of Exeter
Peter Sichel Collection, Middle East Centre Archive, St Antony's College, University of Oxford
Foreign Office and Foreign and Commonwealth Office, digitized in the Arabian Gulf Digital Archive

Other Sources
Abrougui, Afef. "Omani Film Critic Sentenced to Jail Over Facebook Posts." *Global Voices*, November 16, 2016. https://advox.globalvoices.org/2016/11/16/omani-film-critic-sentenced-to-jail-over-facebook-posts/.
Abu-Lughod, Janet. "The Islamic City: Historic Myth, Islamic Essence, and Contemporary Relevance." *International Journal of Middle East Studies* 19, no. 2 (May 1987): 155–76.
———. "Urbanization and Social Change in the Arab world." *Ekistics* 50, no. 300 (May/June 1983): 223–31.
Abu-Lughod, Lila. *Veiled Sentiments: Honor and Poetry in a Bedouin Society*. Berkeley: University of California Press, 1986.
Afraz, Mahboubeh, and Rafaʾt Afraz. *Hamrah Ba Enghelabiyoun-e Omani: Yaddashthay-e Jang-e Zoffar*. Frankfurt: Andeesheh va Peykar Publication, 2018.
Agamben, Giorgio. *Homo Sacer: Sovereign Power and Bare Life*. Stanford: Stanford University Press, 1998.
Ahmed, Mustafa, and ʿIsa Khalfan. "Jalsat qaraʾat kitab: Dhufar thawrat al-riyah al-mawsimiyyah." Streamed live on December 20, 2021. YouTube video, 1:39:44. https://www.youtube.com/watch?app=desktop&v=WW9uhII3bVc.

Ahram, Ariel. *Break All the Borders: Separatism and the Reshaping of the Middle East.* New York: Oxford University Press, 2019.
Aidi, Hisham, Marc Lynch, and Zachariah Mampilly. "Racial Formations in Africa and the Middle East: A Transregional Approach." *Pomeps Studies* 44 (September 2021). https://pomeps.org/wp-content/uploads/2021/09/POMEPS_Studies_44_Web-rev3.pdf.
Akehurst, John. *We Won a War: The Campaign in Oman, 1965–1975.* Salisbury: Michael Russell, 1982.
'Amri, Muhammad Said Duraibi al-. *Dhufar: Al-thawrah fi al-tarikh al-umani al mu'asir.* Beirut: Riad el-Rayyes, 2005.
Azraki, Amir Al-. "Uncovering anti-Blackness in the Arab World." *The Conversation*, June 9, 2021. https://theconversation.com/uncovering-anti-blackness-in-the-arab-world-162060.
Azri, Khalid M. Al-. *Social and Gender Inequality in Oman: The Power of Religious and Political Tradition.* London: Routledge, 2013.
Alhassen, Maytha. "Please Reconsider the Term 'Arab Spring.'" *Huffington Post*, February 10, 2012. https://www.huffpost.com/entry/please-reconsider-arab-sp_b_1268971.
Al-Khalili, Charlotte. "Halaqas, Relational Subjects, and Revolutionary Committees in Syria." *Focaal* 2021, no. 91 (2021): 50–66.
Allan, Diana. *Refugees of the Revolution: Experiences of Palestinian Exile.* Stanford: Stanford University Press, 2014.
Allan, Joanna. *Silenced Resistance: Women, Dictatorships, and Genderwashing in Western Sahara and Equatorial Guinea.* Madison: University of Wisconsin Press, 2019.
Allen, Calvin, and W. Lynn Rigsbee. *Oman under Qaboos: From Coup to Constitution, 1970–1996.* London: Frank Cass, 2000.
Allfree, P. S. *Warlords of Oman.* London: Hale, 1967.
Allinson, Jamie. "A Fifth Generation of Revolution Theory?" *Journal of Historical Sociology* 32, no. 1 (March 2019): 142–51.
AlShehabi, Omar H. *Contested Modernity: Sectarianism, Nationalism, and Colonialism in Bahrain.* London: Oneworld Academic, 2019.
Anonymous. "Some Notes on the Political Situation in Muscat and Oman. Prepared for the visit of Mr. Barran." John Craven Wilkinson Archive, Special Collections, University of Exeter, EUL MS 119/3/29 Box 10/1, May 1965.
Apte, Mahadev. *Humor and Laughter: An Anthropological Approach.* Ithaca: Cornell University Press, 1985.
Arif, Amal. "Heiny Srour." *Alakhbar*, September 17, 2018. https://al-akhbar.com/Cinema/258050.
Arkless, David. *The Secret War: Dhofar, 1971–1972.* William Kimber & Co. Ltd., 1988.
Armbrust, Walter. *Martyrs and Tricksters: An Ethnography of the Egyptian Revolution.* Princeton: Princeton University Press, 2019.
Atheer. "The Sultanate of Oman's First Government School: Al Saidiya." *Atheer*, n.d., accessed June 2, 2022. https://www.atheer.om/en/37883/sultanate-omans-first-government-school-al-saidiya/.
Auyero, Javier, and Claudio Benzecry. "The Practical Logic of Political Domination:

Conceptualizing the Clientelist Habitus." *Sociological Theory* 35, no. 3 (September 2017): 179–99.

Babb, Florence. *After Revolution: Mapping Gender and Cultural Politics in Neoliberal Nicaragua.* Austin: University of Texas Press, 2001.

Badiou, Alain. *Being and Event.* Translated by Oliver Feltham. London: Continuum, 2005.

Barbuscia, Davide. "Oman deficit at $2.3 bln in May as oil revenue declines." *Reuters,* July 1 2021. https://www.reuters.com/world/middle-east/oman-deficit-23-bln-may-oil-revenue-declines-2021-07-01/

Bardawil, Fadi A. *Revolution and Disenchantment: Arab Marxism and the Binds of Emancipation.* Durham: Duke University Press, 2020.

Bayat, Asef. *Revolutionary Life: The Everyday of the Arab Spring.* Cambridge: Harvard University Press, 2021.

———. *Revolution Without Revolutionaries: Making Sense of the Arab Spring.* Stanford: Stanford University Press, 2017.

Beasant, John, and Christopher Ling. *Sultan in Arabia: A Private Life.* Edinburgh: Mainstream Publishing, 2004.

Beaugrand, Claire. "Urban Margins in Kuwait and Bahrain: Decay, Dispossession and Politicization." *City* 18, no. 6 (November 2014): 735–45.

Beblawi, Hazem. "The Rentier State in the Arab World." *Arab Studies Quarterly* 9 no. 4 (Fall 1987): 383–98.

Beblawi, Hazem, and Giacomo Luciani, eds. *The Rentier State.* London: Croom Helm, 1987.

Behrooz, Maziar. *Rebels with a Cause: The Failure of the Left in Iran.* London: I. B. Tauris, 2000.

Bent, Theodore, and Mabel Bent. *Southern Arabia.* London: Smith and Elder, 1900.

Bernal, Victoria. "Equality to Die For?: Women Guerrilla Fighters and Eritrea's Cultural Revolution." *PoLAR: Political and Legal Anthropology Review* 23, no. 2 (November 2000): 61–76.

Beverley, John. *The Failure of Latin America: Postcolonialism in Bad Times.* Pittsburgh: University of Pittsburgh Press, 2019.

bin ʿAqil, Salim. *Uman bain al-tajziʾah wa al-wihdah 1913–1976.* Salalah: Markaz al-ruʾiyyah lil tanmiyyah al-bashriyyah, 2007.

Bin Said, Qaboos. *The Royal Speeches of His Majesty Sultan Qaboos Bin Said.* Muscat: Ministry of Information, 2015.

Binbkhait. "Thawrat Dhufar." July 5, 2009. YouTube video, 1:19, accessed June 15, 2021. https://www.youtube.com/watch?v=FDYzk7Y3PkI.

Bodenhorn, Barbara, and Gabriele vom Bruck. "'Entangled in Histories': An Introduction to the Anthropology of Names and Naming." In *The Anthropology of Names and Naming,* edited by Gabriele vom Bruck and Barbara Bodenhorn, 1–30. Cambridge: Cambridge University Press, 2006.

Bourdieu, Pierre. *Outline of a Theory of Practice.* Cambridge: Cambridge University Press, 1977.

Boustead, Hugh. *The Wind of Morning: The Autobiography of Hugh Boustead.* London: Chatto & Windus, 1971.

Boutieri, Charis. "Bastardy and Irreverence: The Injuries of Kinship in Post-Revolutionary Tunisia." *Hespéris-Tamuda* LV, no. 4 (2020): 131–49.

———. "Events of Citizenship: Left Militantism and the Returns of Revolution in Tunisia." *History and Anthropology* (2020): 1–19.

Bouvard, Marguerite Guzman. *Revolutionizing Motherhood: The Mothers of the Plaza de Mayo.* Wilmington: Scholarly Resources Inc, 1994.

Bristol-Rhys, Jane. *Emirati Women: Generations of Change.* London: Hurst, 2010.

Burdett, A. L. P. ed. *Records of Oman 1966–1971.* 6 vols. Farnham Common: Archive Editions, 2003.

Butler, Judith. *Gender Trouble: Feminism and the Subversion of Identity.* London: Routledge, 1990.

Campbell, Madeline Otis. *Interpreters of Occupation: Gender and the Politics of Belonging in an Iraqi Refugee Network.* Syracuse: Syracuse University Press, 2016.

Certeau, Michel de. *The Practice of Everyday Life.* Translated by Steven Rendall. Berkeley: University of California Press, 1988.

Chalcraft, John T. "Migration and Popular Protest in the Arabian Peninsula and the Gulf in the 1950s and 1960s." *International Labor and Working-Class History,* no. 79 (Spring 2011): 28–47.

Chatty, Dawn. "Rituals of Royalty and the Elaboration of Ceremony in Oman: View from the Edge." *International Journal of Middle East Studies* 41, no. 1 (February 2009): 39–58.

Chay, Clemens. "The Dīwāniyya Tradition in Modern Kuwait: An Interlinked Space and Practice." *Journal of Arabian Studies* 6, no. 1 (2016): 1–28.

Chayanov, Alexander. *The Theory of Peasant Economy.* Manchester: University of Manchester Press, 1966.

Cherstich, Igor, Martin Holbraad, and Nico Tassi. *Anthropologies of Revolution: Forging Time, People, and Worlds.* Berkeley: University of California Press, 2020.

Clapham, Christopher. *Transformation and Continuity in Revolutionary Ethiopia.* Cambridge: Cambridge University Press, 1988.

Clark, Christopher. "Why Should We Think about the Revolutions of 1848 Now?" *The London Review of Books,* March 7, 2019.

Clark, Terence. "Oman: A Century of Oil Exploration and Development." *Asian Affairs* 39, no. 3 (2008): 388–99.

———. *Underground to Overseas: The Story of Petroleum Development Oman.* London: Stacey International, 2007.

Clarke, Morgan. "Closeness in the Age of Mechanical Reproduction: Debating Kinship and Biomedicine in Lebanon and the Middle East." *Anthropological Quarterly* 80, no. 2 (2007): 379–402.

———. *Islam and New Kinship: Reproductive Technology and the Shariah in Lebanon.* New York: Berghahn Books, 2009.

Cobain, Ian. "Britain's Secret Wars." *The Guardian,* September 8, 2016. https://www.theguardian.com/uk-news/2016/sep/08/britains-secret-wars-oman.

Connerton, Paul. *How Societies Remember.* Cambridge: Cambridge University Press, 1989.

Costa, P. "The Study of the City of Zafar (Al Baleed)." *Journal of Oman Studies* 5 (1979): 111–50.

Coulter, Chris. *Bush Wives and Girl Soldiers: Women's Lives through War and Peace in Sierra Leone*. Ithaca: Cornell University Press, 2009.

Crone, Patricia. *Meccan Trade and the Rise of Islam*. Princeton: Princeton University Press, 1987. Facsimile reprint of the first edition. Piscataway: Gorgias Press, 2004.

Dahlgren, Susanne. *Contesting Realities: The Public Sphere and Morality in Southern Yemen*. Syracuse: Syracuse University Press, 2010.

———. "Making Intimate 'Civilpolitics' in Southern Yemen." In *Freedom without Permission: Bodies and Space in the Arab Revolutions*, edited by Frances S. Hasso and Zakia Salime, 80–104. Durham: Duke University Press, 2016.

Das, Veena. *Life and Words: Violence and the Descent into the Ordinary*. Berkeley: University of California Press, 2006.

Deeb, Lara. *An Enchanted Modern: Gender and Public Piety in Shi'i Lebanon*. Princeton: Princeton University Press, 2006.

DeVore, Marc. "A More Complex and Conventional Victory: Revisiting the Dhofar Counterinsurgency, 1963–1975." *Small Wars and Insurgencies* 23, no. 1 (2012): 144–73.

Dhofari Gucci. "Festival of the Negroes 2015." *Dhofari Gucci Blog*, October 23, 2015. http://dhofarigucci.blogspot.com/2015/10/festival-of-negroes-2015.html.

———. "Remaining Prisoners Released." *Dhofari Gucci Blog*, July 5, 2011. http://dhofarigucci.blogspot.com/2011/07/remaining-prisoners-released.html.

———. "Salalah No More." *Dhofari Gucci Blog*, January 23, 2015. http://dhofarigucci.blogspot.com/search/label/Haffa%20Beach.

———. "Tension in Salalah." *Dhofari Gucci Blog*, May 15, 2011. http://dhofarigucci.blogspot.com/2011/05/tension-in-salalah.html.

———. "URGENT: Army Arrest Hundreds in Salalah." *Dhofari Gucci Blog*, May 13, 2011. http://dhofarigucci.blogspot.com/2011/05/urgent-army-arrest-hundreds-of-dhofaris.html.

Diamond, Larry. "Why Are There No Arab Democracies?" *Journal of Democracy* 21, no. 1 (January 2010): 93–104.

Donaghy, Rori. "Oman Arrests Leading Writer over Government Criticism." *Middle East Eye*, April 19, 2016. https://www.middleeasteye.net/news/oman-arrests-leading-writer-over-government-criticism-rights-group.

Donham, Donald L. *Marxist Modern: An Ethnographic History of the Ethiopian Revolution*. Berkeley: University of California Press, 1999.

Donner, Henrike. "Radical Masculinity: Morality, Sociality and Relationships through Recollections of Naxalite Activists." *Dialectical Anthropology* 33, no. 3 (2009): 327–43.

Douglas, Mary. *Purity and Danger: An Analysis of Concepts of Pollution and Taboo*. London: Routledge, 1966.

Dresch, Paul. "Debates on Marriage and Nationality in the United Arab Emirates." In *Monarchies and Nations: Globalisation and Identity in the Arab States of the Gulf*, edited by Paul Dresch and James P. Piscatori, 136–57. London: I. B. Tauris, 2005.

Dresch, Paul. "Foreign Matter: The Place of Strangers in Gulf Society." In *Globalization and the Gulf*, edited by John W Fox, Nada Mourtada-Sabbah and Mohammed Al Mutawa, 402–49. London: Routledge, 2011.

Duschinski, Haley, Mona Bhan, Ather Zia, and Cynthia Mahmood, eds. *Resisting Occupation in Kashmir*. Philadelphia: University of Pennsylvania Press, 2018.
Eickelman, Christine. *Women and Community in Oman*. New York: New York University Press, 1984.
El Shakry, Omnia. "'History without Documents': The Vexed Archives of Decolonization in the Middle East." *The American Historical Review* 120, no. 3 (2015): 920–34.
Embassy of the Sultanate of Oman in London. "Communist Subversion." *Oman*, no. 1 (1973): 7. Arab World Documentation Unit, University of Exeter, A/Omn.5.OMAN/L.
———. "Erroneous P.F.L.O.A.G. Reports." *Oman*, no. 6 (1973): Unnumbered page. Arab World Documentation Unit, University of Exeter, A/Omn.5.OMAN/L.
Engels, Friedrich. *The Origin of the Family, Private Property and the State: In the Light of the Researches of Lewis H Morgan*. 1884. Reprint, London: Lawrence and Wishart, 1972.
Enriquez, Laura. *Children of the Revolution: Violence, Inequality, and Hope in Nicaraguan Migration*. Stanford: Stanford University Press, 2022.
Fanon, Frantz. *Black Skin, White Masks*. Translated by Charles Lam Markmann. New York: Grove Press, 1967.
Feldman, Allen. "Political Terror and the Technologies of Memory: Excuse, Sacrifice, Commodification, and Actuarial Moralities." *Radical History Review* 85, no. 1 (Winter 2003): 58–73.
Fernández-Savater, Amador, Cristina Flesher Fominaya, Luhuna Carvalho, Çiğdem, Hoda Elsadda, Wiam El-Tamami, Patricia Horrillo, Silvia Nanclares, and Stavros Stavrides. "Life after the Squares: Reflections on the Consequences of the Occupy Movements." *Social Movement Studies* 16, no. 1 (2017): 119–51.
Fernandez, Nadine T. *Revolutionizing Romance: Interracial Couples in Contemporary Cuba*. New Brunswick: Rutgers University Press, 2010.
Fiennes, Ranulph. *Where Soldiers Fear to Tread*. London: Hodder and Stoughton, 1975.
Fitchett, Joseph. "End of Britain's War in Arabia." *The Observer*, January 11, 1976.
Foran, John. "Theories of Revolution Revisited: Toward a Fourth Generation?" *Sociological Theory* 11, no. 1 (1993): 1–20.
Foucault, Michel. *Ethics: Subjectivity and Truth*. Vol. 1 of *Essential Works of Foucault, 1954–1984*, edited by Paul Rabinow. Translated by Robert Hurley and others. London: Penguin, 2019.
———. "Is it Useless to Revolt?". In *Foucault and the Iranian Revolution: Gender and the Seductions of Islamism*, edited by Janet Afary and Kevin Anderson, 263–67. Chicago: University of Chicago Press, 2005.
Frederiksen, Martin Demant, and Katrine Bendtsen Gotfredsen. *Georgian Portraits: Essays on the Afterlives of a Revolution*. Winchester: Zero Books, 2017.
Freedom House. *Freedom in the World 2016: The Annual Survey of Political Rights and Civil Liberties*. New York: Rowman and Littlefield, 2017.
Fuccaro, Nelida. *Histories of City and State in the Persian Gulf*. Cambridge: Cambridge University Press, 2009.
Gal, Susan, and Gail Kligman. *The Politics of Gender after Socialism: A Comparative-Historical Essay*. Princeton: Princeton University Press, 2000.

Gardiner, Ian. *In the Service of the Sultan: A First Hand Account of the Dhofar Insurgency.* Barnsley: Pen & Sword Military, 2015.

Gardner, Andrew. "Rumour and Myth in the Labour Camps of Qatar." *Anthropology Today* 28, no. 6 (December 2012): 25–28.

———. "The Transforming Landscape of Doha: An Essay on Urbanism and Urbanization in Qatar." *Jadaliyya*, November 9, 2013. https://www.jadaliyya.com/Details/29778.

Gengler, Justin. *Group Conflict and Political Mobilization in Bahrain and the Arab Gulf: Rethinking the Rentier State.* Bloomington: Indiana University Press, 2015.

Gennep, Arnold van. *The Rites of Passage.* Translated by M. Vizedom and G. Caffee. London: Routledge, 1960.

Ghamari-Tabrizi, Behrooz. *Foucault in Iran: Islamic Revolution After the Enlightenment.* Minneapolis: University of Minnesota Press, 2016.

———. *Remembering Akbar: Inside the Iranian Revolution.* New York: OR Books, 2016.

Ghassani, Salem bin Ahmad al-. *Al-Tariq wa al-dalil.* Salalah: Wizarat al-i'lam, 2010.

Gilbertson, Amanda. "A Fine Balance: Negotiating Fashion and Respectable Femininity in Middle-Class Hyderabad, India." *Modern Asian Studies* 48, no. 1 (2014): 120–58.

Gilroy, Paul. *The Black Atlantic: Modernity and Double Consciousness.* London: Verso, 1993.

Goldman, Wendy Z. *Women, the State and Revolution: Soviet Family Policy and Social Life, 1917–1936.* Cambridge: Cambridge University Press, 1993.

Goodale, Mark. *A Revolution in Fragments: Traversing Scales of Justice, Ideology, and Practice in Bolivia.* Durham: Duke University Press, 2019.

Goode, James. "Assisting Our Brothers, Defending Ourselves: The Iranian Intervention in Oman, 1972–75." *Iranian Studies* 47, no. 3 (2014): 441–62.

Goodfellow, Aaron. *Gay Fathers, their Children, and the Making of Kinship.* New York: Fordham University Press, 2015.

Government of Oman. *Census 2010.* Muscat: National Centre for Statistics and Information, n.d., accessed June 5, 2022. https://www.ncsi.gov.om/Elibrary/LibraryContentDoc/bar_Census%20Final%20Result%202010_388bd9c6-a938-467d-8c92-f6950cc1785f.pdf.

Graham, Robert. "Iran May Withdraw Troops from Oman to Calm Gulf." *Financial Times*, January 14, 1977.

Grandville, B. de la. "Marmul Field, South Oman: Appraisal and Development of Structural and Stratigraphic Trap Oil Field with Reservoirs in Glacial/Periglacial Clastics." *AAPG Bulletin* 65 (1981): 917.

Gross-Wyrtzen, Leslie. "'There Is No Race Here': On Blackness, Slavery, and Disavowal in North Africa and North African Studies." *The Journal of North African Studies* (June 13, 2022).

Guindi, Fadwa El. *Veil: Modesty, Privacy and Resistance.* Oxford: Berg, 1999.

Gulf Centre for Human Rights. "Oman: Writer and Online Activist Saed Al-Darodi Sentenced to Three Months in Prison." February 21, 2016. https://www.gc4hr.org/news/view/1187.

Gulf Committee, The. *Women and the Revolution in Oman.* London: The Gulf Committee, 1975.

Hadad, Qasim. "Dhufar... Thawrat al-riyah al-mawsumiyyah." *al-Quds*, November 19, 2019. https://tinyurl.com/4hzpfpkv.

Hafez, Sherine. *Women of the Midan: The Untold Stories of Egypt's Revolutionaries*. Bloomington: Indiana University Press, 2019.
Halbwachs, Maurice. *On Collective Memory*. Translated by Lewis A. Coser. Chicago: University of Chicago Press, 1992.
Halilovich, Hariz. *Places of Pain: Forced Displacement, Popular Memory and Trans-local Identities in Bosnian War-torn Communities*. Oxford: Berghahn Books, 2015.
Halliday, Fred. *Arabia without Sultans*. Harmondsworth: Penguin, 1974.
———. "Arabia Without Sultans Revisited." *Middle East Report* 204 (Fall 1997): 27–29.
Haremi, Tariq Ziad El. "Documentary Film Tells Untold Stories of UK Troops in Oman's Dhofar War." *Times of Oman*, October 3, 2016. https://timesofoman.com/article/18636-documentary-film-tells-untold-stories-of-uk-troops-in-omans-dhofar-war.
Hashemi, Said al-, ed. *Al-Rabi' al-umani: Qira'ah fi al-siyaqat wa al-dalalat*. Beirut: Dar al-Farabi, 2013.
———. "Al-Umani Zahran Zahir al-Sarimi fi 'al-Bahth 'an watan.'" *al-Quds*, April 25, 2020. https://tinyurl.com/thszusm6.
Hasso, Frances S., and Zakia Salime, eds. *Freedom without Permission: Bodies and Space in the Arab Revolutions*. Durham: Duke University Press, 2016.
Havel, Václav. *The Power of the Powerless: Citizens against the State in Central-Eastern Europe*. Edited by John Keane. London: Hutchinson, 1985.
Hayden, Corinne P. "Gender, Genetics, and Generation: Reformulating Biology in Lesbian Kinship." *Cultural Anthropology* 10, no. 1 (February 1995): 41–63.
Hazelton, Jacqueline L. "The 'Hearts and Minds' Fallacy: Violence, Coercion, and Success in Counterinsurgency Warfare." *International Security* 42, no. 1 (Summer 2017): 80–113.
———. *Bullets not Ballots: Success in Counterinsurgency Warfare*. Cornell: Cornell University Press, 2021.
Hegland, Mary Elaine. *Days of Revolution: Political Unrest in an Iranian Village*. Stanford: Stanford University Press, 2013.
Heim, Bernhard, Marc Joosten, Aurel von Richthofen, and Florian Rupp. "On the Process and Economics of Land Settlement in Oman: Mathematical Modeling and Reasoning in Urban Planning and Design." *Homo Oeconomicus* 35, no. 1 (2018): 1–30.
Helg, Aline. *Slave No More: Self-liberation before Abolitionism in the Americas*. Translated by Lara Vergnaud. Chapel Hill: The University of North Carolina Press, 2019.
Hennebelle, Guy, and Monique Martineau Henebelle. "The Hour of Liberation." April 28, 2021. https://www.sabzian.be/text/the-hour-of-liberation.
Hermez, Sami. *War Is Coming: Between Past and Future Violence in Lebanon*. Philadelphia: University of Pennsylvania Press, 2017.
Higgins, Andrew. *With the SAS and Other Animals: A Vet's Experiences During the Dhofar War 1974*. 2nd ed. Barnsley: Pen and Sword Military, 2015.
Hobbes, Thomas. *Leviathan*. 1615. Reprint, London: Penguin Books, 1985.
Hoffman, Valerie J. *The Essentials of Ibadi Islam*. Syracuse: Syracuse University Press, 2012.
Holbraad, Martin. "Revolución o Muerte: Self-Sacrifice and the Ontology of Cuban Revolution." *Ethnos* 79, no. 3 (2014): 365–87.

Hughes, Dhana. "'Retired' Insurgents: Recreating Life after Sri Lanka's Terror." *Contemporary South Asia* 21, no. 1 (2013): 62–74.
Hughes, Geraint. "Demythologising Dhofar: British Policy, Military Strategy, and Counter-Insurgency in Oman, 1963–1976." *The Journal of Military History* 79, no. 2 (April 2015): 423–56.
———. "A 'Model Campaign' Reappraised: The Counter-Insurgency War in Dhofar, Oman, 1965–1975." *Journal of Strategic Studies* 32, no. 2 (2009): 271–305.
Humphrey, Caroline. *Karl Marx Collective: Economy, Society and Religion in a Siberian Collective Farm.* Cambridge: Cambridge University Press, 1983.
Hurewitz, J. "The Persian Gulf: British Withdrawal and Western Security." *The Annals of the American Academy of Political and Social Science* 401, no. 1 (May 1972): 106–15.
Ibn Battuta. *The Travels of Ibn Battuta, A.D. 1325–1354.* Translated by Hamilton Gibb. Edited by C. Defremery and B. R. Sanguinetti. Vol. 2, Cambridge: Cambridge University Press, 1958.
Ibn Khaldun. *The Muqaddimah: An Introduction to History.* Translated by Franz Rosenthal. New York: Pantheon, 1958.
Ibrahim, Sonallah. *Warda.* Translated by Richard Jocquemond. Paris: Actes Sud, 2005.
———. *Warda.* Translated by Hosam Aboul-Ela. Yale: Yale University Press, 2021.
———. *Wardah.* Cairo: Dar al-mustaqbal al-ʿarabi, 2000.
ʿIkri, ʿAbd al-Nabi. *Dhakirat al-watan wa al-manfa.* Manama: Dar Faradees, 2015.
Imperial War Museum. "Battle of Mirbat (SAS 22)." *Imperial War Museum*, n.d., accessed October 27 2022. https://www.iwm.org.uk/memorials/item/memorial/80550.
Jabob, Mona. "Inhaʾ al-riqq wa tahrir al-marʾah wa tanwir al-mujtamaʿah." *Gulf Centre for Development Policies*, n.d., accessed June 5, 2022. https://gulfpolicies.org/2019-05-18-07-14-32/93-2019-06-26-10-11-31/922-2019-06-26-13-06-42.
———. "Majlis Dhufar." *Mona Jabob Blog*, November 24, 2013. http://munagaboob.blogspot.com/
———. *Qiyadat al-mujtamʿah nahwa al-taghayyur: Al-tajribah al-tarbawiyyah li thawrat Dhufar, 1969–1992.* Beirut: Markaz dirasat al-wihdah al-ʿarabiyyah, 2010.
Jacob, Wilson Chacko. *For God or Empire: Sayyid Fadl and the Indian Ocean World.* Stanford: Stanford University Press, 2019.
Jalabi, Raya. "Oman to Reimpose Nightly Curfew Following Spike in COVID-19 Cases." *Reuters*, June 19, 2021. https://www.reuters.com/world/middle-east/oman-reimpose-nightly-curfew-following-spike-covid-19-cases-2021-06-19/.
———. "Omanis Protest Unemployment in a Rare Show of Discontent." *Reuters*, May 24, 2021. https://www.reuters.com/world/middle-east/omanis-protest-unemployment-rare-show-discontent-2021-05-24/.
Janzen, Jörg. "The Destruction of Resources Among the Mountain Nomads of Dhofar." In *The Transformation of Nomadic Society in the Arab East*, edited by Martha Mundy and Basim Musallam, 160–75. Cambridge: Cambridge University Press, 2000.
———. *Nomads in the Sultanate of Oman: Tradition and Development in Dhofar.* Boulder: Westview Press, 1986.
Jeapes, Tony. *SAS Secret War.* 3rd ed. London: Harper Collins, 1996.

Johnson, Penny, Lamis Abu Nahleh, and Annelies Moors. "Weddings and War: Marriage Arrangements and Celebrations in Two Palestinian Intifadas." *Journal of Middle East Women's Studies* 5, no. 3 (Fall 2009): 11–35.

Jones, Clive. "Military Intelligence and the War in Dhofar: An Appraisal." *Small Wars & Insurgencies* 25, no. 3 (2014): 628–46.

Jones, Jeremy, and Nicholas Ridout. *A History of Modern Oman*. Cambridge: Cambridge University Press, 2015.

Kar, Sohini. "Securitizing Women: Gender, Precaution, and Risk in Indian Finance." *Signs: Journal of Women in Culture and Society* 43, no. 2 (Winter 2018): 301–25.

Kelly, Tobias. "The Attractions of Accountancy: Living an Ordinary Life during the Second Palestinian Intifada." *Ethnography* 9, no. 3 (September 2008): 351–76.

Khalaf, Sulayman N. "Gulf Societies and the Image of Unlimited Good." *Dialectical Anthropology* 17, no. 1 (1992): 53–84.

Khalfan, Bushra. *Al-Bagh: Riwayah*. Ottawa: Mas'a li al-nashr wa al-tawzi', 2018.

Khalfan, Bushra, and Al Roya Newspaper. "Munaqashat riwayat al-Bagh." *Al Roya Newspaper*. March 31, 2018. YouTube video, 10:11, https://www.youtube.com/watch?app=desktop&v=DoUNY6dK_hk.

Khalili, Charlotte Al-. "Rethinking the Concept of Revolution through the Syrian Experience." *Al-Jumhuriya*, May 5, 2021. https://aljumhuriya.net/en/2021/05/05/rethinking-concept-revolution-through-syrian-experience/.

———. "Waiting for the Revolution to End: Syrian Displacement, Time, Subjectivity." London: University College London Press, forthcoming.

Khalili, Charlotte Al-, Narges Ansari, Myriam Lamrani, and Kaya Uzel, eds. *Revolution Beyond the Event: The Afterlives of Radical Politics*. London: University College London Press, forthcoming.

Khalili, Laleh. "Gendered Practices of Counterinsurgency." *Review of International Studies* 37, no. 4 (2011): 1471–91.

———. *Heroes and Martyrs of Palestine: The Politics of National Commemoration*. Cambridge: Cambridge University Press, 2007.

———. *Time in the Shadows: Confinement in Counterinsurgencies*. Stanford: Stanford University Press, 2012.

Kim, Suzy. *Everyday Life in the North Korean Revolution, 1945–1950*. Ithaca: Cornell University Press, 2013.

Knowles, Caroline. *Flip-flop. A Journey Through Globalisation's Backroads*. London: Pluto Press, 2014.

KROAG [Committee for the Revolution in Oman and the Arabian Gulf]. "Experiences of a Health Worker." *News from Oman and Southern Arabia* 37 (1981): 19–23.

———. "Interview with Abdel Samad." *News from Oman and Southern Arabia* 38 (1981): 13–31.

———. "Interview with Hudda." *News from Oman and Southern Arabia* 36 (1980): 47–50.

———. "The Role of Women in the Second Phase of the Revolution (1968–74)." *News from Oman and Southern Arabia* 36 (1980): 25–35.

———. "The Role of Women in the Third Phase of the Revolution (1974–)." *News from Oman and Southern Arabia* 36 (1980): 35–44.

———. "The Traditional Role of Women in the Omani Society." *News from Oman and Southern Arabia* 36 (1980): 19–22.
Kroag. *The Revolution Is Alive: The Liberation Struggle in Oman.* Copenhagen: Kroag, 1979.
Kuper, Adam. *The Invention of Primitive Society: Transformations of an Illusion.* London: Routledge, 1988.
Kwon, Heonik. *Ghosts of War in Vietnam.* Cambridge: Cambridge University Press, 2008.
La Botz, Dan. *What Went Wrong? The Nicaraguan Revolution: A Marxist Analysis.* 2nd ed. Chicago: Haymarket Books, 2018.
Labour Party International Department. "Dhofar After the Revolution." OMA 953.506 DHO Arab World Documentation Unit, University of Exeter, 1982.
Lackner, Helen. *P. D. R. Yemen: Outpost of Socialist Development in Arabia.* London: Ithaca Press, 1985.
Ladwig, Walter C. "Supporting Allies in Counterinsurgency: Britain and the Dhofar Rebellion." *Small Wars & Insurgencies* 19, no. 1 (2008): 62–88.
Lal, Priya. *African Socialism in Postcolonial Tanzania: Between the Village and the World.* Cambridge: Cambridge University Press, 2015.
Lazar, Sian. "Historical Narrative, Mundane Political Time, and Revolutionary Moments: Coexisting Temporalities in the Lived Experience of Social Movements." Special issue, *Journal of the Royal Anthropological Institute* 20, no. S1 (April 2014): 91–108.
———. *The Social Life of Politics: Ethics, Kinship and Union Activism in Argentina.* Stanford: Stanford University Press, 2017.
Lazreg, Marnia. "French Revisionism and the Erasure of the Algerian Revolution." *Rosa Luxemburg Stiftung*, June 21 2022.
Le Renard, Amélie. *A Society of Young Women: Opportunities of Place, Power, and Reform in Saudi Arabia.* Stanford: Stanford University Press, 2014.
Ledeneva, Alena V. *Russia's Economy of Favours: Blat, Networking, and Informal Exchange.* Cambridge: Cambridge University Press, 1998.
Lefebvre, Henri. *Everyday Life in the Modern World.* Translated by Sacha Rabinovitch. London: Allen Lane, 1971.
———. *The Production of Space.* Translated by Donald Nicholson-Smith. Oxford: Blackwell, 1991.
Lévi-Strauss, Claude. *The Elementary Structures of Kinship.* Edited by Rodney Needham. Translated by James Harle Bell and John Richard von Sturmer. London: Eyre & Spottiswoode, 1969.
Liberation Support Movement. "Feature: A New Generation of Women." *LSM News: Quarterly Journal of the Liberation Support Movement* 2, no. 3 (1975).
Liebhaber, Samuel. "Society." In *When Melodies Gather: Oral Art of the Mahra*, edited by Samuel Liebhaber. A Stanford Digital Project: Stanford University Press, 2018.
Limbert, Mandana E. *In the Time of Oil: Piety, Memory, and Social Life in an Omani Town.* Stanford: Stanford University Press, 2010.
———. "Marriage, Status and the Politics of Nationality in Oman." In *The Gulf Family: Kinship Policies and Modernity*, edited by Alanound Alsharekh, 199–213. London: Saqi, 2009.

Linenthal, Edward Tabor. *Preserving Memory: The Struggle to Create America's Holocaust Museum.* New York: Columbia University Press, 2001.

Link, Perry. "China: The Anaconda in the Chandelier." *The New York Review of Books*, April 11, 2002. https://www.nybooks.com/articles/2002/04/11/china-the-anaconda-in-the-chandelier/.

Lorimer, John G. *Gazetteer of the Persian Gulf, Oman and Central Arabia. Vol. 2: Geographical and Statistical.* Calcutta: Superintendent Government Printing, 1908–1915.

Lovell, Julia. *Maoism: A Global History.* London: The Bodley Head, 2019.

Low, Valentine. "Prince Harry Honours SAS Hero in Fiji." *The Times*, October 25, 2018. https://www.thetimes.co.uk/article/prince-harry-honours-sacrifice-of-fijis-sas-hero-gm3mnzr6z.

Luong, Hy. *Revolution in the Village: Tradition and Transformation in North Vietnam, 1925–1988.* Honolulu: University of Hawaii Press, 1992.

Macleod, Arlene Elowe. *Accommodating Protest: Working Women, the New Veiling, and Change in Cairo.* New York: Columbia University Press, 1991.

Mahajan, Nidhi. "Remembering Slavery at the Bin Jelmood House in Qatar." *Middle East Report* 299 (Summer 2021). https://merip.org/2021/08/remembering-slavery-at-the-bin-jelmood-house-in-qatar/.

Mahdavi, Pardis. *Passionate Uprisings: Iran's Sexual Revolution.* Stanford: Stanford University Press, 2008.

Mahdavy, Hussein. "The Patterns and Problems of Economic Development in Rentier States: The Case of Iran." In *Studies in the Economic History of the Middle East*, edited by M. A. Cook, 428–67. London: Oxford University Press, 1970.

Mahfaif. "25 Fibrayir: I'tisamat Salalah." *Tahyati*, March 5, 2011. http://tahyati.blogspot.com/2011/03/25.html.

———. "Min fawa'id al-i'tisamat." *Tahyati*, March 16, 2011. http://tahyati.blogspot.com/2011/03/blog-post_16.html.

Mahmood, Saba. *Politics of Piety: The Islamic Revival and the Feminist Subject.* Princeton: Princeton University Press, 2005.

Makram-Ebeid, Dina. "'Old People are not Revolutionaries': Labor Struggles and the Politics of Value and Stability ('Istiqrar) in a Factory Occupation in Egypt." *Focaal*, November 14, 2014. https://www.focaalblog.com/2014/11/14/dina-makram-ebeid-labor-struggles-and-the-politics-of-value-and-stability-in-a-factory-occupation-in-egypt/.

Maldonado-Torres, Nelson. "On the Coloniality of Being: Contributions to the Development of a Concept." *Cultural Studies* 21, no. 2–3 (2007): 240–70.

Malinowski, Bronislaw. *Argonauts of the Western Pacific: An Account of Native Enterprise and Adventure in the Archipelagoes of Melanesian New Guinea.* London: Routledge, 1922. Reprinted with foreword by Adam Kuper. London: Routledge, 2014.

Malkki, Liisa H. *Purity and Exile: Violence, Memory, and National Cosmology among Hutu Refugees in Tanzania.* Chicago: University of Chicago Press, 1995.

Mampilly, Zachariah Cherian. *Rebel Rulers: Insurgent Governance and Civilian Life During War.* Ithaca: Cornell University Press, 2011.

Mantovan, Giacomo. "'Ils étaient les rois . . .': L'adieu aux armes d'anciens combattants des Tigres tamouls exilés en France." *Migrations Société* 161, no. 5 (2015): 89–104.

Martin, Paul. "Dhufar Rebellion's Eleventh Hour." *The Times*, August 3, 1970.
Matthiesen, Toby. *The Other Saudis: Shiism, Dissent and Sectarianism*. Cambridge: Cambridge University Press, 2014.

———. "Red Arabia: Anti-Colonialism, the Cold War, and the Long Sixties in the Gulf States." In *Routledge Handbook of the Global Sixties*, edited by Chen Jian, Martin Klimke, Masha Kirasirova, Mary Nolan, Marilyn Young, and Joanna Waley-Cohen, 94–105. London: Routledge, 2018.

———. *Sectarian Gulf: Bahrain, Saudi Arabia, and the Arab Spring That Wasn't*. Stanford: Stanford University Press, 2013.

Mauss, Marcel. "A Sociological Assessment of Bolshevism (1924–5)." *International Journal of Human Resource Management* 13, no. 3 (1924–5 [1984]): 331–74.

McConnell, Fiona. "Contextualizing and Politicizing Peace: Geographies of Tibetan *Satyagraha*." In *Geographies of Peace*, edited by Nick Megoran, Fiona McConnell, and Philippa Williams, 131–50. London: I. B. Tauris, 2014.

McMullin, Jaremey. *Ex-Combatants and the Post-Conflict State: Challenges of Reintegration*. London: Palgrave Macmillan, 2013.

MENA Vinyl Project. "Chants révolutionnaires du peuple d'Oman, du Yémen et d'Iran." February 25, 2018. YouTube video, 37:18, accessed June 5, 2022. https://www.youtube.com/watch?v=VhfFWwGg4io.

Meneley, Anne. *Tournaments of Value: Sociability and Hierarchy in a Yemeni Town*. Toronto: University of Toronto Press, 1996.

Ménoret, Pascal. *Joyriding in Riyadh: Oil, Urbanism, and Road Revolt*. Cambridge: Cambridge University Press, 2014.

Metsola, Lalli. "The Struggle Continues? The Spectre of Liberation, Memory Politics and 'War Veterans' in Namibia." *Development and Change* 41, no. 4 (July 2010): 589–613.

Ministry of Defence. "Countering Insurgency." *British Army Field Manual*. 1, no. 10 (2009). http://news.bbc.co.uk/1/shared/bsp/hi/pdfs/16_11_09_army_manual.pdf.

———. "UK Armed Forces Operational Deaths Post World War II." March 26, 2015. https://bit.ly/3iSCSBW.

Mockaitis, Thomas R. *British Counterinsurgency in the Post-Imperial Era*. Manchester: Manchester University Press, 1995.

Molyneux, Maxine. "Mobilization without Emancipation? Women's Interests, the State, and Revolution in Nicaragua." *Feminist Studies* 11, no. 2 (Summer 1985): 227–54.

Montoya, Rosario. *Gendered Scenarios of Revolution: Making New Men and New Women in Nicaragua, 1975–2000*. Tucson: University of Arizona Press, 2012.

Morris, Miranda. "Dhofar: What Made it Different?". In *Oman: Economic, Social and Strategic Developments*, edited by B. R. Pridham, 51–78. London: Croom Helm, 1987.

———. "The Harvesting of Frankincense in Dhofar, Oman." In *Profumi d'Arabia*, edited by Alessandra Avanzini, 231–47. Rome: L'Erma di Bretschneider, 1997.

———, ed. *The Oral Art of Soqoṭra: A Collection of Island Voices*. Edited by Miranda Morris. Leiden: Brill, 2021.

———. "Some Thoughts on Studying the Endangered Modern South Arabian Languages." *Brill's Journal of Afroasiatic Languages and Linguistics* 9, no. 1–2 (January 2017): 9–32.

Muʿammari, Sulayman, and Said al-Hashemi. *Ubaid al-umani hayyan*. Beirut: Dar Suʾal li al-nashr, 2015.

Nakib, Farah Al-. *Kuwait Transformed: A History of Oil and Urban Life*. Stanford: Stanford University Press, 2016.

———. "Kuwait's Modern Spectacle: Oil Wealth and the Making of a New Capital City, 1950–90." *Comparative Studies of South Asia, Africa and the Middle East* 33, no. 1 (2013): 7–25.

———. "Revisiting Ḥaḍar and Badū in Kuwait: Citizenship, Housing, and the Construction of a Dichotomy." *International Journal of Middle East Studies* 46, no. 1 (2014): 5–30.

Navaro-Yashin, Yael. *Faces of the State: Secularism and Public Life in Turkey*. Princeton: Princeton University Press, 2002.

Newsinger, John. *British Counterinsurgency*. 2nd ed. Basingstoke: Palgrave Macmillan, 2015.

Nora, Pierre. "Between Memory and History: Les lieux de mémoire." Special issue, *Representations* 26 (April 1989): 7–24.

———. "Reasons for the Current Upsurge in Memory." *Transit* 22 (2002). https://www.eurozine.com/reasons-for-the-current-upsurge-in-memory/.

Nugent, Daniel. *Spent Cartridges of Revolution: An Anthropological History of Namiquipa, Chihuahua*. Chicago: University of Chicago Press, 1993.

Omani Association for Human Rights. *Torture in the Sultanate of Oman: Lost Liberties and Suppression of Human Rights Activists*. Gulf Centre for Human Rights, 2021. https://www.gc4hr.org/report/view/147.

Orwell, George. *Nineteen Eighty-Four*. London: Secker and Warburg, 1949.

Ottaway, Marina, and David Ottaway. *A Tale of Four Worlds: The Arab Region after the Uprisings*. London: Hurst, 2019.

Owtram, Francis. *A Modern History of Oman: Formation of the State Since 1920*. London: I. B. Tauris, 2004.

Pedwell, Carolyn. *Revolutionary Routines: The Habits of Social Transformation*. Montreal: McGill-Queen's University Press, 2021.

Peteet, Julie. *Landscape of Hope and Despair: Palestinian Refugee Camps*. Philadelphia: University of Pennsylvania Press, 2005.

Peterson, J. E. *Oman's Insurgencies: The Sultanate's Struggle for Supremacy*. London: Saqi, 2007.

Peutz, Nathalie. *Islands of Heritage: Conservation and Transformation in Yemen*. Stanford: Stanford University Press, 2018.

Phillips, Sarah G., and Jennifer S. Hunt. "'Without Sultan Qaboos, We Would Be Yemen': The Renaissance Narrative and the Political Settlement in Oman." *Journal of International Development* 29, no. 5 (July 2017): 645–60.

Piliavsky, Anastasia, ed. *Patronage as Politics in South Asia*. Cambridge: Cambridge University Press, 2014.

Pine, Frances. "Naming the House and Naming the Land: Kinship and Social Groups in Highland Poland." *Journal of the Royal Anthropological Institute* 2, no. 3 (1996): 443–59.

Popular Front for the Liberation of Oman [PFLO]. "9th June Revolution Enters its Tenth Year." *9 June,* June 1974: 1–11.

———. "Al-Alawi Reveals Weakness of Muscat Regime in Front of U.N." *Saut al-Thawra* (November 1977): 14–16.
———. *Al-Qabilah: min aina wa ila aina?* Aden: Popular Front for the Liberation of Oman, 1981.
———. "Annual Military Report," Special issue: 10 Years of Struggle. *Saut al-Thawra* (June 9, 1975): 30.
———. "Astar min tarikh thawrat al-tasi' min yunyu." *Thawrat Uman* 4, no. 40 (1981): 14–15.
———. *In the Path of Self Reconstruction and Perseverance in the Revolutionary War.* N.p.: The Popular Front for the Liberation of Oman, Central Information Committee, 1977.
———. *Sijil al-khalidin, 1965–1979.* N.p.: Popular Front for the Liberation of Oman, n.d., circa 1980.
———. *Uman: Al-insan wa al-thawrah/Oman: Man and Revolution.* Aden: The Popular Front for the Liberation of Oman, 1977.
———. [Special Edition for the 20th Anniversary of the Revolution]. *Saut al-Thawra*, July-August, no. 460, 1985.
Popular Front for the Liberation of Oman and the Arabian Gulf [PFLOAG]. "Internal Statutes for People's Councils in the Dhofar Region [1972]." In *Documents of the National Struggle in Oman and the Arabian Gulf*, edited by The Gulf Committee, 54–56. London: The Gulf Committee, 1974.
———. "National Democratic Working Plan [1971]." In *Documents of the National Struggle in Oman and the Arabian Gulf*, edited by The Gulf Committee, 24–31. London: The Gulf Committee, 1974.
———. "Liberated Area: People's Authority Established in Liberated Area." *Saut al-Thawra* 54 (June 2, 1973): 2.
Powell, Eve Troutt. *A Different Shade of Colonialism: Egypt, Great Britain, and the Mastery of the Sudan.* Berkeley: University of California Press, 2003.
———. *Tell This in My Memory: Stories of Enslavement from Egypt, Sudan, and the Ottoman Empire.* Stanford: Stanford University Press, 2012.
Pridham, B. "Oman: Change or Continuity?". In *Arabia and the Gulf: From Traditional Society to Modern States*, edited by Ian Netton, 132–55. Croom Helm: London, 1986.
Punamäki, Raija-Leena. "Can Ideological Commitment Protect Children's Psychosocial Well-Being in Situations of Political Violence?" *Child Development* 67, no. 1 (1996): 55–69.
Rabi, Uzi. *The Emergence of States in a Tribal Society.* Brighton: Sussex Academic Press, 2006.
Radcliffe-Brown, A. R. *Structure and Function in Primitive Society: Essays and Addresses.* London: Cohen & West, 1952.
Rafeh, Chawki. *Dr Kamel Mohanna: un médecin libanais engagé dans la tourmente des peuples: les choix difficiles.* Translated by Danielle Saleh. Beirut: Dar al-Farabi, 2013.
Ragoné, Helena. "Surrogate Motherhood and American Kinship." In *Kinship and Family: An Anthropological Reader*, edited by Robert Parkin and Linda Stone, 342–61. Maldon: Blackwell, 2004.

Rahal, Malika. "Fused Together and Torn Apart: Stories and Violence in Contemporary Algeria." *History and Memory* 24, no. 1 (2012): 118–51.

Rasheed, Madawi Al-. "Transnational Connections and National Identity: Zanzibari Omanis in Muscat." In *Monarchies and Nations: Globalisation and Identity in the Arab States of the Gulf*, edited by Paul Dresch and James P. Piscatori, 96–113. London: I. B. Tauris, 2005.

Risse, Marielle. *Community and Autonomy in Southern Oman*. New York: Palgrave Macmillan, 2019.

Rivers, Daniel Winunwe. *Radical Relations: Lesbian Mothers, Gay Fathers, and their Children in the United States since World War II*. Chapel Hill: University of North Carolina Press, 2013.

RMC-MENA. "Aghani al-jabhah al-sha'biyyah li tahrir Umaan wa-al-khalij al-'arabi." August 21, 2011. YouTube video, 3:18. https://www.youtube.com/watch?v=KQiT3ommb0o.

Rofel, Lisa. *Other Modernities: Gendered Yearnings in China After Socialism*. Berkeley: University of California Press, 1999.

Rolston, Bill. *Children of the Revolution: The Lives of Sons and Daughters of Activists in Northern Ireland*. Derry: Guildhall, 2011.

Rosendahl, Mona. *Inside the Revolution: Everyday Life in Socialist Cuba*. Ithaca: Cornell University Press, 1997.

Ross, Kristin. *Communal Luxury: The Political Imaginary of the Paris Commune*. London: Verso, 2015.

Saba, Mary Jirmanus. "Heiny Srour on The Hour of Liberation Has Arrived." *Screen Slate*, June 3, 2019. https://www.screenslate.com/articles/heiny-srour-hour-liberation-has-arrived.

Sachedina, Amal. *Cultivating the Past, Living the Modern: The Politics of Time in the Sultanate of Oman*. Ithaca: Cornell University Press, 2021.

Sahlins, Marshall. "What Kinship Is (Part One)." *The Journal of the Royal Anthropological Institute* 17, no. 1 (March 2011): 2–19.

Said, Maha El, Lena Meari, and Nicola Pratt, eds. *Rethinking Gender in Revolutions and Resistance: Lessons from the Arab World*. London: Zed Books, 2015.

Salem, Sara. *Anticolonial Afterlives in Egypt: The Politics of Hegemony*. Cambridge: Cambridge University Press, 2020.

Sarimi, Zahran al-. *Al-Bahth 'an watan: Sirat muwatin umani 'asha al-ghurbah wa al-ightirab*. Beirut: Riad el-Rayyes, 2020.

———. "Al-Qawl al-fasl fi 'awahin al-qawl." *Al-Hiwar*, October 29, 2020. https://www.ahewar.org/debat/show.art.asp?aid=697148.

———. "Ma'athir wa ma'alat al-thawrah al-umaniyyah." *Al-Falaq*, January 18, 2017. https://www.alfalq.com/?p=9050.

Scaglioni, Marta. *Becoming the 'Abid: Lives and Social Origins in Southern Tunisia*. Milan: Ledizioni, 2020.

Schafer, Jessica. *Soldiers at Peace: Veterans of the Civil War in Mozambique*. New York: Palgrave Macmillan, 2007.

Schäfers, Marlene. "Afterlives: An Introduction." *Allegra Lab*, May 2020. https://allegralaboratory.net/afterlives-introduction/.

———. *Voices that Matter: Kurdish Women and the Dilemmas of Representation in Contemporary Turkey.* Chicago: Chicago University Press, 2022.

Scheffler, Samuel. *Death and the Afterlife.* Edited by Niko Kolodny. Oxford: Oxford University Press, 2013.

Schielke, Samuli. *Egypt in the Future Tense: Hope, Frustration, and Ambivalence Before and After 2011.* Bloomington: Indiana University Press, 2015.

Schneider, David. "What is Kinship All About?". In *Kinship Studies in the Morgan Centennial Year*, edited by P. Reining, 32–63. Washington, DC: Anthropological Society of Washington, 1972.

Schwarcz, Vera. "Memory, Commemoration, and the Plight of China's Intellectuals." *The Wilson Quarterly* 13, no. 4 (Autumn 1989): 120–29.

Scott, David. *Conscripts of Modernity: The Tragedy of Colonial Enlightenment.* Durham: Duke University Press, 2004.

Scott, James C. *Domination and the Arts of Resistance: Hidden Transcripts.* New Haven: Yale University Press, 1990.

———. *Seeing Like a State: How Certain Schemes to Improve the Human Condition Have Failed.* New Haven: Yale University Press, 1998.

———. *Weapons of the Weak: Everyday Forms of Peasant Resistance.* New Haven: Yale University Press, 1985.

———. "Revolution in the Revolution: Peasants and Commissars." Special issue, *Theory and Society* 7, no. 1/2 (March 1979): 97–134.

Shah, Alpa. "The Intimacy of Insurgency: Beyond Coercion, Greed or Grievance in Maoist India." *Economy and Society* 42, no. 3 (2013): 480–506.

———. *Nightmarch: Among the Guerrillas of India's Revolutionary Movement.* London: Hurst, 2018.

———. "'The Muck of the Past': Revolution, Social Transformation, and the Maoists in India." *Journal of the Royal Anthropological Institute* 20, no. 2 (2014): 337–56.

Shahri, 'Ali Ahmad al-. *Kayfa ibtadayna wa-kayfa irtaqayna bi al-hadarah al-insaaniyyah min shibh al-jazirah al-'arabiyyah. Dhufar: Kitabatuha wa-nuqushuha al-qadimah.* Dubai: al-Tab'ah 1, 1994.

———. *Lughat 'Ad/The language of Aad.* Salalah: n.p., 2000.

Shahri, Bakheit al-. "Madrasat Khawlah bint Hakim bi Salalah tunaffidh mashru' al-muwatinah al-raqmiyyah." *Oman Observer*, January 11, 2017. https://www.omandaily.om/?p=426098.

Shahri, Muhammad al-. "Bidayat Fawwaz Trabulsi." *Al-Sahah al-umaniyyah*, October 7, 2012. https://tinyurl.com/ycsnvntn.

Shahri, Susan Al. "Female Genital Mutilation (FGM) in Dhofar: The Woman with the Frankincense Burner." *Susan Al Shahri Blog*, June 7, 2011. http://susanalshahri.blogspot.com/2011/06/woman-with-frankincense-burner.html.

———. "The Issue of FGM in Oman." *Susan Al Shahri Blog*, January 1, 2013. http://susanalshahri.blogspot.com/search/label/female%20genital%20mutilation.

———. "Protests in Salalah - Friday Gathering Draws Thousands in Salalah." *Susan Al*

Shahri Blog, March 5, 2011. http://susanalshahri.blogspot.com/2011/03/protests-in-salalah-friday-gathering.html.

Shayne, Julie D. *The Revolution Question: Feminisms in El Salvador, Chile, and Cuba*. New Brunswick: Rutgers University Press, 2004.

Shehabi, Ala'a. "Uncovering Protection Rackets through Leaktivism." *Middle East Research and Information Project* 291, no. 49 (2019): 40–45.

Shelley, Toby. *Endgame in the Western Sahara: What Future for Africa's Last Colony?* London: Zed Books, 2004.

Shryock, Andrew. *Nationalism and the Genealogical Imagination. Oral History and Textual Authority in Tribal Jordan*. Berkeley: University of California Press, 1997.

Sichel, Peter. "Sultanate of Oman Demographic Survey: Dhofar 1977, Musandam 1983." MEC Archive, St Antony's College, Oxford, GB165-0426 Peter Sichel Collection 1/1, 1977.

Silber, Irina Carlota. *Everyday Revolutionaries: Gender, Violence, and Disillusionment in Postwar El Salvador*. New Brunswick: Rutgers University Press, 2010.

Singh, Kaushalendra. "Award Set Up to Boost Arabic Writers." *Oman Daily Observer*, May 3, 2016. https://www.pressreader.com/oman/oman-daily-observer/20160503/281573764896055.

Skocpol, Theda. *States and Social Revolutions: A Comparative Analysis of France, Russia and China*. Cambridge: Cambridge University Press, 1979.

Spivak, Gayatri. "Can the Subaltern Speak?". In *Marxism and the Interpretation of Culture*, edited by Cary Nelson and Lawrence Grossberg, 271–313. Urbana: University of Illinois Press, 1988.

Sprenkels, Ralph. *After Insurgency: Revolution and Electoral Politics in El Salvador*. Notre Dame: University of Notre Dame Press, 2018.

Srour, Heiny, dir. *Sa'at al-thawrah daqqat*. Film, 1974. 1 hr., 2 min.

———. "Visit to Dhofar." *The Gulf Bulletin* 2, (October–November 1971): 7.

Starn, Orin. "Missing the Revolution: Anthropologists and the War in Peru." *Cultural Anthropology* 6, no. 1 (February 1991): 63–91.

Stefansson, Anders. "Coffee after Cleansing? Co-existence, Co-operation, and Communication in Post-conflict Bosnia and Herzegovina." *Focaal* 2010, no. 57 (June 2010): 62–76.

Stoll, David. *Between Two Armies in the Ixil Towns of Guatemala*. New York: Columbia University Press, 1994.

Strathern, Marilyn. "Cutting the Network." *The Journal of the Royal Anthropological Institute* 2, no. 3 (September 1996): 517–35.

———. *Reproducing the Future: Essays on Anthropology, Kinship and the New Reproductive Technologies*. Manchester: Manchester University Press, 1992.

Subhi, Ahlam Khalfan Al. "Women's Representation in Majlis al Shura in Oman: How do Gender Ideology, Islam, and Tribalism Matter?" MA diss., Iowa State University, 2016. https://lib.dr.iastate.edu/etd/15134.

Suleiman, Khalifa. "Fawwaz Trabulsi li Majallat al-falaq." *Al-Falaq*, October 29, 2015. https://www.alfalq.com/?p=7588.

Sultanate of Oman. *Statistical Year Book 2012*. Muscat: National Centre for Statistics and Information, 2013. http://www.ncsi.gov.om.
Szalai, Julia. "Some Aspects of the Changing Situation of Women in Hungary." *Signs* 17, no. 1 (Autumn 1991): 152–70.
Tabook, Salim Bakhit Salim. "Tribal Practices and Folklore of Dhofar, Sultanate of Oman." PhD diss., University of Exeter, 1997.
Ta'i, 'Abdullah ibn Muhammad. *Mala'ikat al-jabal al-akhdar: Qissat al-thawrah al-Umaniyyah fi marhalatiha al-ula*. Kuwait: Sharikat al-rubay'an lil nashr wa al-tawzi', 2009.
Takriti, Abdel Razzaq. "Colonial Coups and the War on Popular Sovereignty." *The American Historical Review* 124, no. 3 (June 2019): 878–909.
———. *Dhufar: thawrat al-riyah al-mawsimiyyah*. Beirut: Jadawel, 2019.
———. *Monsoon Revolution. Republicans, Sultans and Empires in Oman, 1965–1976*. Oxford: Oxford University Press, 2013.
Theidon, Kimberly. "Gender in Transition: Common Sense, Women, and War." *Journal of Human Rights* 6, no. 4 (2007): 453–78.
Thiranagama, Sharika. *In My Mother's House: Civil War in Sri Lanka*. Philadelphia: University of Pennsylvania Press, 2011.
Thomas, Bertram. *Arabia Felix: Across the Empty Quarter of Arabia*. London: Jonathan Cape, 1932.
Thomassen, Bjorn. "Notes Towards an Anthropology of Political Revolutions." *Comparative Studies in Society and History* 54, no. 3 (July 2012): 679–706.
Thompson, E. P. *The Making of the English Working Class*. London: Victor Gollancz, 1963.
Thompson, Robert. *Defeating Communist Insurgency: Experiences from Malaya and Vietnam*. London: Chatto & Windus, 1966.
Thwaites, Peter, and Simon Sloane. *Muscat Command*. London: Leo Cooper, 1995.
Tilly, Charles. *From Mobilization to Revolution*. New York: Random House, 1978.
Toumi, Habib. "GCC Marshall-Style Aid Package for Bahrain, Oman." *Gulf News*, March 2, 2011. https://gulfnews.com/world/gulf/bahrain/gcc-marshall-style-aid-package-for-bahrain-oman-1.770473.
Townsend, J. *Oman: The Making of a Modern State*. London: Croom Helm, 1977.
Trabulsi, Fawwaz. *Dhufar: Shahadah min zaman al-thawrah*. Beirut: Riad el-Rayyes, 2004.
———. "The Liberation of Dhufar." *MERIP Reports*, no. 6 (January 1972): 3–11.
———. *Surat al-fata bil ahmar, ayam fil silm wa al-harb*. Beirut: Riad el-Rayyes, 1997.
Traverso, Enzo. *Left-wing Melancholia: Marxism, History, and Memory*. New York: Columbia University Press, 2017.
Turner, Victor. *The Anthropology of Performance*. New York: PAJ Publications, 1988.
Uehling, Greta Lynn. *Beyond Memory: The Crimean Tatars' Deportation and Return*. New York: Palgrave Macmillan, 2004.
United Nations Ad Hoc Committee on Oman. "Report of the Ad Hoc Committee on Oman." United Nations General Assembly Official Records, Nineteenth Session, Annex 16, A/5846, January 22, 1965.
United Nations Secretary-General. "Report of the Special Representative of the

Secretary-General on his Visit to Oman." General Assembly of the United Nations, Eighteenth Session, Annexes, A/5562, October 8, 1963.

US Embassy Muscat. "Contractor's Guarantee: Road Building Project." September 11, 1979. *Wikileaks Cable: 1979MUSCAT01602_e*. https://search.wikileaks.org/plusd/cables/1979MUSCAT01602_e.html.

———. "Saudi and Kuwaiti Aid for Oman." January 22, 1977. *Wikileaks Cable: 1977MUSCAT00117_c*. https://search.wikileaks.org/plusd/cables/1977MUSCAT00117_c.html.

———. "(U) FMS Sales Data Requestion - Oman." August 22, 1979. *Wikileaks Cable: 1979MUSCAT01490_e*. https://search.wikileaks.org/plusd/cables/1979MUSCAT01490_e.html.

Vacchiano, Francesco and Hafsa Afailal. "'Nothing Will Ever Be the Same Again': Personal Commitment and Political Subjectivation in the 20 February Movement in Morocco." *The Journal of North African Studies* 26, no. 2 (2021): 231–50.

Valéri, Marc. *Oman: Politics and Society in the Qaboos State*. 2nd ed. London: Hurst, 2017.

———. "The Qaboos-State under the Test of the 'Omani Spring': Are the Regime's Answers up to Expectations?". *Dossier du CERI* (September 2011). https://www.sciencespo.fr/ceri/sites/sciencespo.fr.ceri/files/art_mv.pdf.

Vaziri, Parisa. "On 'Saidiya': Indian Ocean World Slavery and Blackness beyond Horizon." *Qui parle* 28, no. 2 (December 2019): 241–80.

Verdery, Katherine. *The Vanishing Hectare: Property and Value in Postsocialist Transylvania*. Ithaca: Cornell University Press, 2003.

———. *What Was Socialism, and What Comes Next?* Princeton: Princeton University Press, 1996.

Vince, Natalya. *Our Fighting Sisters: Nation, Memory and Gender in Algeria, 1954–2012*. Manchester: Manchester University Press, 2015.

Vinitzky-Seroussi, Vered. "Commemorating a Difficult Past: Yitzhak Rabin's Memorials." *American Sociological Review* 67, no. 1 (February 2002): 30–51.

Wagner-Pacifici, Robin, and Barry Schwartz. "The Vietnam Veterans Memorial: Commemorating a Difficult Past." *American Journal of Sociology* 97, no. 2 (September 1991): 376–420.

Wanner, Catherine. *Burden of Dreams: History and Identity in Post-Soviet Ukraine*. Pennsylvania: Penn State University Press, 1998.

Watson, Rubie S. "Making Secret Histories: Memory and Mourning in Post-Mao China." In *Memory, History, and Opposition under State Socialism*, edited by Rubie S. Watson, 65–86. Santa Fe: School for Advanced Research Press, 1994.

———. "Memory, History, and Opposition under State Socialism: An Introduction." In *Memory, History, and Opposition under State Socialism*, edited by Rubie S. Watson, 1–20. Santa Fe: School for Advanced Research Press, 1994.

Wedeen, Lisa. *Ambiguities of Domination: Politics, Rhetoric, and Symbols in Contemporary Syria*. Chicago: University of Chicago Press, 1999.

Weir, Shelagh. *Qat in Yemen: Consumption and Social Change.* London: British Museum Publications, 1985.
West, Harry G. "From Socialist Chiefs to Postsocialist Cadres: Neotraditional Authority in Neoliberal Mozambique." In *Enduring Socialism: Explorations of Revolution and Transformation, Restoration and Continuation*, edited by Harry G. West and Parvathi Raman, 29–43. Oxford: Berghahn Books, 2009.
———. "Girls with Guns: Narrating the Experience of War of FRELIMO's 'Female Detachment.'" *Anthropological Quarterly* 73, no. 4 (October 2000): 180–94.
Weston, Kath. *Families We Choose: Lesbians, Gays, Kinship.* New York: Columbia University Press, 1991.
Wiegink, Nikkie. *Former Guerrillas in Mozambique.* Pennsylvania: University of Pennsylvania Press, 2020.
Wikan, Unni. *Behind the Veil in Arabia: Women in Oman.* Baltimore: Johns Hopkins University Press, 1982.
Wilkinson, John. *Ibâḍism: Origins and Early Development in Oman.* Oxford: Oxford University Press, 2010.
———. *The Imamate Tradition of Oman.* Cambridge: Cambridge University Press, 1987.
Wilson, Alice. "Gifts that Recalibrate Relationships: Marriage Prestations in an Arab Liberation Movement." *Ethnos* 83, no. 2 (2018): 296–315.
———. "Invisible Veterans: Defeated Militants and Enduring Revolutionary Social Values in Dhufar, Oman." *Conflict and Society: Advances in Research* 5, no. 1 (June 2019): 132–49.
———. "Kinship and a Counter-hegemonic Social Order: Former Revolutionaries in Southern Oman." *Journal of the Royal Anthropological Institute* 26, no. 2 (March 2020): 302–20.
———. "Oman's Consultative Council Elections: Shaking up Tribal Hierarchies in Dhufar." *Middle East Report* 281 (Winter 2016): 41–43.
———. "Revolution." In *The Cambridge Encyclopedia of Anthropology* (website), edited by Felix Stein. October 16, 2019. http://doi.org/10.29164/19rev.
———. *Sovereignty in Exile: A Saharan Liberation Movement Governs.* Philadelphia: University of Pennsylvania Press, 2016.
Winegar, Jessica. "A Civilized Revolution: Aesthetics and Political Action in Egypt." *American Ethnologist* 43, no. 4 (November 2016): 609–22.
———. "The Privilege of Revolution: Gender, Class, Space, and Affect in Egypt." *American Ethnologist* 39, no. 1 (February 2012): 67–70.
Wippel, Steffen. "Salalah Globalized: Developing, Fragmenting, and Marketing a 'Secondary City' at Spatio-Temporal Interfaces." In *Gulf Cities as Interfaces*, edited by George Katodrytis and Sharmeen Syed, 69–105. Cambridge: Gulf Research Centre Cambridge, 2016.
———. "Salalah 'Paradise': The Emergence of a New Tourism Destination in Southern Oman." Odense: Syddansk Universitet. Center for Mellemøststudier, 2015.
Wolf, Eric. *Peasant Wars of the Twentieth Century.* New York: Harper & Row, 1969.

Wolin, Richard. *The Wind from the East: French Intellectuals, the Cultural Revolution, and the Legacy of the 1960s*. Princeton: Princeton University Press, 2010.
Wood, Elizabeth A. *The Baba and the Comrade: Gender and Politics in Revolutionary Russia*. Bloomington: Indiana University Press, 1997.
Worrall, James. "Oman: The 'Forgotten' Corner of the Arab Spring." *Middle East Policy* 19, no. 3 (Fall 2012): 98–115.
———. *Statebuilding and Counterinsurgency in Oman: Political, Military and Diplomatic Relations at the End of Empire*. 2nd ed. London: I. B. Tauris, 2018.
Wright, Michelle. *Physics of Blackness: Beyond the Middle Passage Epistemology*. Minneapolis: University of Minnesota Press, 2015.
Yan, Yunxiang. *Private Life under Socialism: Love, Intimacy, and Family Change in a Chinese Village, 1949–1999*. Stanford: Stanford University Press, 2003.
Yanagisako, Sylvia. "Family and Household: The Analysis of Domestic Groups." *Annual Review of Anthropology* 8 (1979): 161–205.
Zarins, Juris. "Aspects of Recent Archaeological Work at al-Balīd (Ẓafār), Sultanate of Oman." *Proceedings of the Seminar for Arabian Studies* 37 (2007): 309–24.
Zubaidi, Ahmad al-. *Ahwal al-qaba'il: 'Ashirat al-inqilab al-inglizi fi Salalah*. Beirut: Dar al-Farabi, 2008.
———. *Imra'ah min Dhufar*. Beirut: Dar al-Farabi, 2013.
———. *Nabsh al-dhakirah: al kitab al-awl: Uman bain 'alamain*. Beirut: Dar Su'al, 2014.
———. *Sanawat al-nar*. Beirut: Dar al-Farabi, 2012.

Index

Letters following a page number indicate the following references - n (note), f (figure), t (table).
Example: 153n7 means [page number] 153, [a note] n, [note number] 7

ʿAbd al-ʿAziz al-Qadi: funeral attendance, 227, 228; return celebrations, 230, 231; return to Oman, 13, 19, 27, 123, 130
ʿAbd al-ʿAziz al-Rawwas, 185, 242
ʿAbd al-Samad, Ahmad, 83, 86
abduction, 32, 93. *See also* parental consent
ʿAbdullah Habib. *See* Habib, ʿAbdullah
absences, chain of, 201, 202, 214–20, 232
Abu Kamil. *See* Qatan, Musallam Said (Abu Kamil)
activism: with the Front, 143, 151, 174; postwar, 92, 93, 206, 219, 220
activist(s), 11, 49, 51, 65, 189–90; Front, 32, 53, 82, 90, 112, 116; imprisonment, 13; memory work, 10, 219; Omani Women's Organization (OWO), 86, 87, 153; political, 10, 31, 166; revolutionary, 49, 68, 237; scholars, 4, 75, 219. *See also* Habib, ʿAbdullah; Halliday, Fred; Salim, Huda ("Mama Huda")
Aden, 51, 55, 88, 106, 150, 209

adolescent recruits, 62–63, 67, 97, 150
Afraz, Mahboubeh, 84, 88, 89, 119, 153, 211
afterlives (term), 3–4, 7, 10–11
afterlives of revolution (concept), 4, 7, 10, 11–13, 19, 64
agency: revolutionary, 35, 56, 97, 213, 232, 237; spatial transformation, 99, 100, 103, 134, 135, 237
agendas, revolutionary, 29, 66, 67–68, 88, 93, 188
agricultural: committees, 75–76; destruction, 118; economies, 51; labor, 72, 76–77; land, 46, 72
agriculture, rain-fed, 40–41, 42
air base (RAF Salalah). *See* RAF Salalah (air base)
air strikes, 33, 61, 82, 93, 95, 118–19
Akhdar, al-Jabal al- (mountains), 43, 47, 104, 215
ʿAlawi, Sayyid Fadhl bin. *See* Sayyid Fadhl bin ʿAlawi
ʿAlawi, Yusuf bin. *See* Yusuf bin ʿAlawi

Al-Bagh. See *Bagh, Al-* (Khalfan)
al-Busaid sultans. *See* Busaid sultans, al-
Algeria, 67, 139, 143, 182
al-Maʿshani tribe. *See* Maʿshani tribe, al- (Qara)
al-nahdah. *See* "renaissance" (*al-nahdah*)
al-Qadi. *See* ʿAbd al-ʿAziz al-Qadi
al-Rawwas. *See* ʿAbd al-ʿAziz al-Rawwas
al-Sarimi, Zahran. *See* Sarimi, Zahran al-
ambiguity: and afterlives of revolution, 19, 198; humor, 224–25, 226; poetry, 28, 209; red lines, 21, 27, 28; return celebrations, 228–29; social camouflage, 198, 239; surveillance, 247n77
ambiguous commemorations, 202, 232–34
ʿAmri, Muhammad al- (researcher), 20, 216
ʿAmri, Musallam bin Muhammad al- (governor for Sadah), 98–99, 111, 112, 113
ancestry, 24, 25, 144–45, 155–56, 159, 267n29
anti-colonial liberation, 37, 38, 53, 210, 239
ʿAqil Salim, Salim, 77, 81, 86, 93, 94
Arabian Peninsula, 145, 148
Arab nationalism, 37, 48, 51. *See also* Movement of Arab Nationalism (MAN)
Arabophone populations, 38, 40, 41–42, 72, 157, 243
archives, 28, 33, 56, 58, 65, 212
areas, government-controlled. *See* government-controlled areas
Arkless, David, 112, 115, 118
arrest(s), 27, 75, 85, 122; in 1994, 132, 225; in 2011, 241
authoritarianism, 5, 19, 20, 35, 69, 135
authoritarian rule, 15, 61, 99, 135, 138
authorities, governing: and governed constituencies, 14; "hearts and minds" campaign, 17; hostility, 201; inequality, 72; kinship practices, 142; of "liberated territories," 66; national narratives, 203; red lines, 21; resistance of concern, 10, 19

ʿAwqad, 43t, 125, 133
Azri, Khalid Al-, 21, 29

Bagh, Al- (Khalfan), 219, 224
bahharah families, 40, 71, 144, 241
Bahrain, 10, 14, 53, 73, 135, 227
Baleed, al-, 39, 40, 214
Baluchi, 46, 54, 105, 106, 267n29
Battle of Mirbat. *See* Mirbat, Battle of
"big opportunities," 111–12, 120
Black Hand, The (*al-kaff al-aswad*), 50, 53, 90
blackness, 25, 145, 155, 180
blockade(s): civilian casualties, 30, 60; effects, 76; "hearts and minds" campaign, 16; intensification, 33, 112; landmines, 137; livelihoods, 132; spatial transformation, 117, 120; starvation, 51, 56, 106
bombing, 33, 61, 82, 93, 118–19. *See also* air strikes
books, prohibited, 20, 170, 216–17, 222, 274n101
boomtown (Salalah), 113, 121–22
Britain's Royal Air Force (RAF). *See* RAF (Royal Air Force), Britain's
British Army Training Team (BATT), 112–13
British counterinsurgency: acknowledgment, 213; backers, 6; censorship, 56, 58; experts, 14; plan, 104; report, 218; soldiers, 26, 152
British involvement, 55–56, 112
British military intervention, 45, 47, 56, 274n98
budget for counterinsurgency, 15, 57, 108; budget deficit, 55, 121
Busaid dynasty, al-, 2, 37, 43, 48, 215, 216
Busaid sultans, al-, 2, 45, 46, 166

camels, 41, 94, 108, 118, 134
candidates, women, 190–91, 193–94, 271n53
Canning Award, 44. *See also* subsidies
capture, 32, 33, 59, 115, 116, 127
Carden, Derrick, 52, 55

casualties, civilian, 30, 58, 60–61
casualties, military, 59t, 60
cattle: destruction, 16, 118; ownership, 89; stealing, 115; tending, 75, 77, 264n145; water resources, 107
caves, 33, 41, 50, 119, 146, 211
celebrations, return, 7, 130, 228–29, 231
censorship: authoritarian, 3, 27, 232; British counterinsurgency, 56, 58; Front, 85; Omani government. *See* Omani government (censorship); self-censorship, 21, 27–28, 220, 232
census data, 38, 42, 43t. *See also* population estimates
China, 51–52, 53, 205, 206, 232
circumlocution, 23, 206–7, 220, 221, 224–25, 226
civil action teams (CATs), 109
civilian casualties, 30, 58, 60–61
classified documents, 28, 56
client(s): electoral success, 241; exploitation, 71; fishing families, 40, 41, 144, 183, 242, 270n45; herders, 41, 77, 271n55; inequality, 100; marriages, 149; participation in celebrations, 146, 267n33
"close marriage," 145, 152, 154, 162, 166, 167
coastal plain, 112, 113
coastal plain (*jarbib*), 40, 42
coercion, role of, 15, 16, 99, 120, 125, 217
collective identities: cultivating, 73, 85, 202, 210; fostering, 202–3, 204, 207, 227; multiple, 210; reproduction of, 146
colonialist narratives, 6, 232. *See also* anti-colonial liberation
Commander of the Sultan's Armed Forces (CSAF), 95, 99
commemoration, acts of (definition), 202
commemoration, fragmented, 203, 234
commemoration culture, 201, 212–13
"common good, the" (*al-maslahah al-'ammah*), 126–27, 134, 200
concern, resistance of. *See* resistance of concern

conformity: "close marriage," 162; conservatism, 189; contact with unrelated men, 1; female fighters, 128; with official silence, 190; revolutionary participation, 88; social pressure, 87, 234
Congress, DLF (1965), 50
Congress, PFLOAG (1968): emancipation, 53, 74, 78, 90, 92; Maoist influence, 52, 53; Marxist-inspired agendas, 75; persuasion to change sides, 112; religiosity, 95; Revolution Camp, 81; treason, 76
Congress, PFLOAG (1971), 75, 86, 96
consciousness, feminist, 129, 196, 198–99
consent: interlocutor, 20, 29, 190; mutual, 15; parental, 32, 84, 93–94
conservatism, 104, 189, 195, 198, 237
constraints, political, 66, 198
constraints, research, 5, 23, 28
Consultative Council (Oman), 22, 240, 241, 271n53
containment: food supplies, 106, 221; normality, 114; spatial transformation, 120; strategies, 56; surrender, 127; and winning the war, 107. *See also* blockade(s)
contested meanings: breaking official silence, 217; collective identities, 210; myth, 236; political control, 100; reproduction of hierarchies, 174; social convention, 17; social order, 138, 140, 166
counterhegemonic social order, 139, 144, 154–55, 160, 163, 167–68; marriage, 157, 162
counterhegemonic values, 17, 18, 20, 31, 143
counterhistories: commemoration culture, 201; everyday, 3–7, 170; and hostility, 234; kinship practices, 138; messiness, 64, 97; official silence, 232; revolutionary defeat, 236; revolutionary social values, 199
counterinsurgency, model. *See* "model counterinsurgency"

counterinsurgency agendas, 35, 54–61
counterinsurgency interventions, 37, 110
creativity, 172, 173
CSAF (Commander of the Sultan's Armed Forces), 95, 99
Cuba, 53, 222
cultural resources, 202, 205–6, 207, 226, 233
culture, commemoration, 201, 212–13

Darodi, Said al-, 242
decolonization, 6, 36, 47, 202, 208, 212, 232, 234; political process, 36, 38
defeat, military. *See* military defeat
defeat, revolutionary, 168, 235, 236
deficit, counterinsurgency budget, 55, 121
democracy, 10, 14, 15, 51, 203
demonstrations, 61, 65, 235, 239, 241
desert, 38, 41–42, 73, 108, 133, 174
destruction (of): agricultural resources, 13, 60, 107, 118; counterinsurgency violence, 30; essential resources, 60, 106, 117, 119; evidence, 221; housing. *See* housing, destruction of; livelihoods, 60, 211; people, 119; plans, 95; Rakhyut, 118
development, economic, 57, 100, 103–4, 112, 126, 134–35. *See also* investment
Dhufar (description), 38–44
Dhufar Charitable Association (DCA), 49–50, 240
Dhufar Force (DF), 72, 106
Dhufari nationalism, 50, 242–43
Dhufar Liberation Front (DLF): founded, 50; activist, 112; emancipation, 90; nationalism, 242; radio broadcasts, 95; support, 51, 98
Dhufar Soldiers' Organization (DSO), 49–50
Dhufar University, 24, 157
disappointment: defeat, 9, 89, 235; domestic tasks, 198; female fighters, 237; new generations, 4; official commemoration, 206; in the revolution, 153

disciplinary measures, 19, 84, 96, 120, 125, 219
discrimination, 24–25, 26, 68, 74, 116, 180
discussion groups, political, 78–79, 86, 87f, 88
displacement, 79, 122
DLF (Dhufar Liberation Front). *See* Dhufar Liberation Front (DLF)
domestic roles, 153, 178, 198
driving, car (women), 187, 195

East Africa, 24, 126
economic development, 57, 100, 103–4, 112, 126, 134–35. *See also* investment
economic future, 112, 130, 131, 243, 244
education, access to formal, 74, 81, 195
egalitarianism, values of, 2, 7, 16, 27, 31, 242
electoral candidacy, 21, 27, 190, 191, 192, 271n55
electoral leagues, 158, 193, 194, 240–41
electoral success, 190, 241
emancipation (of enslaved persons), 24, 67, 77, 90
emancipation (of women), 67, 78–79, 86, 90, 91, 192
emancipation, social, 53, 62, 74, 96–97, 182
enacting: gendered egalitarianism, 186, 197; meanings of the past, 202, 204, 233, 236; social egalitarianism, 185, 199; social inclusivity, 242; values, 170, 196, 239
engagement, active (programs), 34, 93
enslaved heritage, 24, 25, 40, 50, 70, 71. *See also sumur*
enslavement, 24, 25, 53, 70, 71, 77
environmental degradation, 13, 16, 30, 118, 131, 132. *See also* grazing resources; land mines
essays, 85, 211, 223, 224, 274n88
ethical dilemmas of research, 20–29
ethnographic lens, 30, 36

events, life cycle, 137, 168
everyday (conceptual discussion), 17–20, 172–75. *See also* quotidian interactions
exile, bases for, 12, 53, 56, 72, 182, 237; People's Democratic Republic of Yemen (PDRY), 12, 79, 112, 128, 153, 169; Saudi Arabia, 47; Yemen, 2, 130, 156, 219
experience, lived, 9, 84, 186
experiential gaps, 84, 87, 88, 89, 97
exploitation, colonial, 37, 38, 46, 47, 48
expropriation, 46, 131
ex-revolutionaries, contributions of, 127, 134, 200
extraordinary acts, 19, 186–96, 197, 236; feminist consciousness, 35, 196, 198

face coverings, 132, 147, 175, 270n45
Fakhro, Laila. *See* Salim, Huda ("Mama Huda")
family histories, 61, 223, 237
family units, 138, 146, 155, 159
female fighters, 81; captured, 115; future of, 116; gender emancipation, 79, 91; images, 79, 80f, 237; numbers, 257n95
Female Labor Force Participation (FLP), 188t
feminist consciousness, 129, 196, 198–99
feud. *See* revenge killings
fieldwork. *See* research methods
firaq (Dhufari pro-government paramilitaries): families, 121, 124, 132; history, 216, 223; inequalities, 120; leaders, 57, 122; naming practices, 213; numbers, 59t, 108; orientalism, 218; recruitment, 110, 112–13, 114–15, 116, 117, 152; salaries, 16
fire bombing. *See* bombing
food supplies, 51, 106, 221
forums, 61, 76, 185, 196, 199
frameworks, 63, 64, 97, 237
frankincense, 39, 41, 113, 214, 249n6
free status, 25, 77, 132, 149, 155, 157
Front, the (*al-jabhah*), overview, 2, 23

funeral attendance, 226–28, 234. *See also* mourning
future, economic, 112, 130, 131, 243, 244

galsah gatherings, 176–84, 177f, 185, 196
"Gardens Mall," 156, 157, 158, 159, 175
Gardiner, Ian, 132, 212, 213
gatherings, evening, 165, 169, 170, 198, 216, 224. *See also galsah* gatherings
gendered subjectivities, 65, 115, 197
gender emancipation, 79, 86, 91–92, 237
gender segregation, 146, 177–78
General Command (the Front), 52, 77, 150
generation, first (changing sides), 111–21; released prisoners, 111–12
generation, second (changing sides), 121–27
generation, third and fourth (changing sides), 127–30
generations, new, 4, 155, 160, 162, 167, 243
geographical zones, 39; coastal plain (*jarbib*), 40, 42; desert, 38, 41–42, 73, 108, 133; *jabal* (mountains), description, 16, 40–41. *See also* Akhdar, al-Jabal al- (mountains); Qara, Jabal al- (mountains)
gestures: ambiguity, 225–26; commentary, 216; cumulative, 172; egalitarianism, 67; groups of men, 176–77, 178; repetitions, 172; silence, 193; suggestive avoidance, 238
Ghaidah, al-, 79, 81, 82, 88, 119, 208
Ghassani, al- (tribe), 124–25, 265n170
Ghassani, Salim al-, 150, 265n170
gifts, cash (*maghbur*), 148, 166, 271n47
goal(s), revolutionary: achievement, 185, 236; ambitious, 239; failure, 9–10, 11, 12, 170, 238; matched, 31; parallel, 185; prioritization, 150; undermining of, 67; understanding of, 50, 62, 66; unfulfilled, 144
goats, 41, 107
"good governance" approach, 57, 110

governance: British advisors, 250n37; Gulf monarchies, 13–15; inequalities, 111, 120; investment, 66; revolutionary, 237, 243; strategies, 16
governing authorities. *See* authorities, governing
government-controlled areas: coastal plain, 112, 113; destruction of housing, 99; health care, 15; "hearts and minds" campaign, 30; new settlements, 113, 122; patronage networks, 152; Salalah, 105; spatial transformation, 117
government sanction, 24, 125, 229, 234, 241
graduate(s): access to formal education, 81, 195; "the common good," 126, 128; disappointment, 198; friendships, 82, 150; gender segregation, 179; kinship practices, 149; labor force participation, 188–89, 237
Graham, John, 99, 101, 113
graves: missing, 217; mourning at, 13, 61, 201; poems, 209; unmarked, 161, 225
grazing resources, 13, 41, 117–18, 132
groups, political discussion, 78–79, 86, 87f, 88
groups of men, 169, 176–77, 178. *See also galsah* gatherings
guerrilla fighters, 34, 54, 165
Gulf Cooperation Council (GCC), 129, 135
Gulf monarchies: authoritarian rule, 99; governance, 13–15; marriage, 148; political loyalty, 16; revenues, 121, 130; spatial transformation, 35, 100–105, 135

Habib, 'Abdullah: arrest, 27, 225; breaking official silence, 61; imprisonment, 13, 21, 161, 201, 248n96; online activities, 28
Hadhramawt region (Yemen), 38, 42, 43–44, 214
Hafah, al-, 40, 71, 106, 125, 131, 221
Halliday, Fred: adolescent recruits, 62–63, 150; arrests, 75; contradiction, 84–85; PFLOAG camp, 91f; religiosity, 96; revolutionary participation, 88–89; women's emancipation, 79
Hamrin Congress (1968). *See* Congress, PFLOAG (1968)
Harvey, Mike, 107, 117
Hawf: air strikes, 82, 118, 119; clinic, 208, 210; marriage, 128; revolutionary institutions, 79, 81
Hawley, Donald, 98–99, 118–19
health care: access, 15, 45, 81, 131, 215; clinics, 112–13, 150, 208, 210, 219; in the Front, 57; hospitals, 84, 150, 156–59, 163, 190, 208; naming practices, 209; revolutionary social change, 66, 92, 93, 126
"hearts and minds" campaign: colonialist narratives, 6; Marxist-inspired programs, 34; "model counterinsurgency," 57, 110; myths, 217; patronage, limits of, 13, 15, 16, 17; revolutionary defeat, 235, 236; winning, 30–31
Hepworth, C. (Captain), 107, 212
herders, 31, 41, 76–77, 107, 133
hierarchies, postrevolutionary, 151–53
hierarchies, reproduction of, 75, 138–39, 160, 166, 174–75, 185; kinship, 144–49; postrevolutionary, 152–53
Higgins, Andrew, 115–16, 120, 121–22, 211
hinterland, 38, 42, 43, 44, 48, 221
Ho Chi Minh, 208, 209, 210
Hormuz, Strait of, 31, 55
hospitals, 84, 150, 156–59, 190, 208
hostility: governing authorities, 201; political circumstances, 69, 97, 200, 233; political ghosts, 218; toward communism, 34, 150; toward the Front, 93; unaccompanied women, 187
housing, destruction of: during counterinsurgency, 60, 85, 99, 107; during resistance to postwar Omani authorities, 16, 125–26
housing, public (*sha'biyat*), 124, 125

Huda Salim ("Mama Huda"). *See* Salim, Huda ("Mama Huda")
"Huda's children," 149, 153
Humeau, Jean-Michel, 5f, 80f, 82, 83f
humor, 202, 206, 210, 224–25, 226, 233

Ibadhis, 43, 44, 101, 102, 260n9, 270n32
Ibadhism, 43, 260n9, 266n193, 270n32
Ibn Khaldun, 140–41, 266n8
Ibrahim, Sonallah, *Warda*, 212, 218
imagination, 69, 118, 137, 220, 239, 244
imprisonment: of journalists, 21, 161, 201, 217, 225; life, 127; official silence, 13, 61; pardons, 240
inclusivity, social: anti-colonial liberation, 239; evening gatherings, 198; formal organizations, 242; funerals, 227, 228; *galsah* gatherings, 184; initiatives, 91; positionality, 26; revolutionary values, 240; values of, 27, 186
independence: from Britain, 47, 49, 51, 55; Dhufari, 50, 130; of women, 86, 171, 196. *See also* anti-colonial liberation
indoctrination, 32, 77, 150, 268n44
inequality, social, 35, 70–74, 76, 78, 96, 169; challenging, 100, 196; cultivation, 111, 120, 135–36; gendered, 187; labor force, 188; material, 274n92; naturalizing, 141; new variations, 67, 127; reproduction, 78
influences, long-term, 4, 10, 12, 239–44
intelligence service (*mukhabarat*), 127, 128
intentionality, 163–66
interlocutor consent, 20, 29, 190
internationalized counterinsurgency, 36, 37, 38, 54
internet sites, 28, 223–24
internet use. *See* online activities
interracial marriage, 26, 155–57, 182
intersectionality, 9, 196, 198. *See also* kinship, intersections of
intimacy, 67, 132, 158, 168, 200

investment: in civilian governance, 66; in commemoration, 203, 213; in counterinsurgency, 221; in economic development, 112; against future insurgency, 47; in infrastructure, 46; in services, 46; in social development, 112; in social values, 199
Iranian casualties, 58, 59
Iranian counterinsurgency personnel, 56, 108, 125, 218
Iranian volunteers, 53, 84, 88, 119, 153, 211
Islam: and counterinsurgency, 95, 126, 213; and the Front, 32, 94, 95–96. *See also* Ibadhism
Islamic practices, 71, 126, 146
Islamic Republic of Iran, 65, 218

jabal (mountains), description, 16, 40–41. *See also* Akhdar, al-Jabal al- (mountains); Qara, Jabal al- (mountains)
jabbali people: blockades, 106, 132; displacement, 121; food supplies, 221; Islam, 95, 126; overview, 41–42; public housing, 124; status groups, 146; students, 116; transhumant pastoralism, 72
jabhah, al- ("the Front"), overview, 2, 23
Jabob, Mona, 82, 93, 189
Jalali prison, 111
Jeapes, Tony, 114, 117, 120, 122, 124, 222
Jordanians, 108, 125

Kathiri tribes, 108, 114, 125, 145, 216
Khalfan, Bushra, 243; *Al-Bagh*, 219, 224
kidnapping, 32, 93. *See also* parental consent
killed, numbers, 59t, 60, 116
killing(s): those who pray, 96; revenge, 32–33, 76, 125, 151; Salalah–Thumrait road, 50
kinship, intersections of, 142, 153, 166, 167, 168
kinship, rethinking (postwar), 139–44

kinship, revolutionary, 138, 149–51, 164
kinship practices: counterhegemonic social order, 139, 144, 154, 160, 163, 166–68; long-standing, 141–42; "normal" life, 137–38, 144, 166; revolutionary, 149; subjectivities, 151
kinship relations, postwar, 18, 141, 167
kinship reproducing hierarchy, 144–49, 166
Kuwait: activists, 53; financial resources, 54, 124, 179; independence, 49; modernization, 102; university, 150. *See also* Dhufar Charitable Association (DCA)

labor, waged, 128, 188, 189
labor force participation, 128–29, 188, 189, 197, 224, 237
land mines, 30, 137, 248n103
Landon, Tim, 108–9, 110, 131
legitimacy, political, 7–8, 102, 203, 204, 211, 213
Leninist-Marxist turn. *See* Marxist-Leninist turn
liberation, anti-colonial, 37, 38, 53, 210, 239
Libya, 53, 82, 229, 234
lieux de mémoire, 203, 205, 214, 216, 217, 221
liminality, 9, 65–66, 238–39
lived experience, 9, 30, 84, 174, 186
livelihood: destruction, 60, 99, 211; disruption, 39, 100, 113, 132
livestock: destruction, 16, 60, 107, 117–18; movement, 94, 133, 134; ownership, 89; prices, 31; stealing, 114–15; subsidies, 15; tending, 41, 72, 77, 106, 258n145, 264n145. *See also* camels; cattle

maghbur (cash gifts), 148, 166, 271n47
Mahra: families, 125, 148; governorate, 79, 83f; tribes, 41, 70, 108, 144, 149
majlis al-shura (National Council), 191, 192, 193
mall, the, 158, 159, 175, 176, 269n24

MAN (Movement of Arab Nationalism), 48, 49–50
Maoist influence, 51, 52–53, 66, 83, 84
Mao Tse Tung, 52, 81
marginalization: challenging, 67, 218, 233; current forms of, 69; of former revolutionaries., 198; minorities, 204; resistance against, 174; social segregation, 180; spatial transformation, 103; vulnerable to, 71; of women, 193. *See also bahharah* families; *sumur*
marriage gifts, 71, 91, 142, 145; *maghbur* (cash gifts), 148, 166, 271n47
marriage(s), 42, 70, 92, 151, 163, 169; "close," 145, 152, 154, 162, 166, 167; interracial, 25–26, 155–57, 182; postwar, 138, 139, 164–65; revolutionary, 78, 89, 149, 155, 157, 159–60. *See also* wedding parties
Marxism-Leninism, 83, 90, 91, 95, 149
Marxist-inspired: agendas, 49, 74, 75, 90, 237; programs, 34–35, 236; scholars, 141
Marxist-Leninist turn, 50, 52, 53, 55, 84, 242
Ma'shani tribe, al- (Qara), 48, 145
Masoud, Said, 88, 111–12
Mazoon bint 'Ali Ahmad, 48, 145
memory work, 10, 218–20, 224, 233, 243
men, contact with unrelated, 1, 3, 184
men, groups of, 169, 176–77, 178
messiness (conceptual discussion), 63–65
methods, research, 20–29
military casualties, 59t, 60
military defeat: after, 3; disappointment, 9, 89; domestic roles, 153; effects, 126, 152; formal commemoration, 210; revolutionary institutions, 81
military intervention, 13, 30, 47, 56, 104, 274n98
military spending, 108, 266n203
Ministry of Information (Oman), 11, 20, 216
minorities, 204, 238
Mirbat, 106, 133, 212, 217, 253n129, 274n92
Mirbat, Battle of, 212, 217, 253n129, 274n92

mobility: government-controlled areas, 113; seasonal movement, 39, 41–42, 133–34; transhumant pastoralism, 41, 72; women, unaccompanied, 1, 187; women driving, 187, 195

mobilization, revolutionary, 4, 8, 75, 161, 168

"model counterinsurgency," 37, 57, 60, 110

modernization: Dhufar, 29, 31, 35, 100; Gulf monarchies, 101, 102; Oman, 200, 205, 214, 233, 236

Modern South Arabian languages (MSAL): museum, 214; poetry, 28, 61, 207, 209–10, 248n99; Shahri, 40, 41, 209; song, 207, 209–10; speakers, 42, 70, 214

Mohanna, Kamel, 91–92, 208, 210–11, 219, 220

monsoon (*kharif*), 39, 40, 133–34, 146, 148, 239. *See also* post-monsoon (*sarb*); pre-monsoon

Monsoon Revolution (Takriti), 224, 243

Morris, Miranda, 126, 129, 150

mosques, 49, 95, 126, 131, 214, 266n193

mountains (*jabal*). *See jabal* (mountains), description

mourning: circumlocution, 206; cultural resources, 207; gatherings, 133, 226–27; at graves, 13, 61, 201; the past, 129, 131, 205; rituals, 226–28, 273n84

movement, seasonal, 39, 40, 41–42, 125, 133–34

Movement of Arab Nationalism (MAN), 48, 49–50

MSAL (Modern South Arabian languages). *See* Modern South Arabian languages (MSAL)

Mubarak, President (Egypt), 6, 143

mukhabarat (intelligence service), 127, 128

Musallam bin Muhammad al-'Amri. *See* 'Amri, Musallam bin Muhammad al- (governor for Sadah)

Muscat (description), 43. *See also* Busaid dynasty, al-

Muscat (Dhufar comparison), 38, 43–44, 187, 269n25

Muscat and Oman (political entity), 49, 50, 52, 55–56, 73, 105; Dhufar dependency, 38, 44. *See also* Seeb, Treaty of

mutiny (1970), 52–53, 85

myth(s): British involvement, 55; challenging, 29; commemoration culture, 213; ethnographic lens, 30, 36; "hearts and minds," 217; "model counterinsurgency," 37, 60; revolutionary agency, 56; transformation of Oman, 134

nahdah, al- ("renaissance"), 35, 101, 126, 161, 214

naming practices, 160, 161, 209, 213, 226

napalm, 33, 118

narratives, colonialist, 6, 232

narratives, conventional, 6, 35, 98, 102, 233, 235–36; challenges, 212; myths, 36

National Charter, 52, 77

National Council (*majlis al-shura*), 191, 192, 193

National Day, 214, 215, 216

National Democratic Front for the Liberation of Oman and the Arabian Gulf (NDFLOAG), 53

nationalism: Arab, 37, 48, 51; Dhufari, 50, 242–43; variations, 85, 206, 207. *See also* Movement of Arab Nationalism (MAN)

national narratives, 200, 203, 206

networks, social, 3, 138, 162

news, 1, 3, 230

newspapers, 54f, 60, 209, 216

normality: containment, 114; gender segregation, 177; intimacy, 158; for militants, 167; "normal" life, 17, 18, 137–38, 143–44, 164, 166; political violence, 197; reclaiming, 137–38, 139–40, 143–44, 153, 166; reproducing, 137–38; surveillance, 170

normalization, 18, 141, 172, 215, 237

official commemoration, 200–203, 205–7, 212–15, 225–26; commemorative culture (Front, the), 211, 213; disappointment, 206; effects, 232; historical urgency, 210; *lieux de mémoire*, 203, 205; National Day, 214; obstacles, 202; participation, 214, 215, 225; supplementation, 206–7
officially silenced revolution (term), 11
official silence, breaking, 29, 61
official silence, challenges to, 29, 161, 205–6, 232
oil exploration, 47, 55, 73
oil revenues, 35, 46, 47, 54, 103, 130
Omani government (censorship): circumventing, 11, 61, 218; effectiveness, 29; and memory work, 219–20, 224, 233, 243; officially silenced revolution (term), 11; prohibited books, 222
Omani Women's Organization (OWO), 86, 87, 153
online activities: essays, 274n88; forums, 61; imprisonment, 248n96; internet sites, 28, 223–24; memory work, 224; news, 230; self-censorship, 27
Operation Taurus, 115, 120
organizations, formal, 170, 242
orientalism, 46, 116, 120, 202, 218, 232
outcomes, problematic, 67, 68, 84, 88, 89
"out of place" kinship, 139, 154–63, 164, 167–68

paramilitaries, pro-government, 15, 31, 33, 54, 77, 85. *See also firaq* (Dhufari pro-government paramilitaries)
parental consent, 32, 84, 93–94
participation, revolutionary, 86, 88
pastoralists, 41, 51, 72, 92, 95, 140. *See also* herders; transhumant pastoralism
patronage, limits of, 13–17
patronage networks, 17, 112, 124, 152, 166, 186
People's Democratic Republic of Yemen (PDRY): air strikes, 95, 118; bases for exile, 12, 79, 112, 128, 153, 169; fall of, 152; female fighters, 116; political support, 127–28, 129–30; revolutionary bases, 79, 157, 173; revolutionary schools, 83f; supply routes, 51, 108. *See also* Ghaidah, al-; Hawf
People's Republic of South Yemen (PRSY), 55; supplies from, 51
People's School, 82, 210
persuasion: to cease resistance, 108, 135; to change sides, 110, 112, 114; internal governance affairs, 250n37; material advantages, 109; parental consent, 93; recruitment, 107; to return to Oman, 13, 127, 128, 130
Petroleum Development Oman (PDO), 47, 49–50, 114, 118, 251n59
PFLOAG (1968–1971). *See* Popular Front for the Liberation of the Occupied Arabian Gulf (PFLOAG)
PFLOAG (1971–1974). *See* Popular Front for the Liberation of Oman and the Arabian Gulf (PFLOAG)
phrases, 95, 192
PLA (Popular Liberation Army). *See* Popular Liberation Army (PLA)
plain, coastal (*jarbib*), 40, 42
poetry, 28, 61, 146, 207–8, 209–10, 224; revolutionary, 209, 220, 223
polarized representations, 65, 97, 235–36
political agendas, 97, 103, 135
political change, 65, 76, 104, 243
political circumstances, 69, 97, 128, 200, 233
political control, 73, 100, 134
political discussion groups, 78–79, 86, 87f, 88
political ghosts, 128, 200, 207
political loyalty, 14, 16, 104, 111
political opposition: formal exilic, 236, 240; suppression, 2, 13–14, 132, 138; undermining, 123
political repression, 4, 14, 168, 198, 202, 238

Popular Front for the Liberation of Oman (PFLO), 53, 54f
Popular Front for the Liberation of Oman and the Arabian Gulf (PFLOAG): air strikes, 119; Central Command, 89; fighters, 5f, 79, 80f; General Command, 77; name change, 53, 210; newspaper, 209; pay, 81; rally, 5f, 80f
Popular Front for the Liberation of the Occupied Arabian Gulf (PFLOAG), 5f, 52, 91f
Popular Liberation Army (PLA): adolescent recruits, 62; arrests, 75; fighters, 77, 79, 108, 115, 116; name, 81; naming practices, 209; punishment, 85
population estimates, 42t, 45. *See also* census data
ports, 39, 43, 44, 101, 121, 130
Portuguese presence, 44, 111, 225
positionality, 23, 26
post-monsoon (*sarb*), 40, 42, 95, 134, 148
prayer, 32, 95, 96, 126
pre-monsoon, 1, 41, 106
prisoners, released, 111–12, 241
privilege, 77, 185, 187, 191, 196, 270n45
"privilege of revolution," 171, 198
privilege of revolutionary afterlives, 171, 196, 198
problematic outcomes, 67, 68, 84, 88, 89
pro-government paramilitaries, Dhufari. *See firaq* (Dhufari pro-government paramilitaries)
programs, revolutionary, 34, 64, 67, 88
prohibited books, 20, 170, 216–17, 222, 274n101
protestors, 12, 17, 153, 235, 241, 242
public circulation (women), 187–88, 189
public housing (*sha'biyat*), 124, 125
punishment: imprisonment, 161, 242; intrafamilial, 151; religiosity, 32; resistance of concern, 167; risk, 174; and school attendance, 94; severe, 211; of traitors, 33, 85

Qaboos bin Said, Sultan (overview), 2, 35, 48, 56, 102, 213
Qaboos bin Said, Sultan (photograph), 109f
Qaboos bin Said, Sultan (speeches), 101, 214, 215, 260n8
Qadi, al-. *See* 'Abd al-'Aziz al-Qadi
Qara, Jabal al- (mountains), 39, 40, 41
Qara tribes, 41, 108–9, 145, 146, 149. *See also* Ma'shani tribe, al- (Qara)
Qatan, Musallam Said (Abu Kamil), 81–82, 119
quotidian interactions: contradictions, 173, 175; evening gatherings, 198; limitations, 170, 197, 239; new forms, 172; "normal" life, 17, 18

radio broadcasts, 50, 77, 81, 86, 95, 209
RAF (Royal Air Force), Britain's, 47–48, 57, 98, 105, 112, 250n26
RAF Salalah (air base), 40, 48, 57, 250n26, 251n64, 252n98
Rakhyut, 40, 96, 117, 118, 259n179
Rawwas, al-. *See* 'Abd al-'Aziz al-Rawwas
Raysut, 121, 130
recruits, adolescent, 62–63, 67, 97, 150
red lines, 21, 27, 28, 230, 231
reintegration, postwar social, 142, 151, 153, 154
released prisoners, 111–12, 241
religiosity, 32, 95–96, 189
"renaissance" (*al-nahdah*), 35, 101, 126, 161, 214
repression, political, 4, 14, 168, 198, 202, 238
reproduced values, 3, 136, 170, 237
research constraints, 5, 23, 28, 184
research dilemmas, 5, 19, 20–29
research methods, 20–29
research safety, 2, 19, 20, 22–23, 27, 201
resettlement, 34, 117
resistance of concern: authoritarian rule, 138–39; counterhegemonic values, 143, 144; naming practices, 161; perceived absence, 10, 18–20, 27, 167. *See also* protestors

resources for survival, 13, 60, 107, 117, 120
return to Oman, 13, 19, 122–23, 127–30, 154, 202; celebrations, 7, 130, 131, 229
revenge killings, 32–33, 76, 125, 151
revenues: access, 14, 46; oil, 35, 46, 47, 54, 103, 130; state, 108, 121
revolution, the (*al-thawrah*), overview, 7–13, 22–23, 37
revolutionary agency, 35, 56, 97, 213, 232, 237
revolutionary agendas, 29, 66, 67–68, 88, 93, 188
revolutionary defeat, 168, 235, 236
revolutionary institutions, 79, 81, 83
revolutionary kinship, 138, 149–51, 164
revolutionary programs, 34, 64, 67, 88
revolutionary school(s): air strikes, 95; graduates, 126, 149, 150, 237; indoctrination, 32, 150; parental consent, 93; pupils, 83f, 153, 182, 221; revolutionary agency, 35; revolutionary mobilization, 4. *See also* People's School; Salim, Huda ("Mama Huda")
revolutionary social change, 88, 91, 92, 93, 126, 173; conceptualization of, 63–64; legacies, 24, 90, 97, 237; unpacking, 65–70
revolutionary subjectivities, 149, 151
Revolution Camp: female fighters, 79, 81, 189, 198; internal contradictions, 84; prayer, 96; recruits, 62, 150
road, Salalah–Thumrait. *See* Salalah–Thumrait road
Royal Air Force (RAF), Britain's. *See* RAF (Royal Air Force), Britain's

sacrifice: "the common good," 134, 200; health care, 150; liminality, 9; Marxist-Leninist turn, 50; modernization, 233; punishment, 85; revolutionary failures, 68
Sadah (town), 98–100, 106, 111, 113, 120, 262n58

sadah families, 40, 70–71, 78, 149, 157, 249n16
SAF (Sultan's Armed Forces), 33, 55, 59t, 96, 105–7, 109–10
safety, research, 2, 19, 20, 22–23, 27, 201
Said bin Taimur, Sultan (overview), 35, 38, 45, 55, 107, 145
Saidiyyah school, al-, 74, 207
Salalah (description), 1, 40, 147f, 177f. *See also* boomtown (Salalah)
Salalah air base. *See* RAF Salalah (air base)
Salalah–Thumrait road, 43, 50, 56
salaries, 16, 144, 188, 192, 229
Salim, Huda ("Mama Huda"), 82, 119, 149
Salim ʿAqil Salim. *See* ʿAqil Salim, Salim
Samad, Ahmad ʿAbd al-. *See* ʿAbd al-Samad, Ahmad
sanctions, government, 24, 125, 229, 234, 241
sarb (post-monsoon), 40, 42, 95, 134, 148
Sarimi, Zahran al-, 219, 224, 236, 243
SAS (Special Air Service): British military intervention, 56; and female fighters, 115; investment, 112–13; officers, 109–10; spatial transformation, 125; tribalization, 114; welfare services, 122. *See also* British Army Training Team (BATT)
Saudi Arabia, 38, 47, 54, 55, 124
Saut al-Thawra (newspaper), 54f, 60, 209
Sayyid Fadhl bin ʿAlawi, 44, 216
school attendance, 93, 94
school types, 45, 73, 74, 82, 207, 210. *See also* revolutionary school(s)
seasonal movement, 39, 40, 41–42, 125, 133–34
Seeb, Treaty of, 45, 47, 215
segregation, gender, 146
segregation, social, 162, 164, 180
self-censorship, 21, 27–28, 220, 232
sentencing, 7, 240, 242
settlement(s): air strikes, 118; boomtown (Salalah), 121; new, 113, 122, 124; patterns, 41; surveillance, 34; temporary, 146

sha'biyat (public housing), 124, 125
shahrah, 41, 145, 146, 241, 267n33
Shahri (language), 40, 41, 209
silence, official. *See* officially silenced revolution (term)
slavery. *See* enslavement
slogans, 17, 37, 49, 66, 95
SOAF (Sultan of Oman's Air Force), 105, 118
social backgrounds: all, 79, 228; different, 70, 164, 179, 183, 184; high-ranking, 128; low-ranking, 128, 240
social camouflage, 171, 198, 234, 239
social convention, 17, 174, 238
social differentiation, 8, 71, 270n32
social inequality. *See* inequality, social
social interactions, 172, 184, 202, 236, 239
social order, contested, 138, 140, 166, 167, 174. *See also* counterhegemonic social order
social pressure, 87, 198, 234, 269n24
social respectability, 189, 270n45
Southwest Asia and North Africa (SWANA): demonstrations, 65; discrimination, 25; illness, 156; Islamic practices, 146; protests, 223, 235, 241; revolutions, 4; uprisings (2010–2011), 5
spaces, unofficial, 184, 196
spatial transformation: blockade(s), 120; of Gulf monarchies, 35, 100–105; ports, 130; of postwar Dhufar, 99, 121, 124, 125, 127, 134–35; revolutionary agency, 237; of wartime Dhufar, 36, 117, 121, 134–35
Special Air Service (SAS). *See* SAS (Special Air Service)
Sri Lanka, 11, 17, 139
Srour, Heiny, 62–63, 84, 93, 94
starvation: blockades, 33, 56, 106; civilian casualties, 60; food supplies, 51; "hearts and minds" campaign, 16, 30, 57; parental consent, 93; revolutionary participation, 88; threat, 73
state power, 5, 8, 24, 65–66, 68, 207

state revenues, 108, 121
status groups, 144–46, 149, 164, 181; stratified, 144–45, 151, 152, 155
stipends, 15–16, 116, 129–30, 132
stories, 22–23, 26, 215, 220–21, 223, 224
subjectivities: changes in, 69; cultivation of, 172; gendered, 65, 115, 197; national, 65; new, 68, 93; political, 65, 142; revolutionary, 149, 151
subsidies: and Britain, 47, 57, 103, 251n56; livestock, 15; and loyalty, 14; salaries, 188; from Zanzibar, 44
subsistence economy: context, 70; frankincense, 30, 39; livestock, 114; oil exploration, 55; resources for survival, 13, 60, 107; targeting of, 16
subversion, 172, 174
Sultan of Oman's Air Force (SOAF), 105, 118
Sultan Qaboos bin Said. *See* Qaboos bin Said, Sultan (overview)
Sultan Said bin Taimur. *See* Said bin Taimur, Sultan (overview)
Sultan's Armed Forces (SAF), 33, 55, 59t, 96, 105–7, 109–10
Sultan Taimur bin Faisal. *See* Taimur bin Faisal, Sultan
sumur: ancestry, 24, 267n29; discrimination, 24–26, 180; enslavement, 70, 71; expropriation, 131; face covering, 270n45; inequality, 70, 187–88; marriage, 149, 155, 156; status groups, 144–45, 146, 149, 155; women candidates, 191
surrender, 59t, 82, 112, 116, 122, 127
surveillance: ambiguity, 234, 247n77; authoritarian, 18, 238, 239; facilitation, 170; of former revolutionaries, 130; investment, 221; political threat, 242; research safety, 19, 20, 22–23, 201, 220, 223; settlements, 34; social camouflage, 198
survival, resources for, 13, 60, 107, 117, 120

Tabook, Salim, 146, 150, 164
Taimur bin Faisal, Sultan, 45, 70
Takriti, Abdel Razzaq, *Monsoon Revolution*, 224, 243
Taurus, Operation, 115, 120
thawrah, al- (the revolution), overview, 22–23, 37
Thomas, Bertram, 70, 71
threat, political, 49, 242
Tiananmen Square, 205, 207
Trabulsi, Fawwaz, 85, 211, 219, 224
transformation of Oman, 103, 127, 134
transhumant pastoralism, 40, 41, 72, 125
trauma, 17, 85, 118–19, 139, 151, 220
treason, 32–33, 76, 85
Treaty of Seeb. *See* Seeb, Treaty of
tribalization, 111, 114, 115, 122, 144, 267n29
tribal membership, 39, 71, 72, 77, 144
Trucial Oman, 38, 53

UN General Assembly, 49, 73
university, 24, 128, 150, 157, 179, 225
unofficial commemoration (circumlocution), 23, 206–7, 220, 221, 224–25, 226. *See also* humor
unofficial commemoration (socially inflected space), 184, 196, 271n47; *lieux de mémoire*, 203, 205, 214, 216, 217, 221
unofficial commemoration (written and oral texts), 206, 224; poetry. *See* poetry; stories, 215, 220–21, 223, 224
USSR, 51, 182

values, counterhegemonic, 17, 18, 20, 31, 143
values, reproduced, 3, 136, 168, 170, 171, 236–37
values, revolutionary social, 181–86; formal organization, 242; maintenance, 162, 175, 199; recreation, 240; reproduction, 168, 171, 236
values of egalitarianism, 2, 7, 16, 27, 31, 242
Voice of the Arabs, 50, 95

Warda (Ibrahim), 212, 218
water resource(s): access, 91f, 169; control of, 75, 145; severe shortages, 41, 111; threats, 34, 120, 125; transportation, 113, 121; wells, 107, 264n145. *See also* blockade(s)
Watts, John, 109–10
wedding parties, 147, 148, 163
welfare provisions, 57, 84, 110, 122
welfare services, 31, 99, 100, 122, 124, 126. *See also* health care
welfare states, 14, 238
wells, 107, 108, 122, 264n145
Western Sahara, 24, 67, 142, 182, 235
whiteness, 6, 24, 25, 155, 183, 217
winning: elections, 190, 193; friends, 106; "hearts and minds," 10, 13, 15, 30, 31; lucrative contracts, 114; persuasion, 127; support, 108; the war, 11, 12, 56, 107, 134, 235–36
women, unaccompanied, 1, 187
women candidates, 190–91, 193–94, 271n53
women driving, 187, 195
women fighters. *See* female fighters
women's emancipation, 67, 78–79, 86, 90, 91, 192
wounded, numbers, 59t, 60

Yafaʿi tribe, 124–25, 131
Yemen: bases for exile, 219, 237; borders, 38, 41; conference (1992), 12; return from, 31, 129, 156; revolutionary institutions, 81; revolutionary schools, 94, 126; rulers, 42; southern, 2, 79; war, 28. *See also* Ghaidah, al-; Hawf; People's Democratic Republic of Yemen (PDRY); People's Republic of South Yemen (PRSY)
YouTube, 223, 230, 241
Yusuf bin ʿAlawi, 50, 95, 112, 152

Zanzibar, 24, 44, 126

The authorized representative in the EU for product safety and compliance is:
Mare Nostrum Group
B.V Doelen 72
4831 GR Breda
The Netherlands

www.ingramcontent.com/pod-product-compliance
Lightning Source LLC
Chambersburg PA
CBHW031900220426
43663CB00006B/700